UNDERGRADUATE TEXTS IN COMPUTER SCIENCE

Editors
David Gries
Fred B. Schneider

Springer

New York
Berlin
Heidelberg
Barcelona
Budapest
Hong Kong
London
Milan
Paris
Santa Clara
Singapore
Tokyo

UNDERGRADUATE TEXTS IN COMPUTER SCIENCE

Pankaj Jalote

AN INTEGRATED APPROACH TO SOFTWARE ENGINEERING

Second Edition

With 108 Illustrations

Springer

Pankaj Jalote
Department of Computer Science
    and Engineering
Indian Institute of Technology
Kanpur 208016
India

Series Editors
David Gries
Fred B. Schneider
Department of Computer Science
Cornell University
Upson Hall
Ithaca, NY 14853-7501
USA

Library of Congress Cataloging-in-Publication Data
Jalote, P.
    An integrated approach to software engineering / Pankaj Jalote. –
2nd ed.
        p. cm. – (Undergraduate texts in computer science)
    Includes bibliographical references and index.
    ISBN 0-387-94899-6 (alk. paper)
    1. Software engineering   I. Title.   II. Series.
QA76.758.J35 1997
005.1–dc20   96-38869

Printed on acid-free paper.

Production managed by Steven Pisano; manufacturing supervised by Johanna Tschebull.
Camera-ready copy prepared from the author's LaTeX files.
Printed and bound by R.R. Donnelley and Sons, Harrisonburg, VA.
Printed in the United States of America.

9 8 7 6 5 4 3 2

ISBN 0-387-94899-6 Springer-Verlag New York Berlin Heidelberg SPIN 10664474

Preface to the Second Edition

A lot has changed in the fast-moving area of software engineering since the first edition of this book came out. However, two particularly dominant trends are clearly discernible: focus on software processes and object-orientation. A lot more attention is now given to software processes because process improvement is considered one of the basic mechanisms for improving quality and productivity. And the object-oriented approach is considered by many one of the best hopes for solving some of the problems faced by software developers.

In this second edition, these two trends are clearly highlighted. A separate chapter has been included entitled "Software Processes." In addition to talking about the various development process models, the chapter discusses other processes in software development and other issues related to processes. Object-orientation figures in many chapters. Object-oriented analysis is discussed in the chapter on requirements, while there is a complete chapter entitled "Object-Oriented Design." Some aspects of object-oriented programming are discussed in the chapter on coding, while specific techniques for testing object-oriented programs are discussed in the chapter on testing. Overall, if one wants to develop software using the paradigm of object-orientation, all aspects of development that require different handling are discussed. Most of the other chapters have also been enhanced in various ways. In particular, the chapters on requirements specification and testing have been considerably enhanced.

The focus of the book remains an introductory course on software engineering; advanced topics are still not included. The basic case study–based approach of the book has been preserved. In addition to the structured design of the case study, the object-oriented design of the case study has been performed, and the design is described in the book. The structured design has now been implemented in C (in the first edition the coding was done in Pascal), keeping in mind the growing popularity of the C language in commercial establishments. The object-oriented design has been coded in C++. Again, C++ was chosen mostly due to its high availability and popularity. Both the C and C++ code of the case study are available to readers from the home page for the book.

Metrics-based software development has been steadily gaining importance. This trend has been reflected in the book by placing greater emphasis on the role of metrics in software development. The use of some of the metrics in effecting the development process has been demonstrated on the case study. For example, metrics were used to evaluate, and then change, the design of the case study. Similarly, the C code was evaluated and then changed to reduce the complexity. Tools that were developed for metrics extraction and evaluation are also being made available through the home page.

A home page has been created on the Web for this edition of the book, through which some of the documents and code of the case study and some of the tools used can be obtained. The URL of the home page is

http://www.springer-ny.com/supplements/jalote/

The following material is available through the home page (these are discussed at appropriate places in the book):

1. Design specifications for the structured design of the case study (both the initial and the final versions).
2. The C code implementing the final structured design of the case study (both the initial and the final versions).
3. The C++ code implementing the object-oriented design of the case study.
4. The following tools which have been used in the case study:
   - dmetric—to evaluate the complexity of a design.
   - complexity—to evaluate the complexity of a C program.
   - style—to evaluate the style of a C program.
   - ccov—a test coverage analyzer for C programs.

I would like to express my gratitude to many people who readily clarified issues and provided feedback on various parts of the book. These include Frank McGarry; Professors Victor Basili, Alan Davis, Ginaluigi Caldiera, Harish Karnik, and Mary Jean Harrold; and many others. I am particularly grateful to Kamal K. Mantri, S. Haripriya, and G. Aditya Kiran for developing the C and C++ code for the case study, developing the tools used for evaluation, and performing experiments with the tools and various designs. I would also like to express my thanks to Infosys Technologies Ltd., Bangalore, where I am spending my sabbatical, for providing the necessary help to finish this edition. Comments about the book are welcome and can be sent by email to **jalote@iitk.ernet.in**.

Pankaj Jalote

Preface to the First Edition

It is now clear that development of large software systems is an extremely complex activity which is full of various opportunities to introduce errors. Software engineering is the discipline that attempts to provide methods to handle this complexity and enable us to produce reliable software systems with maximum productivity.

This book offers an integrated approach to software engineering. The "integrated" approach is different from others because the different topics are not covered in isolation. A running case study is employed, which is used throughout the book, illustrating the different activities of software development on the same project. Most of the major outputs of the project, such as the project plan, design document, code, test plan, test report, and so on, are shown for the case study.

It is important, and very instructive, to not only teach the principles of software engineering but also apply them to a software development project so that all aspects of development can be seen clearly on a project. Such an approach, besides explaining the principles, also offers a case study which can be used as a model for a software development project by a student.

Integration is further achieved by combining software metrics with the different development phases, instead of having a separate chapter on the subject. It is recognized that metrics are used for controlling and assessing a software project and are employed throughout the life cycle. In the book, for each phase, relevant metrics and their use is discussed in the chapter for that phase. This conveys the right idea that metrics is not really a separate topic, complete in itself, but is integrated with the different activities of software development. Similarly, for each phase, quality assurance activities and the control activities that need to be performed while the activities of that phase are being done are described in the chapter for the particular phase.

The sequence of chapters is essentially the same as the sequence of activities performed during software development. All activities, including quality assurance and control activities, that should be performed during a particular phase are grouped in one chapter. This is particularly useful for a project-based introductory course in software engineering in which both the students and the instructor can follow the chapters in the order given both in the lectures as well as in the project.

This book is for students who have not had previous training in software engineering, and it is suitable for a one-semester course. In order to limit the scope of the book and focus it for an introductory course, advanced topics like software reuse, reverse engineering, development environments, and so on, have not been included. It was felt that in an introductory course, rather than trying to give a flavor of all the topics, it would be best to introduce the student to the discipline of software engineering as well as to some of the important topics, and to prepare the student for taking advanced courses in the area of software engineering. This need was further felt since in the undergraduate computer science curriculum of most universities, the students have no exposure to software engineering prior to the introductory course, and often do not have any other follow-up course before they graduate. One of the goals of the book, then, is to include only as much material as can be covered in a one-semester course, which may be the only software engineering course in a computer science student's education.

I am grateful to my colleagues Victor R. Basili and Dieter Rombach for their valuable inputs during the conceptual stages. I am particularly grateful to students in the software engineering courses that I taught at the University of Maryland and the Indian Institute of Technology, Kanpur. Teaching and interacting with the students had a great influence on the final form of the book. Students in my course at the Indian Institute of Technology, particularly Sandeep Sharma and Samudrala Sridhar, deserve special thanks for helping with the case study.

Contents

1

Introduction

The evolution of electronic computers began in the 1940s. Early efforts in the field of computing were focused on designing the hardware, as that was the challenge, and hardware was where most technical difficulties existed. In the early computing systems, there was essentially no operating system; the programs were fed with paper tapes or by switches. With the evolution of second-generation machines in the 1950s, early concepts of operating systems evolved and single-user operating systems came into existence. High-level languages, particularly FORTRAN and Cobol, along with their compilers were developed. There was a gradual trend toward isolating the user from the machine internals, so the user could concentrate on solving the problem at hand rather than getting bogged down in the machine details.

With the coming of the multiprogramming operating systems in the early 1960s, the usability and efficiency of the computing machines took a big leap. Prices of hardware also decreased, and awareness of computers increased substantially since their early days. With the availability of cheaper and more powerful machines, higher-level languages, and more user-friendly operating systems, the applications of computers grew rapidly. In addition, the nature of software engineering evolved from simple programming exercises to developing software systems, which were much larger in scope, and required great effort by many people. The techniques for writing simple programs could not be scaled up for developing software systems, and the computing world found itself in the midst of a "software crisis." Two conferences, sponsored by the NATO Science Committee, were held in Europe in the 1960s to discuss the growing software crisis and the need to focus on software development. The term *software engineering* was coined at these meetings.

The use of computers is growing very rapidly. Now computer systems are used in such diverse areas as business applications, scientific work, video games, air traffic control, aircraft control, missile control, hospital management, airline reservations, and medical diagnostic equipment. There is probably no discipline that does not use computer systems now—even artists, linguists, and filmmakers use it. With this increased use of computers the need for software is increasing dramatically. Furthermore, the complexity of these systems is also increasing—imagine the complexity of the software for aircraft control or a telephone network monitoring system. Actually, the complexity of applications and software systems has grown much faster than our ability to deal with it. Consequently, many years after the software crisis was first declared, we find that it has not yet ended. Software engineering is the discipline whose goal is to deal with this problem.

In this chapter we first define our problem domain and discuss the major reasons for the "software problem." Then we discuss the major problems that software engineering faces. This is followed by the basic approach followed by software engineering to handle the software crisis. In the rest of the book we discuss in more detail the various aspects of the software engineering approach.

1.1   The Software Problem

Let us first discuss what we mean by *software*. Software is not merely a collection of computer programs. There is a distinction between a program and a programming systems product. A *program* is generally complete in itself and is generally used only by the author of the program. There is usually little documentation or other aids to help other people use the program. Because the author is the user, the presence of "bugs" is not a major concern; if the program crashes, the author will fix the program and start using it again. These programs are not designed with such issues as portability, reliability, and usability in mind.

A *programming system product*, on the other hand, is used largely by people other than the developers of the system. The users may be from different backgrounds, so a proper user interface is provided. There is sufficient documentation to help these diverse users use the system. Programs are thoroughly tested before operational use, because users do not have the luxury of fixing bugs that may be detected. And because the product may be used in a variety of environments, perhaps on a variety of hardware platforms, portability is a key issue.

Clearly, a program to solve a problem and a programming systems product to solve the same problem are two entirely different things. Obviously, much more effort and resources are required for a programming systems product. Brooks estimates [Bro75] that as a rule of thumb, a programming systems product costs approximately ten times as much as a corresponding program. The software industry is largely interested in developing programming systems products, and most commercial software systems or packages fall in this category. The programming systems product is also sometimes called *production* or *industrial\quality software*.

IEEE defines *software* as the collection of computer programs, procedures, rules, and associated documentation and data [IEE87]. This definition clearly states that software is not just programs, but includes all the associated documentation and data. This implies that the discipline dealing with the development of software should not deal only with developing programs, but with developing all the things that constitute software. Overall, we can say that software engineering is largely concerned with the development of industrial-quality software, where software is as defined earlier. In the rest of the book *software* means industrial-quality software.

1.1.1 Software Is Expensive

Over the past decades, with the advancement of technology, the cost of hardware has consistently decreased. For example, the cost per bit of memory decreased more than 50 fold in two decades [Dav93]. The situation with the processors is similar; virtually every year newer and faster processors are introduced that provide many times the compute power of earlier mainframe computer systems at a cost that is a fraction of those mainframe systems. On the other hand, the cost of software is increasing. As a result, the HW/SW ratio for a computer system has shown a reversal from the early years, as is shown in Figure 1.1 [Boe76].

The main reason for the high cost of software is that software development is still labor-intensive. To get an absolute idea of the costs involved, let us consider the current state of practice in the industry. Delivered lines of code (DLOC) is by far the most commonly used measure of software size in the industry. (We will discuss the issue of software size later in the book.) As the main cost of producing software is

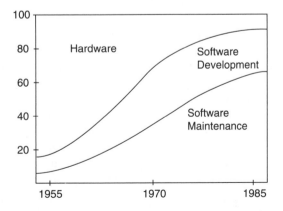

FIGURE 1.1. Hardware-software cost trends [Boe76].

in the manpower employed, the cost of developing software is generally measured in terms of person-months of effort spent in development. And productivity is frequently measured in the industry in terms of DLOC per person-month.

The current productivity in the software industry for writing fresh code ranges from 300 to 1000 DLOC per person-month. That is, for developing software, the average productivity per person, per month, over the entire development cycle is about 300 to 1000 DLOC. And software companies charge the client for whom they are developing the software upwards of $100,000 per person-year or more than $8,000 per person-month (which comes to about $50 per hour). With the current productivity figures of the industry, this translates into a cost per line of code of approximately $8 to $25. In other words, each line of delivered code costs between $8 and $25 at current costs and productivity levels! And even moderately sized projects easily end up with software of 50,000 LOC. (For projects like the software for the space shuttle, the size is millions of lines of code.) With this productivity, such a software project will cost between $0.5 million and $1.25 million!

Given the current compute power of machines, such software can easily be used on a workstation or a small network with a server. This implies that software that can cost more than a million dollars can run on hardware that costs at most tens of thousands of dollars, clearly showing that the cost of hardware on which such an application can run is a fraction of the cost of the application software! This example clearly shows that not only is software very expensive, it indeed forms the major component of the total automated system, with the hardware forming a very small component.

1.1.2   Late, Costly, and Unreliable

There are many instances quoted about software projects that are behind schedule and have heavy cost overruns. The software industry has gained a reputation of not being able to deliver on time and within budget. Consider the example of the U.S. Air Force command-and-control software project [Boe81]. The initial estimate given by the winning contractor was $400,000. Subsequently, the cost was renegotiated to $700,000, to $2,500,000, and finally to $3,200,000. The final project completion cost was almost 10 times the original estimate! Take another example from [Mcf89]. A Fortune 500 consumer products company plans to get an information system developed in nine months at the cost of $250,000. Two years later, after spending $2.5 million, the job was still not done, and it was estimated that another $3.6 million would be needed. The project was scrapped (evidently, the extra cost of $3.6 million was not worth the returns!). Many such disaster examples are given in [Mcf89, Rot89].

A survey reported in [Rot89] states that of the 600 firms surveyed, more than 35% reported having some computer-related development project that they categorized as a *runaway*. And a runaway is not a project that is somewhat late or somewhat over budget—it is one where the budget and schedule are out of control. The problem has become so severe that it has spawned an industry of its own; there are consultancy companies that advise how to rein such projects, and one such company had more than $30 million in revenues from more than 20 clients [Rot89].

Similarly, a large number of instances have been quoted regarding the unreliability of software; the software does not do what it is supposed to do or does something it is not supposed to do. In one defense survey, it was reported that more than 70% of all the equipment failures were due to software! And this is in systems that are loaded with electrical, hydraulic, and mechanical systems. This just indicates that all other engineering disciplines have advanced far more than software engineering, and a system comprising of the products of various engineering disciplines finds that software is the weakest component. Failure of an early Apollo flight was also attributed to software. Similarly, failure of a test firing of a missile in Asia was attributed to software problems. Many banks have lost millions of dollars due to inaccuracies and other problems in their software [Neu88].

Overall, the software industry has gained a reputation of not delivering software within schedule and budget and of producing software systems of poor quality. There are numerous instances of projects that enforce this view. In fact, a whole column in *Software Engineering Notes* is dedicated to such instances. It is clear that cost and schedule overruns and the problem of reliability are major contributors to the software crisis.

A note about the cause of unreliability in software: Software failures are different from failures of, say, mechanical or electrical systems. Products of these other engineering disciplines fail because of the change in physical or electrical properties of the system caused by aging. A software product, on the other hand, never wears out due to age. In software, failures occur due to bugs or errors that get introduced during the design and development process. Hence, even though a software may fail after operating correctly for some time, the bug that causes that failure was there from the start! It only got executed at the time of the failure. This is quite different from other systems, where if a system fails, it generally means that sometime before the failure the system developed some problem (due to aging) that did not exist earlier.

1.1.3 Problem of Change and Rework

Once the software is delivered and deployed, it enters the *maintenance* phase. All systems need maintenance, but for other systems it is largely due to problems that are introduced due to aging. Why is maintenance needed for software, when software does not age? Software needs to be maintained not because some of its components wear out and need to be replaced, but because there are often some residual errors remaining in the system that must be removed as they are discovered.

It is commonly believed that the state of the art today is such that almost all software that is developed has residual errors, or bugs, in them. Many of these surface only after the system has been in operation, sometimes for a long time. These errors, once discovered, need to be removed, leading to the software getting changed. This is sometimes called *corrective maintenance*.

Even without bugs, software frequently undergoes change. The main reason is that software often must be upgraded and enhanced to include more features and provide more services. This also requires modification of the software. It has been argued that once a software system is deployed, the environment in which it operates changes. Hence, the needs that initiated the software development also change to reflect the needs of the new environment. Hence, the software must adapt to the needs of the changed environment. The changed software then changes the environment, which in turn requires further change. This phenomenon is sometimes called the *law of software evolution*. Maintenance due to this phenomenon is sometimes called *adaptive maintenance*.

Though maintenance is not considered a part of software development, it is an extremely important activity in the life of a software product. If we consider the total life of software, the cost of maintenance generally exceeds the cost of developing the software! The maintenance-to-development-cost ratio has been variously suggested as 80:20, 70:30, or 60:40. Figure 1.1 also shows how the maintenance costs are increasing.

Maintenance work is based on existing software, as compared to development work that creates new software. Consequently, maintenance revolves around understanding existing software and maintainers spend most of their time trying to understand the software they have to modify. Understanding the software involves understanding not only the code but also the related documents. During the modification of the software, the effects of the change have to be clearly understood by the maintainer because introducing undesired side effects in the system during modification is easy. To test whether those aspects of the system that are not supposed to be modified are operating as they were before modification, *regression testing* is done. Regression testing involves executing old test cases to test that no new errors have been introduced.

Thus, maintenance involves understanding the existing software (code and related documents), understanding the effects of change, making the changes—to both the code and the documents—testing the new parts (changes), and retesting the old parts that were not changed. Because often during development, the needs of the maintainers are not kept in mind, few support documents are produced during development to help the maintainer. The complexity of the maintenance task, coupled with the neglect of maintenance concerns during development, makes maintenance the most costly activity in the life of software product.

Maintenance is one form of change or software rework that typically is done after the software development is completed and the software has been deployed. However, there are other forms of changes that lead to rework during the software development itself.

One of the biggest problems in software development, particularly for large and complex systems, is that what is desired from the software (i.e., the requirements) is not understood. To completely specify the requirements, *all* the functionality, interfaces, and constraints have to be specified before software development has commenced! In other words, for specifying the requirements, the clients and the developers have to *visualize* what the software behavior should be once it is developed. This is very hard to do, particularly for large and complex systems. So, what generally happens is that the requirements are "frozen" when it is believed that they are generally in good shape, and then the development proceeds. However, as time goes by and the understanding of the system improves, the clients frequently discover additional requirements they had not specified earlier. This leads to requirements getting changed when the development may have proceeded to the coding, or even testing, stage! This change leads to *rework*; the requirements, the design, the code all have to be changed to accommodate the new or changed requirements.

Just uncovering requirements that were not understood earlier is not the only reason for this change and rework. Software development of large and complex systems can take a few years. And with the passage of time, the needs of the clients change. After all, the current needs, which initiate the software product, are a reflection of current times. As times change, so do the needs. And, obviously, the clients want the system deployed to satisfy their most current needs. This change of needs while the development is going on also leads to rework.

In fact, changing requirements and associated rework are a major problem of the software industry. It is estimated that rework costs are 30 to 40% of the development cost [Boe87]. In other words, of the total development effort, rework due to various changes consume about 30 to 40% of the effort! No wonder change and rework is a major contributor to the software crisis. However, unlike the issues discussed earlier, the problem of rework and change is not just a reflection of the state of software development, as changes are frequently initiated by clients as their needs change. However, change is a reality that has to be dealt with properly.

1.2   Software Engineering Problem

It is clear that the current state of software leaves much to be desired. A primary reason for this is that approaches to software development are frequently ad hoc and programming-centered. The ad hoc or programming-centered approach (which considers developing software essentially as a programming exercise) may work for small projects, but for the problem domain that we are interested in (i.e., large industrial-quality software), these approaches generally do not work. If we have to control this software crisis, some methodical approach is needed for software development. This is where software engineering comes in. *Software engineering* is defined as [IEE87]:

> *Software engineering* is the systematic approach to the development, operation, maintenance, and retirement of software.

Another definition from the economic and human perspective is given by Boehm [Boe81] by combining the dictionary's definition of engineering with its definition of software. His definition states:

> *Software Engineering* is the application of science and mathematics by which the capabilities of computer equipment are made useful to man via computer programs, procedures, and associated documentation.

The use of the terms *systematic approach* or *mathematics and science* for the development of software means that software engineering provides methodologies for developing software as close to the scientific method as possible. That is, these methodologies are repeatable, and if the methodology is applied by different people, similar software will be produced. In essence, the goal of software engineering is to take software development closer to science and away from being an art. Note also that the focus of software engineering is not developing software *per se*, but methods for developing software. That is, the focus is on developing methods that can be used by various software projects.

The phrase *usable to man* emphasizes the needs of the user and the software's interface with the user. This definition implies that user needs should be given due importance in the development of software, and the final program should give importance to the user interface. With this definition of software engineering, let us now discuss a few fundamental problems that software engineering faces.

1.2.1   The Problem of Scale

A fundamental problem of software engineering is the problem of scale; development of a very large system requires a very different set of methods compared to developing a small system. In other words, the methods that are used for developing small systems generally *do not scale up* to large systems. An example will illustrate this point. Consider the problem of counting people in a room versus taking a census of a country. Both are essentially counting problems. But the methods used for counting people in a room (probably just go row-wise or column-wise) will just not work when taking a census. Different set of methods will have to be used for conducting a census, and the census problem will require considerably more management, organization, and validation, in addition to counting.

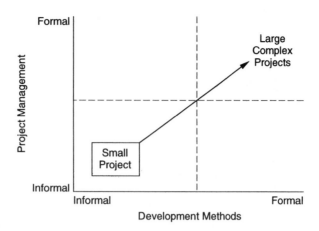

FIGURE 1.2. The problem of scale.

Similarly, methods that one can use to develop programs of a few hundred lines cannot be expected to work when software of a few hundred thousand lines needs to be developed. A different set of methods have to be used for developing large software. Any large project involves the use of technology and project management. For software projects, by technology we mean the methods, procedures, and tools that are used. In small projects, informal methods for development and management can be used. However, for large projects, both have to be much more formal, as shown in Figure 1.2.

As shown in the figure, when dealing with a small software project, the technology requirement is low (all you need to know is how to program and a bit of testing) and the project management requirement is also low (who needs formal management for developing a 100-line program?). However, when the scale changes to large systems, to solve such problems properly, it is essential that we move in both directions—the methods used for development need to be more formal, and the project management for the development project also needs to be more formal. For example, if we leave 50 bright programmers together (who know how to develop small programs well) without formal management and development procedures and ask them to develop an on-line inventory control system for an automotive manufacturer, it is highly unlikely that they will produce anything of use. To successfully execute the project, a proper method of development has to be used and the project has to be tightly managed to make sure that methods are indeed being followed and that cost, schedule, and quality are under control.

Though there is no universally acceptable definition of what is a "small" project and what is a "large" project, one can use the definitions used in the COCOMO cost model (to be discussed later in the book) to get an idea of scale. According to this model, a project is *small* if its size in thousands of delivered lines of code

(KDLOC) is 2 KDLOC, *intermediate* if the size is 8 KDLOC, *medium* if the size is 32 KDLOC, and *large* if the size is 128 KDLOC (or larger).

1.2.2   Cost, Schedule, and Quality

An engineering discipline, almost by definition, is driven by practical parameters of cost, schedule, and quality. A solution that takes enormous resources and many years may not be acceptable. Similarly, a poor-quality solution, even at low cost, may not be of much use. Like all engineering disciplines, software engineering is driven by the three major factors: cost, schedule, and quality. In some contexts, cost and quality are considered the primary independent factors, as schedule can be modeled as cost or considered as an independent variable whose value is more or less fixed for a given cost. We will also consider these as the primary driving factors.

We have already seen that the current state of affairs is that producing software is very expensive. Clearly, a practical and consistent goal on software engineering is to come up with methods of producing software more cheaply. Cost is a consistent driving force in software engineering.

The cost of developing a system is the cost of the resources used for the system, which, in the case of software, are the manpower, hardware, software, and other support resources. Generally, the manpower component is predominant, as software development is largely labor-intensive and the cost of the computing systems (the other major cost component) is now quite low. Hence, the cost of a software project is measured in terms of person-months, i.e., the cost is considered to be the total number of person-months spent in the project. To convert this to a dollar amount, it is multiplied with the dollar cost per person-month. In defining this unit cost for a person-month, the other costs are included (called *overheads*). In this manner, by using person-months for specifying cost, the entire cost can be modeled.

Schedule is an important factor in many projects. Business trends are dictating that the time to market of a product should be reduced; that is, the cycle time from concept to delivery should be small. Any business with such a requirement will also require that the cycle time for building a software needed by the business be small. Similarly, there are examples, particularly in the financial sector, where the window of opportunity is small. Hence, any software needed to exploit this window of opportunity will have to be done within a small cycle time. Due to these types of applications, where a reduced cycle time is highly desirable even if the costs become higher, there is a growing interest in *rapid application development (RAD)*.

One of the major factors driving any production discipline is quality. In the current times, quality is the main "mantra," and business strategies are designed around quality. Clearly, developing methods that can produce high-quality software is

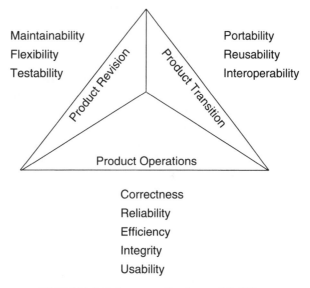

Maintainability
Flexibility
Testability

Portability
Reusability
Interoperability

Product Operations

Correctness
Reliability
Efficiency
Integrity
Usability

FIGURE 1.3. Software quality factors [CM78].

another fundamental goal of software engineering. However, while cost is generally well understood, the concept of quality in the context of software needs further discussion. We can view quality of a software product as having three dimensions [CM78]:

- Product Operation
- Product Transition
- Product Revision

The first factor, product operations, deals with quality factors such as correctness, reliability, and efficiency. Product transition deals with quality factors like portability and interoperability. Product revision is concerned with those aspects related to modification of programs, including factors such as maintainability, and testability. These three dimensions and the different factors for each are shown in Figure 1.3 [CM78].

Correctness is the extent to which a program satisfies its specifications. Reliability is the property that defines how well the software meets its requirements. Efficiency is a factor in all issues relating to the execution of software; it includes such considerations as response time, memory requirement, and throughput. Usability, or the effort required to learn and operate the software properly, is an important property that emphasizes the human aspect of the system. Maintainability is the effort required to locate and fix errors in operating programs. Testability is the effort required to test to ensure that the system or a module performs its intended function. Flexibility is the effort required to modify an operational program (perhaps to enhance its functionality). Portability is the effort required to transfer the software from one hardware configuration to another. Reusability is the extent to which parts of the software can be reused in other related applications. Interoperability is the effort required to couple the system with other systems.

There are two important consequences of having multiple dimensions to quality. First, software quality cannot be reduced to a single number (or a single parameter). And second, the concept of quality is project-specific. For some ultra-sensitive project, reliability may be of utmost importance but not usability, while in some commercial package for playing games on a PC, usability may be of utmost importance and not reliability. Hence, for each software development project, a project-specific quality objective must be specified before the development starts, and the goal of the development process should be to satisfy that quality objective.

Despite the fact that there are many factors, reliability is generally accepted to be main quality criteria. As unreliability of software comes due to presence of defects in the software, one measure of quality is the number of defects in the software per unit size (generally taken to be thousands of lines of code, or KLOC). With this as the major quality criteria, the quality objective of software engineering becomes to reduce the number of defects per KLOC as much as possible. Due to this, defect tracking is another essential activity that must be done in a software project, in addition to tracking cost. Current best practices in software engineering have been able to reduce the defect density to less than 1 defect per KLOC. It should be pointed out that before this definition of quality is used, what a defect is has to be clearly defined. A *defect* could be some problem in the software that causes the software to crash or a problem that causes an output to be not properly aligned or one that misspells some word, etc. The exact definition of what is considered a defect will clearly depend on the project or the standards of the organization developing the project (typically it is the latter).

1.2.3 The Problem of Consistency

Though high quality, low cost (or high productivity), and small cycle time are the primary objectives of any project, for an organization there is another goal: consistency. An organization involved in software development does not just want low cost and high quality for a project, but it wants these *consistently*. In other words, a software development organization would like to produce consistent quality with consistent productivity. Consistency of performance is an important factor for any organization; it allows an organization to predict the outcome of a project with reasonable accuracy, and to improve its processes to produce higher-quality products and to improve its productivity.

Achieving consistency is an important problem that software engineering has to tackle. As can be imagined, this requirement of consistency will force some standardized procedures to be followed for developing software.

1.3   The Software Engineering Approach

Based on the preceding discussions, we can say that the basic objective of software engineering is to: *Develop methods and procedures for software development that can scale up for large systems and that can be used to consistently produce high-quality software at low cost and with a small cycle time.* That is, the key objectives are consistency, low cost, high quality, small cycle time, and scalability.

The basic approach that software engineering takes is to separate the development process from the developed product (i.e., the software). The premise is that the development process, or the software process, controls the quality, scalability, consistency, and productivity. Hence to satisfy the objectives, one must focus on the software process. Design of proper software processes and their control then becomes the primary goal of software engineering. It is this focus on process that distinguishes it from most other computing disciplines. Most other computing disciplines focus on some type of product—algorithms, operating system, databases, etc.—while software engineering focuses on the process for producing the products. It is essentially the software equivalent of "manufacturing engineering."

The software process must necessarily have components of project management, in addition to procedures for development. Otherwise, as we discussed, scalability will not be achieved. To better manage the development process and to achieve consistency, it is essential that the software development be done in phases. Hence, a phased development process is central to the software engineering approach. Besides having a phased development process, it is essential that monitoring of a project for quality and cost involve objective means rather than subjective methods. Otherwise, the scalability is limited: it is possible to handle a small project without measuring anything and using "gut-feel" type of management, but such methods are unlikely to work for projects that involve many people (possibly hundreds) and last many months. We briefly discuss these fundamental approaches here. The software process, being the central concept of software engineering, is discussed in detail in the next chapter.

1.3.1   Phased Development Process

A development process consist of various phases, each phase ending with a defined output. The phases are performed in an order specified by the process model being followed. The main reason for having a phased process is that it breaks the problem of developing software into successfully performing a set of phases, each handling a different concern of software development. This ensures that the cost of development is lower than what it would have been if the whole problem was tackled together. Furthermore, a phased process allows proper checking for quality and progress at some defined points during the development (end of phases). Without this, one would have to wait until the end to see what software has been produced. Clearly, this will not work for large systems. Hence, for managing the complexity, project tracking, and quality, all the development processes consist of a set of phases. A phased development process is central to the software engineering approach for solving the software crisis.

Various process models have been proposed for developing software. In fact each organization that follows a process has its own version. We will discuss some of the common models in the next chapter. The different processes can have different activities. However, in general, we can say that any problem solving in software must consist of these activities: requirement specification for understanding and clearly stating the problem, design for deciding a plan for a solution, coding for implementing the planned solution, and testing for verifying the programs. For small problems, these activities may not be done explicitly, the start and end boundaries of these activities may not be clearly defined, and no written record of the activities may be kept. However, for large systems, where the problem-solving activity may last a couple of years and where many people are involved in development, performing these activities implicitly without proper documentation and representation will clearly not work, and each of these four problem solving activities has to be done formally. In fact, for large systems, each activity can itself be extremely complex, and methodologies and procedures are needed to perform it efficiently and correctly. Each of these activities is a major task for large software projects. These basic phases are briefly described here; each one of them will be discussed in more detail during the course of the book (there is at least one chapter for each of these phases).

Requirements Analysis

Requirements analysis is done in order to understand the problem the software system is to solve. The problem could be automating an existing manual process, developing a new automated system, or a combination of the two. For large systems that have many features, and that need to perform many different tasks, understanding the requirements of the system is a major task. The emphasis in requirements analysis is on identifying *what* is needed from the system, not *how* the system will achieve its goals. This task is complicated by the fact that there are often at least two parties involved in software development—a client and a developer. The developer has to develop the system to satisfy the client's needs. The developer usually does not understand the client's problem domain, and the client often does not understand the issues involved in software systems. This causes a communication gap, which has to be adequately bridged during requirements analysis.

In most software projects, the requirements phase ends with a document describing all the requirements. In other words, the goal of the requirements specification phase is to produce the *software requirements specification* document (also called the *requirements document*). The person responsible for the requirements analysis is often called the *analyst*.

There are two major activities in this phase: problem understanding or analysis and requirement specification. In problem analysis, the analyst has to understand the problem and its context. Such analysis typically requires a thorough understanding of the existing system, parts of which have to be automated. A clear understanding is needed of the important data entities in the system, major centers where action is taken, the purpose of the different actions that are performed, and the inputs and outputs. This requires interacting with clients and end users, as well as studying the existing manuals and procedures. With the analysis of the current system, the analyst can understand the reasons for automation and what effects the automated system might have.

Understanding the existing system is usually just the starting activity in problem analysis, and it is relatively simple. The goal of this activity is to understand the requirements of the new system that is to be developed. Understanding the properties of a system that does not exist is more difficult and requires creative thinking. The problem is more complex because an automated system offers possibilities that do not exist otherwise. Consequently, even the client may not really know the needs of the system. The analyst has to make the client aware of the new possibilities, thus helping both client and analyst determine the requirements for the new system.

Once the problem is analyzed and the essentials understood, the requirements must be specified in the requirement specification document. For requirement specification in the form of a document, some specification language has to be selected (e.g., English, regular expressions, tables, or a combination of these). The requirements document must specify all functional and performance requirements; the formats of inputs and outputs; and all design constraints that exist due to political, economic, environmental, and security reasons. In other words, besides the functionality required from the system, all the factors that may effect the design and proper functioning of the system should be specified in the requirements document. A preliminary user manual that describes all the major user interfaces frequently forms a part of the requirements document.

Software Design

The purpose of the design phase is to plan a solution of the problem specified by the requirements document. This phase is the first step in moving from the problem domain to the solution domain. In other words, starting with *what* is needed, design takes us toward *how* to satisfy the needs. The design of a system is perhaps the most critical factor affecting the quality of the software; it has a major impact on the later phases, particularly testing and maintenance. The output of this phase is the *design document*. This document is similar to a blueprint or plan for the solution and is used later during implementation, testing, and maintenance.

The design activity is often divided into two separate phases—*system design* and *detailed design*. *System design*, which is sometimes also called *top-level design*, aims to identify the modules that should be in the system, the specifications of these modules, and how they interact with each other to produce the desired results. At the end of system design all the major data structures, file formats, output formats, and the major modules in the system and their specifications are decided.

During *detailed design*, the internal logic of each of the modules specified in system design is decided. During this phase further details of the data structures and algorithmic design of each of the modules is specified. The logic of a module is usually specified in a high-level design description language, which is independent of the target language in which the software will eventually be implemented.

In system design the focus is on identifying the modules, whereas during detailed design the focus is on designing the logic for each of the modules. In other words, in system design the attention is on *what* components are needed, while in detailed design *how* the components can be implemented in software is the issue. A *design methodology* is a systematic approach to creating a design by application of a set of techniques and guidelines. Most methodologies focus on system design.

Coding

Once the design is complete, most of the major decisions about the system have been made. However, many of the details about coding the designs, which often depend on the programming language chosen, are not specified during design. The goal of the coding phase is to translate the design of the system into code in a given programming language. For a given design, the aim in this phase is to implement the design in the best possible manner.

The coding phase affects both testing and maintenance profoundly. Well-written code can reduce the testing and maintenance effort. Because the testing and maintenance costs of software are much higher than the coding cost, the goal of coding should be to reduce the testing and maintenance effort. Hence, during coding the focus should be on developing programs that are easy to read and understand, and not simply on developing programs that are easy to write. Simplicity and clarity should be strived for during the coding phase.

An important concept that helps the understandability of programs is *structured programming*. The goal of structured programming is to linearize the control flow in the program. That is, the program text should be organized as a sequence of statements, and during execution the statements are executed in the sequence given in the program. For structured programming, a few single-entry-single-exit constructs should be used. These constructs include selection (if-then-else) and iteration (while-do, repeat-until, etc.). With these constructs it is possible to construct a program as a sequence of single-entry-single-exit constructs.

Testing

Testing is the major quality control measure used during software development. Its basic function is to detect errors in the software. During requirements analysis and design, the output is a document that is usually textual and nonexecutable. After the coding phase, computer programs are available that can be executed for testing purposes. This implies that testing not only has to uncover errors introduced during coding, but also errors introduced during the previous phases. Thus, the goal of testing is to uncover requirement, design, and coding errors in the programs. Consequently, different levels of testing are used.

The starting point of testing is *unit testing*. In this, a module is tested separately and is often performed by the coder himself simultaneously along with the coding of the module. The purpose is to exercise the different parts of the module code to detect coding errors. After this, the modules are gradually integrated into subsystems, which are then integrated to eventually form the entire system. During integration of modules, *integration testing* is performed to detect design errors by focusing on testing the interconnection between modules.

After the system is put together, *system testing* is performed. Here the system is tested against the system requirements to see if all the requirements are met and if the system performs as specified by the requirements. Finally, *acceptance testing* is performed to demonstrate to the client, on the real-life data of the client, the operation of the system.

Testing is an extremely critical and time-consuming activity. It requires proper planning of the overall testing process. Frequently the testing process starts with a *test plan* that identifies all the testing-related activities that must be performed and specifies the schedule, allocates the resources, and specifies guidelines for testing. The test plan specifies conditions that should be tested, different units to be tested, and the manner in which the modules will be integrated together. Then for different test units, a *test case specification document* is produced, which lists all the different test cases, together with the expected outputs. During the testing of the unit, the specified test cases are executed and the actual result compared with the expected output. The final output of the testing phase is the *test report* and the *error report*, or a set of such reports (one for each unit tested). Each test report contains the set of test cases and the result of executing the code with these test cases. The error report describes the errors encountered and the action taken to remove the errors.

1.3.2 Project Management and Metrics

As stated earlier, a phased development process is central to the software engineering approach. However, a development process does not specify how to allocate resources to the different activities in the process. Nor does it specify things like schedule for the activities, how to divide work within a phase, how to ensure that each phase is being done properly, what the risks for the project are and how to mitigate them, etc. Without properly handling these issues, it is unlikely that the cost and quality objectives can be met. These types of issues generally fall in the domain of project management. This implies that even for properly using a phased development process, project management must be treated as an integral part of the development project. Effective project management is another basic technique that software engineering uses to satisfy its objectives.

The management activities in a project typically revolve around a *plan*. A software plan forms the baseline that is used heavily for project monitoring and control during project execution. This makes planning the most important management activity in a project. It can be safely said that without proper project planning a software project is very unlikely to meet its objectives. We will devote a complete chapter to project planning.

All project management activities require information, upon which the management decisions are based. Otherwise, even the essential questions—is the schedule is being met, what is the extent of cost overrun, is quality objectives being met, etc.—cannot be answered. And information that is subjective is only marginally better than no information (e.g., Q: how close are you to finishing? A: We are almost there). Hence, for effective project management, objective data is needed. For this, software metrics are used.

Software metrics are quantifiable measures that could be used to measure different characteristics of a software system or the software development process. There are two types of metrics used for software development: *product metrics* and *process metrics*. *Product metrics* are used to quantify characteristics of the product being developed, i.e., the software. *Process metrics* are used to quantify characteristics of the process being used to develop the software. Process metrics aim to measure such considerations as productivity, cost and resource requirements, effectiveness of quality assurance measures, and the effect of development techniques and tools.

Metrics and measurement are necessary aspects of managing a software development project. For effective monitoring, the management needs to get information about the project: how far it has progressed, how much development has taken place, how far behind schedule it is, the quality of the development so far, etc. Based on this information, decisions can be made about the project. Without proper metrics to quantify the required information, subjective opinion would have to be used, which is often unreliable and goes against the fundamental goals of engineering. Hence, we can say that metrics-based management is also a key component in the software engineering strategy to achieve its objectives.

1.4   Summary

Software cost now forms the major component of a computer system's cost. Software is currently extremely expensive to develop and is often unreliable. The goal of software engineering is to face this "software problem." In this chapter, we have discussed a few basic points regarding software and software engineering:

1. Software is not just a set of computer programs but comprises programs and associated data and documentation. The main problems for software development currently are: high cost, low quality, and frequent changes causing rework.

2. Software engineering is the discipline that aims to provide methods and procedures for developing software systems. The basic problem of software engineering is the problem of scale; the techniques used to solve small problems do not scale up to solve large and complex problems. And the main controlling factors are cost, schedule, quality, and consistency. The basic objective of software engineering is to develop methods for developing software that can scale up and be used to consistently develop high-quality software at low cost.

3. The fundamental approach of software engineering to achieve its objective is to separate the development process from the products. Software engineering focuses on the process with the belief that the quality of products developed using a process are influenced mainly by the process. The process used for development need to be a phased process in order to achieve the software engineering objectives. As effective project management is critical to the success of a large development project, metrics-based project management is another basic approach software engineering uses.

1.5   Overview of the Book

This book has a total of nine chapters. Each major phase is discussed in a separate chapter. Due to the importance of software processes and the planning activity in the management process, these are discussed in separate chapters. The order of presentation of the chapters on various activities is the same as the order in which the different activities are performed in a typical development project. **A running case study is used in the book**, which is taken through the different phases in the development process. The activity of each phase is performed for the case study, and the major outputs are given in the relevant chapters. The following documents of the case study are either given in the book or are available from the home page: requirements document, project plan, system design document, design document for object-oriented design, code (both for function-oriented design and object-oriented design), test plan, and test case specification. The URL of the home page is **http://www.springer-ny.com/supplements/jalote.** Some tools that have been used for evaluating the design, code, or testing of the case study are also available from the home page.

The structure of most chapters in this book is similar. Most chapters begin by discussing the fundamental concepts for that particular phase. Then the methods for performing the activity for that phase are discussed. This is followed by the verification methods used for that phase. Metrics relevant to the phase are discussed next, along with some discussion on how metrics can be used for monitoring and control activities for that phase. Most chapters end with a discussion of the case study and a description of the case study outputs for that particular phase. Here we give a brief outline of each of the chapters.

As the concept of process is central to the software engineering approach, **Chapter 2** is devoted to "Software Processes." First, the three major entities of software engineering - processes, projects, and products - are defined. The major component processes of a software process are then identified, along with the basic properties of a software process. Then each component process is discussed in some detail through the rest of the chapter. Various models that have been proposed for the development process are discussed. The role of metrics in the project management process and the process management process is also discussed.

Chapter 3 is entitled "Software Requirements Analysis and Specification" and discusses the different aspects of this phase. The desirable qualities of the requirements document are discussed, along with the different aspects the document should specify. Different approaches for problem analysis and representation are covered, and a brief description of some of the tools available for requirements analysis is included. The validation methods and metrics of interest for this phase are described. The chapter ends with problem analysis and the requirements document for the case study.

Chapter 4 is entitled "Planning a Software Project" and discusses the different issues relating to software development project planning. The topics covered are cost estimation, schedule and milestone plan, personnel plan, team structure, software quality assurance plans, configuration management plans, project monitoring plans, and risk management. For cost and schedule planning, different models are described. In quality assurance plans, general methods of monitoring, including reviews, are discussed. For risk management, different activities for performing risk management are discussed. A project plan for the case study is then presented.

Chapter 5 discusses "Function-Oriented Design." We consider design as a two-level process combining system design and detailed design (detailed design is discussed in Chapter 7.). For system design, two major approaches have emerged—function-oriented design and object-oriented design. In Chapter 5 we first discuss the basic principles of design, including problem partitioning, divide and conquer, top-down refinement, modularity and abstraction. We then describe one design technique: the structured design methodology, which is a widely used function-oriented design methodology. Different methods for verifying a system design, and metrics applicable for a function-oriented system design are also discussed. For the case study, we follow the structured design methodology and give the entire system design. We also demonstrate how metrics are used to improve the design of the case study.

In **Chapter 6** we discuss "Object-Oriented design." The basic principles behind the object-oriented design are first discussed, followed by a design methodology. Some metrics that can be applied to an object-oriented design are then described. The chapter ends with a complete description of the object-oriented design for the case study.

In **Chapter 7** we discuss the issue of "Detailed Design." The first step in designing a module is to specify the module formally and understand it clearly. We discuss some methods of formally specifying modules that support functional or data abstractions. For detailed design we discuss the method of stepwise refinement and the program design language (PDL). Different methods for verification and some metrics for complexity, cohesion, and coupling are discussed.

Chapter 8, "Coding", discusses the issues relating to programming. The basic principles for developing programs are discussed. These include structured programming, information hiding, programming style, and internal documentation. Many methods for verification exist for programs. In this chapter we discuss code reading, data flow analysis, symbolic execution, program proving, unit testing, code reviews and walkthroughs. Metrics discussed include size metrics and complexity analysis.

Chapter 9, the last chapter, discusses "Testing." We first clarify the concepts of faults, errors, failures, and reliability. Different levels of testing that are usually used and their various purposes are defined. The importance of the psychology of testing is discussed, as are the two basic approaches to testing (functional testing and structural testing). Different heuristics for generating test cases for functional testing are described. For the structural testing approach, control flow-based testing, data flow-based testing, and mutation testing are discussed. The issues and techniques for testing object-oriented programs are described next. The basic metric we describe is reliability assessment, and we describe one model for reliability estimation. The test plan and the test case specifications for the case study are given.

Exercises

1. Suppose a program for solving a problem costs C, and a programming product for solving that problem costs 9C. Where do you think this extra 8C cost is spent? Suggest a possible breakdown of this extra cost.

2. If the primary goal is to make software maintainable, list some of the things you *will* do and some of the things you *will not* do during 1) design, 2) coding, and 3) testing.

3. If you are given extra time to improve the reliability of the final product developing a software product, how would you distribute this extra time?

4. List some possible problems that can come up if the methods you use for developing small software are used for developing large software systems.

5. Suggest ways of reducing the cost due to rework.

6. Suggest some ways to detect software errors in the early phases (when implementation is not yet complete).

7. What are the major reasons for having a phased process? How does it help in project management?

8. If absolutely no metrics are used, can you manage, or even define, a project? What is the bare minimum set of metrics that you must use for a development project?

2

Software Processes

As we saw in the previous chapter, the concept of process is at the heart of the software engineering approach. According to Webster, the term *process* means "a particular method of doing something, generally involving a number of steps or operations." In software engineering, the phrase *software process* refers to the method of developing software.

A software process is a set of activities, together with ordering constraints among them, such that if the activities are performed properly and in accordance with the ordering constraints, the desired result is produced. The desired result is, as stated earlier, high-quality software at low cost. Clearly, a process that does not scale up (i.e., cannot handle large software projects) or cannot produce good-quality software (i.e., good-quality software is not the outcome) is not a suitable process. In this chapter, we will discuss the concept of software processes, the component processes of a software process, and some models that have been proposed.

2.1 Software Process

In an organization whose major business is software development, there are typically many processes simultaneously executing. Many of these do not concern software engineering, though they do impact software development. These could be considered nonsoftware-engineering process models [RV95]. Business process models, social process models, and training models, are all examples of processes that come under this. These processes also affect the software development activity but are beyond the purview of software engineering.

The process that deals with the technical and management issues of software development is called a *software process*. Clearly, many different types of activities need to be performed to develop software. As we have seen earlier, a software development project must have at least development activities and project management activities. All these activities together comprise the software process. As different type of activities are being performed, which are frequently done by different people, it is better to view the software process as consisting of many component processes, each consisting of a certain type of activity. Each of these component processes typically has a different objective, though these processes obviously cooperate with each other to satisfy the overall software engineering objective.

In this section we will define the major component processes of a software process and what their objectives are. Before we do that, let us first clearly understand the three important entities that repeatedly occur in software engineering—software processes, software projects, and software products—and their relationship.

2.1.1   Processes, Projects, and Products

A software process, as mentioned earlier, specifies a method of developing software. A software project, on the other hand, is a development project in which a software process is used. And software products are the outcomes of a software project. Each software development project starts with some needs and (hopefully) ends with some software that satisfies those needs. A software process specifies the abstract set of activities that should be performed to go from user needs to final product. The actual act of executing the activities for some specific user needs is a software project. And all the outputs that are produced while the activities are being executed are the products (one of which is the final software). One can view the software process as an abstract type, and each project is done using that process as an instance of this type. In other words, there can be many projects for a process (i.e., many projects can be done using a process), and there can be many products produced in a project. This relationship is shown in Figure 2.1.

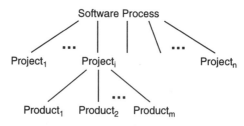

FIGURE 2.1. Processes, projects, and products.

A pertinent question that comes up is if the sequence of activities is provided by the process, what is the difficulty in following it in a project? First, the sequence of activities specified by the process is typically at an abstract level because they have to be usable for a wide range of projects. Hence, "implementing" them in a project is not straightforward. To clarify this, let us take the example of traveling. A process for traveling to a destination will be something like this: Set objectives for the travel (tourism, business, meeting friends, etc.), determine the optimal means of traveling (this will depend on the objective), if driving is best determine what type of vehicle is most desired (car, truck, or camper), get a detailed map to reach the destination, plan details of the trip, get sufficient money, rent the car, etc. If flying to the destination is best, then book flights, reserve a car at the destination if needed, etc. In a sense, the process provides a "checklist," with an ordering constraint (e.g., renting a car as a first step is suboptimal). If one has to go from New York to Orlando (a specific project), then even with this process, a considerable effort is required to reach Orlando. And this effort is not all passive; one has to be alert and active to achieve this goal (e.g., preparing a map and following the map are not passive or trivial tasks).

Overall, the process specifies activities at an abstract level that are not project-specific. It is a generic set of activities that does not provide a detailed roadmap for a particular project. The detailed roadmap for a particular project is the *project plan* that specifies what specific activities to perform for this particular project, when, and how to ensure that the project progresses smoothly. In our travel example, the project plan to go from New York to Orlando will be the detailed marked map showing the route, with other details like plans for night halts, getting gas, and breaks.

It should be clear that it is the process that drives a project. A process limits the degrees of freedom for a project by specifying what types of activities must be done and in what order. Further restriction on the degrees of freedom for a particular project are specified by the project plan, which, in itself, is within the boundaries established by the process (i.e., a project plan cannot include performing an activity that is not there in the process). With this, the hope is that one has the "shortest" (or the most efficient) path from the user needs to the software satisfying these needs.

As each project is an instance of the process it follows, it is essentially the process that determines the expected outcomes of a project. Due to this, the focus of software engineering is heavily on the process.

2.1.2 Component Software Processes

The three basic type of entities that software engineering deals with—processes, project, and products—require different processes. The major process dealing with products is the development process responsible for producing the desired product (i.e., the software) and other products (e.g., user manual, and requirement specification). The basic goal of this process is to develop a product that will satisfy the customer. A software project is clearly a dynamic entity in which activities are performed, and project management process is needed to properly control this dynamic activity, so that the activities do not take the project astray but all activities are geared toward reaching the project goal. For large projects, project management is perhaps even more important than technical methods for the success of the project. Hence, we can clearly identify that there are two major components in a software process—a development process and a project management process—corresponding to the two axes in Figure 1.2. The development process specifies the development and quality assurance activities that need to be performed, whereas the management process specifies how to plan and control these activities so that project objectives are met.

The development process and the project management process both aim at satisfying the cost and quality objectives of the project. However, as we have seen, change and rework in a project occur constantly, and any software project has to deal with the problems of change and rework satisfactorily. As the development processes generally cannot handle change requests at an arbitrary point in time, to handle the inevitable change and rework requests another processes called *software configuration control process*, is generally used. The objective of this component process is to primarily deal with managing change, so that the cost and quality objectives are met and the integrity of the products is not violated despite these change requests.

Overall, for a particular project, to satisfy the objectives and handle the realities of software, at least three major constituent processes are needed: development process, project management process, and configuration control process. (One can think of other processes too, e.g., training process or business process, but these can be considered minor processes as far as software engineering is considered.) It should be clear that both the project management process and the configuration control process depend on the development process. As the management process aims to control the development process, it clearly depends on the activities in the development process. Though the configuration control process is not as closely tied to the development process as the management process is, what changes to allow and how to process and manage a change depend on the development process, as the effect of the change depends on methods used. For this reason there is some sort of primacy of the development process, which is reflected in the fact that models have generally been proposed for the development processes. The management process, for example, is typically developed after the development process has been adopted.

These three constituent processes focus on the projects and the products. In fact, they can be all considered as comprising *product engineering processes*, as their main objective is to produce the desired product. If the software process can be viewed as a static entity, then these three component processes will suffice. However, a software process itself is a dynamic entity, as it must change to adapt to our increased understanding about software development and availability of newer technologies and tools. Due to this, a process to manage the software process is needed.

The process management process deals with the software process; its basic objective is to improve the software process. By *improvement*, we mean that the capability of the process to produce quality goods at low cost is improved. For this, the current software process is studied, frequently by studying the projects that have been done using the project. Based on the analysis of the existing process, various aspects of the development, project management, configuration management, or other minor processes that affect software development are improved, thereby improving the software process. The whole process of understanding the current process, analyzing its properties, determining how to improve, and then affecting the improvement is dealt with by the process management process.

The relationship between these major component processes is shown in Figure 2.2. These component processes are distinct not only in the type of activities performed in them, but typically also in the people who perform the activities specified by the process. In a typical project, development activities are performed by programmers, designers, testing personnel, librarians, writers, etc.; the project management process activities are performed by the project management; configuration control process activities are performed by a group generally called the *configuration control board*; and the process management process activities are performed by a group called the *software engineering process group (SEPG)*.

In the rest of this chapter we will discuss each of these processes further. However, in the rest of the book we will focus primarily on processes relating to product engineering, as process management is an advanced topic beyond the scope of this book. The rest of the book essentially discusses various components of a development process (frequently called *methodologies* for the particular phase of the development process), and for each component discusses its relationship with

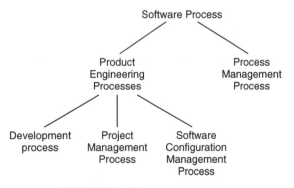

FIGURE 2.2. Software processes.

the project management process. We will use the term *software process* to mean product engineering processes, unless specified otherwise.

2.2   Characteristics of a Software Process

Before we discuss the constituent processes of a software process, let us discuss some desirable characteristics of the software process (besides the fact that it should provide effective development, management, and change management support). The fundamental objectives of a process are the same as that of software engineering (after all, the process is the main vehicle of satisfying the software engineering objectives), namely, *optimality* and *scalability*. *Optimality* means that the process should be able to produce high-quality software at low cost, and *scalability* means that it should also be applicable for large software projects. To achieve these objectives, a process should have some properties. We will discuss some of the important ones in this section.

2.2.1   Predictability

Predictability of a process determines how accurately the outcome of following a process in a project can be predicted before the project is completed. Predictability can be considered a fundamental property of any process. In fact, if a process is not predictable, it is of limited use. Let us see why.

We have seen that effective project management is essential for the success of a project, and effective project management revolves around the project plan. A project plan typically contains cost and schedule estimates for the project, along with plans for quality assurance and other activities. Any estimation about a project is based on the properties of the project, and the capability or past experience of the organization. For example, a simple way of estimating cost could be to say, "this project A is very similar to the project B that we did 2 years ago, hence A's cost will be very close to B's cost." However, even this simple method implies that the process that will be used to develop project A will be same as the process used for project B, *and* the process is such that following the process the second time will produce similar results as the first time. That is, this assumes that the process is *predictable*. If it was not predictable, then there is no guarantee that doing a similar project the second time using the process will incur a similar cost.

Similar is the situation with quality. The fundamental basis for quality prediction is that quality of the product is determined largely by the process used to develop it. Using this basis, quality of the product of a project can be estimated or predicted by seeing the quality of the products that has been produced in the past by the process being used in the current project. In fact, effective management of quality assurance activities largely depends on the predictability of the process. For example, for effective quality assurance, one method is to estimate what types and quantity of errors will be detected at what stage of the development, and then use to determine if the quality assurance activities are being performed properly. This can only be done if the process is predictable; based on the past experience of such a process one can estimate the distribution of errors for the current project. Otherwise, how can anyone say whether detecting 10 errors per 100 lines of code (LOC) during testing in the current project is "acceptable"? With a predictable process, if the process is such that one expects 10 errors per 100 LOC during testing, this means that the testing of this project was probably done properly. But, if past experience with the process shows that about 20 errors per 100 LOC are detected during testing, then a careful look at the testing of the current project is necessary.

It should be clear that if we want to use the past experience to control costs and ensure quality, we must use a process that is predictable. With low predictability, the experience gained through projects is of little value. A predictable process is also said to be *under statistical control* [Hum89]. A process is under statistical control if following the same process produces similar results. This is shown in Figure 2.3; the y-axis represents some property of interest (quality, productivity, etc.), and x-axis represents the projects. The dark line is the expected value of the property for this process. Statistical control implies that most projects will be within a bound around the expected value.

Statistical control also implies that the predictions for a process, which are generally based on the past performance of the process, are only probabilistic. If 20 errors per 100 LOC have been detected in the past for a process (which is under statistical control), then it is expected that with a high probability, this is the range of errors that will be detected during testing in future projects. Still, it is possible that in some projects this may not happen. This may happen if the programmer was very good, had a bout of excellence, or the code was easy, etc. Due to this, any data about

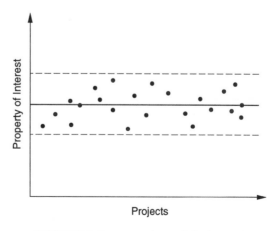

FIGURE 2.3. Process under statistical control.

the current project beyond the range suggested by the process, implies that the data and the project should be carefully examined and allowed to "pass through" only if clear evidence is found that this is a "statistical aberration."

It should be clear that if one hopes to consistently develop software of high quality at low cost, it is necessary to have a process that is under statistical control. A predictable process is an essential requirement for ensuring good quality and low cost. Note that this does not mean that one can never produce high-quality software at low cost without following such a process. It is always possible that a set of bright people might do it. However, what this means is that without such a process, such things cannot be repeated. Hence, if one wants quality consistently across many projects, having a predictable process is essential. Because software engineering is interested in general methods that can be used to develop different software, a predictable process forms the backbone of the software engineering methods.

2.2.2   Support Testability and Maintainability

We have already seen that in the life of software the maintenance costs generally exceed the development costs. Clearly, if we want to reduce the overall cost of software or achieve "global" optimality in terms of cost rather than "local" optimality in terms of development cost only, the goal of development should be to reduce the maintenance effort. That is, one of the important objectives of the development project should be to produce software that is easy to maintain. And the process should be such that it ensures this maintainability.

Frequently, the scftware produced is not easily maintainable. This clearly implies that the development process used for developing software frequently does not have maintainability as a clear goal. One possible reason for this is that the developers frequently develop the software, install it, and then hand it over to a different set of people called maintainers. The maintainers frequently don't even belong to the organization that developed the software but rather to the organization that contracted out the development. In such a situation, clearly there is no incentive for the developers to develop maintainable software, as they don't have to put in the effort for maintenance. This situation can only be alleviated if the developers are made responsible for maintenance, at least for a couple of years after the delivery of software.

Even in development, coding is frequently given a great degree of importance. We have seen that a process consists of phases, and a process generally includes requirements, design, coding, and testing phases. Of the development cost, an example distribution of effort with the different phases is shown in Table 2.1.

The exact numbers will differ with organization and the nature of the process. However, there are some observations we can make. First is that coding consumes only a small percentage of the development effort. This is against the common

Requirements	10%
Design	20%
Coding	20%
Testing	50%

TABLE 2.1. Effort distribution with phases.

Writing programs	13%
Reading programs and manuals	16%
Job communication	32%
Others (including personal)	39%

TABLE 2.2. How programmers spend their time.

naive notion that developing software is largely concerned with writing programs and that programming is the major activity.

Another way of determining the effort spent in programming is to study how programmers spend their time in a software organization. A study conducted in Bell Labs to determine how programmers spend their time, as reported in [Fai85], found the distribution shown in Table 2.2.

This data clearly shows that programming is not the major activity where programmers spend their time. Even if we take away the time spent in "other" activities, the time spent by a programmer writing programs is still less than 25% of the remaining time. It also shows that job communication, which includes meetings, writing memos, discussions, etc., consumes the most time of the programmers. In the study reported by Boehm [Boe81], it was found that programmers spend less than 20% of their time programming. Both these studies show that writing programs does not consume much of the programmers' time. It is 15 to 25% of the total time spent on projects. These data provide additional validation that coding is not the major activity in software development.

The second important observation from the data about effort distribution with phases is that testing consumes the most resources during development. This is, again, contrary to the common practice, which considers testing a side activity that is often not properly planned. Underestimating the testing effort often causes the planners to allocate insufficient resources for testing, which, in turn, results in unreliable software or schedule slippage.

Overall, we can say that the goal of the process should not be to reduce the effort of design and coding, but to reduce the cost of testing and maintenance. Both testing and maintenance depend heavily on the design and coding of software, and these costs can be considerably reduced if the software is designed and coded to make testing and maintenance easier. Hence, during the early phases of the development process the prime issues should be "can it be easily tested" and "can it be easily modified."

2.2.3 Early Defect Removal and Defect Prevention

The notion that programming is the central activity during software development is largely due to programming being considered a difficult task and sometimes an "art." Another consequence of this kind of thinking is the belief that errors largely occur during programming, as it is the hardest activity in software development and offers many opportunities for committing errors. It is now clear that errors can occur at any stage during development. An example distribution of error occurrences by phase is:

Requirements analysis	20%
Design	30%
Coding	50%

As we can see, errors occur throughout the development process. However, the cost of correcting errors of different phases is not the same and depends on when the error is detected and corrected. The relative cost of correcting requirement errors as a function of where they are detected is shown in Figure 2.4 [Boe81].

As one would expect, the greater the delay in detecting an error after it occurs, the more expensive it is to correct it. As the figure shows, an error that occurs during the requirements phase, if corrected during acceptance testing, can cost up to 100 times more than correcting the error during the requirements phase itself. The reason for this is fairly obvious. If there is an error in the requirements, then the design and the code will be effected by it. To correct the error after the coding is done would require both the design and the code to be changed, thereby increasing the cost of correction.

The main moral of this section is that we should attempt to detect errors that occur in a phase during that phase itself and should not wait until testing to detect errors. This is not often practiced. In reality, sometimes testing is the sole point where errors are detected. Besides the cost factor, reliance on testing as the primary source for error detection, due to the limitations of testing, will also result in unreliable software. Error detection and correction should be a continuous process that is done throughout software development. In terms of the development phases, this means that we should try to verify the output of each phase before starting with the next.

Detecting errors soon after they have been introduced is clearly an objective that should be supported by the process. However, even better is to provide support for *defect prevention*. It is generally agreed that all the defect removal methods that exist today are limited in their capability and cannot detect all the defects that are

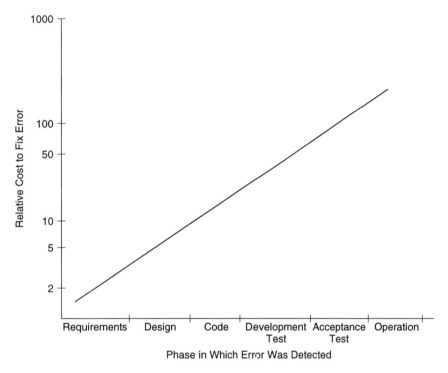

FIGURE 2.4. Cost of correcting errors[Boe81].

introduced. (Why else are there bugs in most software that are released and are then fixed in later versions?) Furthermore, the cost of defect removal is generally high, particularly if they are not detected for a long time. Clearly, then, to reduce the total number of residual defects that exist in a system at the time of delivery and to reduce the cost of defect removal, an obvious approach is to prevent defects from getting introduced. This requires that the process of performing the activities should be such that fewer defects are introduced. The method generally followed to support defect prevention is to use the development process to learn (from previous projects) so that the methods of performing activities can be improved.

2.2.4   Process Improvement

As mentioned earlier, a process is also not a static entity. Improving the quality and reducing the cost of products are fundamental goals of any engineering discipline. In the context of software, as the productivity (and hence the cost of a project) and quality are determined largely by the process, to satisfy the engineering objectives of quality improvement and cost reduction, the software process must be improved.

Having process improvement as a basic goal of the software process implies that the software process used is such that it supports its improvement. This requires that there be means for evaluating the existing process and understanding the weaknesses in the process. Only when support for these activities is available can process improvement be undertaken. And, as in any evaluation, it is always preferable to have a quantifiable evaluation rather than a subjective evaluation. Hence, it is important that the process provides data that can be used to evaluate the current process and its weaknesses.

Having process improvement as a fundamental objective requires that the software process be a closed-loop process. That is, the process must learn from previous experiences, and each project done using the existing process must feed information back into the process itself, which can then use this information for self-improvement. As stated earlier, this activity is largely done by the process management component of the software process. However, to support this activity, information from various other processes will have to flow to the process management process. In other words, to support this activity, other processes will also have to take an active part.

2.3   Software Development Process

In the software development process we focus on the activities directly related to production of the software, for example, design, coding, and testing. A development process model specifies some activities that, according to the model, should be performed, and the order in which they should be performed. As stated earlier, for cost, quality, and project management reasons, development processes are generally phased.

As the development process specifies the major development and quality assurance activities that need to be performed in the project, the development process really forms the core of the software process. The management process is decided based on the development process. Due to the importance of development process, various models have been proposed. In this section we will discuss some of the major models. As processes consist of a sequence of steps, let us first discuss what should be specified for a step.

2.3.1   A Process Step Specification

A production process is a sequence of steps. Each step performs a well-defined activity leading toward the satisfaction of the project goals, with the output of one step forming the input of the next one. Most process models specify the steps that need to be performed and the order in which they need to be performed. However, when implementing a process model, there are some practical issues like when to initiate a step and when to terminate a step that need to be addressed. Here we discuss some of these issues.

As we have seen, a process should aim to detect defects in the phase in which they are introduced. This requires that there be some verification and validation (V&V) at the end of each step. (In verification, consistency with the inputs of the phase is checked, while in validation the consistency with the needs of user is checked.) This implies that there is a clearly defined output of a phase, which can be verified by some means and can form input to the next phase (which may be performed by other people). In other words, it is not acceptable to say that the output of a phase is an idea or a thought in the mind of someone; the output must be a formal and tangible entity. Such outputs of a development process, which are not the final output, are frequently called the *work products*. In software, a work product can be the requirements document, design document, code, prototype, etc.

This restriction that the output of each step be some work product that can be verified suggests that the process should have a small number of steps. Having too many steps results in too many work products or documents, each requiring V&V, and can be very expensive. Due to this, at the top level, a development process typically consists of a few steps, each satisfying a clear objective and producing a document used for V&V. How to perform the activity of the particular step or phase is generally not an issue of the development process. This is an issue addressed by *methodologies* for that activity. We will discuss various methodologies for different activities throughout the book.

As a development process typically contains a sequence of steps, the next issue that comes is when a phase should be initiated and terminated. This is frequently done by specifying the entry criteria and exit criteria for a phase. The *entry criteria* of a phase specifies the conditions that the input to the phase should satisfy in order to initiate the activities of that phase. The *output criteria* specifies the conditions that the work product of this phase should satisfy in order to terminate the activities of the phase. The entry and exit criteria specify constraints of when to start and stop an activity. It should be clear that the entry criteria of a phase should be consistent with the exit criteria of the previous phase.

The entry and exit criteria for a phase in a process depend largely on the *implementation* of the process. For example, for the same process, one organization may have the entry criteria for the design phase as "requirements document signed by the client" and another may have "no more than X errors detected per page in the requirement review." As each phase ends with some V&V activity, a common exit criteria for a phase is "V&V of the phase completed satisfactorily," where *satisfactorily* is defined by the organization based on the objectives of the project and its experience in using the process. The specification of a step with its input, output, and entry and exit criteria is shown in Figure 2.5.

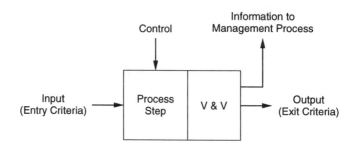

FIGURE 2.5. A step in a development process.

Besides the entry and exit criteria for the input and output, a development step needs to produce some information for the management process. We know that the basic goal of the management process is to control the development process. For controlling a process, the management process needs to have precise knowledge about the development process activities. As the management process is executed by a logically separate group of people, the information about the development process must flow from the development process to the management process. This requires that a step produce some information for the management process. The nature of this information is specified by the management process, based on its needs. (Note the tight coupling of the management process with the development process.) This information (and other such information from previous steps) is used by the management process to exert control on the development process. The flow of information from a step and exercise of control is also shown in Figure 2.5.

Generally, the information flow from a step is in the form of summary reports describing the amount of resources spent in the phase, schedule information, errors found in the V&V activities, etc. This type of information flow at defined points in the development process makes it possible for the project management (i.e., the people executing the management process) to get precise information about the development process, without being directly involved in the development process or without going through the details of all activities of a phase.

It should be clear that the entry and exit criteria and the nature of information flow depends on how the process is implemented in an organization and on the project. Consequently, process models typically do not specify these. However, they must be specified by an organization, if it wishes to adopt a process model for software development.

2.3.2   Waterfall Model

We now discuss some of the common process models that have been proposed. The simplest process model is the *waterfall model*, which states that the phases are organized in a linear order. There are various variations of the waterfall model depending on the nature of activities and the flow of control between them. In a typical model, a project begins with feasibility analysis. On successfully demonstrating the feasibility of a project, the requirements analysis and project planning begins. The design starts after the requirements analysis is complete, and coding begins after the design is complete. Once the programming is completed, the code is integrated and testing is done. On successful completion of testing, the system is installed. After this, the regular operation and maintenance of the system takes place. The model is shown in Figure 2.6.

In this book, we will only discuss the activities related to the development of software. Thus, we will only discuss phases from requirements analysis to testing. The requirements analysis phase is mentioned as "analysis and planning." *Planning* is a critical activity in software development. A good plan is based on the requirements of the system and should be done before later phases begin. However, in practice, detailed requirements are not necessary for planning. Consequently, planning usually overlaps with the requirements analysis, and a plan is ready before the later phases begin. This plan is an additional input to all the later phases.

With the waterfall model, the sequence of activities performed in a software development project is: requirement analysis, project planning, system design, detailed design, coding and unit testing, system integration and testing. This is the order the different phases will be discussed in this book, keeping the sequence as close as possible to the sequence in which the activities are performed.

Linear ordering of activities has some important consequences. First, to clearly identify the end of a phase and the beginning of the next, some certification mechanism has to be employed at the end of each phase. This is usually done by some verification and validation means that will ensure that the output of a phase is consistent with its input (which is the output of the previous phase), and that the output of the phase is consistent with the overall requirements of the system.

The consequence of the need for certification is that each phase must have some defined output that can be evaluated and certified. That is, when the activities of a phase are completed, there should be some product that is produced by that phase. And the goal of a phase is to produce this product. The outputs of the earlier phases are often called *work products* (or *intermediate products*) and are usually in the form of documents like the requirements document or design document. For the coding phase, the output is the code. From this point of view, the output of a software project is not just the final program along with the user documentation, but also the requirements document, design document, project plan, test plan, and test results.

Let us now consider the rationale behind the waterfall model. There are two basic assumptions for justifying the linear ordering of phases in the manner proposed by the waterfall model [Boe81]:

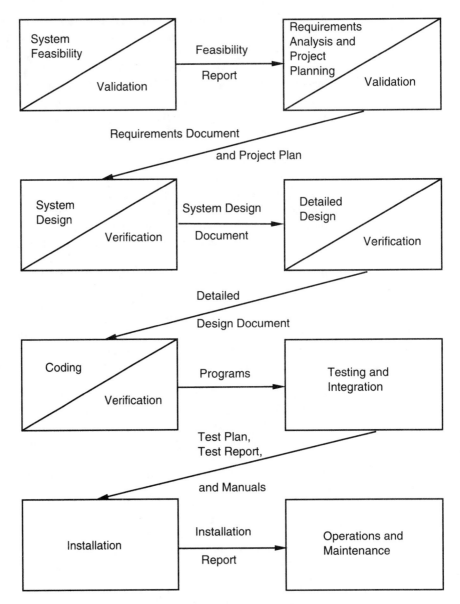

FIGURE 2.6. The waterfall model.

1. For a successful project resulting in a successful product, all phases listed in the waterfall model must be performed anyway.

2. Any different ordering of the phases will result in a less successful software product.

A successful software product is one that satisfies all the objectives of the development project. These objectives include satisfying the requirements and performing the development within time and cost constraints. Generally, for any reasonable size project, all the phases listed in the model must be performed explicitly and formally. Informally performing the phases will work only for very small projects.

The second reason is the one that is now under debate. For many projects, the linear ordering of these phases is clearly the optimum way to organize these activities. However, some argue that for many projects this ordering of activities is unfeasible or suboptimum. We will discuss some of these ideas shortly. Still, the waterfall model is conceptually the simplest process model for software development that has been used most often.

Project Outputs in Waterfall Model

As we have seen, the output of a project employing the waterfall model is not just the final program along and documentation to use it. There are a number of intermediate outputs that must be produced to produce a successful product. Though the set of documents that should be produced in a project is dependent on how the process is implemented, the following is a set of documents that generally forms the minimum set that should be produced in each project:

- Requirements document
- Project plan
- System design document
- Detailed design document
- Test plan and test reports
- Final code
- Software manuals (e.g., user, installation, etc.)
- Review reports

Except for the last one, these are the outputs of the phases, and they have been briefly discussed. To certify an output product of a phase before the next phase begins, reviews are often held. Reviews are necessary, especially for the requirements and design phases, because other certification means are frequently not available. Reviews are formal meetings to uncover deficiencies in a product and will be discussed in more detail later. The review reports are the outcome of these reviews.

Limitations of the Waterfall Model

The waterfall model, although widely used, has received some criticism. Here we list some of these criticisms:

1. The waterfall model assumes that the requirements of a system can be frozen (i.e. baselined) before the design begins. This is possible for systems designed

to automate an existing manual system. But for new systems, determining the requirements is difficult as the user does not even know the requirements. Hence, having unchanging requirements is unrealistic for such projects.

2. Freezing the requirements usually requires choosing the hardware (because it forms a part of the requirements specification). A large project might take a few years to complete. If the hardware is selected early, then due to the speed at which hardware technology is changing, it is likely that the final software will use a hardware technology on the verge of becoming obsolete. This is clearly not desirable for such expensive software systems.

3. The waterfall model stipulates that the requirements be completely specified before the rest of the development can proceed. In some situations it might be desirable to first develop a part of the system completely and then later enhance the system in phases. This is often done for software products that are developed not necessarily for a client (where the client plays an important role in requirements specification), but for general marketing, in which case the requirements are likely to be determined largely by the developers themselves.

4. It is a document driven process that requires formal documents at the end of each phase. This approach tends to make the process documentation-heavy and is not suitable for many applications, particularly interactive applications, where developing elaborate documentation of the user interfaces is not feasible. Also, if the development is done using fourth-generation languages or modern development tools, developing elaborate specifications before implementation is sometimes unnecessary.

Despite these limitations, the waterfall model is the most widely used process model. It is well suited for routine types of projects where the requirements are well understood. That is, if the developing organization is quite familiar with the problem domain and the requirements for the software are quite clear, the waterfall model works well.

2.3.3   Prototyping

The goal of a prototyping-based development process is to counter the first two limitations of the waterfall model. The basic idea here is that instead of freezing the requirements before any design or coding can proceed, a throwaway prototype is built to help understand the requirements. This prototype is developed based on the currently known requirements. Development of the prototype obviously undergoes design, coding, and testing, but each of these phases is not done very formally or thoroughly. By using this prototype, the client can get an actual feel of the system, because the interactions with the prototype can enable the client to better understand the requirements of the desired system. This results in more stable requirements that change less frequently.

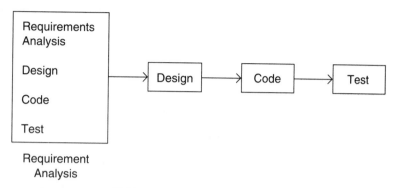

FIGURE 2.7. The prototyping model.

Prototyping is an attractive idea for complicated and large systems for which there is no manual process or existing system to help determine the requirements. In such situations, letting the client "play" with the prototype provides invaluable and intangible inputs that help determine the requirements for the system. It is also an effective method of demonstrating the feasibility of a certain approach. This might be needed for novel systems, where it is not clear that constrains can be met or that algorithms can be developed to implement the requirements. In both situations, the risks associated with the projects are being reduced through the use of prototyping. The process model of the prototyping approach is shown in Figure 2.7.

A development process using throwaway prototyping typically proceeds as follows [GS81]. The development of the prototype typically starts when the preliminary version of the requirements specification document has been developed. At this stage, there is a reasonable understanding of the system and its needs and of which needs are unclear or likely to change. After the prototype has been developed, the end users and clients are given an opportunity to use the prototype and play with it. Based on their experience, they provide feedback to the developers regarding the prototype: what is correct, what needs to be modified, what is missing, what is not needed, etc. Based on the feedback, the prototype is modified to incorporate some of the suggested changes that can be done easily, and then the users and the clients are again allowed to use the system. This cycle repeats until, in the judgment of the prototypers and analysts, the benefit from further changing the system and obtaining feedback is outweighed by the cost and time involved in making the changes and obtaining the feedback. Based on the feedback, the initial requirements are modified to produce the final requirements specification, which is then used to develop the production quality system.

For prototyping for the purposes of requirement analysis to be feasible, its cost must be kept low. Consequently, only those features are included in the prototype that will have a valuable return from the user experience. Exception handling, recovery, and conformance to some standards and formats are typically not included in prototypes. In prototyping, as the prototype is to be discarded, there is no point in implementing those parts of the requirements that are already well understood. Hence, the focus of the development is to include those features that are not properly understood. And the development approach is "quick and dirty" with the focus on quick development rather than quality. Because the prototype is to be thrown away, only minimal documentation needs to be produced during prototyping. For example, design documents, a test plan, and a test case specification are not needed during the development of the prototype. Another important cost-cutting measure is to reduce testing. Because testing consumes a major part of development expenditure during regular software development, this has a considerable impact in reducing costs. By using these type of cost-cutting methods, it is possible to keep the cost of the prototype less than a few percent of the total development cost.

Prototyping is often not used, as it is feared that development costs may become large. However, in some situations, the cost of software development without prototyping may be more than with prototyping. There are two major reasons for this. First, the experience of developing the prototype might reduce the cost of the later phases when the actual software development is done. Secondly, in many projects the requirements are constantly changing, particularly when development takes a long time. We saw earlier that changes in requirements at a late stage during development substantially increase the cost of the project. By elongating the requirements analysis phase (prototype development does take time), the requirements are "frozen" at a later time, by which time they are likely to be more developed and, consequently, more stable. In addition, because the client and users get experience with the system, it is more likely that the requirements specified after the prototype will be closer to the actual requirements. This again will lead to fewer changes in the requirements at a later time. Hence, the costs incurred due to changes in the requirements may be substantially reduced by prototyping. Hence, the cost of the development after the prototype can be substantially less than the cost without prototyping; we have already seen how the cost of developing the prototype itself can be reduced.

Prototyping is catching on. It is well suited for projects where requirements are hard to determine and the confidence in obtained requirements is low. In such projects, a waterfall model will have to freeze the requirements in order for the development to continue, even when the requirements are not stable. This leads to requirement changes and associated rework while the development is going on. Requirements frozen after experience with the prototype are likely to be more stable. Overall, in projects where requirements are not properly understood in the beginning, using the prototyping process model can be the most effective method for developing the software. It is an excellent technique for reducing some types of risks associated with a project. We will further discuss prototyping when we discuss requirements specification and risk management.

2.3.4 Iterative Enhancement

The iterative enhancement model [BT75] counters the third limitation of the waterfall model and tries to combine the benefits of both prototyping and the waterfall model. The basic idea is that the software should be developed in increments, each increment adding some functional capability to the system until the full system is implemented. At each step, extensions and design modifications can be made. An advantage of this approach is that it can result in better testing because testing each increment is likely to be easier than testing the entire system as in the waterfall model. Furthermore, as in prototyping, the increments provide feedback to the client that is useful for determining the final requirements of the system.

In the first step of this model, a simple initial implementation is done for a subset of the overall problem. This subset is one that contains some of the key aspects of the problem that are easy to understand and implement and which form a useful and usable system. A *project control list* is created that contains, in order, all the tasks that must be performed to obtain the final implementation. This project control list gives an idea of how far the project is at any given step from the final system.

Each step consists of removing the next task from the list, designing the implementation for the selected task, coding and testing the implementation, performing an analysis of the partial system obtained after this step, and updating the list as a result of the analysis. These three phases are called *the design phase*, *implementation phase*, and *analysis phase*. The process is iterated until the project control list is empty, at which time the final implementation of the system will be available. The iterative enhancement process model is shown in Figure 2.8.

The project control list guides the iteration steps and keeps track of all tasks that must be done. Based on the analysis, one of the tasks in the list can include redesign of defective components or redesign of the entire system. However, redesign of the system will generally occur only in the initial steps. In the later steps, the design would have stabilized and there is less chance of redesign. Each entry in the list is a task that should be performed in one step of the iterative enhancement process

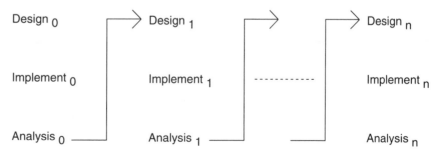

FIGURE 2.8. The iterative enhancement model.

and should be simple enough to be completely understood. Selecting tasks in this manner will minimize the chances of error and reduce the redesign work. The design and implementation phases of each step can be performed in a top-down manner or by using some other technique.

One effective use of this type of model is for product development, in which the developers themselves provide the specifications and therefore have a lot of control on what specifications go in the system and what stay out. In fact, most products undergo this type of development process. First, a version is released that contains some capability. Based on the feedback from users and experience with this version, a list of additional desirable features and capabilities is generated. These features form the basis of enhancement of the software, and are included in the next version. In other words, the first version contains some core capability. And then more features are added to later versions.

However, in a customized software development, where the client has to essentially provide and approve the specifications, it is not always clear how this process can be applied. Another practical problem with this type of development project comes in generating the business contract—how will the cost of additional features be determined and negotiated, particularly because the client organization is likely to be tied to the original vendor who developed the first version. Overall, in these types of projects, this process model can be useful if the "core" of the application to be developed is well understood and the "increments" can be easily defined and negotiated. In client-oriented projects, this process has the major advantage that the client's organization does not have to pay for the entire software together; it can get the main part of the software developed and perform cost-benefit analysis for it before enhancing the software with more capabilities.

2.3.5 The Spiral Model

This is a recent model that has been proposed by Boehm [Boe88]. As the name suggests, the activities in this model can be organized like a spiral that has many cycles. The radial dimension represents the cumulative cost incurred in accomplishing the steps done so far, and the angular dimension represents the progress made in completing each cycle of the spiral. The model is shown in Figure 2.9 [Boe88].

Each cycle in the spiral begins with the identification of objectives for that cycle, the different alternatives that are possible for achieving the objectives, and the constraints that exist. This is the first quadrant of the cycle (upper-left quadrant). The next step in the cycle is to evaluate these different alternatives based on the objectives and constraints. The focus of evaluation in this step is based on the risk perception for the project. Risks reflect the chances that some of the objectives of the project may not be met. Risk management will be discussed in more detail later in the book. The next step is to develop strategies that resolve the uncertainties

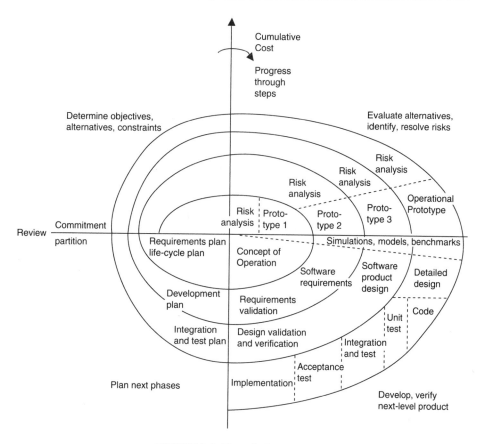

FIGURE 2.9. The spiral model [Boe88].

and risks. This step may involve activities such as benchmarking, simulation, and prototyping. Next, the software is developed, keeping in mind the risks. Finally the next stage is planned.

The development step depends on the remaining risks. For example, if performance or user-interface risks are considered more important than the program development risks, the next step may be an evolutionary development that involves developing a more detailed prototype for resolving the risks. On the other hand, if the program development risks dominate and the previous prototypes have resolved all the user-interface and performance risks, the next step will follow the basic waterfall approach.

The risk-driven nature of the spiral model allows it to accommodate any mixture of a specification-oriented, prototype-oriented, simulation-oriented, or some other type of approach. An important feature of the model is that each cycle of the spiral is completed by a review that covers all the products developed during that cycle, including plans for the next cycle. The spiral model works for development as well as enhancement projects.

In a typical application of the spiral model, one might start with an extra *round zero*, in which the feasibility of the basic project objectives is studied. These project objectives may or may not lead to a development/enhancement project. Such high-level objectives include increasing the efficiency of code generation of a compiler, producing a new full-screen text editor and developing an environment for improving productivity. The alternatives considered in this round are also typically very high-level, such as whether the organization should go for in-house development, or contract it out, or buy an existing product. In *round one*, a concept of operation might be developed. The objectives are stated more precisely and quantitatively and the cost and other constraints are defined precisely. The risks here are typically whether or not the goals can be met within the constraints. The plan for the next phase will be developed, which will involve defining separate activities for the project. In *round two* the top-level requirements are developed. In *succeeding rounds* the actual development may be done.

This is a relatively new model; it can encompass different development strategies. In addition to the development activities, it incorporates some of the management and planning activities into the model. For high-risk projects this might be a preferred model.

2.4   Project Management Process

Proper management is an *integral* part of software development. A large software development project involves many people working for a long period of time. We have seen that a development process typically partitions the problem of developing software into a set of phases. To meet the cost, quality, and schedule objectives, resources have to be properly allocated to each activity for the project, and progress of different activities has to be monitored and corrective actions taken, if needed. All these activities are part of the project management process.

The project management process component of the software process specifies all activities that need to be done by the project management to ensure that cost and quality objectives are met. Its basic task is to ensure that, once a development process is chosen, it is implemented optimally. The focus of the management process is on issues like planning a project, estimating resource and schedule, and monitoring and controlling the project. In other words, the basic task is to plan the detailed implementation of the process for the particular project and then ensure that the plan is followed. For a large project, a proper management process is essential for success.

2.4.1   Phases of Management Process

The activities in the management process for a project can be grouped broadly into three phases: planning, monitoring and control, and termination analysis. Project management begins with planning, which is perhaps the single largest responsibility of the project management. The goal of this phase is to develop a *plan* for software development following which the objectives of the project can be met successfully and efficiently. Proper planning is recognized as a critical ingredient for a successful project. The project plan provides the fundamental basis for project management. A software plan is usually produced before the development activity begins and is updated as development proceeds and data about progress of the project becomes available. During planning, the major activities are cost estimation, schedule and milestone determination, project staffing, quality control plans, and controlling and monitoring plans.

In cost and schedule estimation, the total cost and time needed for successfully completing the project are estimated. In addition, cost and schedule for the different activities of the development process to be used are also estimated, as the development process only specifies the activities, not the cost and time requirement for them. In addition to estimating the effort and schedule for various activities and components in the project, the project plan plans for all the software quality assurance activities that need to be performed in order to ensure that quality objectives are met. A plan also provides methods for handling change and methods for monitoring a project. Project planning is undoubtedly the single most important management activity, and output of this forms the basis of monitoring and control. We will devote one full chapter later in the book to project planning.

Project monitoring and control phase of the management process is the longest in terms of duration; it encompasses most of the development process. It includes all activities the project management has to perform while the development is going on to ensure that project objectives are met and the development proceeds according to the developed plan (and update the plan, if needed). As cost, schedule, and quality are the major driving forces, most of the activity of this phase revolves around monitoring factors that affect these. Monitoring potential risks for the project, which might prevent the project from meeting its objectives, is another important activity during this phase. And if the information obtained by monitoring suggests that objectives may not be met, necessary actions are taken in this phase by exerting suitable control on the development activities.

Monitoring a development process requires proper information about the project. Such information is typically obtained by the management process from the development process. As shown earlier in Figure 2.5, the implementation of a development process model should be such that each step in the development process produces information that the management process needs for that step. That is, the development process provides the information the management process needs. However, interpretation of the information is part of monitoring and control.

For example, suppose that after the design is done, the development process provides the information that the design took three times the effort that was projected in the plan. The experience about the general distribution of effort (as shown in Table 2.1) suggests that the total cost of the project is likely to be much larger than was estimated earlier. When this situation is observed during project monitoring as part of project control, corrective action has to be exerted on the project, as without it the chances of meeting the cost, schedule, and quality objectives are low. The corrective actions could be to reduce the scope of the project, renegotiate the cost and schedule, add more manpower, use better tools, etc.

Whereas monitoring and control lasts the entire duration of the project, the last phase of the management process—termination analysis—is performed when the development process is over. The basic reason for performing termination analysis is to provide information about the development process. Remember that a project is an instantiation of the process. To understand the properties of the process, data from many projects that used the process will be needed. Using the predictability property of the process, this data about the process can be used to make predictions and estimations about future projects. The data about the project is also needed to analyze the process. For these reasons, the termination analysis phase is needed. We will discuss the use of project data for predicting and process improvement later in the chapter.

The temporal relationship between the management process and the development process is shown in Figure 2.10. This is an idealized relationship showing that planning is done before development begins, and termination analysis is done after development is over. As the figure shows, during the development, from the various phases of the development process, quantitative information flows to the monitoring and control phase of the management process, which uses the information to exert control on the development process.

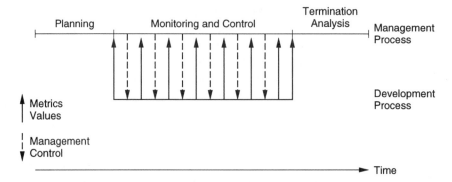

FIGURE 2.10. Temporal relationship between development and management process.

2.4.2   Metrics, Measurement, and Models

For effective project monitoring, the information coming from the development process to the management process should be objective and quantitative data about the project. If the information obtained is not quantitative, then subjective judgments will have to be used, which an engineering discipline needs to minimize. The need for quantitative data from the process requires that software metrics be used.

Software metrics are quantifiable measures that could be used to measure different characteristics of a software system or the software development process. All engineering disciplines have metrics (such as metrics for weight, density, wavelength, and temperature) to quantify various characteristics of their products. Software metrics is an emerging area. Because the software has no physical attributes, conventional metrics are not much help in designing metrics for software. A number of metrics have been proposed to quantify things like the size, complexity, and reliability of a software product.

Intricately tied to metrics is measurement. Metrics provide the scale for quantifying qualities; actual measurement must be performed on a given software system in order to use metrics for quantifying characteristics of the given software. An analogy in the physical world is that centimeters is the metric of length, but to determine the length of a given rod, one must measure it using some means like a measuring tape. The measurement method must be objective and should produce the same result independent of the measurer.

Values for some metrics can be directly measured; others might have to be deduced by other measurement (an analogy could be that the distance between two points can be deduced by measuring the speed of a vehicle and measuring the time it takes to traverse the given distance). If a metric is not measured directly, we call the metric *indirect*. Some factors, like many software quality parameters, cannot be measured directly either because there are no means to measure the metric directly, or because the final product whose metric is of interest still does not exist. For example, it is desirable to predict the quality of software during the early phases of development, such as after design. Because the software does not yet exist, the metric will have to be predicted from the factors that can be measured after design. Similarly, the reliability of a software cannot, in general, be measured directly, even though precise definition and metrics for reliability exist. It has to be estimated from other measurements that *are* possible.

For estimating, *models* are needed. A model is a relationship of the predicted variable (the property of interest) that other variables that can be measured. That is, if there is some metric of interest which cannot be measured directly, then we build models to estimate the metric value based on the value of some other metrics that we *can* measure. The model may be determined based on empirical data or it may be analytic [CDS86]. As these models capture the relationships whose exact nature depends on the process, building a model is an issue that concerns process management; we will discuss it later in this chapter.

It should be clear that metrics, measurement, and models go together. Metrics provide a quantification of some property, measurements provide the actual value for the metrics, and models are needed to get the value for the metrics that cannot be measured directly (i.e., provide the measurement indirectly by using a model). Let us now try to understand how metrics are used in the project management process.

All metrics must have a purpose; otherwise why should we collect them? Generally, the purpose in some way will be related to achieving the basic objective of low cost and high quality. Any metric that does not help directly or indirectly in improving the product quality or reducing its cost is of academic interest only. For example, let's take a metric that gives for code (or some other document) the total frequency of occurrence of different alphabets. This is a bona-fide metric that quantifies something precisely, and it can be measured easily. It may be of some use to linguists or people involved in encryption, but it is of no practical use as far as software engineering is concerned.

Let us consider a more commonly used metric. Many metrics have been proposed for measuring the "complexity" of code, or design—it seems that knowing the complexity of the code is interesting. However, "interestingness" is not of much use to us—we are interested in cost, schedule, and quality. Hence, unless we can relate complexity to these parameters, a complexity metric is of little use (regardless of the claim of how "accurately" it measures complexity). Fortunately, in this case, complexity is related to some quality parameters, as a complex program is generally harder to modify (hence has low modifiability) and is difficult to code and debug (and thus requires more effort).

However, this is not the complete picture. If we are interested in measuring complexity, say, for the purpose of improving the maintainability or the error-detection process, we must first establish a clear relationship between the chosen metric and the property of interest, because most of the quality properties cannot be directly measured and hence have to be estimated from other measurements. Unless this relationship is established, any metric is as good as any other (in fact, the frequency metric mentioned earlier can also be claimed to be a complexity metric). Hence, it is very important that relationships of a metric are established with some quality or cost parameter. For example, in the case of complexity, if we choose the cyclomatic complexity (described later in the book), some correlation of the metric values and maintainability or number of errors must first be established. If it is shown that there is a strong correlation between the cyclomatic complexity of a module and the number of errors made in that module, then the metric can be used to estimate the "error proneness" of a module: a high-complexity module can be "highlighted" as error prone, and then measures can be taken to improve the quality of that module. In other words, once the relationship with a parameter of interest is established, the metric value for a project can be used to improve the parameter with which the correlation is established.

Establishing a relationship with the property of interest with some metrics that we can measure is essentially building models. The exact nature of the model depends on the process and is discussed later in the chapter. Once the models are known for the process being used, the value of some measurable metrics can be used to estimate other values of interest that have a direct bearing on cost and quality. These can then be used by project management—at the very least they provide objective means for project monitoring. In fact, all quantitative data flowing from the development process to the management process is essentially some metric values. Therefore, one can say that metrics (and measurement and models for estimation) are essential for objective and data-based project management. Without metrics, project management activities will have to depend on subjective evaluation and information, which as we have said, goes against the fundamental goal of engineering.

It is important to understand this role of software metrics. Many metrics have been proposed in literature, and most of them have been proposed without any studies about their correlation with anything. However, now relationships of many metrics have been established with some parameters that affect cost or quality of the project. In this book, for each major development activity, we will define some metrics that can be used for that activity, but we will focus primarily on the metrics for which some relationships have been established. It should be pointed out that a relationship between a metric and some parameter may be "local," i.e., it holds for some type of processes and some environments (which influence the actual process implementation) and not for other types of processes. That is, the exact nature of the relationship may not be "global" and is more likely to depend on local conditions.

2.5 Software Configuration Management Process

Throughout development, software consists of a collection of items (such as programs, data, and documents) that can easily be changed. During software development, the design, code, and even requirements are often changed, and the changes occur at any time during the development. This easily changeable nature of software and the fact that changes often take place require that changes be done in a controlled manner. *Software configuration management (SCM)* [BHS79, Ber84, IEE87] is the discipline for systematically controlling the changes that take place during development. The IEEE defines SCM as "SCM is the process of identifying and defining the items in the system, controlling the change of these items throughout their life cycle, recording and reporting the status of items and change requests, and verifying the completeness and correctness of items" [IEE87].

Software configuration management is a process independent of the development process largely because most development models cannot accommodate changes at any time during development. Development processes handle "normal" changes, such as changes in code while the programmer is developing it, changes in requirements during the requirements phase, etc. However, most cannot properly handle changes like requirements changes while coding is being done, code changes during system acceptance testing, etc. As such changes are a fact of life (requirements do change after the requirements phase is over and the requirements have been "finalized," and bugs are found in a module even after it has been coded and "handed over"), they are handled by the software configuration management activities. The changes themselves are still performed by the development team, but approving the change, evaluating the impact of the change, decide what needs to be done to accommodate a change request, etc. are issues that are handled by SCM. In a way, the development process is brought under the configuration control process, so that changes are allowed in a controlled manner, as shown in Figure 2.11 for a waterfall-type development process model [Whi91]. Note that SCM directly controls only the products of a process (most products of phases are called *baselines*, as discussed later) and only indirectly influences the activities producing the product.

The basic reason for having SCM, as with any other activities for a project, is that it has beneficial effects on cost, schedule, and quality of the product being developed. As we saw earlier, cost, schedule, and quality are the fundamental concerns that drive a software project. Changes, and rework required for the changes, can have an enormous adverse effect on the cost and quality of the product being developed. (We saw earlier that changes and rework can consume up to 50% of the development effort. If left uncontrolled, this can go much higher.) The fundamental reason for having the SCM process is to control the changes so that they have minimal effect on cost, schedule, and quality.

Though configuration management is more general than change management, managing changes is its primary task, and it is this aspect of it that we will focus on here. Much of the material here is based on [Whi91, BHS80]. We will only briefly discuss the issues of system building, version management, etc., which sometimes also come under SCM; the user is referred to [Whi91] for discussion of these topics. With this, SCM can be considered as having three major components:

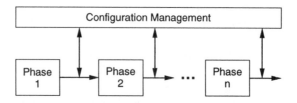

FIGURE 2.11. Configuration management and development process.

- Software configuration identification
- Change control
- Status accounting and auditing

These three components of SCM are directly derived from the IEEE definition of SCM. In the rest of this section, we will discuss these three components.

2.5.1   Configuration Identification

The first requirement for any change management is to have a clearly agreed-on basis for change. That is, when a change is done, it should be clear *to what* the change has been applied. This requires *baselines* to be established. A baseline, once established, forms the basis of change [BHS80]. A *baseline change* is the changing of the established baseline, which is controlled by SCM.

A baseline also forms a reference point in the development of a system and is generally formally defined after the major phases in development. At the time it is established, a software baseline represents the software in the most recent state. After baseline changes (made through SCM), the state of the software is defined by the most recent baseline and the changes that were made. Some of the common baselines are functional or requirements baseline, design baseline, and product or system baseline. *Functional or requirements baseline* is generally the requirements document that specifies the functional requirements for the software. *Design baseline* consists of the different components in the software and their designs. *Product or system baseline* represents the developed system. It should be clear that a baseline is established only after the product is relatively stable. For example, there is no point establishing the first rough draft of the SRS (which has not yet been reviewed) as the baseline, as it is still a "working" document. Only when the requirements are "frozen," is the baseline established. We will discuss this issue more later. Though other project-specific baselines can be established (for example, documents like plans and test case specifications can be baselined), we will assume that only these baselines exist.

Though the goal of SCM is to control the establishment and changes to these baselines, treating each baseline as a single unit for the purposes of change is undesirable, as the change may be limited to a very small portion of the baseline. For example, suppose only one module in a large system is changed. If we do not consider the product baseline for the system as consisting of many modules (or module hierarchies), then this change will be viewed as changing the product baseline, and a finer, module-level control cannot be established on this change.

For this reason, a baseline can consist of many software configuration items (SCIs), or *items*. An SCI is a document or an artifact that is explicitly placed under configuration control and that can be regarded as a basic unit for modification. A baseline essentially is an arrangement of a set of SCIs [BHS80]. That is, a baseline is a set of SCIs and the relationship between them. For example, a requirements baseline may consist of many requirement SCIs (i.e., each requirement is an SCI) and how these SCIs are related in the requirements baseline (e.g. in which order they appear). With a baseline consisting of many SCIs, a new issue arises for SCM: how to "build" a baseline from the SCIs. The basic problem of system building is how to get a consistent system from the SCIs, particularly when the SCIs might be getting changed and multiple versions of an SCI may exist (see the discussion later). In other words, the system building procedure has to be such that it rebuilds the system if an SCI changes to make sure that the changes are reflected in the system and selects the proper version of SCIs. The first part of this problem is sometimes handled by tools like the Makefile [Fel79]. Makefile requires a definition of the system in terms of its components, dependencies between components, and how the system is to be constructed from the components. When a system build is done using the Makefile, it rebuilds the system if any of the components it depends on has changed since the last time the system was built. More advanced tools are needed to solve the issue of incorporating versions in a flexible manner. We will not discuss this aspect of SCM further; the reader is referred to [Whi91] for more information.

Because the baseline consists of the SCIs and SCI is the basic unit for change control, the SCM process starts with identification of configuration items. There are no hard and fast rules for SCI selection, except that SCI should be a part of some baseline, and once identified, it is given an identifiable name and becomes the unit of change control. Frequently, the requirements or functional baseline has just one SCI—the requirements document. However, if desired, different chapters, sections, or even paragraphs can be treated as SCIs (provided they are labeled properly for referencing). Similarly, the design baseline frequently consists of a single SCI—the design document. Again, if needed, different portions of the design can be designated SCIs.

At the code level, that is, for the product baseline, generally multiple SCIs exist. Other approaches are also possible. Multiple SCIs are used at the code level, because usually the change volume is the largest at the code level (almost any change requires some changes in the code). Furthermore, frequently a large number of developers are involved during the coding activity, with different developers responsible for different parts. By having a finer granularity for SCI, assigning responsibility for change becomes easier, making it easier to control and track changes. For defining SCIs, one practice is to have each separately compilable module as an SCI, with the name of the module being the name of the SCI. Another approach is to have each file (consisting of some modules or definitions) treated as an SCI, with the name of the file being the name of the SCI.

It should be clear that the SCIs being managed by SCM are not independent of one another and there are dependencies between various SCIs. An SCI X is said to *depend* on another SCI Y, if a change to Y might require a change to be made to X for X to remain correct or for the baselines to remain consistent [Whi91].

A change request, though, might require changes be made to some SCIs; the dependency of other SCIs on the ones being changed might require that other SCIs also need to be changed. Clearly, the dependency between the SCIs needs to be properly understood when changes are being made. However, though it is possible to specify the dependencies, they are frequently not explicitly documented but are derived from the nature of the SCIs. For example, the SCI representing the design document depends on the SCI representing the requirements document. Frequently, in design documents, each design item specifies which requirements it implements. If a design baseline is considered as composed of many SCIs, this information can be used to understand the dependencies between different items in requirements and in design. In code, an SCI representing a module might depend on another module SCI, depending on the relationship between them. This dependency can generally be obtained from the design specifications. While doing change control, these dependencies are used to decide what needs to be changed for a change request.

2.5.2   Change Control

Once the SCIs are identified and their dependencies understood, the change control procedures of SCM can be applied. Most of the decisions regarding the change are generally taken by the *configuration control board (CCB)*, which is a group of people responsible for configuration management, headed by the *configuration manager (CM)*. For smaller projects, the CCB might consist of just one (full-time or part-time) person (the CM). Typically, for a project, the constitution of the CCB and the procedures it will follow are specified in the software configuration management plans. We will generally use CM to refer to the CCB.

Let us come back to the issue of what exactly is under the control of SCM. Typically, while an SCI is under development and is not visible to other SCIs, it is considered being in the *working* state. An SCI in the working state is not under SCM and can be changed freely. Once the developer is satisfied that the SCI is stable enough for it to be used by others, the SCI is given to the CM for review, and the item enters the state "under review." Once an item is in this state, it is considered as "frozen," and any changes made to a private copy that the developer may have made are not recognized. The CM reviews the SCI (or gets it reviewed), and if it is approved, enters it into a *library*, after which the item is formally under SCM. The basic purpose of this review is to make sure that the item is of satisfactory quality and is needed by others, though the exact nature of review will depend on the nature of the SCI and the actual practice of SCM. For example, the review might entail checking if the item meets its specifications or if it has been properly unit tested. If the item is not approved, the developer may be given the item back and the SCI enters the

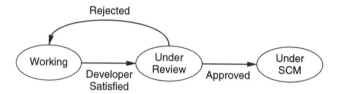

FIGURE 2.12. SCM life cycle of an item

working state again. This "life cycle" of an item from the SCM perspective, which is an enhancement from the one described in [Whi91], is shown in Figure 2.12.

Once an SCI is in the library, it cannot be modified, even by the author/developer, without the permission of the CM. An SCI under SCM can be changed only if the change has been approved by the CM. In such a case, the SCI is checked out of the library, the change made to the SCI, and then the modified SCI is given back to the CM, who reviews it again to ensure that the change is properly done and then checks the item back in the library. This aspect of SCM is sometimes called *library management* and can be done with the aid of tools. Frequently, the changed SCI does not replace the old copy; instead a new version of the SCI is created because the old version might be used in some working system (frequently the older version of the system to which the SCI belongs), and if the new version is not fully compatible with the old version, we would not like to disturb the working of the systems that use the old version. In other words, after implementing an approved change to an SCI, both the old and new versions of the SCI may exist in the library. The old version may be used in some older versions of the system, and the new one may be used in some later versions of the system. Clearly, with multiple versions of SCIs and multiple versions of systems using different versions of SCIs, *version management* becomes extremely important. Even if only one version of each SCI is maintained, it is desirable to know the change history and the version number of the SCI. This is frequently done by keeping a change log with the SCI and appropriately numbering the versions. We do not discuss the version management aspect of SCM further in this book; the reader is referred to [Whi91] for further information.

A change is initiated by a *change request (CR)*. The reason for change can be anything. However, the most common reasons are requirement changes, changes due to bugs, platform changes, and enhancement changes. The CR for a change generally consists of three parts. The first part describes the change, reason for change, the SCIs that are affected, the priority of the change, etc. The second part, filled by the CM, describes the decision taken by the CCB on this CR (approved, not approved), the actions the CM feels need to be done to implement this change (no action, change of documentation, change of software, etc.), and any other comments the CM may have. The third part is filled by the implementor who later implements the change. The implementor may also maintain a change log to facilitate the undoing of the change, if needed. The CR is assigned a unique number by the CCB, which is used to refer to it. A CR will contain the following information:

> CR ID
> About the change request
>> Items to be changed
>> Description of change
>> Reasons for change
>> Priority of change
>> Originator
> CCB comments
>> CR approved/rejected
>> Actions needed
>> Comments
> Implementation information
>> Status of change implementation
>> Comments

The CM evaluates the CR primarily by considering the effect of change on cost, schedule, and quality of the project and the benefits likely to come due to this change. The cost-benefit analysis may require interaction with the change originator and may require some negotiations. Once the CR is accepted and the actions that need to be taken to maintain consistency of the software are identified by the CM, the project manager will generally take over and plan and schedule the change implementation. The cost and schedule for implementing the CR is also sometimes recorded in the CR itself. The CR is then generally implemented by the person responsible for the SCI, generally the programmer if the SCI is a code module. Any comments regarding the change implementation are also recorded in the CR. Hence, a CR form not only contains the change request, but a summary of all the activities related to the change. By looking at the CR form, the status of a change request can be determined.

One of the most common reasons for a CR is the discovery of some bug or problem in the software. Frequently, the change requests originating due to faults are made on a different form called a *fault report (FR)*. FRs are generally treated as high-priority CRs, especially if the fault being reported is serious. An FR is also assigned a unique ID by the CM. Besides requesting the change, FRs are used to track the status of known bugs in the system. An FR form will generally contain:

> FR ID
> Fault information
>> Description of the fault
>> Severity of the fault
>> Item suspected of being faulty
>> Effect of the fault

                    Circumstances and environment data that caused the fault to
                        manifest itself
                    Possible fixes
                    Originator
                CCB comments
                    Approved/rejected
                    Priority
                    Comments
              Fault fixing information
                    Items changed
                    Comments

Some changes might effect the baselines, while others might not have any effect
on the baselines. If a CR affects the baseline, then the baseline has to be updated.
This is generally done by the CM, who controls the baselines. Frequently, changes
to baselines are appended to the baselines, particularly if the baseline is a paper
document like the requirements document. If too many baseline changes are made,
then the baseline may be revised to create an updated baseline incorporating all
the changes.

2.5.3   Status Accounting and Auditing

Incorporating changes, after they have been approved, takes time. So the changes
to items occur over a period of time. Some mechanisms are needed to record the
current status of a CR/FR, which can be used by a manager to determine the status
of all the change requests. Though the role of status accounting is more general,
we will limit our discussion to status of CRs/FRs. The aim of status accounting is
to answer questions like what is the status of a CR (approved or not), what is the
status of an approved CR, what is the frequency of CRs, what is the average time
and effort for fixing a CR, and what is the number of CRs per SCI.

For status accounting, the main source of information is the CRs and FRs themselves. Generally, a field in the CR/FR is added that specifies its current status.
The status could be active (i.e., change is being performed), completed, or not
scheduled. Information about dates and efforts can also be added to the CR. The
information from the CRs/FRs can be used to prepare a summary (e.g., all the CRs
that are still pending, all the FRs that are still "not closed"), which can be used by
the project manager and the CCB to track all the changes.

Auditing has a different role. In general, an audit for a process is performed by
auditors (who are different from the people implementing the process). The main
objective of an audit is to determine if the specified process is being followed
and whether the specified process satisfies the goals of the process. The same
is done for SCM auditing. Records of past changes are evaluated by the auditor
to determine if the SCM procedures are being followed, and the procedures are

evaluated to ensure that the SCM goals are met. One impact of auditing is that while performing SCM, enough information has to be recorded such that an SCM audit can be performed. Generally, a periodic auditing is performed. The period of the audit may be small in the start but may increase as the processes become well established and institutionalized.

2.6 Process Management Process

A software process is not a static entity—it has to change to improve so that the products produced using the process are of higher quality and are less costly. Reducing cost and improving quality are fundamental goals of engineering. For producing software it implies that the software process must continually be improved, as cost and quality of products are determined to a great extent by the process. As stated earlier, this is the objective of the process management process. It should be emphasized that process management is quite different from project management. In process management the focus is on improving the process that improves the general quality and productivity for the products produced using the process. In project management the focus is on executing the current project and ensuring that the objectives of the project are met. The time duration of interest for project management is typically the duration of the project, while process management works on a much larger time scale as each project is viewed as providing a data point for the process.

Process management is an advanced topic beyond the scope of this book. Interested readers are referred to the book by Humphrey [Hum89]. We will only briefly discuss some aspects here. However, one aspect of process management is to build models for the process by which the nature of the relationship between some metric values for the process can be captured. As these models directly affect project management, we will discuss this issue in some detail.

2.6.1 Building Estimation Models

It is not always easy to define metrics to quantify many quality attributes (e.g. usability), and for many others where metrics can be defined it is not easy to measure the value (e.g. reliability). In such cases, it is important to build models that can be used to estimate or predict the (quality) parameter of interest by using the metric values that can be measured and the model. These models can then be used for project management in predicting various parameters of interest for the project.

Such models are generally process-specific as the property of interest depends on the process. That is, if the process changes, the value of the property will change even if the input values (i.e., the metrics that have been measured) are the same. For example, suppose there is a strong correlation between the value of some complexity metric and total testing effort. The actual correlation will clearly depend on the process. A process using good tools and methods will consume less effort than an ad-hoc process not using any tools, even for the same complexity.

Though the models capture properties of the process, they are used heavily in project management. As discussed earlier, project management uses the models to predict some values of interest, and these predicted values can then be used for project monitoring. For example, there is a strong dependence of the total effort required for a project on the project size. However, the actual nature of the dependence depends on the process—a very efficient process with high productivity will consume a lot less effort for the same project compared to an inefficient process. Once the model for a particular process is built, it can be used for effort estimation by projects using this process. In fact, this is how cost and schedule estimation is done for processes.

Hence, we can say that models capture some aspects of the process that are quite often important for project management. Hence, for effective project management, it is important that appropriate models be built for the process.

A model for the software process (or a part of it) can be represented as [CDS86]

$$y = f(x_1, x_2, \ldots, x_n).$$

The dependent variable y is the metric of interest (e.g., total effort, reliability, etc.). $x_1, x_2, \ldots, x_n$ are *independent* variables that typically represent some metric values that can be measured when this model is to be applied. The function f is really the model itself that specifies how y depends on these independent variables for the process. A model may be *theoretical* or *data-driven*. In a theoretical model, the relationship between the dependent and independent variables is determined by some existing relationships that are known. Such models are independent of data. Data-driven models are generally the result of statistical analysis of the data collected about the process from previous projects. In these models, one hypothesizes some model, whose actual parameters are then determined through the analysis of data. Many of the process models used in project management are data-driven. Collecting data for building such models is the major reason for the termination analysis phase of the management process.

Let us briefly discuss how data-driven models are constructed. It is clear that for data-driven models, data from past projects is needed to obtain the model. The larger the data set, the more accurate the model. The goal of building a model is to determine the relationship between a metric of interest and some other metric values. The simplest such model is one with only one independent variable, that is, to determine the relationship between two variables, say, y (variable of interest) and x (variable whose value could be measured).

The first question is whether there is any relationship between them. Suppose for the last n projects we have the values of y and x and our data set is $(x_1, y_1), (x_2, y_2),$

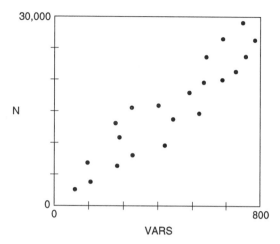

FIGURE 2.13. N versus *VARS*.

..., (x_n, y_n). This can be done graphically by drawing a *scatter plot* [CDS86], in which points for all the $x - y$ pairs are drawn. If the graph, containing n points, shows some pattern, one can say that there is some relationship between them. For example, the scatter plot of the total length of Pascal programs (N) and the number of different variables (*VARS*) is shown in Figure 2.13 (adapted from [CDS86]). The scatter plot clearly shows that there is a relationship between N and *VARS*. It also suggests that the relationship is probably linear, though the relationship is not perfect.

Existence of relationship between the two variables can also be determined by determining the *correlation* between them. Correlation, in the statistical sense, implies that an interval change in one variable is accompanied by an interval change in the other variable. The strength of the correlation is captured by the *correlation coefficient*. If we assume that the relationship is *linear* then the correlation coefficient r can be determined by the following equation [CDS86]:

$$r = \frac{1}{n-1} \sum \frac{(x - \bar{x})}{s_x} \frac{(y - \bar{y})}{s_y}$$

where $\bar{x}$ and $\bar{y}$ represent the means of the values of x and y, and s_x and s_y are the standard deviations of the samples of x and y. Incorporating the equations for standard deviation and means, one gets [CDS86]

$$r = \frac{n \sum (xy) - (\sum x)(\sum y)}{\sqrt{(n \sum x^2 - (\sum x)^2)(n \sum y^2 - (\sum y)^2)}}.$$

If $r = 1$, it implies that there is a perfect correlation. In such a case, all the points in the scatter plot will lie exactly on a straight line (i.e., one line will pass through all the points). When there is no (linear) relationship between x and y, the value of r is close to 0. As this is a statistical analysis, its accuracy will depend on the size of the data set (i.e., the larger n is, the more accurate the correlation).

This method determines if there is a linear correlation between two variables and the strength of the correlation. It does not determine the exact nature of the relationship. That is, the correlation coefficient analysis does not specify the straight line that can capture the linear relationship between the two. It is desirable to represent the linear relationship between the variables in terms of an equation. That is, if y is the dependent variable and x is the independent variable, we are looking for the constants a and b such that the equation

$$y = ax + b$$

closely represents the equation capturing the relationship between x and y. To determine the constants a and b, typically a *regression analysis* needs to be done. The basic idea in regression analysis is to fit a line through the data points in the scatter plot so that the sum of squares of the distance from the line of the points is minimized. With this as the objective, these coefficients can be determined as [CDS86]

$$a = \frac{(x_i - \bar{x})(y_i - \bar{y})}{\sum(x_i - \bar{x})^2}$$
$$b = \bar{y} - a\bar{x}$$

The line specified by these coefficients is called the *regression line*. This regression line captures the linear relationship between y and x. Note that a regression line can be "fitted" with any data set; whether fitting a line is proper or not is determined by the correlation coefficient.

Once such a model between two variables is built for a process (and the two variables have been shown to have a strong correlation), the y value for a project can be estimated if its x value is known. That is, if for an ongoing project only the x value can be measured but the desire of the project management is to estimate the value of the variable y, this equation can be used for estimation. So, what is being done is that from the data of the completed projects (or the past projects) for which both the x and y values are known, the equation representing the relationship between x and y is determined, which is then used by the project management to estimate the value of y for projects where only x is known. Note that this approach implies that the process is under statistical control.

If the variable of interest y is thought to be dependent on more than one variable, then *multivariate regression* can be performed on the data set from the past projects. If the relationship between the two variables is not linear, then sometimes data transformation can be done to convert it into a linear relation. After this transformation, linear regression can be applied. For example, suppose y and x are believed to be related by a nonlinear equation of the type

$$y = ax^b$$

This equation can be converted into a linear equation by taking a log on both sides, giving the equation $\log y = \log a + b \log x$. Now if we consider $\log y$ as Y and $\log x$ as X we have a linear equation, and we can perform the regression analysis on the data set $(\log x_1, \log y_1), \ldots, (\log x_n, \log y_n)$. By regression analysis constants $\log a$ and b will be determined. From this, the original nonlinear equation can be determined. We leave the details of this as an exercise.

Perhaps the most common example of using the models built this way is in cost estimation, where total effort is modeled as a function of the size of the project. The model for the process to be used for a project can be used to estimate the cost of the project, once the size is estimated (or determined). We will see these models in more detail when we discuss cost estimation in Chapter 4.

The values of the measured variables is used in project management in other ways. Rather than building formal models in the manner described earlier, imprecise models are developed, which then form guidelines for project management. For example, an informal model may be constructed with some module complexity metric (say cyclomatic complexity), as follows. Based on experience with earlier projects it is seen that modules with cyclomatic complexity values greater than 10 show a lot of errors. Based on this experience, a model is built that those modules with a complexity greater than 10 are generally "error prone." Based on this model, the project management can require that all modules whose cyclomatic complexity is greater than 10 have to be reviewed, or tested individually. In other words, the cyclomatic complexity number is not being used to predict some other value, but it is being used directly for project management (in this case to ensure that quality objectives are met). Note that even this type of use requires developing some sort of model. Only the model need not be precise. Still, whether a complexity of 10 is acceptable or not (which essentially is the model here) has to be decided for the organization. In some cases, as these models are approximate, models from other organizations can also be used.

If, on the other hand, the project management wants to use the cyclomatic complexity to estimate the number of errors that exist in a module or the effort that will be required to test the module, then an estimation model needs to be built as described earlier. In other words, a model for predicting the total number of errors or the total testing effort will have to be built from the complexity metric being used (assuming that a strong correlation exists).

2.6.2 Process Improvement and Maturity

There is now considerable interest in improving the software process as it is recognized that only by improving the process can the quality and productivity be improved. Process improvement requires understanding the current process and its deficiencies and then taking actions to remove the deficiencies. This is possible only if the current process is under statistical control. Otherwise, even characterizing the process is not possible, leave aside improving it. Process improvement is an advanced topic beyond the scope of this book. We only present some basic ideas here. We present two frameworks that have been used by various organizations to improve their process.

Capability Maturity Model

To improve its software process, an organization needs to first understand the status of the current status and then develop a plan to improve the process. It is generally agreed that changes to a process are best introduced in small increments and that it is not feasible to totally revolutionize a process. The reason is that it takes time to internalize and truly follow any new methods that may be introduced. And only when the new methods are properly implemented will their effects be visible. Introducing too many new methods for the software process will make the task of implementing the change very hard.

If we agree that changes to a process must be introduced in small increments, the next question is out of a large set of possible enhancements to a process, in what order should the improvement activities be undertaken? Or what small change should be introduced first? This depends on the current state of the process. For example, if the process is very primitive there is no point in suggesting sophisticated metrics-based project control as an improvement strategy; incorporating it in a primitive process is not easy. On the other hand, if the process is already using many basic models, such a step might be the right step to further improve the process. Hence, deciding what activities to undertake for process improvement is a function of the current state of the process. Once some process improvement takes place, the process state may change, and a new set of possibilities may emerge. This concept of introducing changes in small increments based on the current state of the process has been captured in the Capability Maturity Model (CMM) framework. The CMM framework provides a general roadmap for process improvement. We give a brief description of the CMM framework here; the reader is referred to [Hum89, P+93] for more details.

Software process capability describes the range of expected results that can be achieved by following the process [P+93]. The process capability of an organization determines what can be expected from the organization in terms of quality and productivity. The goal of process improvement is to improve the process capability. A *maturity level* is a well-defined evolutionary plateau toward achieving a mature software process [P+93]. Based on the empirical evidence found by examining the processes of many organizations, the CMM suggests that there are five well-defined maturity levels for a software process. These are initial (level 1), repeatable, defined, managed, and optimizing (level 5). The CMM framework says that as process improvement is best incorporated in small increments, processes go from their current levels to the next higher level when they are improved. Hence, during

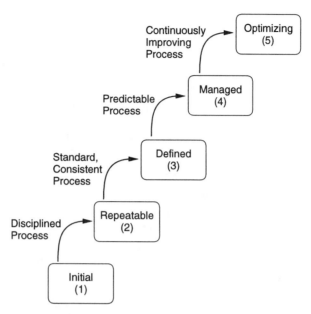

FIGURE 2.14. Capability Maturity Model [P⁺93].

the course of process improvement, a process moves from level to level until it reaches level 5. This is shown in Figure 2.14 [P⁺93].

The CMM provides characteristics of each level, which can be used to assess the current level of the process of an organization. As the movement from one level is to the next level, the characteristics of the levels also suggest the areas in which the process should be improved so that it can move to the next higher level. Essentially, for each level it specifies the areas in which improvement can be absorbed and will bring the maximum benefits. Overall, this provides a roadmap for continually improving the process.

The *initial process* (level 1) is essentially an ad hoc process that has no formalized method for any activity. Basic project controls for ensuring that activities are being done properly and that the project plan is being adhered to are missing. In crisis the project plans and development processes are abandoned in favor of a code-and-test type of approach. Success in such organizations depends solely on the quality and capability of individuals. The process capability is unpredictable as the process constantly changes. Organizations at this level can benefit most by improving project management, quality assurance, and change control.

In a *repeatable process* (level 2), policies for managing a software project and procedures to implement those policies exist. That is, project management is well developed in a process at this level. Some of the characteristics of a process at this level are: project commitments are realistic and based on past experience with similar projects, cost and schedule are tracked and problems resolved when they arise, formal configuration control mechanisms are in place, and software project standards are defined and followed. Essentially, results obtained by this process can be repeated as the project planning and tracking is formal.

At the *defined level* (level 3) the organization has standardized on a software process, which is properly documented. A software process group exists in the organization that owns and manages the process. In the process each step is carefully defined with verifiable entry and exit criteria, methodologies for performing the step, and verification mechanisms for the output of the step. In this process both the development and management processes are formal.

At the *managed level* (level 4) quantitative goals exist for process and products. Data is collected from software processes, which is used to build models to characterize the process. Hence, measurement plays an important role in a process at this level. Due to the models built, the organization has a good insight in the process and its deficiencies. The results of using such a process can be predicted in quantitative terms.

At the *optimizing level* (level 5), the focus of the organization is on continuous process improvement. Data is collected and routinely analyzed to identify areas that can be strengthened to improve quality or productivity. New technologies and tools are introduced and their effects measured in an effort to improve the performance of the process. Best software engineering and management practices are used throughout the organization.

This CMM framework can be used to improve the process. Improvement requires first assessing the level of the current process. This is typically done through the use of a detailed questionnaire, whose answers are used to judge the current level. Based on the current level, the areas in which maximum benefits can be derived are known from the framework. For example, for improving a process at level 1 (or for going from level 1 to level 2), project management and the change control activities must be made more formal. The complete CMM framework provides more details about which particular areas need to be strengthened to move up the maturity framework. This is generally done by specifying the key process areas of each maturity level, which in turn, can be used to determine which areas to strengthen to move up. Some of the key process areas of the different levels are shown in Figure 2.15 [P+93].

Though the CMM framework specifies the process areas that should be improved to increase the maturity of the process, it does not specify how to bring about the improvement. That is, it is essentially a framework that does not suggest detailed prescriptions for improvement, but guides the process improvement activity along the maturity levels such that process improvement is introduced in increments and the improvement activity at any time is clearly focused. Many organizations have successfully used this framework to improve their processes and hundreds of

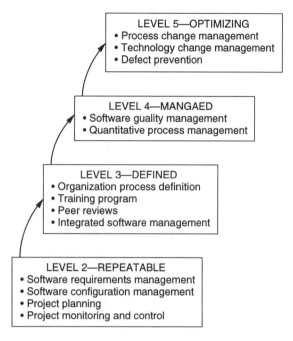

FIGURE 2.15. Some key process areas [P⁺93].

organizations have undergone formal or self-assessment of their capability. It is a major driving force for process improvement.

Quality Improvement Paradigm and GQM

A somewhat different approach for improving a process is taken by the Quality Improvement Paradigm (QIP) [BR88, BR94]. QIP does not specify levels or what areas to focus on for improvement. It gives a general method for improving a process, essentially implying that what constitutes improvement of a process depends on the organization to which the process belongs and its objectives. The basic idea behind this approach is to understand the current process, set objectives for improvement, and then plan and execute the improvement actions. The QIP consists of six basic steps [BR88, BR94]:

- *Characterize.* Understand the current process and the environment it operates in.
- *Set Goals.* Based on the understanding of the process and the environment and objectives of the organization, set quantifiable goals for performance improvement. The goals should be reasonable.
- *Choose Process.* Based on the characterization and goals, choose the component processes that should be changed to meet the goals.

- *Execute.* Execute projects using the processes and provide feedback data.

- *Analyze.* Analyze the data at the end of each project. From the analysis, determine problems and make recommendations for improvements to be applied on future projects.

- *Package.* Based on the experience gained from many projects, define and formalize the changes to be made to processes and expectation from the new processes.

An important component of the QIP is the feedback cycle from the projects. The basic input for process improvement is provided by collecting appropriate data about existing projects. However, for the data to be useful for process improvement, it is imperative that data collection be very focused, and it should be clear how data is to be used in analysis. Collecting data randomly, just because the data is available, is of little use and leads to large volumes of useless data.

For collecting proper data that will serve the purpose of process improvement, the Goal/Question/Metrics (GQM) paradigm is frequently used. The GQM paradigm suggests a general framework for collecting data from projects that can be used for a specific purpose [BW84, BCR94]. The basic premise behind this approach is that there is no "general set" of metrics to be collected. An organization must specify its goals before measuring anything. Then these goals should be translated to specific data along with a framework to evaluate the data collected. In other words, what should be measured and how it should be evaluated depends on the goals of the organization. The fact that many organizations tend to measure and track at least some metrics like effort spent, total number of errors found, and time spent is because most organizations have some similar goals like keeping the cost within projections and keeping the quality high. The similarity of some basic goals gives rise to a sort of "minimal set" of measures that every organization must keep track of. In general, however, the measurement must be for satisfying some objective of the organization.

GQM proposes that to start the measurement activity we must set quality or productivity goals at some level (e.g., process level or a specific project level). An example of the goal could be to reduce the total number of field defects found in the products released by the organization. In this example, the goal is to improve the quality of the process so that fewer defects pass by. An organization may have many goals. For each goal, a set of questions has to be derived that, if answered satisfactorily, will let us see whether or not we are achieving the goal, that is, obtain a set of questions that define the goal. For example, if the goal is to reduce the number of field defects, a question could be what is currently the quality of the released products. The next step consists of defining metrics that need to be collected to answer these questions that have been framed for each goal. In other words, what data should be collected to provide an objective answer to each question? For example, for the question given earlier, one metric could be the number of field defects per KLOC, found within one year of the release of the product. Finally, data collection mechanisms have to be decided.

GQM is a top-down approach that starts from the objectives and works its way down to the metrics needed. Though it is a general framework that can be used for metrics collection for project management, it is frequently used in the context of process improvement. The QIP and GQM have been used successfully by many organizations to improve their processes.

2.7 Summary

There are three important entities that software engineering deals with—processes, projects, and products. Processes relate to the general method of doing something, project is an instance where a process is applied, and products are the outcomes of projects. A software process consists of different component processes that deal with these entities. The development process focuses on the development of products, project management deals with the activities needed to manage a development project, the configuration management process deals with change that takes place during a project, and the process management process deals with the issue of managing changes to the process itself and process improvement.

We have seen that a software process, comprising at least these four component processes, must have some features in order to satisfy the basic software engineering objectives. The basic property is that the process must be predictable, that is, following the same process produces more or less similar results. The process must also support testability and maintainability, as testing and maintenance are the activities that consume the most resources. The process should support defect removal and prevention throughout development, as the longer a defect stays, the more costly it is to remove it. And the process must be self-improving.

Then we studied the four major component processes of the software process. The software development process is traditionally the one that has been most emphasized as it deals with the development and quality activities of software development. Various process models have been proposed. The waterfall model is conceptually the simplest model of software development, where the requirement, design, coding, and testing phases are performed in linear progression. There is a defined output after each phase, which is certified before the next phase begins. It is the most widely used model, even though it has limitations. Another major model is the prototyping model, where a prototype is built before building the final system. Iterative enhancement and the spiral model are other models.

Project management consists of three major phases—planning, monitoring and control, and termination analysis. Much of project management revolves around the project plan, which is produced during the planing phase. The monitoring and control phase requires accurate data about the project to reach project management, which uses this data to determine the state of the project and exercise any control it desires. For this purpose, metrics play an essential role in providing the project management quantified data about the state of development and of the products produced.

The software configuration management process deals with the change that is inevitable in a software development project. The development models cannot typically handle change, which can come at any time during development. And changes can have strong effects on cost and quality. Hence, to ensure that the cost and quality objectives are met, the development project is put under the configuration management process. Basically, the process takes change requests, analyzes them, schedules the changes to be done, and then tracks the changes. The basic objective is to see that the cost and quality are not sacrificed by the change activity. This process is typically performed by the configuration control board.

The process management process is frequently performed by the software engineering process group. A basic objective of this process is to study the existing process and characterize it so that its expected outcomes are known and can be used for project management. For this, models quantifying expected outcomes for the process are built, based on past projects. The other major activity of this process is to improve the process so that the cost and quality of future products are improved. Process management is an advanced topic that will not be discussed further in this book.

In the rest of the book we will focus on the various activities that are generally performed during a software development project. That is, the activities that are generally performed in the development processes are discussed in more detail in the rest of the book. For each activity, some of the activities relating to project management are also discussed.

Exercises

1. What are the other (minor) component processes in a software process? Describe the purpose of each.
2. How can you determine if a process is under statistical control for a property of interest (say cost)?
3. What are the major outputs in a development project that follows the prototyping model?
4. Draw a process model to represent your current approach to developing software.
5. Which of the development process models discussed in this chapter would you follow for the following projects? Give justifications.

(a) A simple data processing project.

(b) A data entry system for office staff who have never used computers before. The user interface and user-friendliness are extremely important.

(c) A new system for comparing fingerprints. It is not clear if the current algorithms can compare fingerprints in the given response time constraints.

(d) A spreadsheet system that has some basic features and many other desirable features that use these basic features.

(e) A new missile tracking system. It is not known if the current hardware/software technology is mature enough to achieve the goals.

(f) An on-line inventory management system for an automobile industry.

(g) A flight control system with extremely high reliability. There are many potential hazards with such a system.

6. It is reasonable to assume that if software is easy to test, it will be easy to maintain. Suppose that by putting extra effort in design and coding you increase the cost of these phases by 15%, but you reduce the cost of testing and maintenance by 5%. Will you put in the extra effort?

7. What are software metrics? What is the role of metrics in project management? What is the role of metrics in process management?

8. Give specific examples of some metrics that can be used to control a software project.

9. Give specific examples of some metrics that can be used to manage and improve a software process.

10. Suppose the relationship between y and x is of the form $y = ax^b$. Given data from past projects, specify how a and b can be determined.

11. Suppose you can measure the number of defects detected during the various reviews and testing. However, the customer requires an estimate of the number of defects remaining at delivery time. How will you build a model to predict this? Assume the existence of any data you need.

3

Software Requirements Analysis and Specification

As we mentioned earlier, a fundamental problem of software engineering is the problem of scale. The complexity and size of applications employing automation, and consequently the complexity and size of software systems, are continuously increasing. As the scale changes to more complex and larger software systems, new problems occur that did not exist in smaller systems (or were of minor significance), which leads to a redefining of priorities of the activities that go into developing software. Software requirement is one such area, to which little importance was attached in the early days of software development, as the emphasis was on coding and design. The tacit assumption was that the developers understood the problem clearly when it was explained to them, generally informally.

As systems grew more complex, it became evident that the goals of the entire system could not be easily comprehended. Hence the need for a more rigorous requirements phase arose. Now, for large software systems, requirements analysis is perhaps the most difficult and intractable activity; it is also very error-prone. Many software engineers believe that the software engineering discipline is weakest in this critical area.

Some of the difficulty is due to the scope of this phase. The software project is initiated by the client's needs. In the beginning, these needs are in the minds of various people in the client organization. The requirement analyst has to identify the requirements by talking to these people and understanding their needs. In situations where the software is to automate a currently manual process, many of the needs can be understood by observing the current practice. But no such methods exist for systems for which manual processes do not exist (e.g., software for a missile control system) or for "new features," which are frequently added when automating an existing manual process. For such systems, the requirements problem is complicated by the fact that the needs and requirements of the system many not be known even to the user—they have to be visualized and created.

Hence, identifying requirements necessarily involves specifying what some people have in their minds (or what will come to their minds when they visualize it). As the information in their minds is by nature not formally stated or organized, the input to the software requirements specification phase is inherently informal and imprecise, and it is likely to be incomplete. When inputs from multiple people are to be gathered, as is often the case, these inputs are likely to be inconsistent as well.

The requirements phase translates the ideas in the minds of the clients (the input), into a formal document (the output of the requirements phase). Thus, the output of the phase is a set of formally specified requirements, which hopefully are complete and consistent, while the input has none of these properties. Clearly, the process of specifying requirements cannot be totally formal; any formal translation process producing a formal output must have a precise and unambiguous input. This is why the software requirements activity cannot be fully automated, and any method for identifying requirements can be at best a set of guidelines.

In this chapter we will discuss what requirements are, why requirement specification is important, how requirements are analyzed and specified, how requirements are validated, and some metrics that can be applied to requirements. It ends with the SRS of the running case used throughout the book.

3.1   Software Requirements

IEEE defines a requirement as "(1) A condition of capability needed by a user to solve a problem or achieve an objective; (2) A condition or a capability that must be met or possessed by a system ... to satisfy a contract, standard, specification, or other formally imposed document...." [IEE87]. Note that in software requirements we are dealing with the requirements of the proposed system, that is, the capabilities that the system, which is yet to be developed, should have. It is because we are dealing with specifying a system that does not exist in any form (the manual form of existence does not generally have the same capability as the eventual automated system) that the problem of requirements becomes complicated. Regardless of how the requirements phase proceeds, it ultimately ends with the Software Requirements Specification (SRS). Generally, the SRS is a document that completely describes *what* the proposed software should do without describing *how* the software will do it. The basic goal of the requirements phase is to produce the SRS, which describes the complete external behavior of the proposed software [Dav93].

However, producing the SRS is easier said than done. A basic limitation for this is that the user needs keep changing as the environment in which the system was to function changes with time. This happens more in complex applications, where all the needs may not be known to any set of people during the requirements phase. This leads to a request for requirement changes even after the requirements phase is done and the SRS is produced. The problem gets worse because frequently the SRS and the process of requirements analysis and specification give additional ideas to clients about what is needed from the system. Hence, requirement changes are a fact of life for most complex systems.

Changing requirements is a continuous irritant for software developers and frequently leads to bitterness between the client and developers. Though many changes come due to the changing needs of the client, many of the change requests have their origin in incorrect interpretation or specification of the requirements. These errors come in the SRS largely due to the requirements phase not being done thoroughly and the client and the requirement analysts not performing the task rigorously. Change requests that have their origins in these types of errors in the SRS can clearly be avoided, or at least reduced considerably, by properly performing the requirements phase.

Even while accepting that some requirement change requests are inevitable, there are still pressing reasons why a thorough job should be done in the requirements phase to produce a high-quality and relatively stable SRS. Let us first look at some of these reasons.

3.1.1 Need for SRS

The origin of most software systems is in the need of a client, who either wants to automate an existing manual system or desires a new software system. The software system itself is created by the developer. Finally, the completed system will be used by the end users. Thus, there are three major parties interested in a new system: the client, the users, and the developer. Somehow the requirements for the system that will satisfy the needs of the clients and the concerns of the users have to be communicated to the developer. The problem is that the client usually does not understand software or the software development process, and the developer often does not understand the client's problem and application area. This causes a communication gap between the parties involved in the development project. A basic purpose of software requirements specification is to bridge this communication gap. SRS is the medium through which the client and user needs are accurately specified; indeed SRS forms the basis of software development. A good SRS should satisfy all the parties—something very hard to achieve—and involves trade-offs and persuasion.

Another important purpose of developing an SRS is helping the clients understand their own needs. As we mentioned earlier, for software systems that are not just automating existing manual systems, requirements have to be visualized and created. Even where the primary goal is to automate an existing manual system, new requirements emerge as the introduction of a software system offers new potential for features, such as providing new services, performing activities in a different manner, and collecting data, that were either impossible or infeasible without a software system. In order to satisfy the client, which is the basic quality objective of software development, the client has to be made aware of these potentials and aided in visualizing and conceptualizing the needs and requirements of his organization. The process of developing an SRS usually helps in this, as it forces the client and the users to think, visualize, interact, and discuss with others (including the requirement analyst) to identify the requirements. Hence one of the main advantages is:

- An SRS establishes the basis for agreement between the client and the supplier on what the software product will do.

This basis for agreement is frequently formalized into a legal contract between the client (or the customer) and the developer (the supplier). So, through SRS, the client clearly describes what it expects from the supplier, and the developer clearly understands what capabilities to build in the software. Without such an agreement, it is almost guaranteed that once the development is over, the project will have an unhappy client, which almost always leads to unhappy developers. (The classic situation is, client: "Hey! there is a bug"; Developer: "No, it is a software feature.") Actually, the reality of the situation is that even with such an agreement, the client is frequently not satisfied! A related, but important, advantage is:

- An SRS provides a reference for validation of the final product.

That is, the SRS helps the client determine if the software meets the requirements. Without a proper SRS, there is no way a client can determine if the software being delivered is what was ordered, and there is no way the developer can convince the client that all the requirements have been fulfilled.

Although, providing the basis of agreement and validation should be strong enough reasons for both the client and the developer to do a thorough and rigorous job of requirement understanding and specification, there are other very practical and pressing reasons for having a good SRS.

We have seen that the primary forces driving a project are cost, schedule, and quality. Consequently, anything that has a favorable effect on these factors should be considered desirable. Boehm found (as reported in [Dav93]) that in some projects 54% of all the detected errors were detected after coding and unit testing was done and that 45% of these errors actually originated during requirement and early design stages. That is, a total of approximately 25% errors occur during requirement and early design stages. A report on errors in the A-7 project shows that about 80 errors were detected in the requirements document over a period of few months that resulted in change requests [BW81]. Another report indicates that more than 500 errors were found in an SRS that was earlier approved (as reported in [Dav93]). Similarly, another project reported that more than 250 errors were found in a previously reviewed SRS by stating the requirements in a structured manner and using tools to analyze the document [Dav89].

It is clear that many errors are made during the requirements phase. And an error in the SRS will most likely manifest itself as an error in the final system implementing the SRS; after all, if the SRS document specifies a wrong system (i.e., one that will not satisfy the client's objectives), then even a correct implementation of the SRS will lead to a system that will not satisfy the client. Clearly, if we want a high-quality final software that has few errors, we must begin with a high-quality SRS. In other words, we can conclude that:

- A high-quality SRS is a prerequisite to high-quality software.

Finally, we show that the quality of SRS has an impact on cost (and schedule) of the project. We have already seen that errors can exist in the SRS. We saw earlier that the cost of fixing an error increases almost exponentially as time progresses. That is, a requirement error, if detected and removed after the system has been developed can cost up to 100 times more than removing it during the requirements phase itself. Based on the data given in [BW81], which reported that on an average it took about 2.4 person-hours to make a change to the requirements to correct an error (this average was without considering the outliers; with the outliers the average was about 5.0 person-hours), we assume that the average cost of fixing a requirement error in the requirement phase is about 2 person-hours. From this and the relative cost of fixing errors as reported in a multicompany study in [Boe76, Boe81] (these costs were reflected graphically in Figure 1.1), the approximate average cost of fixing requirement errors (in person-hours) depending on the phase is shown in Table 3.1.

Clearly, we can have a tremendous reduction in the project cost by reducing the errors in the SRS. A simplified example will illustrate this point. Using the costs given earlier, by investing an additional 100 person-hours in the requirements phase, an average of about 50 new requirements errors will be detected and removed. (This oversimplification is likely to hold only for the errors detected early in the phase. As the number of remaining errors is reduced, the effort required to detect each error is likely to increase.) If these errors are not detected in the requirements phase, they will be detected in some later phase. In the A-7 project the following

Phase	Cost (person-hours)
Requirements	2
Design	5
Coding	15
Acceptance test	50
Operation and maint.	150

TABLE 3.1. Cost of fixing requirement errors

distribution was found [BW81]: of the requirements errors that remain after the requirements phase, about 65% are detected during design, 2% during coding, 30% during testing, and 3% during operation and maintenance. This type of distribution can be expected in general, as most of the requirements errors are likely to be caught in the design phases and the acceptance test phase, while the rest will be caught in other phases. Assume that these 50 requirement errors, if not removed, would have been detected (and fixed) in the later phases with the distribution given earlier. The total cost of fixing the errors in this case will be

$$32.5 * 5 + 1 * 15 + 15 * 50 + 1.5 * 150 = 1152 \text{ person-hours!}$$

In other words, by investing additional 100 person-hours in the requirements phase in this example, the development cost could be reduced by 1152 person-hours—a net reduction in cost of 1052 person-hours!

This can be viewed in another manner. An error that remains in the requirements will be detected in the later phases with the following probabilities: 0.4 in design, 0.1 in coding and unit testing, 0.4 in acceptance testing, 0.1 during operation and maintenance. And the cost of fixing a requirement error in these phases was given earlier. Hence, the expected cost of fixing a requirement error that is not removed during the requirements phase is $0.4 * 5 + 0.1 * 15 + 0.4 * 50 + 0.1 * 150 = 38.5$ person-hours. Therefore, if the expected effort required to detect and remove an error during the requirements phase is less than this, it makes economic sense to spend the extra effort in the requirements phase and remove the error.

This is not the complete story. We know that requirements frequently change. As mentioned earlier, though some of the changes are inevitable due to the changing needs and perceptions, many changes come as the requirements were not properly analyzed and not enough effort was expended to validate the requirements. With a high-quality SRS, requirement changes that come about due to improperly analyzed requirements should be reduced considerably. And as changes tend to escalate the cost and throw the project schedule haywire, a reduction in the requirement change traffic will reduce the project cost, in addition to improving its chances of finishing on schedule.

Let us illustrate this with another simplified example. It is estimated that 20 to 40% of the total development effort in a software project is due to rework, much of which occurs due to change in requirements [Boe87]. The cost of the requirement phase is typically about 6% of the total project cost, according to the COCOMO model [Boe81] (the model is discussed in more detail in Chapter 4). Consider a project whose total effort requirement is estimated to be 50 person-months. For this project, the requirements phase consumes about 3 person-months. If by spending an additional 33% effort in the requirements phase we reduce the total requirement change requests by 33%, then the total effort due to rework (assuming all rework is due to requirement change requests) will reduce from 10 to 20 person-months to 6 to 12 person-months, resulting in a total saving of 5 to 11 person-months, i.e., a saving of 10–22% of the total cost! From these, we can conclude that

- A high-quality SRS reduces the development cost.

Hence, the quality of the SRS impacts customer (and developer) satisfaction, system validation, quality of the final software, and the software development cost. The critical role the SRS plays in a software development project should be evident from these. One will assume that these reasons will ensure that every software project has a high-quality SRS as its starting point. Unfortunately, that is not common practice in the industry. Due to lack of understanding of the role and importance of SRS, and in an effort to "speed up" development and "cut costs" by eliminating "nonessential" activities (which frequently means anything other than coding) many software projects start with a low-quality SRS that is incomplete and full of ambiguities. And the results are consistent with this practice—most of the projects have cost and schedule overruns (rather than reducing cost and time, as is the intention) and the software industry has developed a reputation of providing poor-quality products.

3.1.2 Requirement Process

The requirement process is the sequence of activities that need to be performed in the requirements phase and that culminate in producing a high-quality document containing the software requirements specification (SRS). Whereas the process ends in producing an SRS, its starting point depends on whether the software to be developed is a stand-alone software problem only or is one in which software is a component of the system that requires a combination of hardware and software [Dav93]. In the case where only the software is needed to solve the problem, the requirement process starts when the problem has been identified or a new idea for software arises [Dav93]. In the other case, where a system comprising hardware and software is expected to form the solution of the problem at hand, the starting point of the project is the system requirements specification. This is followed by a system design, which determines what parts of the solution belong to hardware and what parts belong to software. Once the system design is done, the scope of software is defined and the software requirements phase is initiated.

In much of the book, we will focus on the case where the software forms the complete solution. In such a situation, as mentioned earlier, the origin of most software development projects is the need of some clients, and the requirements for the software are originally in the minds of the clients and the users of the software. To satisfy the ultimate objective of the requirements phase—to produce a high-quality SRS document—the requirements process has to ensure that as far as possible all the requirements of the software are elicited and analyzed, clearly specified in the document describing the SRS, and that the SRS if of high-quality.

Due to this, the requirements phase typically consists of three basic activities: *problem or requirement analysis*, *requirement specification*, and *requirements validation*. The first aspect, perhaps the hardest and most nebulous, deals with understanding the problem, the goals, the constraints, etc. Problem analysis starts with some general "statement of need" or a high-level "problem statement." During analysis the problem domain and the environment are modeled in an effort to understand the system behavior, constraints on the system, its inputs and outputs, etc. The basic purpose of this activity is to obtain a thorough understanding of what the software needs to provide. The understanding obtained by problem analysis forms the basis of the second activity—requirements specification—in which the focus is on clearly specifying the requirements in a document. Issues, such as representation, specification languages, and tools, are addressed during this activity. As analysis produces large amounts of information and knowledge with possible redundancies; properly organizing and describing the requirements is an important goal of this activity. The final activity focuses on validating that what has been specified in the SRS are indeed all the requirements of the software and making sure that the SRS is of good quality. The requirements process terminates with the production of the validated SRS.

Though it seems that the requirements process is a linear sequence of these three activities, in reality it is not so for anything other than trivial systems. In most real systems, there is considerable overlap and feedback between these activities. So, some parts of the system are analyzed and then specified while the analysis of the other parts is going on. Furthermore, if the validation activities reveal problems in the SRS, it is likely to lead to further analysis and specification. However, in general, for a part of the system, analysis precedes specification and specification precedes validation. This requirement process is shown in Figure 3.1.

As shown in the figure, from the specification activity we may go back to the analysis activity. This happens as frequently some parts of the problem are analyzed and then specified before other parts are analyzed and specified. Furthermore, the process of specification frequently shows shortcomings in the knowledge of the problem, thereby necessitating further analysis. Once the specification is "complete" it goes through the validation activity. This activity may reveal problems in the specifications itself, which requires going back to the specification step, or may reveal shortcomings in the understanding of the problem, which requires going back to the analysis activity.

During requirements analysis the focus is on understanding the system and its requirements. For a complex system, this is a hard task, and the time-tested method of "divide-and-conquer," i.e., decomposing the problem or system into smaller parts and then understanding the parts and their relationships, is inevitably applied to manage the complexity. Also, for managing the complexity and the large volume of information that becomes available during analysis, various structures are used during analysis to represent the information to help view the system as a series

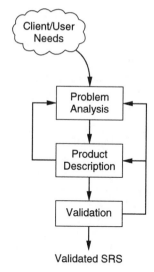

FIGURE 3.1. The requirement process.

of abstractions. Examples of these structures are data flow diagrams and object diagrams (more about these in the next section). For a portion of the system, analysis typically precedes specification. Once the analysis is complete and the structures built, the system part has to be specified.

The transition from analysis to specification, though, seems as if it should be simple; this is not so. In fact, this transition can be quite hard. The reason for this transition being hard is the different objectives of the two activities. In specification, we have to specify only what the software is supposed to do, i.e., focus on the external behavior of the system. In order to identify all the external behaviors, the *structure* of the problem and its various components need to be clearly understood besides understanding its inputs and outputs. However, the structure itself may not be of much use in specification, as its focus is exclusively on the external behavior or the eventual system, not the internal structure of the problem domain. Due to this, one should not expect that once the analysis is done, specification will be straightforward. Furthermore, many "outputs" of the analysis are not used directly in the SRS. This does not mean that these outputs are not useful—they are essential in modeling the problem that leads to the proper understanding of the requirements, which is a prerequisite to specification. Hence, the use of the analysis activity and structures that it built may be indirect, aiding understanding rather than directly aiding specification.

It is worth noting that some similarities exist in the analysis activity and the design activity. As pointed out by Davis [Dav93], the basic problem during software design is the same—managing the complexity. The approach used there is similar—decomposition and building structures to represent the system as a series of abstractions. Due to this similarity, the approaches used for problem analysis and design are frequently similar (e.g., data flow diagrams and object diagrams are used in analysis as well as design). However, although the approaches are similar, the objective of the two activities is completely different. Whereas analysis deals with the problem domain with the basic objective of understanding the problem, design deals with the solution domain with the basic objective of optimizing the design (with respect to some criteria that is typically specified in the requirements) [Dav93]. Due to this, the application of similar approaches produces different structures during analysis and design. It is sometimes mistakenly believed that the structures produced during analysis will and should be carried through in design. This comes from a basic misunderstanding about the objectives of the two activities. Though some of the structures may eventually get used in design, this should be done only if the analysis structures are consistent with the design objective.

Finally, there is the issue of the level of detail that the requirement process should aim to uncover and specify. This is also an issue that cannot be easily resolved and that depends on the objective of the requirement specification phase. We have stated that the objective of the SRS is to specify *what* is needed from the system, not *how* the system will provide it. The main problem comes because *how* at one level of abstraction may be *what* at a lower level of abstraction [Dav93]. Though one can construct various levels of abstraction where *what* at a lower level is *how* at a higher level, two levels can clearly be seen as pertinent to software requirement, depending on the objective of the requirement activity.

If the objective is to define the overall broad needs of the system, the requirements can be very abstractly stated. Generally, the purpose of such requirements is to perform some feasibility analysis or use the requirements for competitive bidding. At the lower level are the requirements where all the behavior and external interfaces of the software are clearly specified. Such requirements are clearly very detailed and are suitable for software development. It can be seen that the requirements (or the *what*) at the lower level can be viewed as specifying the *how* when viewed from the higher level of abstraction.

An example can illustrate this point. Suppose a car manufacturer wants to have an inventory control system. At an abstract level, the requirements of the inventory control system could be stated in terms of the number of parts it has to track, level of concurrency it has to support, whether it will be on-line or batch processing, what types of information and reports it will provide (e.g., status of each item on demand, purchase orders for items that are low in inventory, consumption patterns), etc. Requirements specification at this level of abstraction can be used to estimate the costs and perform a cost-benefit analysis. It can also be used to invite tenders from various developers. However, such a requirements specification is of little use for a developer given the contract to develop the software. That developer needs to know the exact format of the reports, all the queries that can be performed and their structure, total number of terminals the system has to support, the structure of the major databases that will exist, etc. These are all specifying the external behavior of the software, but when viewed from the higher level of abstraction they can be considered as specifying how the abstract requirements should be implemented (e.g., the details of a report can be viewed as defining how the basic objective of providing information is satisfied).

As should be clear, the abstract requirement level is not suitable for software development. Hence, we will focus mostly on the requirements at the lower level in which all the details about external behavior that are needed for the developer to build a software system are specified. That is, we view the SRS as providing all the detailed information needed by a software developer for properly developing the system. However, it is worth pointing out that even when obtaining the detailed requirements is the objective, abstract requirements can still play a useful role for complex systems. As the problem analysis starts with some initial description of the system's behavior or needs, the abstract requirements can play this role (besides being used for competitive bidding and/or feasibility analysis). In other words, specifying the requirements at an abstract level is likely to be useful in producing the SRS that contains the detailed requirements of the system.

The next three sections will be devoted to providing a more detailed description of the activities in the three major activities in the requirements phase: analysis, specification, and verification.

3.2   Problem Analysis

The basic aim of problem analysis is to obtain a clear understanding of the needs of the clients and the users, what exactly is desired from the software, and what the constraints on the solution are [Dav93]. Analysis leads to the actual specification. In this section we will focus on the analysis. Specification is discussed in the next section. People performing the analysis (often called *requirement analysts* or just *analysts*) are also responsible for specifying the requirements.

Analysis involves interviewing the clients and end users. These people and the existing documents about the current mode of operation are the basic source of information for the analysts. Typically, analysts research a problem by asking questions of the client and the user and by reading existing documents. The process of obtaining answers to questions that might arise in an analyst's mind continues until the analyst feels that "all" the information has been obtained.

As mentioned earlier, frequently the client and the users do not understand or know all their needs, because the potential of the new system is often not fully appreciated. The analysts have to ensure that the real needs of the clients and the users are uncovered, even if they don't know them clearly. That is, the analysts are not just collecting and organizing information about the client's organization and its processes, but they also act as *consultants* who play an *active* role of helping the clients and users identify their needs. Due to this, it is extremely important that the analysts thoroughly understand the client's organization and its purpose, the problem domain, and the purpose of automation. In other words, for the duration of the analysis, the analyst has to "get in the shoes" of the clients and users. Only then can it help bring out those needs that even the client and the users don't know initially.

In the rest of this section, we discuss the problem of analysis in more detail. First we discuss some important issues relating to analysis and some principles used during analysis. Then we discuss the various approaches to analysis.

3.2.1   Analysis Issues

As analysis is the activity that feeds information to the specification activity; it is essential that during analysis a complete and consistent set of specifications emerge for the system. For achieving this, the first major problem is to obtain the necessary information. As mentioned earlier, people and existing documents are a major source of information. Besides this, brainstorming between the clients/users and the analysts also reveals the desired properties of the eventual system.

Generally, during analysis, a massive amount of information is collected in the form of answers to questions, questionnaires, information from documentation, ideas, and so forth. As it is important to have the complete set of requirements, it is essential that this gathered information be organized so that it can be evaluated for completeness. Furthermore, due to the nature of the problem, determining completeness will require that the client play an active role during this evaluation. This requires that the information be properly organized. Hence, the second major problem of analysis is how to organize the information obtained so the information can be effectively evaluated for completeness and consistency.

The third major problem during analysis is resolving the contradictions that may exist in the information from different parties. This is essential to ensure that the final specifications are consistent. The contradictions occur because the perceived goals of the system may be quite different for the end users and the client. The analyst has the thankless job of resolving the contradictions and obtaining a "consensus," which frequently involves performing trade-offs, for example, between functionality and cost (or schedule). Conflicts that arise during analysis should not be "pushed under the rug." Instead, the analysts should try to have the conflicts surface and then resolve them.

Finally, the fourth major problem is avoiding internal design. The reasons for the temptation to do design during analysis and why such temptations should be resisted were discussed earlier.

It should be clear that information organization plays an important role in obtaining information and resolving conflicts. While collecting information, the real difficulty arises in the later stages when it is not clear what information is missing. Once what needs to be determined is known, determining it is usually not hard. And for this, properly structuring the existing information is very important. A good structuring of information can "guide" the analyst and help him determine the areas of incompleteness. Similar is the case with conflict resolution; identifying conflicts also requires good structuring of the existing information. For this reason, the modeling techniques that have been proposed for analysis (we will discuss some later in this section) place a heavy emphasis on structuring information.

Clearly, during analysis the interpersonal skills of an analyst are just as important as—if not more than—as the technical skills. Interviewing the users and clients requires good communication skills. The situation can be more complex if some users are reluctant to part with the information they possess. (Many people believe that knowledge is power; such people are likely to be reluctant to part with their knowledge, particularly if it is to be used to develop an automated system that might diminish their role.) Careful dealing is required to make sure that all that needs to be known is found out. During resolution of conflicts, good communication and interpersonal skills are important tools the analyst needs. Here, we will focus on analysis techniques only; no further discussion on interpersonal skills is provided.

The basic principle used in analysis is the same as in any complex task: divide and conquer. That is, *partition* the problem into subproblems and then try to understand each subproblem and its relationship to other subproblems in an effort to understand the total problem. This is applied recursively by treating each subsystem as a system in its own right. However, to employ partitioning for analysis, the immediate question that comes is "partition with respect to what?" Generally, during analysis, partitioning is done with respect to *objects* or *functions*. That is, most analysis techniques view the problem as consisting of objects or functions, and aim to identify the objects or functions and the hierarchies and relationships between them.

In the requirements phase, an *object* is an entity in the real world that has clearly defined boundaries and an independent existence. By considering real-world objects, the focus of the analysis stays on the problem domain, rather than the solution domain. Due to this problem, analysis reveals objects like sensors, manager, automobile, etc., but does not include implementation objects like trees and queues. (During design, when we model the solution domain, the implementation objects become important.) A *function* is a task, service, process, mathematical function, or activity that is now being performed in the real world or has to be performed by the system that will be built to solve the real-world problem [Dav93].

The concepts of *state* and *projection* can sometimes also be used effectively in the partitioning process. A state of a system represents some conditions about the system. Frequently, when using state, a system is first viewed as operating in one of the several possible states, and then object-based or function-based analysis is performed for each state. This approach is sometimes used in real-time software or process-control software. For example, a chemical plant that has to be controlled through digital computers can be considered to be in one of the following states: startup, running, or shutdown (additional states can also be defined, such as exceptional processing or emergency shutdown, etc.). In each state, the expected behavior of the control system is different. Hence, after defining the states of the system, for each state a function-based or object-based analysis can be performed for each of the three states, resulting in a clear understanding of what needs to be done by the control system in all three states.

In *projection*, a system is defined from multiple points of view [YZ80]. Projecting a three-dimensional object on the three different two-dimensional planes is a similar process. While using projection, different viewpoints of the system are defined and the system is analyzed from these different perspectives separately using an object-based or function-based approach. The different "projections" obtained are combined to form the analysis for the complete system. The advantage of using projection is that trying to analyze the system from a global viewpoint is difficult and error-prone, and one is more likely to forget some features of the system. Analyzing the system from the different perspectives is easier, as it limits and focuses the scope of the study. For example, an operating system can be analyzed from the perspective of a general user, a system programmer, or a system administrator (many operating system manuals are divided in this manner). By using the different perspectives, it is easy to ensure that the analysis is indeed complete.

There are three basic approaches to problem analysis: informal approaches based on structured communication and interaction, conceptual modeling–based approaches, and prototyping. The informal approaches don't use any "methodologies" for problem analysis; the analyst relies on his experience and uses questionnaires, forms, interviews, etc. to elicit information about the problem and the client needs. In the conceptual modeling–based approaches, a formal model is built for the problem. Such approaches use the principle of partitioning for building the model. Modeling approaches frequently produce some formal structures representing some aspects of the problem. In prototyping, the problem is analyzed and requirements understood through the feedback from the users and clients with working a prototype system.

It should be clear from this that whereas problem analysis and understanding is an essential step before specifying (what will you specify otherwise?), modeling is not. The basic purpose of problem analysis is to understand the problem and its constraints—modeling is a means for this. Due to this, modeling is not a necessary step in the requirements phase; the problem can be understood or analyzed through other means, formal or informal.

In the remainder of this section we will discuss a few methods for problem analysis. We will describe one function-oriented modeling approach and one object-oriented modeling approach, and will discuss briefly some other modeling approaches. We will also discuss the informal approach and the prototyping approach. As the goal of analysis is to understand the problem domain, an analyst must be familiar with different methods of analysis and pick the approach that he feels is best suited to the problem at hand.

3.2.2 Informal Approach

The informal approach to analysis is one where no defined methodology is used. Like in any approach, the information about the system is obtained by interaction with the client, end users, questionnaires, study of existing documents, brainstorming, etc. However, in this approach no formal model is built of the system. The problem and the system model are essentially built in the minds of the analysts (or the analysts may use some informal notation for this purpose) and are directly translated from the minds of the analysts to the SRS.

Frequently, in such an approach, the analyst will have a series of meetings with the clients and end users. In the early meetings, the clients and end users will explain to the analyst about their work, their environment, and their needs as they perceive them. Any documents describing the work or the organization may be given, along with outputs of the existing methods of performing the tasks. In these early meetings, the analyst is basically the listener, absorbing the information provided. Once the analyst understands the system to some extent, he uses the next few meetings to seek clarifications of the parts he does not understand. He may document the information in some manner (he may even build a model if he wishes), and he may do some brainstorming or thinking about what the system should do. In the final few meetings, the analyst essentially explains to the client what he understands the system should do and uses the meetings as a means of verifying if what he proposes the system should do is indeed consistent with the objectives of the clients. An initial draft of the SRS may be used in the final meetings.

The informal approach to analysis is used widely and can be quite useful. The reason for its usefulness is that conceptual modeling–based approaches frequently do not model all aspects of the problem and are not always well suited for all the problems. Besides, as the SRS is to be validated and the feedback from the validation activity may require further analysis or specification (see Figure 3.1), choosing an informal approach to analysis is not very risky—the errors that may be introduced are not necessarily going to slip by the requirements phase. Hence such approaches may be the most practical approach to analysis in some situations.

3.2.3 Structured Analysis

The structured analysis technique [Ros77, DeM79] uses function-based decomposition while modeling the problem. It focuses on the functions performed in the problem domain and the data consumed and produced by these functions. The structured analysis method helps an analyst decide what type of information to obtain at different points in analysis, and it helps organize information so that the analyst is not overwhelmed by the complexity of the problem. It is a top-down refinement approach, which was originally called *structured analysis and specification* and was proposed for producing the specifications. However, we will limit our attention to the analysis aspect of the approach. Before we describe the approach, let us the describe the data flow diagram and data dictionary on which the technique relies heavily.

Data Flow Diagrams and Data Dictionary

Data flow diagrams (also called *data flow graphs*) are commonly used during problem analysis. Data flow diagrams (DFDs) are quite general and are not limited to problem analysis for software requirements specification. They were in use long before the software engineering discipline began. DFDs are very useful in understanding a system and can be effectively used during analysis.

A DFD shows the flow of data through a system. It views a system as a function that transforms the inputs into desired outputs. Any complex system will not perform this transformation in a "single step," and a data will typically undergo a series of transformations before it becomes the output. The DFD aims to capture the transformations that take place within a system to the input data so that eventually the output data is produced. The agent that performs the transformation of data from one state to another is called a *process* (or a *bubble*). So, a DFD shows the movement of data through the different transformations or processes in the system. The processes are shown by named circles and data flows are represented by named arrows entering or leaving the bubbles. A rectangle represents a source or sink and is a net originator or consumer of data. A source or a sink is typically outside the main system of study. An example of a DFD for a system that pays workers is shown in Figure 3.2.

In this DFD there is one basic input data flow, the weekly timesheet, which originates from the source *worker*. The basic output is the paycheck, the sink for which is also the worker. In this system, first the employee's record is retrieved, using the employee ID, which is contained in the timesheet. From the employee record, the rate of payment and overtime are obtained. These rates and the regular and overtime hours (from the timesheet) are used to compute the pay. After the total pay is determined, taxes are deducted. To compute the tax deduction, information from the tax-rate file is used. The amount of tax deducted is recorded in the employee and company records. Finally, the paycheck is issued for the net pay. The amount paid is also recorded in company records.

Some conventions used in drawing this DFD should be explained. All external files such as employee record, company record, and tax rates are shown as a labeled

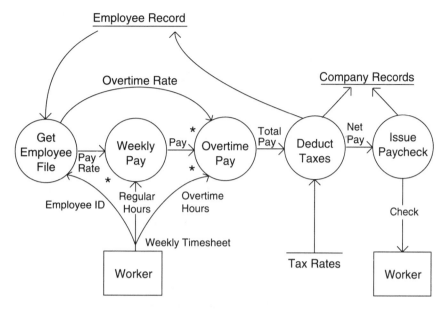

FIGURE 3.2. DFD of a system that pays workers.

straight line. The need for multiple data flows by a process is represented by a
"*" between the data flows. This symbol represents the AND relationship. For
example, if there is a "*" between the two input data flows A and B for a process,
it means that A AND B are needed for the process. In the DFD, for the process
"weekly pay" the data flow "hours" and "pay rate" both are needed, as shown in
the DFD. Similarly, the OR relationship is represented by a "+" between the data
flows.

This DFD is an abstract description of the system for handling payment. It does
not matter if the system is automated or manual. This diagram could very well
be for a manual system where the computations are all done with calculators, and
the records are physical folders and ledgers. The details and minor data paths are
not represented in this DFD. For example, what happens if there are errors in the
weekly timesheet is not shown in this DFD. This is done to avoid getting bogged
down with details while constructing a DFD for the overall system. If more details
are desired, the DFD can be further refined.

It should be pointed out that a DFD is *not* a flowchart. A DFD represents the flow
of data, while a flowchart shows the flow of control. A DFD does not represent
procedural information. So, while drawing a DFD, one *must not* get involved in
procedural details, and procedural thinking must be consciously avoided. For example, considerations of loops and decisions must be ignored. In drawing the DFD,
the designer has to specify the major transforms in the path of the data flowing

from the input to output. *How* those transforms are performed is *not* an issue while drawing the data flow graph.

There are no detailed procedures that can be used to draw a DFD for a given problem. Only some directions can be provided. One way to construct a DFD is to start by identifying the major inputs and outputs. Minor inputs and outputs (like error messages) should be ignored at first. Then starting from the inputs, work toward the outputs, identifying the major transforms in the way. An alternative is to work down from the outputs toward the inputs. (Remember that it is important that procedural information like loops and decisions not be shown in the DFD, and the designer should not worry about such issues while drawing the DFD.) Following are some suggestions for constructing a data flow graph [YC79, DeM79]:

- Work your way consistently from the inputs to the outputs, or vice versa. If you get stuck, reverse direction. Start with a high-level data flow graph with few major transforms describing the entire transformation from the inputs to outputs and then refine each transform with more detailed transformations.
- Never try to show control logic. If you find yourself thinking in terms of loops and decisions, it is time to stop and start again.
- Label each arrow with proper data elements. Inputs and outputs of each transform should be carefully identified.
- Make use of * and + operations and show sufficient detail in the data flow graph.
- Try drawing alternate data flow graphs before settling on one.

Many systems are too large for a single DFD to describe the data processing clearly. It is necessary that some decomposition and abstraction mechanism be used for such systems. DFDs can be hierarchically organized, which helps in progressively partitioning and analyzing large systems. Such DFDs together are called a *leveled DFD set* [DeM79].

A leveled DFD set has a starting DFD, which is a very abstract representation of the system, identifying the major inputs and outputs and the major processes in the system. Then each process is refined and a DFD is drawn for the process. In other words, a bubble in a DFD is expanded into a DFD during refinement. For the hierarchy to be consistent, it is important that the net inputs and outputs of a DFD for a process are the same as the inputs and outputs of the process in the higher-level DFD. This refinement stops if each bubble is considered to be "atomic," in that each bubble can be easily specified or understood. It should be pointed out that during refinement, though the net input and output are preserved, a refinement of the data might also occur. That is, a unit of data may be broken into its components for processing when the detailed DFD for a process is being drawn. So, as the processes are decomposed, data decomposition also occurs.

weekly timesheet =
   Employee_name +
   Employee_Id +
   [Regular_hours + Overtime_hours] *

pay_rate =
   [Hourly | daily | weekly] +
   Dollar_amount

Employee_name =
   Last + First + Middle_initial

Employee_Id =
   digit + digit + digit + digit

FIGURE 3.3. Data dictionary.

In a DFD, data flows are identified by unique names. These names are chosen so that they convey some meaning about what the data is. However, the precise structure of data flows is not specified in a DFD. The *data dictionary* is a repository of various data flows defined in a DFD. The associated data dictionary states precisely the structure of each data flow in the DFD. Components in the structure of a data flow may also be specified in the data dictionary, as well as the structure of files shown in the DFD. To define the data structure, different notations are used. These are similar to the notations for regular expressions (discussed later in this chapter). Essentially, besides sequence or composition (represented by +) selection and iteration are included. Selection (represented by vertical bar "|") means one OR the other, and repetition (represented by "*") means one or more occurrences. In the DFD shown earlier, data flows for weekly timesheet are used. The data dictionary for this DFD is shown in Figure 3.3.

Most of the data flows in the DFD are specified here. Some of the more obvious ones are not shown here. The data dictionary entry for weekly timesheet specifies that this data flow is composed of three basic data entities—the employee name, employee ID, and many occurrences of the two-tuple consisting of regular hours and overtime hours. The last entity represents the daily working hours of the worker. The data dictionary also contains entries for specifying the different elements of a data flow.

Once we have constructed a DFD and its associated data dictionary, we have to somehow verify that they are "correct." There can be no formal verification of a DFD, because what the DFD is modeling is not formally specified anywhere against which verification can be done. Human processes and rules of thumb must be used for verification. In addition to the walkthrough with the client, the analyst should look for common errors. Some common errors are [DeM79]:

- Unlabeled data flows
- Missing data flows; information required by a process is not available.
- Extraneous data flows; some information is not being used in the process.
- Consistency not maintained during refinement.
- Missing processes
- Contains some control information

Perhaps the most common error is unlabeled data flow. If an analyst cannot label the data flow, it is likely that he does not understand the purpose and structure of that data flow. A good test for this type of error is to see that the entries in the data dictionary are precise for all data flows.

To check if there are any missing data flows, for each process in the DFD the analyst should ask, "Can the process build the outputs shown from the given inputs?" Similarly, to check for redundant data flows, the following question should be asked: "Are all the input data flows required in the computation of the outputs?"

In a leveled set of DFDs it is important that consistency be maintained. Consistency can easily be lost if new data flows are added to the DFD during modification. If such changes are made, appropriate changes should be made in the parent or the child DFD. That is, if a new data flow is added in a lower-level DFD, it should also be reflected in the higher-level DFDs. Similarly, if a data flow is added in a higher-level DFD, the DFDs for the processes affected by the change should also be appropriately modified.

The DFDs should be carefully scrutinized to make sure that all the processes in the physical environment are shown in the DFD. It should also be ensured that none of the data flows is actually carrying control information. A data flow without any structure or composition is a potential candidate for control information.

The Method

Now let us return to the structured analysis method. The basic system view of this approach is that each system (whether manual or automated, existing or conceptual) can be viewed as a transformation function operating within an environment that takes some inputs from the environment and produces some outputs for the environment. And as the overall transformation function of the entire system may be too complex to comprehend as a single function, the function should be partitioned into subfunctions that together form the overall function. The subfunctions can be further partitioned and the process repeated until we reach a stage where each function can be comprehended easily. And the basic approach used to uncover the functions being performed in the system (or the functions that are part of the overall system function) is to track the data as it flows through the system—from the input to the output. It is believed that in any complex system the data transformation from the input to the output will not occur in a single step; rather the data will be transformed from the input to the output in a series of transformations starting from the input and culminating in the desired output. By understanding the "states" the data is in as it goes through the transformation series, the functions in the system can be identified; each transformation of the data in the transformation series is performed by a transformation function. Hence, by tracking as the data flows through the system, the various functions being performed by a system can be identified. As this approach can be modeled easily by data flow diagrams, DFDs are used heavily in this method.

The first step in this method is to study the "physical environment." During this, a DFD of the current nonautomated (or partially automated) system is drawn, showing the input and output data flows of the system, how the data flows through the system, and what processes are operating on the data. This DFD might contain specific names for data flows and processes, as used in the physical environment. For example, names of departments, persons, local procedures, and organizational files can occur in the DFD for the physical environment. While drawing the DFD for the physical environment, an analyst has to interact with the users to determine the overall process from the point of view of the data. This step is considered complete when the entire physical data flow diagram has been described and the user has accepted it as a true representation of the operation of the current system. The step may start with a *context diagram* in which the entire system is treated as a single process and all its inputs, outputs, sinks, and sources are identified and shown.

The basic purpose of analyzing the current system is to obtain a logical DFD for the system, where each data flow and each process is a logical entity or operation, rather than an actual name. Drawing a DFD for the physical system is only to provide a reasonable starting point for drawing the logical DFD. Hence, the next step in the analysis is to draw the logical equivalents of the DFD for the physical system. During this step, the DFD of the physical environment is taken and all specific physical data flows are represented by their logical equivalents (for example, file 12.3.2 may be replaced by the employee salary file). Similarly, the bubbles for physical processes are replaced with logical processes. For example, a bubble named "To_John's_office" in the physical system might be replaced by "issue checks" in the logical equivalent. Bubbles that do not transform the data in any form are deleted from the DFD. This phase also ends when the DFD has been verified by the user.

In the first two steps, the current system is modeled. The next step is to develop a logical model of the new system after the changes have been incorporated, and a DFD is drawn to show how data will flow in the new system. During this step the analyst works in the logical mode, specifying only what needs to be done, not how it will be accomplished. No separation between the automated and nonautomated processes is made.

No general rules are provided for constructing the DFD for the new system. The new system still does not exist; it has to be invented. Consequently, what will be the data flows and major processes in this new system must be determined by the analyst, based on his experience and vision of the new system. No rules can be provided for this decision. However, before this can be done, the boundaries of change have to be identified in the logical DFD for the existing system. This DFD models the entire system, and only parts of it may be modified in the new system. Based on the goals of the clients and a clear concept about what the client wants to change, the boundaries of change have to be established in the logical DFD. The DFD for the new system will replace only that part of the existing DFD within this boundary. The inputs and outputs of the new DFD should be the same as the inputs and outputs for the DFD within the boundary.

The next step is to establish the man-machine boundary by specifying what will be automated and what will remain manual in the DFD for the new system. Note that even though some processes are not automated, they could be quite different from the processes in the original system, as even the manual operations may be performed differently in the new system. Often there is not just one option for the man-machine boundary. Different possibilities may exist depending on what is automated and the degree of automation. The analyst should explore and present the different possibilities.

The next two steps are evaluating the different options and then packaging or presenting the specifications.

For drawing a DFD, a top-down approach is suggested in the structured analysis method. In the structured analysis method, a DFD is constructed from scratch when the DFD for the physical system is being drawn and when the DFD for the new system is being drawn. The second step largely performs transformations on the physical DFD. Drawing a DFD starts with a top-level DFD called the context diagram, which lists all the major inputs and outputs for the system. This diagram is then refined into a description of the different parts of the DFD showing more details. This results in a leveled set of DFDs. As pointed out earlier, during this refinement, the analyst has to make sure consistency is maintained and that net input and output are preserved during refinement.

Clearly, the structured analysis provides methods for organizing and representing information about systems. It also provides guidelines for checking the accuracy of the information. Hence, for understanding and analyzing an existing system, this method provides useful tools. However, most of the guidelines given in the structured analysis are only applicable in the first two steps, when the DFD for a current system is to be constructed. For analyzing the target system and constructing the DFD or the data dictionary for the new system to be built (done in step three), this technique does not provide much guidance. Of course, the study and understanding of the existing system will help the analyst in this job, but there is no direct help from the method of structured analysis.

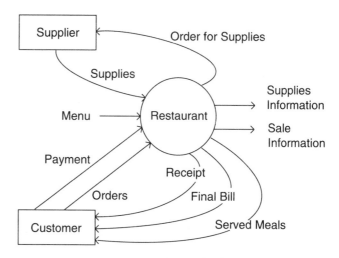

FIGURE 3.4. Context diagram for the restaurant.

An Example

A restaurant owner feels that some amount of automation will help make her business more efficient. She also believes that an automated system might be an added attraction for the customers. So she wants to automate the operation of her restaurant as much as possible. Here we will perform the analysis for this problem. Details regarding interviews, questionnaires, or how the information was extracted are not described. First let us identify the different parties involved.

Client: The restaurant owner

Potential Users: Waiters, cash register operator

The context diagram for the restaurant is shown in Figure 3.4. The inputs and outputs of the restaurant are shown in this diagram. However, no details about the functioning of the restaurant are given here. Using this as a starting point, a logical DFD of the physical system is given in Figure 3.5 (the physical DFD was avoided for this as the logical DFD is similar to the physical and there were no special names for the data or the processes in the physical system). Observing the operation of the restaurant and interviewing the owner were the basic means of collecting raw information for this DFD.

Now we must draw a DFD that models the new system to be built. After many meetings and discussions with the restaurant owner, the following goals for the new system were established:

- Automate much of the order processing and billing.
- Automate accounting.

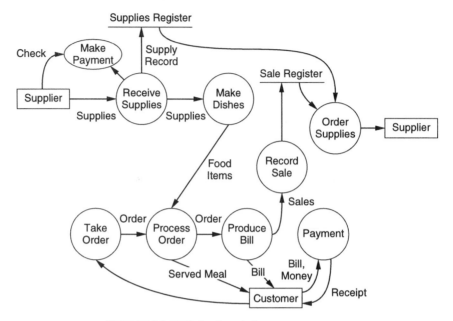

FIGURE 3.5. DFD for the existing restaurant system

- Make supply ordering more accurate so that leftovers at the end of the day are minimized and the orders that cannot be satisfied due to nonavailability are also minimized. This was currently being done without a careful analysis of sales.

- The owner also suspects that the staff might be stealing/eating some food/supplies. She wants the new system to help detect and reduce this.

- The owner would also like to have statistics about sales of different items.

With these goals, we can define the boundaries for change in the DFD. It is clear that the new system will affect most aspects of the previous system, with the exception of making dishes. So, except for that process, the remaining parts of the old system all fall within our boundary of change. The DFD for the new system is shown in Figure 3.6. Note that although taking orders might remain manual in the new system, the process might change, because the waiter might need to fill in codes for menu items. That is why it is also within the boundary of change.

The DFD is largely self-explanatory. The major files in the system are: Supplies file, Accounting file, Orders file, and the Menu. Some new processes that did not have equivalents earlier have been included in the system. These are "check for discrepancy," "accounting reports," and "statistics." Note that the processes are consistent in that the inputs given to them are sufficient to produce the outputs. For example, "checking for discrepancy" requires the following information to produce the report: total supplies received (obtained from the supplies file), supplies left at

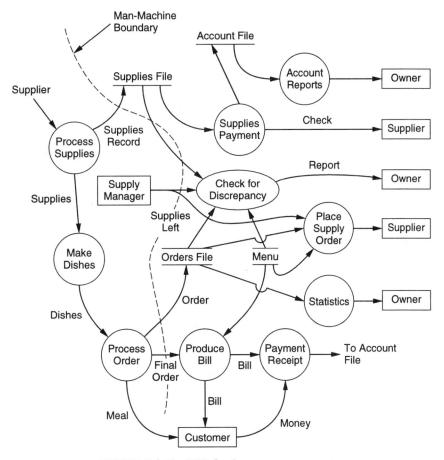

FIGURE 3.6. The DFD for the new restaurant system.

the end of the day, total orders placed by the customers (from the orders file), and the consumption rate for each menu item (from the menu). All these are shown as inputs to the process. Supplies required for the next day are assessed from the total orders placed in the day and the orders that could not be satisfied due to lack of supplies (both kept in the order file). To see clearly if the information is sufficient for the different processes, the structure and exact contents of each of the data flows has to be specified. The data dictionary for this is given in Figure 3.7.

The definitions of the different data flows and files are self-explanatory. Once this DFD and the data dictionary have been approved by the restaurant owner, the activity of understanding the problem is complete. After talking with the restaurant owner the man-machine boundary was also defined (it is shown in the DFD). Now remains such tasks as determining the detailed requirements of each of the bubbles shown in the DFD, determining the nonfunctional requirements, deciding codes

Supplies_file =
  [date +
  [item_no + quantity + cost]*]*

Orders_file
  [date +
  [menu_item_no + quantity + status]*]*

status = satisfied | unsatisfied

order =
  [menu_item_no + quantity]*

menu =
  [menu_item_no + name + price + supplies_used]*

supplies_used =
  [supply_item_no + quantity]*

bill =
  [name + quantity + price]* +
  total_price +
  sales_tax +
  service_charge +
  grand_total

discrepancy_report =
  [supply_item_no + amt_ordered + amt_left + amt_consumed + descr]*

FIGURE 3.7. Data dictionary for the restaurant.

for the items in the menu and in the supply list. Further refinement for some of the bubbles might be needed. For example, it has to be determined what sort of accounting reports or statistics are needed and what their formats should be. Once these are done, the analysis is complete and the requirements can then be compiled in a requirements specification document.

3.2.4 Object-Oriented Modeling

As mentioned earlier, while analyzing the problem domain, the problem can be partitioned with respect to its functionality or with respect to objects. Object-oriented modeling (or object-oriented analysis) uses the latter approach. During analysis, an object represents some entity or some concept in the problem domain. An object contains some state information and provides some services to entities outside the objects. The state of the object can be accessed or modified only through the services it provides.

In object-oriented modeling, a system is viewed as a set of objects. The objects interact with each other through the services they provide. Some objects also interact with the users through their services such that the users get the desired services. Hence, the goal of modeling is to identify the objects that exist in the problem domain, define the objects by specifying what state information they encapsulate and what services they provide, and identify relationships that exist between objects, such that the overall model is such that it supports the desired user services. Such a model of a system is called its *object model*.

Object-oriented modeling and systems have been getting a lot of attention in the recent past. The basic reason for this is the belief that object-oriented systems are going to be easier to build and maintain. It is also believed that transition from object-oriented analysis to object-oriented design (and implementation) will be easy, and that object-oriented analysis is more immune to change because objects are more stable than functions. That is, in a problem domain, objects are likely to stay the same even if the exact nature of the problem changes, while this is not the case with function-oriented modeling. Many approaches to object-oriented modeling and design have been proposed [CY90, Boo94, Fir93, EKW92]. Goals of many of these techniques regarding what to produce are quite similar, and their approaches and notations are also similar. A brief comparison of these techniques is given in [EJW95]. Here, we briefly describe the approach proposed in [CY90], though the notation we use is similar to the one proposed in [R+91].

Basic Concepts and Notation

In understanding or modeling a system using an object modeling technique, the system is viewed as consisting of *objects*. Each object has certain *attributes*, which together define the object. Separation of an object from its attributes is a natural method that we use for understanding systems (a man is separate from his attributes of height, weight, etc.). In object-oriented systems, attributes hold the state (or define the state) of an object. An attribute is a pure data value (like integer, string, etc.), not an object.

Objects of similar type are grouped together to form an *object class* (or just *class*). An object class is essentially a type definition, which defines the state space of objects of its type and the operations (and their semantics) that can be applied to objects of that type. Formation of classes is also a general technique used by humans for understanding systems and differentiating between classes (e.g., an apple tree is an instance of the class of trees, and the class of trees is different from the class of birds).

An object also provides some *services* or *operations*. These services are the only means by which the state of the object can be modified or viewed from outside.

For operating a service, a *message* is sent to the object for that service. In general, these services are defined for a class and are provided for each object of that class. Encapsulating services and attributes together in an object is one of the main features that distinguishes an object modeling approach from data modeling approaches, like the ER diagrams (discussed later).

Object diagrams represent the object model graphically using a precise notation. In an object diagram, an object class is represented as a portrait-style rectangle divided into three parts. The top part contains the name of the class. The middle part lists the attributes that objects of this class possess. And the third part lists the services provided by objects of this class

Through the concepts discussed so far we can model objects or classes. But the relationship between classes and objects cannot be modeled. And entities and classes are related in the real world (e.g., a house object contains many room objects, or the house class is a special form of the general accommodation class). To model these, two types of structures are used: *generalization-specialization* and *aggregation* (also called *assembly*). The generalization-specialization structure can be used by a class to inherit all or some attributes and services of a general class and add more attributes and services. This structure is modeled in object-oriented modeling through *inheritance*. By using a general class and inheriting some of its attributes and services and adding more, one can create a class that is a specialized version of the general class. And many specialized classes can be created from a general class, giving us class hierarchies. The aggregation structure models the whole-part relationship. An object may be composed of many objects; this is modeled through the aggregation structure. The representation of these in a class diagram is shown in Figure 3.8.

In addition to these, instances of a class may be related to objects of some other class. For example, an object of the class Employer may be related to many objects of the class Employee. This relationship between objects also has to be captured if

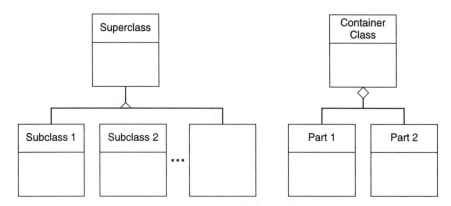

FIGURE 3.8. Class structures.

a system is to be modeled properly. This is captured in object modeling through *associations*. An association is shown in the object diagram by having a line between the two classes. The *multiplicity* of an association specifies how many instances of one class may relate to an instances of the other class through this association. An association between two classes can be one-to-one (i.e., one instance of one class is related to exactly one instance of the other class), one-to-many, or some other special cases. Multiplicity is specified by having a solid ball (•) on the line adjacent to the class representing zero or more instances of the class may be related to an instance of the other class. The relationship may be necessary, that is, an instance cannot exist without being related to another object by this relationship, or it may be optional. In the object diagram, a hollow circle on the line next to the class implies that the participation of an object of that class in the association is optional (i.e., zero or one).

We now have the basic components of an object-oriented model: objects, classes (for classification), inheritance (for modeling generalization-specialization), and aggregation (for modeling whole-part relationship), and associations (for modeling relationships between instances). Using these, a system can be modeled.

Let us illustrate the use of some of these relationships and their representation through the use of an example. Suppose a system is being contemplated for a drugstore that will compute the total sales of the drugstore along with the total sales of different chemists that man the drugstore. The drugs are of two major types—off-the-shelf and prescription drugs. The system is to provide help in procuring drugs when out of stock, removing them when expired, replenishing the off-the-shelf drugs when needed, etc. A model of the system is shown in Figure 3.9.

Let us briefly explain this object diagram. It has five classes of objects, each with a defined name, some attributes, and services. For example, an object of class Chemist has the attributes Name, Registration number, and Address. It has one service ChemistSales(), which computes the total sales by this chemist. The Drug-Store class is an aggregation of the class Medicine and the class Chemist (representing that a drugstore is composed of medicines and chemists). A Medicine may either be Off-the-shelf or Prescription. The object class Medicine has some attributes like Name, Quantity in stock, and Expiry-date, and has services like Expired() (to list the expired medicines), OutOfStock() (to list medicines that are no longer in stock), etc. These attributes and services are inherited by the two specialized classes. In addition to these, the Off-the-shelf class has another attribute qty-on-shelf, representing how many have been put on the shelf and have services related to shelf stock. On the other hand, the Prescription class has Refrigeration-needs and Warnings as specialized attributes and services related to them. There are various associations in this model. For example, there is an association between Sale and Medicine. This association is one to many, that is, one sale could be of many medicines. Similarly, Drug-Store is associated to Medicine and Chemist, and Chemist is associated with Sale.

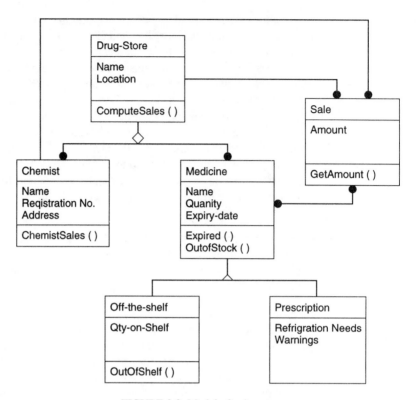

FIGURE 3.9. Model of a drugstore.

Performing Analysis

Now that we know what an object model of a system consists of, the next question that arises is how to obtain the object model for a system. In other words, how do we actually perform the analysis? As mentioned earlier, because the input to the analysis activity (or the requirements activity) is informal and fuzzy and the output is formal, there can be no "algorithm" to perform the analysis or generate the SRS. Hence, any method for performing analysis is, at best, a set of guidelines that have been found to be useful in practice. Here we briefly discuss the set of guidelines given in [CY90], according to which the major steps in the analysis are:

- Identifying objects
- Identifying structures
- Identifying attributes
- Identifying associations
- Defining services

Identifying Objects. An object during analysis is an encapsulation of attributes on which it provides some exclusive services [CY90]. It represents something in the problem space. It has been argued that though things like interfaces between components, functions, etc. are generally volatile and change with changing needs, objects are quite stable in a problem domain.

To identify analysis objects, start by looking at the problem space and its description. Obtain a brief summary of the problem space. In the summary and other descriptions of the problem space, consider the nouns. Frequently, nouns represent entities in the problem space which will get modeled as objects. Structures, devices, events remembered, roles played, locations, organizational units, etc. are good candidates to consider. A candidate should be included as an object if the system needs to remember something about the object, the system needs some services from the object to perform its own services, and the object has multiple attributes (i.e., it is a high-level object encapsulating some attributes). If the system does not need to keep information about some real-world entity or does not need any services from the entity, it should not be considered as an object for modeling. Similarly, carefully consider objects that have only one attribute; such objects can frequently be included as attributes in other objects.

Identifying Structures. Structures represent the hierarchies that exist between object classes. All complex systems have hierarchies. In object modeling, the hierarchies are defined between classes that capture generalization-specialization and whole-part relationships. In generalization-specialization, the class being refined is generally called the *superclass* and the specialized class is called the *subclass*. The attributes and services of the superclass are inherited by the subclasses. The subclasses can add more attributes and services (or redefine the attributes and services of the superclass) to specialize. For example, a general class of reading material may have the attributes of title and publisher. Then there may be subclasses books, magazines, and newspapers. The class book, besides the inherited attributes of reading-material, may have the attributes of ISBN number and author name that are specific to the class of books. Similarly, the magazine may have the attributes of frequency of publication, and its scope (political, humor, fashion, etc.). An assembly structure is used to model an object as a collection of components. For example, a library is composed of books, magazines, and audio-visual objects.

To identify the classification structure, consider the objects that have been identified as a generalization and see if there are objects in the problem space that can be considered as specializations of this. The specializations should be meaningful for the problem domain. For example, if the problem domain does not care about the material used to make some objects, there is no point in specializing the objects based on the material they are made of. Similarly, consider objects as specializations and see if there are other objects that have similar attributes. If so, see if a generalized class can be identified of which these are specializations. Once again, the structure obtained must naturally reflect the hierarchy in the problem domain; it should not be "extracted" simply because some objects have some attributes with the same names.

To identify assembly structure, a similar approach is taken. Consider each object as an assembly and identify its parts or components. See if the system needs to keep track of the parts. If it does, then the parts must be reflected as objects; if not, then the parts should not be modeled as separate objects. Then consider each object as a part and see to which object it can be considered as belonging. Once again, this separation is maintained only if the system needs it. As before, the structures identified should naturally reflect the hierarchy in the problem domain and should not be "forced."

Identifying Attributes. Attributes add detail about the object and are the repositories of data for the object. For example, for a person object class, the attributes could be the name, sex, and address. The data stored in forms of values of attributes are hidden from outside the objects and are accessed and manipulated only by the service functions for that object. Which attributes should be used to define an object depend on the problem and what needs to be done. For example, while modeling a hospital system, for the object person attributes of height, weight, and date of birth may be needed, though these may not be needed for a database for a county that keeps track of populations in various neighborhoods.

To identify attributes, consider each object and see which attributes for the object are needed by the problem domain. This is frequently a simple task. Then position each attribute properly using the structures; if the attribute is a common attribute, it should be placed in the superclass, while if it is specific to a specialized object it should be placed with the subclass. While identifying attributes, new objects may also get defined or old objects may disappear (e.g., if you find that an object really is an attribute of another object).

Identifying Associations. Associations capture the relationship between instances of various classes. For example, an instance of the class company may be related to an instance of the class person by an "employs" relationship. Note that there is no relationship between the class company and the class person; their instances are related. This is similar to what is done in ER modeling. And like in ER modeling, an instance connection may be of 1:1 type representing that one instance of this type is related to exactly one instance of another class. Or it could be 1:M, indicating that one instance of this class may be related to many instances of the other class. As indicated earlier, the multiplicity of an association is represented by a solid ball (●) and the optional nature by a circle. There are M:M connections, and there are sometimes multiway connections, but these are not very common. The associations between objects are derived from the problem domain directly once the objects have been identified. An association may have attributes of its own; these are typically attributes that do not naturally belong to either object. Though in many situations they can be "forced" to belong to one of the two objects without losing any information, it should not be done unless the attribute naturally belongs to the object.

Defining Services. An object performs a set of predefined services. A service is performed when the object receives a message for it. Services really provide the active element in object-oriented modeling; they are the agent of state change or "processing." It is through the services that desired functional services can be provided by a system. To identify services, first identify the *occur* services, which are needed to create, destroy, and maintain the instances of the object. These services are generally not shown in the object diagrams. Other services depend on the type of services the system is providing. A method for identifying the services is to define the system states and then in each state list the external events and required responses. For each of these, identify what services the different objects should possess.

The object diagram clearly gets large and complex for large systems. To handle the complexity, it is suggested to have a *subject layer* in which the object model is partitioned into various subjects, with each subject containing some part of the diagram. Typically, a subject will contain many related objects.

An Example

Let us consider the example of the restaurant, whose structured analysis was performed earlier. By stating the goals of the system (i.e., automate the bill generation for orders given by customers, obtain sale statistics, determine discrepancy between supplies taken and supplies consumed, automate ordering of supplies) and studying the problem domain (i.e., the restaurant with customer, supplier, menu, etc.), we can clearly see that there are at least the following objects: Restaurant, Restaurant owner, Bill, Menu, CustomerOrder, Supplier, SupplyOrder, Supply handling (unit), and Dishes. Each of these entities plays an important role in the system. We consider this as the starting point and the initial object layer. By looking at the objectives and scope of the system, we find that no information about the Supplier or the Operator needs to be maintained in the system. Hence, they need not be modeled in the system as objects. For the same reason, entities like Dishes and Restaurant owner are not modeled as objects. The initial object layer is shown in Figure 3.10. Note that this is the initial layer, which will further evolve, and new objects may get added and some of these may eventually not be needed.

Now let us try to identify structure between these classes. Clearly, a Restaurant is an aggregation of Menu and Supply handling. As dishes, operator, etc. are not considered objects, they do not show up as components of Restaurant. Further, a Menu is an aggregation of many MenuItems. This requires us to add the object MenuItem in the object layer. Similarly, the SupplyOrder is an aggregation of (many) SupplyItems. This also requires us to add SupplyItem as a new object

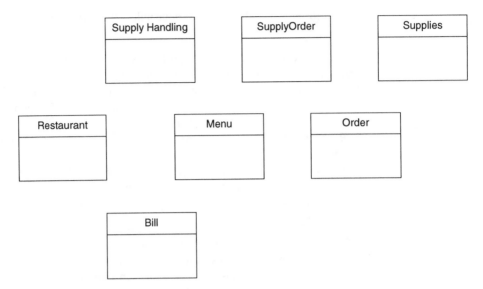

FIGURE 3.10. Initial object layer for the restaurant example.

to the object layer. Furthermore, the association between SupplyOrder and SupplyItem has an attribute quantity, reflecting the quantity ordered for a particular
item by an order. There is no generalization-specialization hierarchy in this.

Many attributes of various items can be directly identified. A MenuItem has attributes of Number, Name, Price, Supplies used (i.e., which supplies it uses and
quantity; this is needed to detect discrepancies in consumption and supplies used).
Similarly, SupplyItem has Item name and Unit price as attributes.

With this, we are ready to identify relationships between objects. The Supply
handling (unit) is related to (many) SupplyOrder. Similarly, an Order (by a
customer) is related to many MenuItem. Furthermore, this association has an attribute of its own—quantity. The quantity of the particular MenuItem ordered in
a particular Order is naturally a property of the association between the specific
Order and the specific MenuItem.

Finally, we have to identify the service layer. Keeping our basic services of the
system in mind (generate sale statistics, bill, discrepancy report, sale order), we
define services of various objects. Supply handling object has the services Cred-
itSupply() (used to record the receipt of supplies), DebitSupply() (used to record
the supplies taken out), and PlaceOrder() (to place order of supplies). For SupplyOrder, one service is identified—ProduceCheck() to produce the check for the
particular order. The object Order has one service—ProduceBill()—to produce the
bill for the particular order. Handling the bill as essentially something generated
for each order, we remove the object Bill from the object layer. The main object
Restaurant has the services SaleStat() to generate the sale statistics for which it

will require all order information (which it will obtain through its association with
Order). It also has the service Discrepancy() to generate a discrepancy report. For
this, it will need to find out what items have been consumed their quantity, and
how much supply was debited. The former it can obtain from all the orders and the
latter from Supply handling. The final object diagram is shown in Figure 3.11.

3.2.5 Other Modeling Approaches

Many other languages and related processors have been proposed for requirement
analysis and specification. Most of these are not general and cater to some application area. Here we briefly discuss some of the techniques. These approaches
typically are designed for both analysis and specification; they provide means for
organizing information and producing reports.

Before we describe the languages, a word of caution is in order. All these languages provide means for organizing and specifying requirements, but they do not
provide much help in determining the requirements. This is not a shortcoming of
the languages but rather is a feature of the requirement specification problem. Because in the beginning the requirements are in the minds of the people, no language
or automated tool can uncover them. Determining the requirements is necessarily
a human process. These languages help in writing the requirements in a manner
useful in later activities. The processors for the languages are often capable of
performing cross checking and some amount of consistency checking.

SADT

Structured analysis and design technique (SADT) [Ros77, RS77] is designed for
information processing systems. It has a graphical language based on the concept
of blueprints used in civil engineering. A model in SADT is a hierarchy of diagrams supporting a top-down approach for analysis and specification. Embedded
in the diagrams is text in natural language. Hence, the specification language is a
combination of a precisely defined graphical language and a natural language.

A diagram in an SADT model is either an activity diagram or a data diagram. Each
diagram consists of *boxes* and *arrows*. Boxes represent parts of a whole and arrows
represent the interfaces between different parts. Each diagram may be accompanied
by some text.

The hierarchy of diagrams starts with the *context diagram*, which is the most
abstract description of the problem. The problem is then refined into subproblems
that are shown as another diagram. Each of the subproblems in this diagram can
be further refined by constructing its diagram. Each diagram represents a limited
amount of detail about a well-defined subproblem of a higher-level diagram. As
the refinement proceeds, our understanding of the problem becomes more detailed

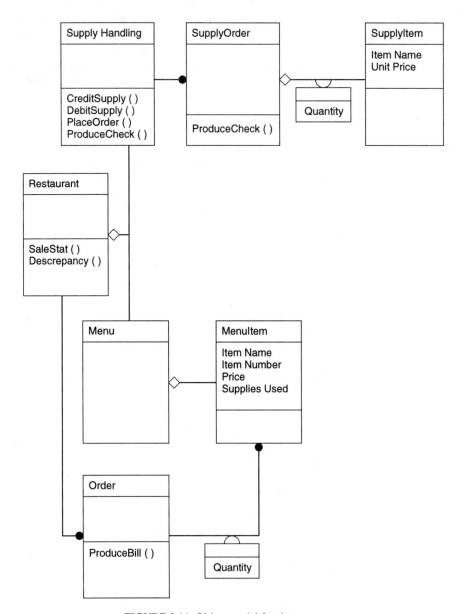

FIGURE 3.11. Object model for the restaurant.

and accurate. This method of refinement exposes the details about the problem gradually, which helps the analyst manage the analysis activity.

Again, the basic components of the SADT diagram are boxes and arrows entering or leaving the boxes. The idea behind the diagrams is similar to that of a DFD, except that the notation is different and there are precise rules for interpretation of arrows, depending on which side of the box they enter. Furthermore, loops might exist in diagrams in SADT, while loops are rare in DFDs.

A box represents a *transformation* (like a bubble does in the DFD). The arrows entering a box from the left represent things that will be transformed. What these are transformed into are shown by arrows leaving from the right. Arrows entering from the top of a box represent some sort of *control* that affects the transformation of the box. The control arrows are meant to ensure that the transformation is applied only when circumstances are appropriate or conditions are correct. Arrows entering from the bottom of a box represent *mechanisms* needed to perform the transformation. The boxes are labeled by "verbs" representing *happenings*, while the arrows are labeled by "nouns" representing *things*.

When a part of the diagram is refined into another diagram, the overall arrows in the parent diagram should be preserved in the refinement. That is, in general, the arrows going in and coming out of a diagram is a refinement of a box in a parent diagram should be the same as the arrows going in and coming out of the box in the parent diagram. This is similar to the consistency requirement imposed on a leveled set of DFDs in the structured analysis approach.

Note that just like in DFD, the refinement does not produce a design. The analysis stays in the problem domain, and during refinement we try to find the different parts of the problem. The solution to the problem is not an issue during analysis.

As an example consider the system that pays workers described by the DFD in Figure 3.2. The context diagram for this is shown in Figure 3.12, and the diagram after one refinement is shown in Figure 3.13.

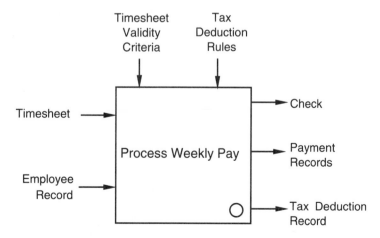

FIGURE 3.12. Context diagram for the pay system.

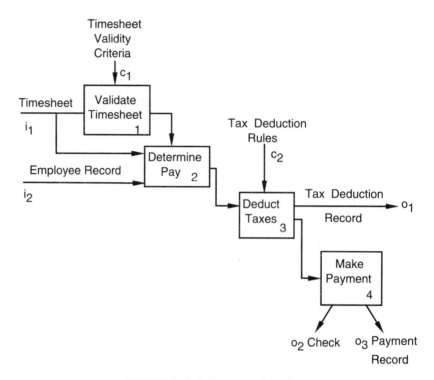

FIGURE 3.13. Refinement of the diagram.

In the context diagram, different inputs and outputs are identified. Note that timesheet validity criteria and tax deduction rules are identified as control inputs. This
overall problem is broken into subproblems during refinement. During the refinement four different boxes are identified. The overall inputs and outputs remain the
same (as they should). Note that the output of "validate timesheet" is the control
input to the "determine pay" box. The boxes, inputs, and outputs in the refinement
have been given numbers, according to the convention of the SADT diagrams.

PSL/PSA

The Problem Statement Language (PSL) [TH77] is designed to specify the requirements of information systems. It is a textual language, as opposed to many other
techniques that are a combination of graphical and textual. Problem Statement
Analyzer (PSA) is the processor that processes the requirements stated in PSL; it
produces some useful reports and analyses.

In PSL, a system contains a set of objects, each object having properties and defined
relationships. The major parts of a system description are system input/output flow,
system structure, and data structure. The system input/output flow deals with the

interaction of the system with the environment and specifies all the inputs received and all the outputs produced. System structure defines the hierarchies among the different objects, and data structure defines the relationships among the data used within the system.

PSA operates on the database of information collected from the PSL description of the requirements. A number of reports can be produced, including the data dictionary, data flow diagrams, a database modification report, summary reports, reference reports, and analysis reports. The data-base modification report lists all changes made to the database since the last report. Summary reports produce an overview of all the objects defined and their properties. Analysis reports produce information about inputs and outputs and any consistency problems that have been uncovered.

The PSL method is fundamentally the same as the structured analysis method. The problem description revolves around *process* descriptions. A process is similar to a bubble in a DFD or a box in the SADT diagram. In PSL, a process is described textually. Just like in DFD, the PSL specification identifies the different inputs and outputs. In addition, for a hierarchical decomposition, a PSL description of a process specifies its subparts (children) and the process of which it is a part (the parent). A PSL description also specifies the existing procedure used in the process and the dependencies between an output and different inputs. An example of the process description for the overall procedure of the pay-processing system, whose context diagram was shown in Figure 3.12 is given in Figure 3.14. The specification format used is similar to the one described in [TH77].

Refinement can proceed by providing process specifications for the subparts identified in the process description. As we can see, the basic information in a PSL description is similar to the information in a DFD or an SADT diagram. The approach of top-down refinement based on refining processes is also similar to other methods.

RSL/REVS

The requirements statement language (RSL) [Alf77] was specifically designed for specifying complex real-time control systems. The requirement engineering validation system (REVS) is a set of tools to support the development of requirements in RSL. REVS consists of a translator for the requirements written in RSL, a centralized database in which the translator deposits information, and a set of tools for processing the information in the database.

RSL uses a flow-oriented approach to specify real-time systems. For each flow, the stimulus and the final response are specified. In between, the major processing steps are specified. Flows can be specified in RSL as requirement networks (R-NETS), which can be represented graphically or textually. REVS contains tools to help specify flow paths and to check completeness and consistency of information, as

PROCESS
   Pay-processing
DESCRIPTION
   This process performs actions for paying workers based on
   their weekly timesheets.

GENERATES
   Pay check, payment report, tax deduction report
RECEIVES
   Weekly timesheet, employee record, tax deduction rules.
SUBPARTS ARE
   validate_timesheet, determine_pay, deduct_taxes, make_payment

PART OF
   Worker management system
DERIVES
   total_pay
      USING
         timesheet, daily_rate and overtime_rate
         (from employee_record)
   tax_deduction
      USING
         tax_deduction_rules, total_pay
   payment_check
      USING
         total_pay, tax_deduction
PROCEDURE
   1.   Check validity of timesheet
   2.   Compute total pay
   3.   Deduct taxes
   4.   Generate paycheck
HAPPENS
   Once every week

FIGURE 3.14. Process description for the top-level process.

well as a simulation package. It also has the ability to generate reports and specific
analyses.

Unlike other approaches, there is control information specified in RSL. This is
because RSL is primarily designed for real-time control systems, where control
information is an essential component for completely describing system requirements.

Entity-Relationship Modeling

If the application is primarily a database application, the entity-relationship (ER) approach can be used effectively for modeling some parts of the problem. The ER modeling approach was proposed in the middle 1970s [Che76] to help design information systems and is still widely used for designing databases.

The main focus of ER modeling is the data items in the system and the relationships between them. It aims to create a *conceptual schema* (also called the *ER model*) for the data from the user's perspective. The model thus created is a high-level data model that is independent of any database model. The schema can later be used during the development of the database, and there are methods that use the ER models to design databases for the different database models (relational, network, hierarchical). The ER models are frequently represented as entity-relationship diagrams (ER diagrams), though the model can also be represented in more mathematical forms.

The modeling primitives are similar to the primitives in object-oriented modeling, and the notation in ER diagrams is similar to the notation used in object diagrams. In fact, ER modeling represents one of the greatest influences on object-oriented modeling. Here we briefly describe the ER diagram notation and the ER modeling approach; the discussion is based on [Che76, EN89].

The basic units in an ER model are entities, their attributes, entity types, and relationships between the entity types. An entity, like an object in object-oriented modeling, represents something in the real world that may have a physical existence (e.g., person, car) or may only have a conceptual existence (e.g., a course, color, profession). An *entity type* is like a class in object-oriented modeling; it represents the general structures of the entities that belong to that type. An entity type has a set of *attributes* that describe the structure of the entities of that type. For example, the entity type Professor has attributes like name, office number, department to which he belongs, etc. An attribute may be a *composite* attribute consisting of parts that have a meaning of their own. For example, the name attribute can be considered a composite attribute comprising last name, first name, and middle initial. The ER model deals with entity types rather than actual entities.

The entity types represent the various types of entities that exist in the problem and the structure of these entities. However, entities in a system do not exist in isolation, and there are associations between entities. This is captured by *relationship types* in the ER model. The most common relationship is a *binary* relationship, which specifies an association between entities of two types. A binary relation is of *degree* 2. Ternary associations (i.e., with degree 3) are also found, but higher-order associations are generally not found in applications. An instance of a binary relationship type represents an association of two entities, belonging to each of the two types taking part in the relationship. Relationship types may also have attributes.

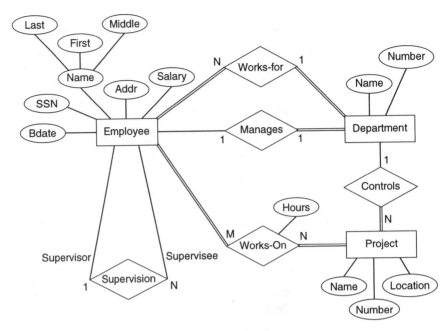

FIGURE 3.15. ER schema for the company database.

Relationships frequently have some constraints on them. The *cardinality ratio* constraint specifies the number of relationship instances an entity can participate in. The three types of cardinality ratios for binary relationships are 1:1, 1:N, and N:M representing one-to-one, one-to-many, and many-to-many associations, respectively. The *participation* constraint specifies whether the participation of a type is total or partial. In a total participation, each entity of an entity type belongs to at least one instance of the relationship. In the partial case, some entities may not be related to any entity of the other type.

The ER diagrams graphically represent the conceptual schema, in which the structure of the entity types, the relationship between entities, and constraints on relationships, are all represented. We illustrate the ER modeling approach by giving an example of an ER model of a company database (adapted from [EN89]). We don't discuss the evolution of this schema; we give only the final schema. The ER diagram for the conceptual schema is given in Figure 3.15 [EN89].

In this example, there are three entity types: Employee, Department, and Project (an entity type is represented by a rectangle). An attribute of an entity is shown as an oval attached to its entity type; if an attribute is composite, its subattributes are shown. For example, an entity of the Employee type has the attributes Bdate, SSN, Name, Address, and Salary. The Name attribute is a composite attribute with the attributes Last, First, and Middle as its components. Relationship types are shown as diamonds. In this example, the relationships are: Works-On, Supervision, Manages, Works-For, and Controls. All of these are binary relationships. The participating entity types of a relationship are shown by lines connecting the entity type to the relationship diamond; the connection is by a double line if the participation of the entity type in the relationship is total. For example, Manages is a relationship between entity types Employee and Department, representing the fact that some employees are also managers of the departments. The participation of the Department entity type is total (all departments must have a manager), whereas the participation of the Employee type is not total (only some entities of the type Employee may be managers). The relationship is 1:1 (also shown in the ER diagram), that is, one employee manages one department. On the other hand, the relationship Works-For is N:1 between Employees and Department, signifying that many employees may work for one department. The relationship Works-On is M:N representing that an employee may work for many departments and a department may have many employees working for it. A relationship can be between entities of the same type, as is the case with Supervision. In this case, the role name of the two entities should be specified (e.g., supervisor and supervisee).

Note that a relationship type may also have attributes. Sometimes, these attributes can be associated with one of the entities that takes part in the relationship, but conceptually they belong to the relationship. For example, the relationship Works-On has an attribute Hours, which specifies the number of hours an employee has spent working for a department. The number of hours is not an attribute of the employee or an attribute of the project; it conceptually belongs to the relationship Works-On. (In this case, as Works-On is an M:N relationship, this attribute cannot be associated with either the employee or the project).

It is clear from this example that the focus of ER modeling is on data in the problem and relationships between data items. For this reason, it is suitable for modeling database applications. Using the ER model, the analyst can expect to get complete knowledge of all the data that exist in the system (including the inputs and outputs) and how the data are related. However, ER modeling does not help much in understanding the functional and processing requirements of the database system. As mentioned earlier, the ER model can also be used later for designing and implementing the database. Here, we have discussed only the basic ER model; it has been extended to reflect concepts like subtyping. The extended model is sometimes called the enhanced-ER (EER) model [EN89].

3.2.6 Prototyping

Prototyping is another method that can be used for problem analysis, which is getting a lot of attention these days. It takes a very different approach to problem analysis as compared to conceptual modeling–based approaches (e.g., structured analysis, object-oriented modeling). In prototyping, a partial system is constructed, which is then used by the client, users, and developers to gain a better understanding of the problem and the needs. Hence, actual experience with a prototype that implements part of the eventual software system are used to analyze the problem and understand the requirements for the eventual software system. A software prototype can be defined as a partial implementation of a system whose purpose is to learn something about the problem being solved or the solution approach [Dav95]. As stated in this definition, prototyping can also be used to evaluate or check a design alternative (such a prototype is called a *design prototype* [Dav95]). Here we focus on prototyping used primarily for understanding the requirements.

The rationale behind using prototyping for problem understanding and analysis is that the client and the users often find it difficult to visualize how the eventual software system will work in their environment just by reading a specification document. Visualizing the operation of the software that is yet to be built and whether it will satisfy the ultimate objectives, merely by reading and discussing the paper requirements, is indeed difficult. This is particularly true if the system is a totally new system and many users and clients do not have a good idea of their needs. The idea behind prototyping is that clients and the users can assess their needs much better if they can see the working of a system, even if the system is only a partial system. Prototyping emphasizes that actual practical experience is the best aid for understanding needs. By actually experimenting with a system, people can say, "I don't want this feature" or "I wish it had this feature" or "This is wonderful."

There are two approaches to prototyping: throwaway and evolutionary [Dav92, Dav95]. In the *throwaway* approach the prototype is constructed with the idea that it will be discarded after the analysis is complete, and the final system will be built from scratch. In the *evolutionary* approach, the prototype is built with the idea that it will eventually be converted into the final system.

The two approaches are very different in how they proceed and what parts of the system they include in the prototype. In throwaway prototyping, as the prototype is to be discarded, there is no point in implementing those parts of the requirements that are already well understood. Hence, the focus of the development is to include those features that are not properly understood. And the development approach is "quick and dirty" with the focus on quick development rather than quality. Experience with this prototype is used to determine if the understanding of requirements when building the prototype is correct. Determining missing requirements is a secondary benefit from this approach.

In contrast, in the evolutionary prototype approach, because the prototype is to be retained, those parts of the system that are well understood are implemented where it is clear they are needed. The development approach is more formal, as the prototype needs to be of the quality standards expected of the final system. The basic focus in this prototype is to elicit missing requirements. By working with a stable system having features that are definitely needed, the client and users can determine which other services and features are needed. This approach works well when the "core" of the system, comprising its critical functions, is well understood.

Whereas the throwaway prototype leads to the prototyping process model, evolutionary prototyping leads to the iterative enhancement process model. Though the evolutionary prototyping is also useful in the context, it is used more to build newer versions of the software rather than for requirements analysis. Furthermore, it is generally harder to implement because building "larger" software from existing software, something that is essential to this approach, is not easy to do and there are no general approaches for it. From the point of view of problem analysis and understanding, the throwaway prototypes are more suited. For the rest of the discussion we limit our attention to throwaway prototypes.

The first question that needs to be addressed when prototyping is being considered for a project is whether or not to prototype. In other words, it is important to clearly understand when prototyping should be done. The requirements of a system can be divided into three sets—those that are well understood, those that are poorly understood, and those that are not known [Dav95]. In a throwaway prototype, the poorly understood requirements are the ones that should be incorporated. Based on the experience with the prototype, these requirements then become well understood, as shown in Figure 3.16

It might be possible to divide the set of poorly understood requirements further into two sets—those critical to design, and those not critical to design [Dav95]. The requirements that can be easily incorporated in the system later are considered noncritical to design. If which of the poorly understood requirements are critical and which are noncritical can be determined, then the throwaway prototype should focus mostly on the critical requirements. Overall, we can say that if the set of poorly understood requirements is substantial (in particular the subset of critical requirements), then a throwaway prototype should be built.

Another approach to determining when to prototype is given in [Dav95]. According to this approach, there are 10 criteria that should be considered when making a decision about whether or not to prototype. These criteria are [Dav95]:

1. Developer's application experience
2. Maturity of application
3. Problem complexity

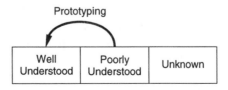

FIGURE 3.16. Throwaway prototyping.

4. Usefulness of early partial functionality

5. Frequency of changes

6. Magnitude of changes

7. Funds and staff profile

8. Access to users

9. Management compatibility

10. Volume of fuzzy requirements

For a project, based on the assessment of these criteria, a decision can be made about whether prototyping should be done, and if yes, what type of prototype should be built. For example, as suggested in [Dav95], a throwaway prototype should be built if the application is new or not well established (criterion 2), the problem complexity is high, if low funding is available in the short term but high funding may be available in the long term (criterion 7), a high access to the users is there, the management is flexible, and there are substantial critical requirements that are fuzzy (the assessment of the rest of the criteria is not relevant).

The development process using a throwaway prototype was discussed earlier in Chapter 2. The development activity starts with an SRS for the prototype. However, developing the SRS for the prototype requires identifying the functions that should be included in the prototype. This decision is typically application-dependent. As mentioned earlier, in general, those requirements that tend to be unclear and vague or where the clients and users are unsure or keep changing their mind, are the ones that should be implemented in the prototype. User interface, new features to be added (beyond automating what is currently being done), and features that may be infeasible, are common candidates for prototyping. Based on what aspects of the system are included in the prototype, the prototyping can be considered *vertical* or *horizontal* [LJZ94]. In horizontal prototyping the system is viewed as being organized as a series of layers and some layer is the focus of prototyping. For example, the user interface layer is frequently a good candidate for such prototyping, where most of the user interface is included in the prototype. In vertical prototyping, a chosen part of the system, which is not well understood, is built completely. This approach is used to validate some functionality or capability of the system.

Development of a throwaway prototype is fundamentally different from developing final production-quality software. The basic focus during prototyping is to keep costs low and minimize the prototype production time. Due to this, many of the bookkeeping, documenting, and quality control activities that are usually performed during software product development are kept to a minimum during prototyping. Efficiency concerns also take a back seat, and often very high-level interpretive languages are used for prototyping. For these reasons, temptation to convert the prototype into the final system should be resisted (if this is desired, then evolutionary prototyping should be used).

Experience is gained by putting the system to use with the actual client and users using it. Constant interaction is needed with the client/users during this activity to understand their responses. Questionnaires and interviews might be used to gather user response.

The final SRS is developed in much the same way as any SRS is developed. The difference here is that the client and users will be able to answer questions and explain their needs much better because of their experience with the prototype. Some initial analysis is also available.

For prototyping for requirements analysis to be feasible, its cost must be kept low. Consequently, only those features that will have a valuable return from the user experience are included in the prototype. Exception handling, recovery, conformance to some standards and formats are typically not included in prototypes. Because the prototype is to be thrown away, only minimal development documents need to be produced during prototyping; for example, design documents, a test plan, and a test case specification are not needed during the development of the prototype. Another important cost-cutting measure is reduced testing. Testing consumes a major part of development expenditure during regular software development. By using cost-cutting methods, it is possible to keep the cost of the prototype to less than a few percent of the total development cost.

The cost of developing and running a prototype can be around 10% of the total development cost [GS81]. However, it should be pointed out that if the cost of prototyping is 10% of the total development cost, it does not mean that the cost of development has increased by this amount. The main reason is that the benefits obtained due to the use of prototype in terms of reduced requirement errors and reduced volume of requirement change requests are likely to be substantial (see the examples given earlier in this chapter), thereby reducing the cost of development itself.

An Example

Consider the example of the restaurant automation discussed earlier. An initial structured analysis of the problem was also shown earlier. During the analysis the restaurant owner was quite apprehensive about the ability and usefulness of the system. She felt that it was risky to automate, as an improper system might cause considerable confusion and lead to a loss of clientele. Due to the risks involved, it was decided to build a throwaway prototype. Note that the basic purpose of the prototype in this situation is not to uncover or clarify requirements but to ascertain the utility of the automated system. Of course, the experience with the prototype will also be used to ensure that the requirements are correct and complete.

The first step in developing a prototype is to prepare an SRS for the prototype. The SRS need not be formal but should identify the different system utilities to be included in the prototype. As mentioned earlier, these are typically the features that are most unclear or where the risk is high. It was decided that the prototype will demonstrate the following features:

1. Customer order processing and billing
2. Supply ordering and processing

The first was included, as that is where the maximum risk exists for the restaurant (after all, customer satisfaction is the basic objective of the restaurant, and if customers are unhappy the restaurant will loose business). The second was included, as maximum potential benefit can be derived from this feature. Accounting and statistics generation were not to be included in the prototype.

The prototype was developed using a database system, in which good facilities for data entry and form (bill) generation exist. The user interface for the waiters and the restaurant manager was included in the prototype. The system was used, in parallel with the existing system, for a few weeks, and informal surveys with the customers were conducted.

Customers were generally pleased with the accuracy of the bills and the details they provided. Some gave suggestions about the bill layout. Based on the experience of the waiters, the codes for the different menu items were modified to an alphanumeric code. They found that the numeric codes used in the prototype were hard to remember. The experience of the restaurant manager and feedback from the supplier were used to determine the final details about supply processing and handling.

3.3 Requirements Specification

The final output is the software requirements specification document (SRS). For smaller problems or problems that can easily be comprehended, the specification activity might come after the entire analysis is complete. However, it is more likely that problem analysis and specification are done concurrently. An analyst typically will analyze some parts of the problem and then write the requirements for that part. In practice, problem analysis and requirements specification activities overlap, with movement from both activities to the other, as shown in Figure 3.1. However, as all the information for specification comes from analysis, we can conceptually view the specification activity as following the analysis activity.

The first question that arises is: If formal modeling is done during analysis, why are the "outputs" of modeling—the structures that are built (e.g., DFD and DD, Object diagrams)—not treated as an SRS? The main reason is that modeling generally focuses on the problem structure, not its external behavior. Consequently, things like user interfaces are rarely modeled, whereas they frequently form a major component of the SRS. Similarly, for ease of modeling, frequently "minor issues" like erroneous situations (e.g., error in output) are rarely modeled properly, whereas in an SRS, behavior under such situations also has to be specified. Similarly, performance constraints, design constraints, standards compliance, recovery, etc. are not included in the model, but must be specified clearly in the SRS because the designer must know about these to properly design the system. It should therefore be clear that the outputs of a model are nowhere near a desirable SRS.

For these reasons, the transition from analysis to specification should also not be expected to be straightforward, even if some formal modeling is used during analysis. It is not the case that in specification the structures of modeling are just specified in a more formal manner. A good SRS needs to specify many things, some of which are not satisfactorily handled during modeling. Furthermore, sometimes the structures produced during modeling are not amenable for translation into external behavior specification (which is what is to be specified in an SRS). For example, the object diagram produced during an OO analysis is of limited use when specifying the external behavior of the desired system.

Essentially, what passes from requirements analysis activity to the specification activity is the knowledge acquired about the system. The modeling is essentially a tool to help obtain a thorough and complete knowledge about the proposed system. The SRS is written based on the knowledge acquired during analysis. As converting knowledge into a structured document is not straightforward, specification itself is a major task, which is relatively independent.

A consequence of this is that it is relatively less important to model "completely," compared to specifying completely. As the primary objective of analysis is problem understanding, while the basic objective of the requirements phase is to produce the SRS, the complete and detailed analysis structures are not as critical as the proponents of a technique make it out to be. In fact, it is possible to develop the SRS without using formal modeling technique. The basic aim of the structures used in modeling is to help in knowledge representation and problem partitioning, the structures are not an end in themselves.

With this, let us start our discussion on requirements specification. We start by discussing the different desirable characteristics of an SRS.

3.3.1 Characteristics of an SRS

To properly satisfy the basic goals, an SRS should have certain properties and should contain different types of requirements. In this section, we discuss some of the desirable characteristics of an SRS and components of a SRS. A good SRS is [IEE87, IEE94]:

1. Correct
2. Complete

3. Unambiguous

4. Verifiable

5. Consistent

6. Ranked for importance and/or stability

7. Modifiable

8. Traceable

The discussion of these properties here is based on [IEE87, IEE94]. An SRS is *correct* if every requirement included in the SRS represents something required in the final system. An SRS is *complete* if everything the software is supposed to do and the responses of the software to all classes of input data are specified in the SRS. Correctness and completeness go hand-in-hand; whereas correctness ensures that what is specified is done correctly, completeness ensures that everything is indeed specified. Correctness is an easier property to establish than completeness as it basically involves examining each requirement to make sure it represents the user requirement. Completeness, on the other hand, is the most difficult property to establish; to ensure completeness, one has to detect the absence of specifications, and absence is much harder to ascertain than determining that what is present has some property.

An SRS is *unambiguous* if and only if every requirement stated has one and only one interpretation. Requirements are often written in natural language, which are inherently ambiguous. If the requirements are specified in a natural language, the SRS writer has to be especially careful to ensure that there are no ambiguities. One way to avoid ambiguities is to use some formal requirements specification language. The major disadvantage of using formal languages is the large effort required to write an SRS, the high cost of doing so, and the increased difficulty reading and understanding formally stated requirements (particularly by the users and clients).

An SRS is *verifiable* if and only if every stated requirement is verifiable. A requirement is verifiable if there exists some cost-effective process that can check whether the final software meets that requirement. This implies that the requirements should have as little subjectivity as possible because subjective requirements are difficult to verify. Unambiguity is essential for verifiability. As verification of requirements is often done through reviews, it also implies that an SRS is understandable, at least by the developer, the client, and the users. Understandability is clearly extremely important, as one of the goals of the requirements phase is to produce a document on which the client, the users, and the developers can agree.

An SRS is *consistent* if there is no requirement that conflicts with another. Terminology can cause inconsistencies; for example, different requirements may use different terms to refer to the same object. There may be logical or temporal conflict between requirements causing inconsistencies. This occurs if the SRS contains two or more requirements whose logical or temporal characteristics cannot be satisfied together by any software system. For example, suppose a requirement states that an event e is to occur before another event f. But then another set of requirements states (directly or indirectly by transitivity) that event f should occur before event e. Inconsistencies in an SRS can be a reflection of some major problems.

Generally, all the requirements for software are not of equal importance. Some are critical, others are important but not critical, and there are some which are desirable but not very important. Similarly, some requirements are "core" requirements which are not likely to change as time passes, while others are more dependent on time. An SRS is ranked for importance and/or stability if for each requirement the importance and the stability of the requirement are indicated. Stability of a requirement reflects the chances of it changing in future. It can be reflected in terms of the expected change volume.

Writing an SRS is an iterative process. Even when the requirements of a system are specified, they are later modified as the needs of the client change. Hence an SRS should be easy to modify. An SRS is *modifiable* if its structure and style are such that any necessary change can be made easily while preserving completeness and consistency. Presence of redundancy is a major hindrance to modifiability, as it can easily lead to errors. For example, assume that a requirement is stated in two places and that the requirement later needs to be changed. If only one occurrence of the requirement is modified, the resulting SRS will be inconsistent.

An SRS is traceable if the origin of each of its requirements is clear and if it facilitates the referencing of each requirement in future development [IEE87]. Forward traceability means that each requirement should be traceable to some design and code elements. Backward traceability requires that it be possible to trace design and code elements to the requirements they support. Traceability aids verification and validation.

Of all these characteristics, completeness is perhaps the most important (and hardest to ensure). One of the most common problem in requirements specification is when some of the requirements of the client are not specified. This necessitates additions and modifications to the requirements later in the development cycle, which are often expensive to incorporate. Incompleteness is also a major source of disagreement between the client and the supplier. The importance of having complete requirements cannot be overemphasized.

3.3.2 Components of an SRS

Completeness of specifications is difficult to achieve and even more difficult to verify. Having guidelines about what different things an SRS should specify will help in completely specifying the requirements. Here we describe some of the system properties that an SRS should specify. The basic issues an SRS must address are:

1. Functionality
2. Performance
3. Design constraints imposed on an implementation
4. External interfaces

Conceptually, any SRS should have these components. If the traditional approach to requirement analysis is being followed, then the SRS might even have portions corresponding to these. However, if, for example, object-oriented analysis is done for problem analysis, then the functional requirements might be specified indirectly by specifying the services on the objects.

Functional Requirements

Functional requirements specify which outputs should be produced from the given inputs. They describe the relationship between the input and output of the system. For each functional requirement, a detailed description of all the data inputs and their source, the units of measure, and the range of valid inputs must be specified.

All the operations to be performed on the input data to obtain the output should be specified. This includes specifying the validity checks on the input and output data, parameters affected by the operation, and equations or other logical operations that must be used to transform the inputs into corresponding outputs. For example, if there is a formula for computing the output, it should be specified. Care must be taken not to specify any algorithms that are not part of the system but that may be needed to implement the system. These decisions should be left for the designer.

An important part of the specification is the system behavior in abnormal situations, like invalid input (which can occur in many ways) or error during computation. The functional requirement must clearly state what the system should do if such situations occur. Specifically, it should specify the behavior of the system for invalid inputs and invalid outputs. Furthermore, behavior for situations where the input is valid but the normal operation cannot be performed should also be specified. An example of this situation is an airline reservation system, where a reservation cannot be made even for valid passengers if the airplane is fully booked. In short, the system behavior for all foreseen inputs and all foreseen system states should be specified. These special conditions are often likely to be overlooked, resulting in a system that is not robust.

Performance Requirements

This part of an SRS specifies the performance constraints on the software system. All the requirements relating to the performance characteristics of the system must be clearly specified. There are two types of performance requirements: static and dynamic.

Static requirements are those that do not impose constraint on the execution characteristics of the system. These include requirements like the number of terminals to be supported, the number of simultaneous users to be supported, and the number of files that the system has to process and their sizes. These are also called *capacity* requirements of the system.

Dynamic requirements specify constraints on the execution behavior of the system. These typically include response time and throughput constraints on the system. Response time is the expected time for the completion of an operation under specified circumstances. Throughput is the expected number of operations that can be performed in a unit time. For example, the SRS may specify the number of transactions that must be processed per unit time, or what the response time for a particular command should be. Acceptable ranges of the different performance parameters should be specified, as well as acceptable performance for both normal and peak workload conditions.

All of these requirements should be stated in measurable terms. Requirements such as "response time should be good" or the system must be able to "process all the transactions quickly" are not desirable because they are imprecise and not verifiable. Instead, statements like "the response time of command x should be less than one second 90% of the times" or "a transaction should be processed in less than one second 98% of the times" should be used to declare performance specifications.

Design Constraints

There are a number of factors in the client's environment that may restrict the choices of a designer. Such factors include standards that must be followed, resource limits, operating environment, reliability and security requirements, and policies that may have an impact on the design of the system. An SRS should identify and specify all such constraints.

Standards Compliance: This specifies the requirements for the standards the system must follow. The standards may include the report format and accounting procedures. There may be audit tracing requirements, which require certain kinds of changes, or operations that must be recorded in an audit file.

Hardware Limitations: The software may have to operate on some existing or predetermined hardware, thus imposing restrictions on the design. Hardware limitations can include the type of machines to be used, operating system available on the system, languages supported, and limits on primary and secondary storage.

Reliability and Fault Tolerance: Fault tolerance requirements can place a major constraint on how the system is to be designed. Fault tolerance requirements often make the system more complex and expensive. Requirements about system behavior in the face of certain kinds of faults is specified. Recovery requirements are often an integral part here, detailing what the system should do if some failure occurs to ensure certain properties. Reliability requirements are very important for critical applications.

Security: Security requirements are particularly significant in defense systems and many database systems. Security requirements place restrictions on the use of certain commands, control access to data, provide different kinds of access requirements for different people, require the use of passwords, and cryptography techniques, and maintain a log of activities in the system.

External Interface Requirements

All the possible interactions of the software with people, hardware, and other software should be clearly specified. For the user interface, the characteristics of each user interface of the software product should be specified. User interface is becoming increasingly important and must be given proper attention. A preliminary user manual should be created with all user commands, screen formats, an explanation of how the system will appear to the user, and feedback and error messages. Like other specifications these requirements should be precise and verifiable. So, a statement like "the system should be user friendly" should be avoided and statements like "commands should be no longer than six characters" or "command names should reflect the function they perform" used.

For hardware interface requirements, the SRS should specify the logical characteristics of each interface between the software product and the hardware components. If the software is to execute on existing hardware or on predetermined hardware, all the characteristics of the hardware, including memory restrictions, should be specified. In addition, the current use and load characteristics of the hardware should be given.

The interface requirement should specify the interface with other software the system will use or that will use the system. This includes the interface with the operating system and other applications. The message content and format of each interface should be specified.

3.3.3 Specification Languages

Requirements specification necessitates the use of some specification language. The language should possess many of the desired qualities (modifiablity, understandablity, unambiguous, and so forth) of the SRS. In addition, we want the language to be easy to learn and use. As one might expect, many of these characteristics conflict in the selection of a specification language. For example, to avoid ambiguity, it is best to use some formal language. But for ease of understanding a natural language might be preferable. Here we describe some of the commonly used languages for requirement specification.

Structured English

Natural languages have been widely used for specifying requirements. The major advantage of using a natural language is that both client and supplier understand the language. Specifying the problem to be solved in a natural language is an expected outcome in the evolution of software engineering. Initially, since the software systems were small, requirements were verbally conveyed using the natural language for expression (in fact, much in-house software development is still done in this manner). Later, as software requirements grew more complex, the requirements were specified in a written form, rather than orally, but the means for expression stayed the same.

The use of natural languages has some important drawbacks. By the very nature of a natural language, written requirements will be imprecise and ambiguous. This goes against some of the desirable characteristics that we stated earlier. Furthermore, efforts to be more precise and complete result in voluminous requirement specification documents, as natural languages are quite verbose.

Due to these drawbacks, there is an effort to move from natural languages to formal languages for requirement specification. However, natural languages are still widely used and are likely to be in use for the near future. To reduce some of the drawbacks, most often natural language is used in a structured fashion. In structured English (choosing English as our natural language), requirements are broken into sections and paragraphs. Each paragraph is then broken into subparagraphs. Many organizations also specify strict uses of some words like "shall," "perhaps," and "should" and try to restrict the use of common phrases in order to improve the precision and reduce the verbosity and ambiguity.

Regular Expressions

Regular expressions can be used to specify the structure of symbol strings formally. String specification is useful for specifying such things as input data, command sequence, and contents of a message. Regular expressions are a useful approach for such cases. Regular expressions can be considered as grammar for specifying the valid sequences in a language and can be automatically processed. They are routinely used in compiler construction for recognition of symbols and tokens.

There are a few basic constructs allowed in regular expressions:

1. Atoms: The basic symbols or the alphabet of the language.
2. Composition: Formed by concatenating two regular expressions. For regular expressions r1 and r2, concatenation is expressed by (r1 r2), and denotes concatenation of strings represented by r1 and r2.
3. Alternation: Specifies the either/or relationship. For r1 and r2, alternation is specified by (r1 | r2) and denotes the union of the sets of strings specified by r1 and r2.

4. Closure: Specifies repeated occurrence of a regular expression. This is the most powerful of the constructs. For a regular expression r, closure is specified by r^*, which means that strings denoted by r are concatenated zero or more times.

With these basic constructs, many data streams can be defined. Hierarchical specifications can also be constructed by using abstract names for specifying the regular expressions and then giving the regular expression specification for those names. For complex data streams, hierarchical specifications can enhance clarity.

Example: Consider a file containing student records. Each student record has the name of the student, followed by the social security number, followed by the sequence of courses the student has taken. This input file can easily be specified as a regular expression.

> Record_file = (Name SSN Courses)*
> Name = (Last First)
> Last, First = $(A \mid B \mid C \mid \ldots \mid Z)(a \mid b \mid c \mid \ldots \mid z)^*$
> SSN = digit digit digit digit digit digit digit digit digit
> digit = $(0 \mid 1 \mid 2 \mid \ldots \mid 9)$
> Courses = $(C\_number)^*$

And C_number can be specified depending on conventions followed (e.g., "CS" followed by a three digit number). Once the regular expression is specified, checking that a given input is a valid string in the language (i.e., has the structure specified by the regular expression) can be done automatically. Tools exist that will generate the analyzers for a given regular expression.

Decision Tables

Decision tables provide a mechanism for specifying complex decision logic. It is formal, table-based notation that can also be automatically processed to check for qualities like completeness and lack of ambiguity.

A decision table has two parts. The top part lists the different conditions, and the bottom part specifies different actions. The table essentially specifies under what combination of conditions what actions are to be performed. It is best to specify the conditions in a manner such that the condition can either be true or false, thus taking only two values. In this case if there are N conditions specified, a complete decision table will have 2^N different combinations listed for which actions must be specified. However, not all the combinations of conditions might be feasible.

Example: Consider the part of a banking system responsible for debiting from accounts. For this part the relevant conditions are:

> C1: The account number is correct.
> C2: The signature matches.

	1	2	3	4	5
C1	N	N	Y	Y	Y
C2		N	N	Y	Y
C3			N	Y	N
A1				X	
A2			X		X
A3		X			

TABLE 3.2. Decision table for the banking example.

C3: There is enough money in the account.

The possible actions are:

A1: Give money.
A2: Give statement that not enough money is there.
A3: Call the vigilance department to check for fraud.

Part of the decision table for this is shown in Table 3.2. The decision rules are the different combinations of conditions that are of interest. For each condition a Y means yes or true, N means no or false, and a blank means that it can be either true or false. If an action is to be taken for a particular combination of the conditions, it is shown by an X for that action. If there is no mark for an action for a particular combination of conditions, it means that the action is not to be performed.

Finite State Automata

Finite state automata (FSA) includes the concept of state and input data streams. An FSA has a finite set of states and specifies transitions between the states. The transition from one state to another is based on the input. An FSA can be specified pictorially, formally as grammar and transition rules, or as a transition table.

FSAs are used extensively for specifying communication protocols. They are not used much in data processing applications.

Example: Consider a simplified version of the alternating bit protocol for data communication. A node can receive a message numbered 0 or 1. When it receives message 0, it sends an acknowledgment and waits for the message 1 to arrive. When message 1 arrives, it sends an acknowledgment and then waits for message 0 to arrive. An FSA specifying this required behavior of the node is shown in Figure 3.17.

State s0 is the state where the node is waiting for message 0 to arrive. When this message arrives, a state transition occurs and the state changes from s0 to s1. The output produced during this transition is the ACK message. Similarly, when the system is in state s1, it is waiting for message 1 to arrive. When the message arrives, it sends the ACK message and changes state to s0.

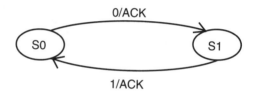

FIGURE 3.17. FSA for the data communication example.

3.3.4   Structure of a Requirements Document

All the requirements for the system have to be included in a document that is clear and concise. For this, it is necessary to organize the requirements document as sections and subsections. There can be many ways to structure a requirements document. Many methods and standards have been proposed for organizing an SRS (see [Dav93] for some examples). One of the main ideas of standardizing the structure of the document is that with an available standard, each SRS will fit a certain pattern, which will make it easier for others to understand (that is one of the roles of any standard). Another role these standards play is that by requiring various aspects to be specified, they help ensure that the analyst does not forget some major property. Here we discuss the organization proposed in the IEEE guide to software requirements specifications [IEE87, IEE94].

The IEEE standards recognize the fact that different projects may require their requirements to be organized differently, that is, there is no one method that is suitable for all projects. It provides different ways of structuring the SRS. The first two sections of the SRS are the same in all of them. The general structure of an SRS is given in Figure 3.18.

1. Introduction
   1.1 Purpose
   1.2 Scope
   1.3 Definitions, Acronyms, and Abbreviations
   1.4 References
   1.5 Overview
2. Overall Description
   2.1 Product Perspective
   2.2 Product Functions
   2.3 User Characteristics
   2.4 General Constraints
   2.5 Assumptions and Dependencies
3. Specific Requirements

FIGURE 3.18. General structure of an SRS.

The introduction section contains the purpose, scope, overview, etc. of the requirements document. It also contains the references cited in the document and any definitions that are used. Section 2 describes the general factors that affect the product and its requirements. Specific requirements are not mentioned, but a general overview is presented to make the understanding of the specific requirements easier. Product perspective is essentially the relationship of the product to other products; defining if the product is independent or is a part of a larger product, and what the principal interfaces of the product are. A general abstract description of the functions to be performed by the product is given. Schematic diagrams showing a general view of different functions and their relationships with each other can often be useful. Similarly, typical characteristics of the eventual end user and general constraints are also specified.

The specific requirements section (section 3 of the SRS) describes all the details that the software developer needs to know for designing and developing the system. This is typically the largest and most important part of the document. For this section, different organizations have been suggested in the standard. These requirements can be organized by the modes of operation, user class, object, feature, stimulus, or functional hierarchy [IEE94]. One method to organize the specific requirements is to first specify the external interfaces, followed by functional requirements, performance requirements, design constraints, and system attributes. This structure is shown in Figure 3.19 [IEE94].

The external interface requirements section specifies all the interfaces of the software: to people, other softwares, hardware, and other systems. User interfaces are clearly a very important component; they specify each human interface the system plans to have, including screen formats, contents of menus, and command structure. In hardware interfaces, the logical characteristics of each interface between the software and hardware on which the software can run are specified. Essentially, any assumptions the software is making about the hardware are listed here. In software interfaces, all other software that is needed for this software to run is specified, along with the interfaces. Communication interfaces need to be specified if the software communicates with other entities in other machines.

In the functional requirements section, the functional capabilities of the system are described. In this organization, the functional capabilities for all the modes of operation of the software are given. For each functional requirement, the required inputs, desired outputs, and processing requirements will have to be specified. For the inputs, the source of the inputs, the units of measure, valid ranges, accuracies, etc. have to be specified. For specifying the processing, all operations that need to be performed on the input data and any intermediate data produced should be specified. This includes validity checks on inputs, sequence of operations, responses to abnormal situations, and methods that must be used in processing to transform the inputs into corresponding outputs. Note that no algorithms are generally specified, only the relationship between the inputs and the outputs (which may be in the

3. Specific Requirements
   3.1 External Interface Requirements
      3.1.1 User Interfaces
      3.1.2 Hardware Interfaces
      3.1.3 Software Interfaces
      3.1.4 Communication Interfaces
   3.2. Functional Requirements
      3.2.1 Mode 1
         3.2.1.1 Functional Requirement 1.1
          :
         3.2.1.n Functional Requirement 1.n
      :
      3.2.m Mode m
         3.2.m.1 Functional Requirement m.1
          :
         3.2.m.n Functional Requirement m.n
   3.3 Performance Requirements
   3.4 Design Constraints
   3.5 Attributes
   3.6 Other Requirements

FIGURE 3.19. One organization for specific requirements [IEE94].

form of an equation or a formula) so that the designer can design an algorithm to produce the outputs from the inputs. For outputs, the destination of outputs, units of measure, range of valid outputs, error messages, etc. all have to be specified.

The performance section should specify both static and dynamic performance requirements. All factors that constrain the system design are described in the performance constraints section. The attributes section specifies some of the overall attributes that the system should have. Any requirement not covered under these is listed under other requirements. Design constraints specify all the constraints imposed on design (e.g., security, fault tolerance, and standards compliance).

There are three other outlines proposed by the IEEE standard for organizing "specific requirements." However, all these outlines are essentially just guidelines. There are other ways a requirements document can be organized. The key concern is that after the requirements have been identified, the requirements document should be organized in such a manner that it aids validation and system design. For different projects many of these sections may not be needed and can be omitted. Especially for smaller projects, some of the sections and subsections may not be necessary to properly specify the requirements.

3.4 Validation

The development of software starts with the requirements document, which is also used to determine eventually whether or not the delivered software system is acceptable. It is therefore important that the requirements specification contains no errors and specifies the client's requirements correctly. Furthermore, as we have seen, the longer an error remains undetected, the greater the cost of correcting it. Hence, it is extremely desirable to detect errors in the requirements before the design and development of the software begin.

Due to the nature of the requirement specification phase, there is a lot of room for misunderstanding and committing errors, and it is quite possible that the requirements specification does not accurately represent the client's needs. The basic objective of the requirements validation activity is to ensure that the SRS reflects the actual requirements accurately and clearly. A related objective is to check that the SRS document is itself of "good quality" (some desirable quality objectives are given later).

Before we discuss validation methods, let us consider the type of errors that typically occur in an SRS. Many different types of errors are possible, but the most common errors that occur can be classified in four types: omission, inconsistency, incorrect fact, and ambiguity. *Omission* is a common error in requirements. In this type of error, some user requirement is simply not included in the SRS; the omitted requirement may be related to the behavior of the system, its performance, constraints, or any other factor. Omission directly affects the external completeness of the SRS. Another common form of error in requirements is *inconsistency*. Inconsistency can be due to contradictions within the requirements themselves or to incompatibility of the stated requirements with the actual requirements of the client or with the environment in which the system will operate. The third common requirement error is *incorrect fact*. Errors of this type occur when some fact recorded in the SRS is not correct. The fourth common error type is *ambiguity*. Errors of this type occur when there are some requirements that have multiple meanings, that is, their interpretation is not unique.

Some projects have collected data about requirement errors. In [Dav89] the effectiveness of different methods and tools in detecting requirement errors in specifications for a data processing application is reported. On an average, a total of more than 250 errors were detected, and the percentage of different types of errors was:

Omission	Incorrect Fact	Inconsistency	Ambiguity
26%	10%	38%	26%

In [BW81] the errors detected in the requirements specification of the A-7 project (which deals with a real-time flight control software) were reported. A total of about 80 errors were detected, out of which about 23% were clerical in nature. Of the remaining, the distribution with error type was:

Omission	Incorrect Fact	Inconsistency	Ambiguity
32%	49%	13%	5%

Though the distributions of errors is different in these two cases, reflecting the difference in application domains and the error detection methods used, they do suggest that the major problems (besides clerical errors) are omission, incorrect fact, inconsistency, and ambiguity. If we take the average of the two data tables, it shows that all four classes of errors are very significant, and a good fraction of errors belong to each of these types. This implies, that besides improving the quality of the SRS itself (e.g., no clerical errors), the validation should focus on uncovering these types of errors. Let us now look at a few common methods of requirements validation.

3.4.1   Requirement Reviews

Because requirements specification formally specifies something that originally existed informally in people's minds, requirements validation must necessarily involve the clients and the users. Requirement reviews, in which the SRS is carefully reviewed by a group of people including representatives of the clients and the users, are the most common method of validation. Reviews can be used throughout software development for quality assurance and data collection, and there is considerable data now to suggest that reviews and inspections, which are manual processes executed on textual documents, are one of the most effective means of detecting errors. As requirements are generally textual documents that cannot be executed, reviews are eminently suitable for requirements validation. We will discuss the general procedure of reviews in the next chapter. Here we only discuss some aspects relevant to requirements reviews.

Requirements review is a review by a group of people to find errors and point out other matters of concern in the requirements specifications of a system. The review group should include the author of the requirements document, someone who understands the needs of the client, a person of the design team, and the person(s) responsible for maintaining the requirements document. It is also good practice to include some people not directly involved with product development, like a software quality engineer.

One way to organize the review meeting is to have each participant go over the requirements before the meeting and mark the items he has doubts about or he feels need further clarification. Checklists can be quite useful in identifying such items. In the meeting, each participant goes through the list of potential defects he has uncovered. As the members ask questions, the requirements analyst (who is the author of the requirements specification document) provides clarifications if there are no errors or agrees to the presence of errors. Other people may need further clarification or join the discussion at any time. The discussions that take place during the review are likely to uncover errors other than the suspected error that may have started the discussion. These discussions form a very important part of the review process.

Alternatively, the meeting can start with the analyst explaining each of the requirements in the document. The participants ask questions, share doubts, or seek clarifications. Errors are uncovered by the participants and the discussion that ensues. Note that the focus of reviews is on group dynamics and synergy for error detection, not on individual capability for detecting errors. In other words, the idea of a structured review meeting is that if the review is held in this manner, the total number of errors detected will be greater than the sum of errors that would be detected if the review participants spent the same amount of time separately reviewing.

Although the primary goal of the review process is to reveal any errors in the requirements, such as those discussed earlier, the review process is also used to consider factors affecting quality, such as testability and readability. During the review, one of the jobs of the reviewers is to uncover the requirements that are too subjective and too difficult to define criteria for testing that requirement.

Checklists are frequently used in reviews to focus the review effort and ensure that no major source of errors is overlooked by the reviewers. A possible checklist that can be used for reviews [Dun84] is given next. A good checklist will usually depend on the project.

- Are all hardware resources defined?
- Have the response times of functions been specified?
- Have all the hardware, external software, and data interfaces been defined?
- Have all the functions required by the client been specified?
- Is each requirement testable?
- Is the initial state of the system defined?
- Are the responses to exceptional conditions specified?
- Does the requirement contain restrictions that can be controlled by the designer?
- Are possible future modifications specified?

Effectiveness: Requirements reviews are probably the most effective means for detecting requirement errors. The data in [BW81] about the A-7 project shows that about 33% of the total requirement errors detected were detected by review processes, and about 45% of the requirement errors were detected during the design phase when the requirement document is used as a reference for design. This clearly suggests that if requirements are reviewed then not only a substantial fraction of the errors are detected by them, but a vast majority of the remaining errors are detected soon afterwards in the design activity.

3.4.2   Other Methods

Requirement reviews remain the most commonly used and viable means for requirement validation. However, there are other approaches that may be applicable for some systems or parts of systems or systems that have been specified formally.

Automated Cross-Referencing

Automated cross-referencing uses processors to verify some properties of requirements. Any automated processing of requirements is possible if the requirements are written in a formal specification language or a language specifically designed for machine processing. We saw examples of such languages earlier. These tools typically focus on checks for internal consistency and completeness, which sometimes leads to checking of external completeness. However, these tools cannot directly check for external completeness (after all, how will a tool know that some requirement has been completely omitted). For this reason, requirement reviews are needed even if the requirements are specified through a tool or in a formal notation.

If the requirements are in machine-processable form, they can be analyzed for internal consistency among different elements of the requirements. Closure properties can also be checked to help uncover incompleteness of requirements. The language processors can also produce cross-reference information, which can then be used in manual analysis.

Effectiveness: The experiments reported in [Dav89, C+83] reveal that through the use of tools (and the languages associated with them) such as REVS and PSL/PSA, many errors can be detected. The two projects reported that 250 to 350 errors were detected by different tools. The data suggests that tools are consistently successful in detecting inconsistency errors in the requirements, followed by ambiguity. They can also detect a fair number of omission type of requirements. However, these experiments do not indicate what fraction of the total requirement errors were detected, i.e., how many slipped by and were caught later. Overall, it can be said that if these languages and tools are used, many errors that can be detected internally from the document itself (inconsistency, ambiguity, etc.) are indeed caught. And the check for internal completeness that these tools can make (e.g., something is referred in one place but is not specified anywhere) frequently leads to detection of missing requirements. However, no tool can directly check for "external completeness" (i.e., the requirements specify all the requirements). Hence, these methods should *not* be considered a means to replace reviews but should be considered as complementary to reviews. To effectively combine the two, the tools can be used to detect the internal errors, thereby freeing the reviewers of this burden and helping focus the review process to the issue of external completeness.

Reading

The goal in reading [Boe84a] is to have someone other than the author of the requirements read the requirements specification document to identify potential problems. By having the requirements read by another person who may have has different "interpretation" of requirements, many of the requirements problems caused by misinterpretations or ambiguities can be identified. Furthermore, if the reader is a person who is interested in the project (like a person from the quality assurance group that will eventually test the system), issues that could cause problems later may be brought to the surface. For example, if a tester reads the requirements, it is likely that the testability of requirements will be well examined.

Reading is effective only if the reader takes the job seriously and reads the requirements carefully. Even with serious readers, reading is limited in scope for catching completeness and consistency errors, particularly for large software systems.

Constructing Scenarios

Scenarios [Boe84a] describe different situations of how the system will work once it is operational. The most common area for constructing scenarios is that of system-user interaction. Constructing scenarios is good for clarifying misunderstandings in the human-computer interaction area. They are of limited value for verifying the consistency and completeness of requirements.

Prototyping

Though prototypes are generally built to ascertain requirements, a prototype can be built to verify requirements. Prototypes can be quite useful in verifying the feasibility of some of the requirements (such as answering the question Can this be done?). A prototype that has been built during problem analysis can also aid validation. For example, if the prototype has most of the user interfaces and they have been approved after use by the client and users, then the user interface, as specified by the prototype, can be considered validated. No further validation need be performed for them.

3.5 Metrics

As we stated earlier, the basic purpose of metrics at any point during a development project is to provide quantitative information to the management process so that the information can be used to effectively control the development process. Unless the metric is useful in some form to monitor or control the cost, schedule, or quality of the project, it is of little use for a project. There are very few metrics that have been defined for requirements, and little work has been done to study the relationship between the metric values and the project properties of interest. This says more about the state of the art of software metrics, rather than the usefulness of having such metrics. In this section, we will discuss some of the metrics and how they can be used. As we will see, some of these are fairly primitive, and their predictive value is limited.

3.5.1   Size Measures

A major problem after requirements are done is to estimate the effort and schedule for the project. For this, some metrics are needed that can be extracted from the requirements and used to estimate cost and schedule (through the use of some model). As the primary factor that determines the cost (and schedule) of a software project is its "size," a metric that can help get an idea of the size of the project will be useful for estimating cost. This implies that during the requirement phase measuring the size of the requirement specification itself is pointless, unless the size of the SRS reflects the effort required for the project. This also requires that relationships of any proposed size measure with the ultimate effort of the project be established before making general use of the metric. We will discuss a few size metrics that are used for requirements. Out of these, the function point has been the most widely used, and significant correlation between the size measured in function points and project cost has been observed. Cost estimation, which is a major reason for estimating size during the requirements phase, is discussed in the next chapter.

Text-Based Measures

A commonly used size metric for requirements is the size of the text of the SRS. The size could be in *number of pages*, *number of paragraphs*, *number of functional requirements* etc. As can be imagined, these measures are highly dependent on the authors of the document. A verbose analyst who likes to make heavy use of illustrations may produce an SRS that is many times the size of the SRS of a terse analyst. Similarly, how much an analyst refines the requirements has an impact on the size of the document. Generally, such metrics cannot be accurate indicators of the size of the project. They are used mostly to convey a general sense about the size of the project. For this purpose they are used quite frequently and their use is not unjustified.

Function Points

Function points [AG83] are one of the most widely used measures of software size. The basis of function points is that the "functionality" of a system, that is, what the system performs, is the measure of the system size. And as functionality is independent of how the requirements of the system are specified, or even how they are eventually implemented, such a measure has a nice property of being dependent solely on the system capabilities. In function points, the system functionality is calculated in terms of the number of functions it implements, the number of inputs, the number of outputs, etc.—parameters that can be obtained after requirements analysis and that are independent of the specification (and implementation) language.

The original formulation for computing the function points uses the count of five different parameters, namely, external input types, external output types, logical internal file types, external interface file types, and external inquiry types. According to the function point approach, these five parameters capture the entire functionality of a system. However, two elements of the same type may differ in their complexity and hence should not contribute the same amount to the "functionality" of the system. To account for complexity, each parameter in a type is classified as *simple*, *average*, or *complex*. The definition of each of these types and the interpretation of their complexity levels is given later [AG83].

Each unique input (data or control) type that is given as input to the application from outside is considered of *external input type* and is counted. An external input type is considered unique if the format is different from others or if the specifications require a different processing for this type from other inputs of the same format. The source of the external input can be the user, or some other application, files. An external input type is considered *simple* if it has a few data elements and affects only a few internal files of the application. It is considered *complex* if it has many data items and many internal logical files are needed for processing them. The complexity is *average* if it is in between. Note that files needed by the operating system or the hardware (e.g., configuration files) are not counted as external input files because they do not belong to the application but are needed due to the underlying technology.

Similarly, each unique output that leaves the system boundary is counted as an *external output type*. Again, an external output type is considered unique if its format or processing is different. Reports or messages to the users or other applications are counted as external input types. The complexity criteria is similar to that of the external input type. For a report, if it contains a few columns it is considered *simple*, if it has multiple columns it is considered *average*, and if it contains complex structure of data and references many files for production, it is considered *complex*.

Each application maintains information internally for performing its functions. Each logical group of data or control information that is generated, used, and maintained by the application is counted as a *logical internal file type*. A logical internal file is *simple* if it contains a few record types, *complex* if it has many record types, and *average* if it is in between.

Files that are passed or shared between applications are counted as *external interface file type*. Note that each such file is counted for all the applications sharing it. The complexity levels are defined as for logical internal file type.

A system may have queries also, where a query is defined as an input-output combination where the input causes the output to be generated almost immediately. Each unique input-output pair is counted as an *external inquiry type*. A query is unique if it differs from others in format of input or output or if it requires different processing. For classifying the query type, the input and output are classified as for external input type and external output type, respectively. The query complexity is the larger of the two.

Each element of the same type and complexity contributes a fixed and same amount to the overall function point count of the system (which is a measure of the functionality of the system), but the contribution is different for the different types, and for a type, it is different for different complexity levels. The amount of contribution of an element is shown in Table 3.3 [AG83, LJ90].

Once the counts for all five different types are known for all three different complexity classes, the raw or unadjusted function point (UFP) can be computed as a weighted sum as follows:

$$UFP = \sum_{i=1}^{i=5} \sum_{j=1}^{j=3} w_{ij} C_{ij},$$

where i reflects the row and j reflects the column in Table 3.3; w_{ij} is the entry in the ith row and jth column of the table (i.e., it represents the contribution of an element of the type i and complexity j); and C_{ij} is the count of the number of elements of type i that have been classified as having the complexity corresponding to column j.

Once the UFP is obtained, it is adjusted for the environment complexity. For this, 14 different characteristics of the system are given. These are data communications, distributed processing, performance objectives, operation configuration load, transaction rate, on-line data entry, end user efficiency, on-line update, complex processing logic, re-usability, installation ease, operational ease, multiple sites, and desire to facilitate change. The degree of influence of each of these factors is taken

Function type	Simple	Average	Complex
External input	3	4	6
External output	4	5	7
Logical internal file	7	10	15
External interface file	5	7	10
External inquiry	3	4	6

TABLE 3.3. Function point contribution of an element.

to be from 0 to 5, representing the six different levels: not present (0), insignificant influence (1), moderate influence (2), average influence (3), significant influence (4), and strong influence (5). The 14 degrees of influence for the system are then summed, giving a total N (N ranges from 0 to 14*5=70). This N is used to obtain a complexity adjustment factor (CAF) as follows:

$$CAF = 0.65 + 0.01N.$$

With this equation, the value of CAF ranges between 0.65 and 1.35. The delivered function points (DFP) are simply computed by multiplying the UFP by CAF. That is,

Delivered Function Points = CAF * Unadjusted Function Points.

As we can see, by adjustment for environment complexity, the DFP can differ from the UFP by at most 35%. The final function point count for an application is the computed DFP.

Function points have been used as a size measure extensively and have been used for cost estimation. Studies have also been done to establish correlation between DFP and the final size of the software (measured in lines of code.) For example, studies reported in [LJ90] suggest that one function point is approximately equal to a little more than 100 lines of Cobol code and approximately equal to about 80 lines of PL1 code. By building models between function points and delivered lines of code (and existing results have shown that a reasonably strong correlation exists between DFP and DLOC so that such models can be built), one can estimate the size of the software in DLOC, if desired.

As can be seen from the manner in which the functionality of the system is defined, the function point approach has been designed for the data processing type of applications. For data processing applications, function points generally perform very well [Kem87] and have now gained a widespread acceptance. For such applications, function points are used as an effective means of estimating cost and evaluating productivity. However, its utility as a size measure for nondata processing types of applications (e.g., real-time software, operating systems, and scientific applications) has not been well established, and it is generally believed that for such applications function points are not very well suited.

A major drawback of the function point approach is that the process of computing the function points involves subjective evaluation at various points and the final computed function point for a given SRS may not be unique and can depend on the analyst. Some of the places where subjectivity enters are: (1) different interpretations of the SRS (e.g., whether something should count as an external input type or an external interface type, whether or not something constitutes a logical internal file, if two reports differ in a very minor way should they be counted as two or one); (2) complexity estimation of a user function is totally subjective and depends entirely on the analyst (an analyst may classify something as complex while someone else may classify it as average) and complexity can have a substantial impact on the final count as the weightage for simple and complex frequently differ by a factor of 2; and (3) value judgments for the environment complexity. These factors make the process of function point counting somewhat subjective. Organizations that use function points try to specify a more precise set of counting rules in an effort to reduce this subjectivity. It has also been found that with experience this subjectivity is reduced [LJ90]. Overall, despite this subjectivity, use of function points for data processing applications continues to grow.

The main advantage of function points over the size metric of DLOC, the other commonly used approach, is that the definition of DFP depends only on information available from the specifications, whereas the size in DLOC cannot be directly determined from specifications. Furthermore, the DFP count is independent of the language in which the project is implemented. Though these are major advantages, another drawback of the function point approach is that even when the project is finished, the DFP is not uniquely known and has subjectivity. This makes building of models for cost estimation hard, as these models are based on information about completed projects (cost models are discussed further in the next chapter). In addition, determining the DFP—from either the requirements or a completed project—cannot be automated. That is, considerable effort is required to obtain the size, even for a completed project. This is a drawback compared to DLOC measure, as DLOC can be determined uniquely by automated tools once the project is completed.

Bang Metric

Bang is another requirement-based metric that has been proposed to quantify the size of the project [DeM82]. The metric assumes that a data flow diagram and data dictionary–based analysis have been performed for the problem and hence is limited in scope to the projects that satisfy this assumption.

The basic data for the bang metric is the count of *functional primitives* that lie inside the man-machine boundary. Functional primitives are the lowest-level bubbles in the data flow diagram (in the portion inside the man-machine boundary). That is, we count those bubbles that are not refined further. For each functional primitive, each data flow coming in or going out is marked with the number of tokens it carries. A token is essentially a data unit in the data flow that is considered independently by this primitive. For example, if a data flow is a record consisting of five fields and each of the field needs to be separately examined in this functional primitive, then this data flow arrow will be marked with the number 5. However, if the entire record is considered as a single unit inside the primitive, then it is considered to have only one token. If TC_i is the total number of tokens involved in the primitive (i.e., going in or out along the data flows), then the contribution of this primitive to the system size is corrected FP increment (CFPI), which is defined as:

$$\text{CFPI}_i = \frac{TC_i * \log_2 TC_i}{2}.$$

The rationale behind this is that by taking $\log_2$, CFPI becomes proportional to the total number of bits needed to uniquely represent all the TC_is. This defines the size of a primitive from the point of view of the number of data tokens it handles. However, it does not distinguish based on the computation the primitive does; two different primitives may perform different amounts of computation of more or less complexity even though they have the same number of tokens. This is handled by categorizing the primitives in 16 different types and assigning different complexity weights for each type. Some of the types, their meanings, and their weights are given next. For a complete list, the reader is referred to [DeM82].

- *Separation or Amalgamation:* Primitives that divide or combine incoming data items. *Weight: 0.6.*
- *Simple Update:* Primitives that perform some updates. *Weight: 0.5.*
- *Verification:* Primitives that perform consistency checks. *Weight: 1.0.*
- *Output Generation:* Primitives involved in outputs. *Weight: 1.0.*
- *Arithmetic:* Primitives that do simple arithmetic. *Weight: 0.7.*
- *Device Management:* Primitives that control devices. *Weight: 2.5.*

Each primitive is classified as belonging to one of the 16 categories. Then the CFPI of that primitive is multiplied by the weight of that category. This gives us the size of the primitive, taking into account the data it processes and the type of processing it does. The final metric of the system is

$$\text{Bang} = \sum_{i=1}^{i=N} \text{CFPI}_i * w_i,$$

where N is the total number of function primitives, CFPI_i is the CFPI of the ith primitive, and w_i is the complexity weight of the ith primitive.

This metric is clearly more detailed than the function point metric, but it has a strong disadvantage; it assumes the existence of a data flow diagram and data dictionary. With some changes, it can be used for data-oriented and hybrid systems [DeM82]. However, there is little data to suggest what type correlation this metric has with project parameters. Overall, as of now, it is more a proposed metric than one that is used commonly.

3.5.2 Quality Metrics

As we have seen, the quality of the SRS has direct impact on the cost of the project. Hence, it is important to ensure that the SRS is of good quality. For this, some quality metrics are needed that can be used to assess the quality of the SRS. Quality of an SRS can be assessed either directly by evaluating the quality of the document by estimating the value of one or more of the quality attributes of the SRS, or indirectly, by assessing the effectiveness of the quality control measures used in the development process during the requirements phase. Quality attributes of the SRS are generally hard to quantify, and little work has been done in quantifying these attributes and determining correlation with project parameters. Hence, the use of these metrics is still limited. However, process based metrics are better understood and used more widely for monitoring and controlling the requirements phase of a project.

Number of Errors Found

This is a process metric that is useful for assessing the quality of requirement specifications. The quality of the requirements is assessed by evaluating the effectiveness of the error detection process (which is generally requirement reviews). The number of errors found can be obtained from the requirement review report. The errors can be categorized into different types (we saw some categorizations earlier).

Once the number of errors of different categories found during the requirement review of the project is known, some assessment can be made about the review process from the size of the project and historical data. This assessment is possible if the development process is under statistical control. In this situation, the error distribution during requirement reviews of a project will show a pattern similar to other projects executed following the same development process. From the pattern of errors to be expected for this process and the size of the current project (say, in function points), the volume and distribution of errors expected to be found during requirement reviews of this project can be estimated. The accuracy of these estimates depends on how well controlled the development process is. From these estimates, it can be determined whether or not the requirement review process was conducted properly (and whether or not further reviews should be scheduled). For example, if much fewer than expected errors were detected, it means that either the SRS was of very high-quality or the requirement reviews were not careful. Further analysis can reveal the true situation. If too many clerical errors were detected and too few omission type errors were detected, it might mean that the SRS was written poorly or that the requirements review meeting could not focus on "larger issues" and spent too much effort on "minor" issues. Again, further analysis will reveal the true situation. Similarly, a large number of errors that reflect ambiguities in the SRS can imply that the problem analysis has not been done properly and many more ambiguities may still exist in the SRS. Some project management decision to control this can then be taken (e.g., build a prototype or do further analysis).

Clearly, review data about the number of errors and their distribution can be used effectively by the project manager to control quality of the requirements. From the historical data, a rough estimate of the number of errors that remain in the SRS after the reviews can also be estimated. This can be useful in the rest of the development process as it gives some handle on how many requirement errors should be revealed by later quality assurance activities.

Change Request Frequency

Requirements rarely stay unchanged. Change requests come from the clients (requesting added functionality, a new report, or a report in a different format, for example) or from the developers (infeasibility, difficulty in implementing, etc.). The frequency of such change requests can be used as a metric. Its basic use is to assess the stability of the requirements and how many changes in requirements to expect during the later stages.

Many organizations have formal methods for requesting and incorporating changes in requirements. Change data can be easily extracted from these formal change approval procedures. The frequency of changes can also be plotted against time. For most projects, the frequency decreases with time. This is to be expected; most of the changes will occur early, when the requirements are being analyzed and understood. During the later phases, requests for changes should decrease.

For a project, if the change requests are not decreasing with time, it could mean that the requirements analysis has not been done properly. Frequency of change requests can also be used to "freeze" the requirements—when the frequency goes below an acceptable threshold, the requirements can be considered frozen and the design can proceed. The threshold has to be determined based on experience and historical data.

Change data (such as in requirements, design, and coding) is used throughout the development cycle for project management. No general rules exist regarding how to use this data. The manner in which this data is to be used is likely to depend on the environment and culture of the developer's organization. This metric can be refined by introducing different categories of changes.

SRS Quality Attributes

The quality metrics discussed earlier are both process-based metrics. Some effort has recently been made to directly quantify some of the quality attributes of the SRS [D+93]. However, no studies have been done on these metrics and no data is available regarding their use. We briefly discuss a couple of these here. For measuring the *unambiguity* attribute of the SRS, specific data from the requirement reviews need to be collected. If during the reviews n_{ui} is the number of requirements all the reviewers interpreted in the same manner and n_r is the total number of requirements, then the unambiguity quality attribute is defined as:

$$Q_U = \frac{n_{ur}}{n_r}.$$

For quantifying completeness, an SRS is considered complete if responses to all classes of input data are specified. (External completeness, i.e., all user requirements are included, is hard to quantify). This completeness definition implies that the function $f(state, stimulus) \rightarrow (state, response)$ is defined for all valid combinations of state and stimulus. Suppose the number of inputs defined in the SRS is n_i, the number of states defined (explicitly or implicitly) is n_s, and the number of unique functions specified is n_u then the completeness quality attribute can be quantified as:

$$Q_C = \frac{n_u}{n_i \times n_s}.$$

This measures the percentage of necessary functions that have been specified. This metric does not capture completeness of nonfunctional requirements and will not work if the inputs or states are not specified completely. As stated earlier, these metrics represent an initial attempt to quantify some of the quality attributes of SRS and their significance has still not been established. In [D⁺93], 24 different attributes are defined, and methods for quantifying many of them are given.

3.6 Summary

Requirements specification is the starting step for the development activities. It is currently one of the weak areas of software engineering. During requirements specifications, the goal is to produce a document of the client's requirements. This document forms the basis of development and software validation. The basic reason for the difficulty in software requirements specification comes from the fact that there are three interested parties—the client, the end users, and the software developer. The requirements document has to be such that the client and users can understand it easily and the developers can use it as a basis for software development. Due to the diverse parties involved in software requirements specification, a communication gap exists. This makes the task of requirements specification difficult.

Given the nature of the problem, it has been claimed that *there is nothing like a perfect requirement* [Dav93]. Hence a practical goal in the requirements phase is to get an SRS of reasonable quality.

There are three basic activities in the requirements phase. The first is problem or requirement analysis. The goal of this activity is to understand such different aspects as the requirements of the problem, its context, and how it fits in the client's organization. The second activity is requirements specification, during which the understood problem is specified or written, producing the SRS. And the third activity is to ensure that the requirements specified in the SRS are indeed what is desired.

There are three main approaches to analysis; unstructured approaches rely on interaction between the analyst, customer, and user to reveal all the requirements (which are then documented). The second is the modeling-oriented approach, in which a model of the problem is built based on the available information. The model is useful in determining if the understanding is correct and in ensuring that all the requirements have been determined. Modeling may be function-oriented or object-oriented. The third approach is the prototyping approach in which a prototype is built to validate the correctness and completeness of requirements.

To satisfy its goals, an SRS should possess certain characteristics. The requirements specification should be complete in that all possible requirements should be specified. It should be consistent, with no conflicting requirements. The requirements should be verifiable, because eventually whether the software satisfies the requirement must be verified. This can only be done if the requirements are verifiable. The requirements specification should also be modifiable and traceable.

To specify the requirements completely, a requirements specification should specify certain properties of the software. First, the SRS should specify all the functions the software is supposed to support. Functional requirements essentially are the input/output behavior specification for the software. Secondly, the SRS should have performance requirements. All requirements relating to performance, such as response time, throughput, and number of concurrent users, should be clearly specified. Thirdly, the SRS should specify the design constraints (those factors that are not really features of the software but constrain the design). Examples of design constraints are standards compliance, operating environment, and hardware limitations. Finally, all the external interfaces of the software should be specified in the SRS. These should include the hardware, software, and human interfaces.

It is important that the final requirements be validated before the next phase of software development starts. As far as possible, all errors from the requirements specifications should be removed before design commences. A number of methods exist for requirements validation. The most commonly used method is requirement review. In this technique, a team of persons, including a representative of the client, reviews the requirements document and ensure that it is complete and consistent.

The main metric of interest for requirements is some quantification of system size. As size is the main factor determining the cost of a project, an accurate size measure can then be used to estimate the cost and schedule of the project. The most commonly used size metric for requirements is the function points. The function point metric attempts to quantify the functionality of the system in terms of five parameters and their complexity levels which can be determined from the requirements of the system. Based on the count of these five parameters for different complexity levels, and the value of fourteen different environment factors, the function point count for a system is obtained. The function point metric can be used for estimating the cost of the system.

Exercises

1. What are the central problems in producing the SRS for a system?

2. Is it possible to have a system that can automatically verify completeness of an SRS document? Explain your answer.

3. Construct an example of an inconsistent (incomplete) SRS.

4. How can you specify the "maintainability" and "user friendliness" of a software system in quantitative terms?

5. For a complete and unambiguous response time requirement, the environmental factors on which the response time depends must be specified. Which factors should be considered, and what units should be chosen to specify them?

6. The basic goal of the requirements activity is to get an SRS that has some desirable properties. What is the role of modeling in developing such an SRS? List three major benefits that modeling provides, along with justifications, for achieving the basic goal.

7. Make a friend of yours as the client. Perform structured analysis and object-oriented analysis for the following:

   (a) An electronic mail system.

   (b) A simple student registration system.

   (c) A system to analyze a person's diet.

   (d) A system to manage recipes for a household.

   (e) A system to fill tax forms for the current year tax laws.

8. Write the SRS for the restaurant example whose analysis is shown in the chapter.

9. In the example for the FSA given in the chapter, assume that a message can get lost during transmission, and a "time out" event occurs at each site to detect the loss of messages. Extend the FSA to model this new system.

10. A library database contains entries that have the name of the book, followed by the author's name, the publisher's name and year of publication, the ISBN number of the book, and finally the number of copies of the book. Each of the data entries is on a new line. Represent this database as a regular expression.

11. Consider the problem of developing software for controlling a small chemical plant. The plant has a number of emergency situations where specified actions have to be taken. Some of these are: (1) if the temperature exceeds T1, then the water shower is turned on; (2) if the temperature is below T2, then the heat is turned on; (3) if the pressure is above P1, the valve v1 is opened, but if it is above P2 (P2>P1), then both values v1 and v2 are opened; (4) if the chemical quantity is more than M and the temperature is more than T3, then the water shower is turned on and a counter chemical is added; (5) if the pressure is above P2 and temperature is above T1, then the water shower is turned on, valves v1 and v2 are opened, and alarm bells are sounded.
Write the requirements for this control system in the form of a decision table.

12. Develop a worksheet for calculating the function point for a given problem specification.

13. Compute the function points for the restaurant example (can use the worksheet).

14. Take some quality attributes for the SRS and try to define some metrics for quantifying them.

CASE STUDY

Problem Analysis

The computer science department in a university offers many courses every semester, which are taught by many instructors. These courses are scheduled based on some policy directions of the department. Currently the scheduling is done manually, but the department would like to automate it. We have to first understand the problem (subject of this section), and then produce a requirements document (described in the next section) based on our understanding of the problem. First we identify the parties involved.

Client: Chairman of the computer science department.

End Users: Department secretary and instructors.

Now we begin to study the current system. After speaking with the instructors, the department chairman, and the secretary, we found that the system operates as follows. Each instructor specifies, on a sheet of paper, the course he is teaching, expected enrollment, and his preferences for lecture times. These preferences must be valid lecture times, which are specified by the department. These sheets are given to the department secretary, who keeps them in the order they are received. After the deadline expires, the secretary does the scheduling. Copies of the final schedule are sent to the instructors. The overall DFD for the system is shown in Figure 3.20.

This DFD was discussed with the chairman and the department secretary and approved by them. We now focus on the scheduling process, which is our main interest. From the chairman we found that the two major policies regarding scheduling are: (1) the post-graduate (PG) courses are given preference over undergraduate (UG) courses, and (2) no two PG courses can be scheduled at the same time.

The department secretary was interviewed at length to find out the details of the scheduling activity. The schedule of the last few semesters, together with their respective inputs (i.e., the sheets) were also studied. It was found that the basic process is as follows. The sheets are separated into three piles—one for PG courses with preferences, one for UG courses with preferences, and one for courses with

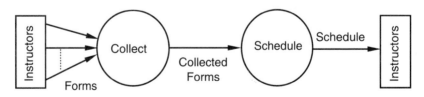

FIGURE 3.20. Top-level DFD for the current scheduling system.

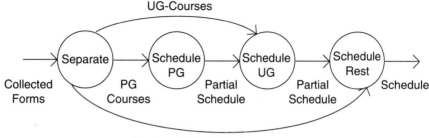

FIGURE 3.21. The DFD for the schedule process.

no preference. The order of the sheets in the three piles was maintained. First the courses in the PG pile were scheduled and then the courses in the UG pile were scheduled. The courses were scheduled in the order they appeared in the pile. During scheduling no backtracking was done, i.e., once a course is scheduled, the scheduling of later courses has no effect on its schedule. After all the PG and UG courses with preferences were processed, courses without any preferences were scheduled in the available slots. It was also found that information about classrooms and the department-approved lecture times was tacitly used during the scheduling. The DFD for the schedule process is shown in Figure 3.21.

The secretary was not able to explain the algorithm used for scheduling. It is likely that some hit-and-miss approach is being followed. However, while scheduling, the following was being checked:

1. Classroom capacity is sufficient for the course.
2. A slot for a room is never allotted to more than one course.

The two basic data flows are the sheets containing preferences and the final schedule. The data dictionary entry for these is shown in Figure 3.22.

Now we have to define the DFD for the new or future automated system. Automating scheduling can affect the preference collection method, so boundaries

collected_forms =
  [instructor_name +
  course_number +
  [preferences]*]

schedule =
  [course_number class_room lecture_time]*

FIGURE 3.22. Data dictionary for the scheduling system.

of change include the entire system. After discussion with the chairman, the instructors, and the secretary, the following decisions were taken regarding what the automated system should do and what the new environment should be:

1. The preferences will be electronically mailed to the secretary by the instructors. The secretary will put these preferences for different courses in a file in the order in which they are received. The secretary will also make entries for all courses for which no response has been given before the deadline. Entries for these courses will have no preferences.

2. The format for each course entry should be similar to the one currently being used.

3. Entries might have errors, so the system should be able to check for errors.

4. The current approach for scheduling should be followed. However, the system should make sure that scheduling of UG courses does not make a PG course without any preference unschedulable. This is not being done currently, but is desired.

5. A reason for unschedulability should be given for the preferences that are not satisfied or for courses that cannot be scheduled.

6. Information about department courses, classrooms, and valid lecture times will be kept in a file.

The DFD for the new logical system (one with automation) is shown in Figure 3.23. The two important data entities are the two files in the DFD. The data dictionary entry for these is given in Figure 3.24.

It is decided that the scheduling process will be automated. The rest (such as combining preferences) will be done manually. Based on the format currently used in the sheets, a detailed format for the course entries was decided and approved by the instructors. A detailed format for the dept_DB file was also chosen and

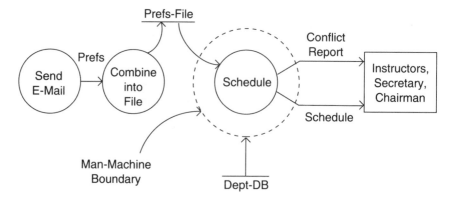

FIGURE 3.23. DFD for the new system.

prefs_file =
  [pref]*

pref =
  course_number + enrollment + [preferences]*

dept_DB =
  [class_rooms]* +
  dept_course_list +
  [valid_lecture_time]*

class_rooms =
  room_no + capacity

FIGURE 3.24. Data dictionary entry for files in the DFD.

approved. The final formats and the requirements are given in the requirements document.

Requirements Specification Document

Abstract: This is the requirements document for the case study that will be used throughout the book. The system to be developed is for scheduling the courses in a computer science department, based on the input about classrooms, lecture times, and time preferences of the different instructors. Different conditions have to be satisfied by the final schedule. This document follows the IEEE standard for a requirements specification document, with some variations.

1. Introduction

1.1. Purpose

The purpose of this document is to describe the external requirements for a course scheduling system. It also describes the interfaces for the system.

1.2. Scope

This document is the only one that describes the requirements of the system. It is meant for use by the developers and will be the basis for validating the final delivered system. Any changes made to the requirements in the future will have to go through a formal change approval process. The developer is responsible for asking for clarifications, where necessary, and will not make any alterations without the permission of the client.

1.3. Definitions, Acronyms, Abbreviations

Not applicable.

1.4. References

Not applicable.

1.5. Developer's Responsibilities Overview

The developer is responsible for (a) developing the system, (b) installing the software on the client's hardware, (c) conducting any user training that might be needed for using the system, and (d) maintaining the system for a period of one year after installation.

2. General Description

2.1. Product Functions Overview

In the computer science department there are a set of classrooms. Every semester the department offers courses, which are chosen from the set of department courses. A course has expected enrollment and could be for graduate students or undergraduate students. For each course, the instructor gives some time preferences for lectures.

The system is to produce a schedule for the department that specifies the time and room assignments for the different courses. Preference should be given to graduate courses, and no two graduate courses should be scheduled at the same time. If some courses cannot be scheduled, the system should produce a "conflict report" that lists the courses that cannot be scheduled and the reasons for the inability to schedule them.

2.2. User Characteristics

The main users of this system will be department secretaries, who are somewhat literate with computers and can use programs such as editors and text processors.

2.3. General Constraints

The system should run on Sun 3/50 workstations running UNIX 4.2 BSD.

2.4. General Assumptions and Dependencies

Not applicable.

3. Specific Requirements

3.1. Inputs and Outputs

The system has two file inputs and produces three types of outputs. These are described here.

Input_file_1: Contains the list of room numbers and their capacity; a list of all the courses in the department catalog; and the list of valid lecture times. The format of the file is:

```
"rooms"
    room1 ":" cap1
    room2 ":" cap2
    ⋮
    ";"
"courses"
    course1 "," course2 "," course3 "," .... ";"
"times"
    time1 "," time2 "," time3 ";"
```

where room1 and room2 are room numbers with three digits, with a maximum of 20 rooms in the building; cap1 and cap2 are room capacities within the range [10, 300]; course1, course2 are course numbers, which are of the form "csddd," where *d* is a digit. There are no more than 30 courses. time1 and time2 are valid lecture times of the form "MWFd" or "MWFdd" or "TTd" or "TTd:dd" or "TTdd:dd". There are no more than 15 such valid lecture times. An example of this file is:

```
rooms
    101 : 25
    115 : 50
    200 : 250 ;
courses
    cs101, cs102, cs110, cs120, cs220, cs412, cs430, cs612, cs630 ;
times
    MWF9, MWF10, MWF11, MWF2, TT9, TT10:30, TT2, TT3:30 ;
```

Input_file_2: Contains information about the courses being offered. For each course, it specifies the course number, expected enrollment, and a number of lecture time preferences. A course number greater than 600 is a post-graduate course; the rest are undergraduate courses. The format of this file is:

```
"course    enrollment        preferences"
    c#1        cap1      pre1 "," pre2 "," pre3 ...
    c#2        cap2      pre1 "," pre2 "," pre3 ...
                            ⋮
                            ⋮
```

where c#1 and c#2 are valid course numbers; cap1 and cap2 are integers in the range [3..250]; and pre1, pre2, and pre3 are time preferences of the instructor (a maximum of 5 preferences are allowed for a course). An example of this file is

course	enrollment	preferences
cs101	180	MWF9, MWF10, MWF11, TT9
cs412	80	MWF9, TT9, TT10:30
cs612	35	
cs630	40	

Output_1: The schedule specifying the class number and time of all the schedulable courses. The schedule should be a table having the lecture times on the x-axis and classroom numbers on the y-axis. For each slot (i.e., lecture time, classroom) the course scheduled for it is given; if no course is scheduled the slot should be blank.

Output_2: List of courses that could not be scheduled and why. For each preference, the reason for inability to schedule should be stated. An example is:

> cs612:   Preference 1: Conflict with cs600.
> Preference 2: No room with proper capacity.

Output_3: Error messages. At the minimum, the following error messages are to be given:

e1. Input file does not exist.
e2. Input-file-1 has error
    e2.1. The course number has wrong format
    e2.2. Some lecture time has wrong format.
    e2.3. Classroom number has wrong format.
    e2.4. Classroom capacity out of range.
e3. Input-file-2 has error
    e3.1. No course of this number.
    e3.2. No such lecture time.
e4. More than permissible courses in the file; later ones ignored.
e5. There are more than permissible preferences; later ones are ignored.

3.2. Functional Requirements

1. Determine the time and room number for the courses such that the following constraints are satisfied:
   (a) No more than one course should be scheduled at the same time in the same room.
   (b) The classroom capacity should be more than the expected enrollment of the course.
   (c) Preference is given to post-graduate courses over undergraduate courses for scheduling.

(d) The post-graduate (undergraduate) courses should be scheduled in the order they appear in the input file, and the highest possible priority of an instructor should be given. If no priority is specified, any class and time can be assigned. If any priority is incorrect, it is to be discarded.

(e) No two post-graduate courses should be scheduled at the same time.

(f) If no preference is specified for a course, the course should be scheduled in any manner that does not violate these constraints.

Inputs: Input_file_1 and Input_file_2.
Outputs: Schedule.

2. Produce a list of all courses that could not be scheduled because some constraint(s) could not be satisfied and give reasons for unschedulability.
Inputs: Input_file_1, and Input_file_2.
Outputs: *Output_2*, i.e., list of unschedulable courses and preferences and why.

3. The data in input_file_2 should be checked for validity against the data provided in input_file_1. Where possible, the validity of the data in input_file_1 should also be checked. Messages should be given for improper input data, and the invalid data item should be ignored.
Inputs: Input_file_1 and Input_file_2.
Outputs: Error messages.

3.3. External Interface Requirements

User Interface: Only one user command is required. The file names can be specified in the command line itself or the system should prompt for the input file names.

3.4. Performance Constraints

[1]. For input_file_2 containing 20 courses and up to 5 preferences for each course, the reports should be printed in less than 1 minute.

3.5. Design Constraints

3.5.1. Software Constraints
The system is to run under the UNIX operating system.

3.5.2. Hardware Constraints

The system will run on a Sun workstation with 16 MB RAM, running UNIX. It will be connected to an 8-page-per-minute printer.

3.6. Acceptance Criteria

Before accepting the system, the developer must demonstrate that the system works on the course data for the last 4 semesters. The developer will have to show through test cases that all conditions are satisfied.

4

Planning a Software Project

Software development is a highly labor-intensive activity. A large software project may involve hundreds of people and span many years. A project of this dimension can easily turn into chaos if proper management controls are not imposed. To complete the project successfully, the large workforce has to be properly organized so that the entire workforce is contributing effectively and efficiently the project. Proper management controls and checkpoints are required for effective project monitoring. Controlling the development, ensuring quality, satisfying the constraints of the selected process model all require careful management of the project.

For a successful project, competent management and technical staff are both essential. Lack of any one can cause a project to fail. Traditionally, computer professionals have attached little importance to management and have placed greater emphasis on technical skills. This is one of the reasons there is a shortage of competent project managers for software projects. Although the actual management skills can only be acquired by actual experience, some of the principles that have proven to be effective can be taught.

We have seen that project management activities can be viewed as having three major phases: project planning, project monitoring and control, and project termination. Broadly speaking, planning entails all activities that must be performed before starting the development work. Once the project is started, project control begins. In other words, during planning all the activities that management needs to perform are planned, while during project control the plan is executed and updated.

Planning may be the most important management activity. Without a proper plan, no real monitoring or controlling of the project is possible. Planning may also be perhaps the weakest activity in many software projects, and many failures caused by mismanagement can be attributed to lack of proper planning. One of the reasons for improper planning is the old thinking that the major activity in a software project is designing and writing code. Consequently, people who make software tend to rush toward implementation and do not spend time and effort planning. No amount of technical effort later can compensate for lack of careful planning. Lack of proper planing is a sure ticket to failure for a large software project. For this reason, we treat project planning as an independent chapter.

The basic goal of planning is to look into the future, identify the activities that need to be done to complete the project successfully, and plan the scheduling and resource allocation for these activities. Ideally, all future activities should be planned. A good plan is flexible enough to handle the unforeseen events that inevitably occur in a large project. Economic, political, and personnel factors should be taken into account for a realistic plan and thus for a successful project.

The *input* to the planning activity is the requirements specification. A very detailed requirements document is not essential for planning, but for a good plan all the important requirements must be known. The output of this phase is the *project plan*, which is a document describing the different aspects of the plan. The project plan is instrumental in driving the development process through the remaining phases. The major issues the project plan addresses are:

> Cost estimation
> Schedule and milestones
> Personnel plan
> Software quality assurance plans
> Configuration management plans
> Project monitoring plans
> Risk management

In the rest of this chapter we will discuss each of these issues and the techniques available for handling the problems in different aspects of project planning.

4.1   Cost Estimation

For a given set of requirements it is desirable to know how much it will cost to develop the software to satisfy the given requirements, and how much time development will take. These estimates are needed *before* development is initiated. The primary reason for cost and schedule estimation is to enable the client or developer to perform a cost-benefit analysis and for project monitoring and control. A more practical use of these estimates is in bidding for software projects, where the developers must give cost estimates to a potential client for the development contract.

For a software development project, detailed and accurate cost and schedule estimates are essential prerequisites for managing the project. Otherwise, even simple questions like "is the project late," "are there cost overruns," and "when is the project likely to complete" cannot be answered. Cost and schedule estimates are also required to determine the staffing level for a project during different phases. It can be safely said that cost and schedule estimates are fundamental to any form of project management and are generally always required for a project.

Cost in a project is due to the requirements for software, hardware, and human resources. Hardware resources are such things as the computer time, terminal time, and memory required for the project, whereas software resources include the tools and compilers needed during development. The bulk of the cost of software development is due to the human resources needed, and most cost estimation procedures focus on this aspect. Most cost estimates are determined in terms of person-months (PM). By properly including the "overheads" (i.e., the cost of hardware, software, office space, etc.) in the dollar cost of a person-month, besides including the direct cost of the person-month, most costs for a project can be incorporated by using PM as the basic measure.

Estimates can be based on subjective opinion of some person or determined through the use of models. Though there are approaches to structure the opinions of persons for achieving a consensus on the cost estimate (e.g., the Delphi approach [Boe81]), it is generally accepted that it is important to have a more scientific approach to estimation through the use of models. In this section we discuss only the model-based approach for cost estimation. Before we discuss the models, let us first understand the limitations of any cost estimation procedure.

4.1.1 Uncertainties in Cost Estimation

One can perform cost estimation at any point in the software life cycle. As the cost of the project depends on the nature and characteristics of the project, at any point, the accuracy of the estimate will depend on the amount of reliable information we have about the final product. Clearly, when the product is delivered, the cost can be accurately determined, as all the data about the project and the resources spent can be fully known by then. This is cost estimation with complete knowledge about the project. On the other extreme is the point when the project is being initiated or during the feasibility study. At this time, we have only some idea of the classes of data the system will get and produce and the major functionality of the system. There is a great deal of uncertainty about the actual specifications of the system. Specifications with uncertainty represent a range of possible final products, not one precisely defined product. Hence, the cost estimation based on this type of information cannot be accurate. Estimates at this phase of the project can be off by as much as a factor of four from the actual final cost.

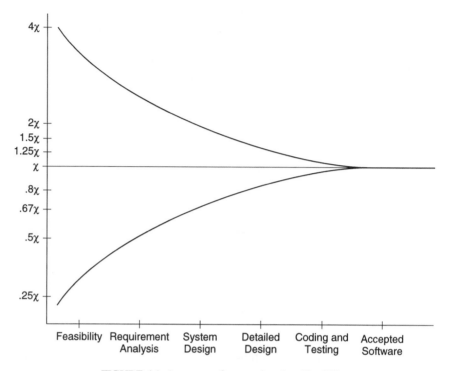

FIGURE 4.1. Accuracy of cost estimation [Boe81].

As we specify the system more fully and accurately, the uncertainties are reduced and more accurate cost estimates can be made. For example, once the requirements are completely specified, more accurate cost estimates can be made compared to the estimates after the feasibility study. Once the design is complete, the estimates can be made still more accurately. The obtainable accuracy of the estimates as it varies with the different phases is shown in Figure 4.1 [Boe81, Boe84b].

Note that this figure is simply specifying the limitations of cost estimating strategies—the best accuracy a cost estimating strategy can hope to achieve. It does not say anything about the existence of strategies that can provide the estimate with that accuracy. For actual cost estimation, cost estimation models or procedures have to be developed. The accuracy of the actual cost estimates will depend on the effectiveness and accuracy of the cost estimation procedures or models employed and the process (i.e., how predictable it is). As mentioned earlier, we will limit our attention to cost estimation models and will not discuss other approaches to cost estimation.

Despite the limitations, cost estimation models have matured considerably and generally give fairly accurate estimates. For example, when the COCOMO model (discussed later) was checked with data from some projects, it was found that the estimates were within 20% of the actual cost 68% of the time. It should also be mentioned that achieving a cost estimate after the requirements have been specified within 20% is actually quite good. With such an estimate, there need not even be any cost and schedule overruns, as there is generally enough slack or free time available (recall the study mentioned earlier that found a programmer spends more than 30% of his time in personal or miscellaneous tasks) that can be used to meet the targets set for the project based on the estimates. In other words, if the estimate is within 20%, the effect of this inaccuracy will not even be reflected in the final cost and schedule.

4.1.2   Building Cost Estimation Models

Let us turn our attention to the nature of cost estimation models and how these models are built. Any cost estimation model can be viewed as a "function" that outputs the cost estimate. As the cost of a project (for the process that is to be followed) depends on the nature of the project, clearly this cost estimation function will need inputs about the project, from which it can produce the estimate. The basic idea of having a model or procedure for cost estimation is that it reduces the problem of estimation to estimating or determining the value of the "key parameters" that characterize the project, based on which the cost can be estimated. The problem of estimation, not yet fully solved, is determining the "key parameters" whose value can be easily determined (especially in the early phases) and how to get the cost estimate from the value of these.

Though the cost for a project is a function of many parameters, it is generally agreed that the primary factor that controls the cost is the size of the project, that is, the larger the project, the greater the cost and resource requirement. Other factors that affect the cost include programmer ability, experience of the developers in the area, complexity of the project, and reliability requirements. In some studies it has been found that programmer ability can have productivity variations of up to a factor of ten. Product complexity has an effect on development effort, as more complex projects that are the same size as simpler projects require more effort. Similarly, reliability requirements have considerable impact on cost; the more the reliability need, the higher the development cost. In fact, the cost increase with reliability is not linear and is often exponential.

The goal of a cost model is to determine which of these many parameters have a "significant" effect on cost and then to discover the relationships between the cost and these characteristics. These characteristics should be such that we can measure or estimate them accurately. The most common approach for determining the significant parameters and their relationship to cost is to build models through regression analysis (model building was discussed in Chapter 2), where cost is the dependent variable and the parameters are the independent variables.

As this approach uses historical data to predict future data points, this approach has one clear implication. This approach can be applied only if the process is under statistical control. If this is not the case, then the past is no reflection of the future, and a regression-type model cannot be used. It also follows that the cost models are process-dependent, as they should be; the cost of developing a software is more if an inefficient process is followed.

The most common approach for estimating effort is to make it a function of a single variable (this is also the simplest from the point of view of model building). Often this variable is the *project size*, and the equation of effort is considered

$$\text{EFFORT} = a * \text{SIZE}^b,$$

where a and b are constants [Bas80]. As discussed in the previous chapter, values for these constants for a particular process are determined through regression analysis, which is applied to data about the projects that has been performed in the past. For example, Watson and Felix [WF77] analyzed the data of more than 60 projects done at IBM Federal Systems Division, ranging from 4000 to 467,000 lines of delivered source code, and found that if the size estimate is in thousands of delivered lines of code (KDLOC), the total effort, E, in person-months (PM) can be given by the equation

$$E = 5.2(\text{KDLOC})^{.91}.$$

A similar study on smaller projects showed that the data fits a straight line quite well, and the equation is of the form

$$\text{EFFORT} = a * \text{SIZE} + b,$$

where a and b are again constants obtained by analysis of data of past projects [Bas80]. These equations suggest that the project cost increases linearly with the size of the final product for small systems but has nonlinear growth for larger projects.

These models have used LOC as the size measure. Similar models have been developed with function point as the size measure [MBM94]. The process of constructing the model is the same—regression analysis on function point size and cost of previously completed projects. An advantage of using function points is that the size in FP can be calculated, while size in LOC will require size estimation be done. However, function point calculation, as discussed in the previous chapter, also involves subjectivity. Due to this, the FP count is not uniquely determined even at the end of the project, unlike the LOC count, which makes the task of getting accurate and consistent data on past projects harder. Note that most of these models will not work for very small projects because for such projects factors other than size become far more important.

4.1.3   On Size Estimation

Though the single-variable cost models with size as the independent variable result in simple-looking models that can be easily obtained from completed projects (for which accurate data about size and cost are known), applying them for estimation is not simple. The reason is that these models now require size as the input, and size of the project is not known early in development (when the estimates are most needed) and has to be estimated. This is particularly true if LOC is used as the measure of size in the model.

So, in a sense, by using size as the main input to the cost model, we have replaced the problem of cost estimation by size estimation. One may then ask, why not directly do cost estimation rather than size estimation? Because size estimation is generally easier than effort estimation. For estimating size, the system is generally partitioned into components it is likely to have. Once the components of the system are known, as estimating something about a small unit is generally much easier than estimating it for a larger system, sizes of components can be generally estimated quite accurately. Once size estimates for components are available, to get the overall size estimate for the system, the estimates of all the components can be added up. Similar property does not hold for cost estimation, as cost of developing a system is *not* the sum of costs of developing the components (there are integration and other costs involved when building a system from developed components). This key feature, that the system property is the sum of the properties of its parts, holds for size but not for cost, and is the main reason that size estimation is easier than cost estimation. For this reason, most cost estimation models, use size estimates in some form.

With the size-based models, if the size estimate is inaccurate, the cost estimate produced by the models will also be inaccurate. Hence, it is important that good estimates for the size of the software be obtained. There is no known "simple" method for estimating the size accurately. In general, there is often a tendency by people to underestimate the size of software. There are many reasons for this [Boe81]. First, people are basically optimistic and have a desire to please others. The way to please others and avoid confrontations in this case is to give a low estimate. Most people give estimates based on previous experiences with similar projects. However, people do not tend to remember their experience completely. Often they tend not to remember the software developed for housekeeping and user interfacing or the support software developed for a project.

When estimating software size, the best way may be to get as much detail as possible about the software to be developed and to be aware of our biases when estimating the size of the various components. By obtaining details and using them for size estimation, the estimates are likely to be closer to the actual size of the final software.

4.1.4 COCOMO Model

Instead of having resource estimates as a function of one variable, resource estimates can depend on many different factors, giving rise to multivariable models. One approach for building multivariable models is to start with an initial estimate determined by using the static single-variable model equations, which depend on size, and then adjusting the estimates based on other variables. This approach implies that size is the primary factor for cost; other factors have a lesser effect. Here we will discuss one such model called the COnstructive COst MOdel (COCOMO) developed by Boehm [Boe81, Boe84b]. This model also estimates the total effort in terms of person-months of the technical project staff. The effort estimate includes development, management, and support tasks but does not include the cost of the secretarial and other staff that might be needed in an organization. The basic steps in this model are:

1. Obtain an initial estimate of the development effort from the estimate of thousands of delivered lines of source code (KDLOC).
2. Determine a set of 15 multiplying factors from different attributes of the project.
3. Adjust the effort estimate by multiplying the initial estimate with all the multiplying factors.

The initial estimate (also called *nominal estimate*) is determined by an equation of the form used in the static single-variable models, using KDLOC as the measure of size. To determine the initial effort E_i in person-months the equation used is of the type $E_i = a * (\text{KDLOC})^b$.

The value of the constants a and b depend on the project type. In COCOMO, projects are categorized into three types—organic, semidetached, and embedded. Organic projects are in an area in which the organization has considerable experience and requirements are less stringent. Such systems are usually developed by a small team. Examples of this type of project are simple business systems, simple inventory management systems, and data processing systems. Projects of the embedded type are ambitious and novel; the organization has little experience and stringent requirements for such aspects as interfacing and reliability. These systems have tight constraints from the environment (software, hardware, and people). Examples are embedded avionics systems and real-time command systems. The semidetached systems fall between these two types. Examples of semidetached systems include developing a new operating system (OS), a database management system (DBMS), and a complex inventory management system. The constants a and b for different systems are given in Table 4.1.

There are 15 different attributes, called *cost driver attributes*, that determine the multiplying factors. These factors depend on product, computer, personnel, and technology attributes (called *project attributes*). Examples of the attributes are required software reliability (RELY), product complexity (CPLX), analyst capa-

System	a	b
Organic	3.2	1.05
Semidetached	3.0	1.12
Embedded	2.8	1.20

TABLE 4.1. Constants for different project types.

Cost Drivers	Rating				
	Very Low	Low	Nom-inal	High	Very High
Product Attributes					
RELY, required reliability	.75	.88	1.00	1.15	1.40
DATA, database size		.94	1.00	1.08	1.16
CPLX, product complexity	.70	.85	1.00	1.15	1.30
Computer Attributes					
TIME, execution time constraint			1.00	1.11	1.30
STOR, main storage constraint			1.00	1.06	1.21
VITR, virtual machine volatility		.87	1.00	1.15	1.30
TURN, computer turnaround time		.87	1.00	1.07	1.15
Personnel Attributes					
ACAP, analyst capability	1.46	1.19	1.00	.86	.71
AEXP, application experience	1.29	1.13	1.00	.91	.82
PCAP, programmer capability	1.42	1.17	1.00	.86	.70
VEXP, virtual machine experience	1.21	1.10	1.00	.90	
LEXP, programming language experience	1.14	1.07	1.00	.95	
Project Attributes					
MODP, modern programming practices	1.24	1.10	1.00	.91	.82
TOOL, use of SW tools	1.24	1.10	1.00	.91	.83
SCHED, development schedule	1.23	1.08	1.00	1.04	1.10

TABLE 4.2. Effort multipliers for different cost drivers.

bility (ACAP), application experience (AEXP), use of modern tools (TOOL), and required development schedule (SCHD). Each cost driver has a rating scale, and for each rating, a multiplying factor is provided. For example, for the product attribute RELY, the rating scale is very low, low, nominal, high, and very high (and in some cases extra high). The multiplying factors for these ratings are .75, .88, 1.00, 1.15, and 1.40, respectively. So, if the reliability requirement for the project is judged to be low then the multiplying factor is .75, while if it is judged to be very high the factor is 1.40. The attributes and their multiplying factors for different ratings are shown in Table 4.2 [Boe81, Boe84b]. The COCOMO approach also provides guidelines for assessing the rating for the different attributes [Boe81].

The multiplying factors for all 15 cost drivers are multiplied to get the effort adjustment factor (EAF). The final effort estimate, E, is obtained by multiplying the initial estimate by the EAF:

$$E = \text{EAF} * E_i.$$

As we discussed earlier, the value of the constants for a cost model depend on the process and thus have to be determined from past data about the usage of that process. COCOMO has instead provided "global" constant values. This might work because it requires some characteristics about the process (e.g., it is well managed), and it provides some means to fine-tune the estimate for a particular process. For example, if the process relies less on tools, the estimate can be "corrected" for this type of process by suitably choosing the value for the TOOL attribute.

Still, there is little data to support that these constants are globally applicable, and to apply COCOMO in an environment, these may need to be tailored for the specific environment. One way is to start with the COCOMO-supplied constants until data for some completed projects is available. With this data, by keeping the exponent in the equations for initial effort estimate fixed, the value of the other constant can be determined through regression analysis so that the data best fits the equation. This will be a simpler regression analysis as only one constant has to be determined rather than two in the standard regression line fitting discussed earlier. With more data, the value of the exponent can also be fine-tuned. Changing both constants together requires a lot more data for regression analysis to be significant. For a particular process or environment, all the attributes might not be significant, and it might be possible to merge some of them into a single attribute. For further details on adapting COCOMO for a particular environment, based on data analysis, the reader is referred to [Boe81].

By this method, the overall cost of the project can be estimated. For planning and monitoring purposes, estimates of the effort required for the different phases is also desirable. In COCOMO, effort for a phase is considered a defined percentage of the overall effort. The percentage of total effort spent in a phase varies with the type and size of the project. The percentages for an organic software project are given in Table 4.3.

Using this table, the estimate of the effort required for each phase can be determined from the total effort estimate. For example, if the total effort estimate for an organic software system is 20 PM, then the percentage effort for the coding and unit testing phase will be $40 + (38 - 40)/(32 - 8) * 20 = 39\%$. The estimate for the effort needed for this phase is 7.8 PM. This table does not list the cost of requirements as a percentage of the total cost estimate because the project plan (and cost estimation) is being done after the requirements are complete. In COCOMO the

Phase	Size			
	Small 2 KDLOC	Intermediate 8 KDLOC	Medium 32 KDLOC	Large 128 KDLOC
Product design	16	16	16	16
Detailed design	26	25	24	23
Code and unit test	42	40	38	36
Integration and test	16	19	22	25

TABLE 4.3. Phase-wise distribution of effort.

detailed design and code and unit testing are sometimes combined into one phase called the *programming phase*.

For the other two types of software systems, the percentages are slightly different, with the percentage for product design and integration and testing increasing slightly and the percentage of coding decreasing slightly. The reader is referred to [Boe81] for further details. An estimate of percentages for project sizes different from the one specified in the table can be obtained by linear interpolation.

Besides phase-wise estimates, the model can be used to estimate the cost of different components or subsystems of the system. For details of this, the reader is referred to [Boe81].

COCOMO provides three levels of models of increasing complexity: basic, intermediate, and detailed. The model described earlier is the intermediate COCOMO model. The detailed model is the most complex. It has different multiplying factors for the different phases for a given cost driver. The set of cost drivers applicable to a system or module is also not the same as the drivers for the system level. However, it might be too detailed for many applications. We will follow the intermediate model described earlier, even for detailed estimates. COCOMO also provides help in determining the rating of different attributes and performing sensitivity and trade-off analysis.

4.1.5 An Example

Suppose a system for office automation must be designed. From the requirements, it was clear that there will be four major modules in the system: data entry, data update, query, and report generator It is also clear from the requirements that this project will fall in the organic category. The sizes for the different modules and the overall system were estimated to be

Data Entry	0.6 KDLOC
Data Update	0.6 KDLOC
Query	0.8 KDLOC
Reports	1.0 KDLOC
TOTAL	3.0 KDLOC

From the requirements, the ratings of the different cost driver attributes were assessed. These ratings, along with their multiplying factors, are:

Complexity	High	1.15
Storage	High	1.06
Experience	Low	1.13
Programmer Capability	Low	1.17

All other factors had a nominal rating. From these, the effort adjustment factor (EAF) is

$$EAF = 1.15 * 1.06 * 1.13 * 1.17 = 1.61.$$

The initial effort estimate for the project is obtained from the relevant equations. We have

$$E_i = 3.2 * 3^{1.05} = 10.14 \, PM.$$

Using the EAF, the adjusted effort estimate is

$$E = 1.61 * 10.14 = 16.3 \, PM.$$

Using the preceding table, we obtain the percentage of the total effort consumed in different phases. The office automation system's size estimate is 3 KDLOC, so we will have to use interpolation to get the appropriate percentage (the two end values for interpolation will be the percentages for 2 KDLOC and 8 KDLOC). The percentages for the different phases are: design—16%, detailed design—25.83%, code and unit test—41.66%, and integration and testing—16.5%. With these, the effort estimates for the different phases are:

System Design	$.16 * 16.3 = 2.6 \, PM$
Detailed Design	$.258 * 16.3 = 4.2 \, PM$
Code and Unit Test	$.4166 * 16.3 = 6.8 \, PM$
Integration	$.165 * 16.3 = 2.7 \, PM.$

These effort estimates will be used later during personnel planning.

4.2 Project Scheduling

Schedule estimation and staff requirement estimation may be the most important activities after cost estimation. Both are related, if phase-wise cost is available.

Here we discuss the schedule estimation. The goal of schedule estimation is to determine the total duration of the project and the duration of the different phases.

First, let us see why the schedule is independent of the person-month cost. A schedule cannot be simply obtained from the overall effort estimate by deciding on average staff size and then determining the total time requirement by dividing the total effort by the average staff size. Brooks has pointed out that person and months (time) are not interchangeable. According to Brooks [Bro75], "... man and months are interchangeable only for activities that require no communication among men, like sowing wheat or reaping cotton. This is not even approximately true of software. . . ."

Obviously, there is some relationship between the project duration and the total effort (in person-months) required for completing the project. But this relationship is not linear; to halve the project duration, doubling the staff-months will not work. The basic reason behind this is that if the staff needs to communicate for the completion of a task, then communication time should be accounted for. Communication time increases with the square of the number of staff. For example, if there are n persons and all need to communicate, then there are n^2 communication paths and each communication path consumes time. Hence, by increasing the staff for a project we may actually increase the time spent in communication. This is often restated as Brook's law: "adding manpower to a late project may make it later."

From this discussion it is clear that we cannot treat the schedule as a variable totally in control of management. Each project will require some time to finish, and this time cannot be reduced by putting more people on the project. Hence, project schedule is an independent variable, which must be assessed for planning. Models are used to assess the project duration.

4.2.1   Average Duration Estimation

Single variable models can be used to determine the overall duration of the project. Generally, schedule is modeled as depending on the total effort (which, in turn, depends on size). Again, the constants for the model are determined from historical data. The IBM Federal Systems Division found that the total duration, M, in calendar months can be estimated by

$$M = 4.1 E^{.36}.$$

In COCOMO, the schedule is determined in a similar manner. The equation for an organic type of software is

$$M = 2.5 E^{.38}.$$

For other project types, the constants vary only slightly. The duration or schedule of the different phases is obtained in the same manner as in effort distribution. The percentages for the different phases are given in Table 4.4.

Phase	Size			
	Small 2 KDLOC	Intermediate 8 KDLOC	Medium 32 KDLOC	Large 128 KDLOC
Product Design	19	19	19	19
Programming	63	59	55	51
Integration	18	22	26	30

TABLE 4.4. Phase-wise distribution of schedule.

In this COCOMO table, the detailed design, coding, and unit testing phases are combined into one "programming phase." This is perhaps done because all these activities are usually done by programmers, while system design and integration are often done by different people, who may or may not be involved in programming activities of the project.

As we can see, these percentages are slightly (but not too much) different from the effort distribution percentages. The percentage of total project duration spent in detailed design, coding, and unit testing is somewhat higher than the percentage of total effort spent in these activities. However, because the percentages are only slightly different, it means that the average staff sizes computed for the different phases will not be too different from the overall average staff size for the project.

4.2.2 Project Scheduling and Milestones

Once we have the estimates of the effort and time requirement for the different phases, a schedule for the project can be prepared. This schedule will be used later to monitor the progress of the project.

A conceptually simple and effective scheduling technique is the Gantt chart, which uses a calendar-oriented chart to represent the project schedule. Each activity is represented as a bar in the calendar, starting from the starting date of the activity and ending at the ending date for that activity. The start and end of each activity become milestones for the project.

Progress can be represented easily in a Gantt chart, by ticking off (or coloring) each milestone when completed. Alternatively, for each activity another bar can be drawn specifying when the activity actually started and ended, i.e., when these two milestones were actually achieved.

The main drawback of the Gantt chart is that it does not depict the dependency relationships among the different activities. Hence, the effect of slippage in one activity on other activities or on the overall project schedule cannot be determined. However, it is conceptually simple and easy to understand, and it is heavily used. It is sufficient for small and medium-sized projects.

For large projects, the dependencies among activities are important to determine which are critical activities, whose completion should not be delayed, and which activities are not critical. To represent the dependencies, PERT charts are often used. A PERT chart is a graph-based chart. It can be used to determine the activities that form the "critical path," which if delayed will cause the overall project to delay. The PERT chart is not conceptually as simple, and the representation is graphically not as clear as Gantt charts. Its use is justified in large projects.

4.2.3   Example Continued

We continue with the office automation example. Recall that the overall size estimate for the project is 3 KDLOC, and the final effort estimate obtained was 16.34 PM. As this is an organic system, the overall duration will be determined by the equation $2.5 * E^{0.38}$. Using this we get the project duration D as

$$D = 2.5 * 16.34^{0.38} = 7.23 \text{ months.}$$

Using the preceding table, which gives the duration of the different phases as a percentage of the total project duration, we can obtain the duration of the different phases. The duration of the different phases is:

System Design	$.19 * 7.23 = 1.37$ M
Programming	$.623 * 7.23 = 4.5$ M
Integration	$.1866 * 7.23 = 1.35$ M

If the project is to start on January 1, then according to this, the project will end in the middle of August. The system design phase will terminate in the middle of February, the programming activity will end in late June, and the rest of the time will be spent in integration and testing. Using these estimates, an overall schedule for the project can be decided.

4.3   Staffing and Personnel Planning

Once the project schedule is determined and the effort and schedule of different phases and tasks are known, staff requirements can be obtained. From the cost and overall duration of the project, the *average* staff size for the project can be determined by dividing the total effort (in person-months) by the overall project duration (in months).

This average staff size is not detailed enough for proper personnel planning, especially if the variation between the actual staff requirement at different phases is large. Typically the staff requirement for a project is small during requirement and design, the maximum during implementation and testing, and drops again during the final phases of integration and testing. Using the COCOMO model, average staff requirement for the different phases can be determined as the effort and schedule for each phase are known. This presents staffing as a step function with time.

For personnel planning and scheduling, it is useful to have effort and schedule estimates for the subsystems and basic modules in the system. At planning time, when the system design has not been done, the planner can only expect to know about the major subsystems in the system and perhaps the major modules in these subsystems.

An approximate method, suitable for many small systems, is to divide the total schedule in terms of the ratio of the sizes of different components. A more accurate method, used in COCOMO, is to start with the sizes of different components (and the total systems). The initial effort for the total system is determined. From this, the *nominal productivity* of the project is calculated by dividing the overall size by the initial effort. Using this productivity, the effort required for each of the modules is determined by dividing the size by nominal productivity. This gives an initial effort estimate for the modules. For each module the rating of the different cost driver attributes is determined. From these ratings the effort adjustment factor (EAF) for each module is determined. Using the initial estimates and the EAFs, the final effort estimate of each module is determined. The final effort estimate for the overall system is obtained by adding the final estimates for the different modules.

It should be kept in mind that these effort estimates for a module are done by treating a module like an independent system, thus including the effort required for design, integration, and testing of the module. When used for personnel planning this should be kept in mind if the effort for the design and integration phases is obtained separately. In that case, the cost of design and integration of a module is included in the design and integration phase effort estimates.

4.3.1 Rayleigh Curve

Staffing in a project, in general, is more a continuous function than a step function with only a few different values. Putnam has proposed a time-dependent continuous function to estimate the staffing at different times throughout the project duration [Put78]. The basis of the model is the observation that there are regular patterns of manpower buildup and phase-out, independent of the type of work being performed (this was earlier observed in hardware development). It was also observed that the staffing pattern followed the Rayleigh curve. For software development, there is the buildup and phase-out curve for each of the different phases, and each curve is a Rayleigh curve. The total staffing pattern, which is determined by summing the different curves, is also a Rayleigh curve, as shown in Figure 4.2.

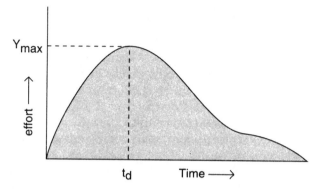

FIGURE 4.2. The Rayleigh curve.

If $\hat{y}$ is the staffing rate in PY/year (person-year per year), then this staffing pattern as a function of time t can be represented by the equation,

$$\hat{y} = 2Kate^{-at_2} \text{ PY/yr},$$

where K is the total manpower required or the total area under the curve from $t = 0$ to infinity. It represents the total person-years used by the project over its entire life cycle. The constant a is the shape parameter, which is determined by the time at which the curve reaches its maximum value. The cumulative manpower used up to time t can be obtained by integrating this equation. Representing the cumulative manpower by y, we have

$$y = K(1 - e^{-at_2}).$$

If $\hat{y}$ peaks at time t_d, the constant a is given by the equation

$$a = 1/2t_d^2.$$

In software projects, it has been observed that t_d corresponds closely to the total development time or the time taken to reach full operational capability. Substituting for a we get

$$\hat{y} = (K/t_d^2)te^{-t_2}/2t_d^2.$$

Integrating this equation from $t = 0$ to t_d we get the total development effort D:

$$D = y(t_d) = K(1 - e^{.5}) = .39K.$$

In other words, the total development cost is approximately 40% of the total life-cycle cost. It was found that the number K/t_d^2 has an interesting property. It represents the difficulty of the system in terms of programming effort required to produce it. When this number is small it corresponds with easy systems; when the number is large it corresponds to difficult systems.

4.3.2   Personnel Plan

Once the schedule and average staff level for each activity is known, the overall personnel allocation for the project can be planned. This plan will specify how many people will be needed for the different activities at different times for the duration of the project.

A method of producing the personnel plan is to make it a calendar-based representation, containing all the months in the duration of the project, by listing the months from the starting date to the ending date. Then, for each of the different tasks identified and for which cost and schedule estimates are prepared, list the number of people needed in each month. The total effort for each month and the total effort for each activity can easily be computed from this plan. The total for each activity should be the same as (or close to) the overall person-month estimate.

Drawing a personnel plan usually requires a few iterations to ensure that the effort requirement for the different phases and activities (and the duration of the different phases) is consistent with the estimates obtained earlier. The ensuring of consistency is made more difficult by the fact that the effort estimates for individual modules include the design and integration effort for those modules, and this effort is also included in the effort for these phases. It is usually not desirable to state staff requirements in a unit less than 0.5 person to make the plan consistent with the estimates. Some difference between the estimates and the totals in the personnel plan is acceptable.

This type of plan, although it has the overall staff requirement, does not distinguish between different types of people. A more detailed plan will list the requirement of people by their specialty; for example, stating how many programmers, analysts, quality assurance people, and so forth are needed at different times.

4.3.3   Example Continued

Now that we have the schedule and effort estimates, we can obtain the cost estimates of the different components. We will use COCOMO to estimate the effort for different modules. For this project we have the following estimates (repeated here for convenience):

Data Entry	0.6 KDLOC
Data Update	0.6 KDLOC
Query	0.8 KDLOC
Reports	1.0 KDLOC
TOTAL	3.0 KDLOC

The initial cost estimate obtained earlier for the total project was 10.14 PM. The nominal productivity for the project is

$$3.0/10.14 = .29 \text{ KDL/PM}.$$

We assume that the cost driver attributes for all the different modules are the same and the EAF for the modules is 1.61 (for a large system, a module should be rated separately, resulting in its own EAF, which might be different from the EAF of others). Using this productivity and EAF, the effort estimate for the different modules can be determined as follows:

Data Entry	$0.6/0.29 \times 1.61$	$= 3.2$ PM
Data Update	$0.6/0.29 \times 1.61$	$= 3.2$ PM
Query	$0.8/0.29 \times 1.61$	$= 4.3$ PM
Reports	$1.0/0.29 \times 1.61$	$= 5.4$ PM.

The total effort estimate for the project is 16.1 PM, which is close to the total estimate obtained earlier (because the EAF for each module was the same as the system EAF in the example shown before). It should again be pointed out that these estimates include the cost of system design and system testing. Using the effort and duration estimates for the different phases obtained earlier, the average staff requirement for the different phases can easily be determined, and we get

System Design	$2.6/1.37$	$= 1.9$ persons
Programming	$11/4.5$	$= 2.4$ persons
Integration	$2.7/1.35$	$= 2$ persons.

Using the estimates for the schedule, the effort for different phases, and the effort for different modules, we can draw a personnel plan. As mentioned earlier, to create a personnel plan that is consistent with the estimates, a few iterations are needed, and the totals in the plan may be somewhat different from the estimates. One plan for this example is shown in Table 4.5.

In this plan we have not included management as a separate activity, as it is a small project and we assume that one of the persons doing the design will be doing the monitoring and control for the duration of the project (and spending a fraction of his or her time on such activity). However, in larger projects, management requirements should be listed separately. Management for a project will require some personnel throughout the project, and the requirement is not likely to vary. Notice that in

	Jan	Feb	Mar	Apr	May	Jun	Jul	Aug	Total
System Design	2	2							3.0
Data Entry		1	1	1					2.0
Update		1	1	1					2.0
Query				1	1	1			2.5
Report				1	1.5	2			4.0
Integration							2	2	3.0
Total	2	2	2	2	2.5	3	2	1	16.5

TABLE 4.5. A personnel plan for the example.

the plan the effort requirement for different phases—system design, programming (for which different modules are listed separately), and integration—is close to the estimates obtained earlier. The duration of the different phases is also close to the duration obtained earlier.

4.3.4 Team Structure

Often a team of people is assigned to a project. For the team to work as a cohesive group and contribute the most to the project, the people in the team have to be organized in some manner. The structure of the team has a direct impact on the product quality and project productivity.

Two basic philosophies have evolved for organizing a team [Man81]: egoless teams and chief programmer teams. Egoless teams consist of ten or fewer programmers. The goals of the group are set by consensus, and input from every member is taken for major decisions. Group leadership rotates among the group members. Due to its nature, egoless teams are sometimes called *democratic teams*. The structure results in many communication paths between people, as shown in Figure 4.3.

The structure allows input from all members, which can lead to better decisions in difficult problems. This suggests that this structure is well suited for long-term research-type projects that do not have time constraints. On the other hand, it is not suitable for regular tasks that are not too complex and that have time constraints. For such tasks, the communication in democratic structure is unnecessary and results in inefficiency.

A chief programmer team, in contrast to egoless teams, has a hierarchy. It consists of a chief programmer, who has a backup programmer, a program librarian, and some programmers. The chief programmer is responsible for all major technical decisions of the project. He does most of the design and he assigns coding of the different parts of the design to the programmers. The backup programmer helps the

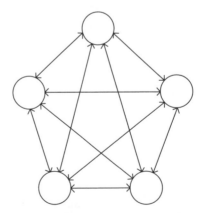

FIGURE 4.3. Communication paths in a democratic team structure.

Chief Programmer

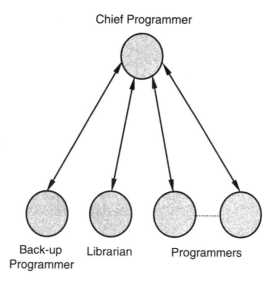

Back-up   Librarian   Programmers
Programmer

FIGURE 4.4. Chief programmer teams.

chief programmer make technical decisions, and takes over as the chief programmer if the chief programmer falls sick or leaves. The program librarian is responsible for maintaining the documentation and other communication-related work. This structure considerably reduces interpersonal communication. The communication paths are shown in Figure 4.4. This kind of structure is well suited for projects with simple solutions and strict deadlines. It is not suitable for difficult tasks where multiple inputs are useful.

A third team structure, called the *controlled decentralized team* [Man81], tries to combine the strengths of the democratic and chief programmer teams. It consists of a project leader who has a group of senior programmers under him, while under each senior programmer is a group of junior programmers. The group of a senior programmer and his junior programmers behaves like an egoless team, but communication among different groups occurs only through the senior programmers of the groups. The senior programmers also communicate with the project leader. Such a team has fewer communication paths than a democratic team but more paths compared to a chief programmer team. This structure works best for large projects that are reasonably straightforward. It is not well suited for very simple projects or research-type projects.

4.4   Software Configuration Management Plans

From the earlier discussions on software configuration management, it should be somewhat clear what the SCM plans should contain. The SCM plan, like other plans, has to identify all the activities that must be performed, give guidelines for performing the activities, and allocate resources for them.

The SCM plan needs to specify the type of SCIs that will be selected and the stages during the project where baselines should be established. Note that in the plan only the type of objects that should be selected can be specified; it may not be possible to identify the exact item, as the item may not exist at the planning time. For example, we can specify that code of any module that is independently unit tested will be considered as SCI. However, we cannot identify the particular modules that will eventually become the SCIs.

For configuration control, the plan has to identify the different members of the configuration control board, the forms to be used for the change requests and fault reporting, and policies, procedures, and tools for controlling the changes.

Finally, an SCM plan should include a plan for configuration accounting and auditing. This part of the plan should state how information on the status of configuration items is to be collected, verified, processed, and reported. It should also specify all the reports that need to be filed by the people identified as responsible for making the changes. It should specify the stages at which major audits must be held, the items to be covered during audits, and the procedures to be used for resolving problems that occur during audits.

4.5 Quality Assurance Plans

To ensure that the final product produced is of high quality, some quality control activities must be performed throughout the development. As we saw earlier, if this is not done, correcting errors in the final stages can be very expensive, especially if they originated in the early phases. The purpose of the software quality assurance plans (SQAP) is to specify all the work products that need to be produced during the project, activities that need to be performed for checking the quality of each of the work products, and the tools and methods that may be used for the SQA activities.

Note that SQAP takes a broad view of quality. It is interested in the quality of not only the final product, but also of the intermediate products, even though in a project we are ultimately interested in the quality of the delivered product. This is due to the fact that in a project it is very unlikely that the intermediate work products are of poor quality, but the final product is of high quality. So, to ensure that the delivered software is of good quality, it is essential to make sure that the requirements and design are also of good quality. For this reason, an SQAP will contain QA activities throughout the project.

The SQAP specifies the tasks that need to be undertaken at different times in the life cycle to improve the software quality and how they are to be managed. These tasks will generally include reviews and audits. Each task should be defined with an entry and exit criterion, that is, the criterion that should be satisfied to initiate the task and the criterion that should be satisfied to terminate the task. Both criteria should be stated so that they can be evaluated objectively. The responsibilities for different tasks should also be identified.

The documents that should be produced during software development to enhance software quality should also be specified by the SQAP. It should identify all documents that govern the development, verification, validation, use, and maintenance of the software and how these documents are to be checked for adequacy.

4.5.1   Verification and Validation (V&V)

SQAP has a general and larger view of software quality and includes different quality criteria. In verification and validation we are most concerned with the correctness of the product. The terms *verification* and *validation* are often used interchangeably, but they have different meanings. *Verification* is the process of determining whether or not the products of a given phase of software development fulfill the specifications established during the previous phase. Verification activities include proving, testing, and reviews. *Validation* is the process of evaluating software at the end of the software development to ensure compliance with the software requirements. Testing is a common method of validation. Clearly, for high reliability we need to perform both activities. Together they are often called *V&V activities*.

The major V&V activities for software development are inspection, reviews, and testing (both static and dynamic). The V&V plan identifies the different V&V tasks for the different phases and specifies how these tasks contribute to the project V&V goals. The methods to be used for performing these V&V activities, the responsibilities and milestones for each of these activities, inputs and outputs for each V&V task, and criteria for evaluating the outputs are also specified. Some of the different V&V activities proposed in the IEEE standards on verification and validation are shown in Figure 4.5 [IEE87].

The two major V&V approaches are testing and inspections. Testing is an activity that can be generally performed only on code. It is an important activity and is discussed in detail in a later chapter. Inspection is a more general activity that can be applied to any work product, including code. Many of the V&V tasks given in Figure 4.5 are such that for them an inspection type of activity is the only possible way to perform the tasks (e.g., traceability and document evaluation). Due to this, inspections play a significant role in verification.

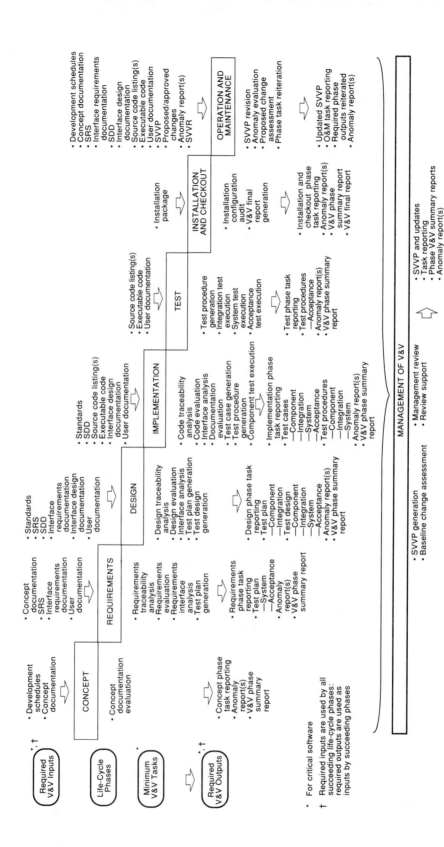

FIGURE 4.5. Software verification and validation plan overview [lee87].

4.5.2 Inspections and Reviews

The software inspection process was started by IBM in 1972 [Fag76], to improve software quality and increase productivity. Much of the earlier interest was focused on inspecting code, as coding seemed to be the major hurdle in a software project. However, it was soon discovered that mistakes occur not only during coding but also during design, and this realization led to design inspections. Of course, now we realize that many times defects in the software are caused by not properly understanding the problem, and this has led to requirement inspections. Today, inspections are widely used and studies have shown that they are an effective method for quality control and tend to enhance productivity.

IEEE defines *inspection* as "a formal evaluation technique in which software requirements, design, or code are examined in detail by a person or a group other than the author to detect faults, violations of development standards, and other problems" [IEE87]. The IEEE *Standard for Software Reviews and Audits* [IEE94], specifies that it is a *formal, peer evaluation* of a software element whose objective is to verify that the software element satisfies its specifications and conforms to standards.

As is clear from the definitions, the purpose of an inspection is to perform a careful scrutiny of the product by *peers*. It is different from a *walkthrough*, which is generally informal and whose purpose is to train or inform someone about a product. In a walkthrough, the author describes the work product in an informal meeting to his peers or superiors to get feedback or inform or explain to them the work product (e.g., a programmer about to leave may use a walkthrough to walk another programmer through his programs to transfer the ownership). Though reviews can also have a meaning different from inspections (e.g., management review of the activities being done), frequently, in the context of software, the term *review* means inspection. We will use these two terms interchangeably.

In an inspection, in contrast to a walkthrough, the meeting and the procedure are much more formal. The inspection of a work product is done by a group of peers, who first inspect the product privately and then get together in a formal meeting to discuss potential defects found by individuals and to detect more defects. In general, an inspection can be held for any technical product, which may include requirements specifications, system design document, detailed design, code, and test plan. There are three reasons for having reviews or inspections:

- Defect removal
- Productivity increase
- Provide information for project monitoring

The primary purpose of inspections is to detect defects at different stages during a project. While defects manifest themselves only in the final output, they can be injected at any phase during product development. As we have seen, the cost of detecting and removing a defect that originated during requirements or design, after the system is implemented, can be 10 to 100 times the cost if the defect was removed at the origin. It is for this reason that reviews are held at many different stages during the project. The most common work products inspected are the requirements document, system design document, detailed design, code, and test plan.

An increase in productivity and a decrease in cost are direct consequences of inspections. Cost is decreased as the defects are detected early in the development, thereby reducing the more expensive corrections that may be needed in the product otherwise. Cost is also reduced because in an inspection the defects are directly found—not just their presence, as is the case with testing. This avoids the costly activity of "debugging." Reviews tend to add to the cost of early phases like requirements specification and design but greatly reduce the cost of later phases, particularly testing, and maintenance.

Besides lowering the cost and improving the reliability of systems, inspections have other quality control benefits. Inspections also help improve software quality by checking properties like standard compliance, modularity, clarity, and simplicity. Another beneficial side effect is that coders and designers learn from defects found in reviews of their work, which enables them to avoid causing similar defects in future projects, thus improving quality and productivity even further.

For monitoring and control, reliable information about the project is needed, which requires some form of evaluation of the various parts of the project. Evaluation of the people responsible for the technical output cannot always be relied on. Inspection by a group that includes people not involved in producing the product being inspected can be a means for obtaining reliable evaluation. One of the purposes of reviews is to provide enough information to management about the project so that management decisions can be made effectively.

It should be stressed that reviews are of products not people. The main purpose is to improve the products. Hence, the review data should *never* be used for personnel evaluation. Inspections will produce good results only if the people responsible for products are willing to let others find defects in their work without fear of jeopardizing their reputation and chances for promotion.

There is another kind of information that can be gathered using reviews that can be useful for setting standards. Which phases have the most defects, the frequency of occurrence of different types of defects, the types of defects caught or that slip by the review process at different stages can all be used to improve the processes and techniques. This kind of information can also be used to evaluate new tools and methodologies.

Inspection Process

The discussion of the inspection process is based on [Hum89, GG94]. An inspection is done by a group of people that usually includes the author or the *producer* of the product under review. *Reviewers* or *inspectors* are mainly peers (i.e., they are not managers or supervisors) not directly responsible for the development of the product but concerned with the product (like designers, other programmers of the project, and testers). A *moderator* guides and controls the inspection activity, and a *recorder* records the results of the inspection [Hum89]. The moderator is the key person with the responsibility of planning and successful execution of the inspection.

As with any major activity, successful implementation of inspections requires a planning phase, an execution phase, and some post-inspection actions [Hum89]. During the planning phase, first the product to be inspected is identified, a moderator is assigned, the objective of the inspection is stated, and the entry criteria that must be satisfied by the product before it can be taken for inspection is specified. The objective could be defect detection, or detection of defects of specific types (e.g., standards violations, design errors, interface errors). It is important to have a clear entry criteria so that the effort spent in inspections is properly used, and minimum quality for the product to be inspected is guaranteed. In general, the entry criteria will ensure that the defects that can be easily detected through tools are detected and removed before the review so that the review effort focuses on those defects that the tools cannot find. However, for code, the review is generally done before any testing, as one of the goals of code reviews is to reduce testing and rework effort. So, for example, for code inspections, an entry criteria could be that the code successfully compiles and has passed some specified source code quality checking tools.

An inspection group is then formed, and an opening meeting is organized by the moderator. During this meeting the objective of the review is explained, roles of the different people are specified, clarifications about the inspection process are given, and the inspection package is distributed to the inspectors. The producer of the product can also give an overview of the product being inspected and background information relating to the construction of the product. The inspection package consists of the document to be inspected, support documents that may be needed to understand the contents of the document, forms to be filled in and checklists to be used. So, for example, for code reviews, the inspection package can consist of the following [Hum89]:

- Program source listing
- Pertinent portions of design or specification document
- Pertinent parts of common definitions (e.g., macros and data structures) that are used by the code
- Any system constraints
- Blank copies of all forms and reports
- Checklists to be used for review

After this, the reviewers individually study the material thoroughly and use the checklists to identify all possible defects. They record all potential errors (or unresolved issues) in the error log form, along with the effort they have spent on the private review. These logs are then submitted to the moderator, who compiles the logs of the different reviewers and gives a copy to the producer so that the producer can study the issues raised by the reviewers before the inspection meeting. For private inspections, properly formed checklists are very important to guide the focus of the reviewers. If based on past experience there is some information about the nature of errors, then such information can be used to design an effective checklist. With good checklists, most of the defects can be detected during individual inspections.

Once all the preparation activities are completed, the stage is set for the inspection meeting. Before scheduling the meeting, the moderator makes sure all the preparatory activities have been satisfactorily completed (e.g., all reviewers have submitted their error logs). The meeting begins with the producer discussing each of the issues raised by the reviewers. The producer either explains why the issue listed is not an error or accepts it as a defect (to be fixed later). He may seek clarification about other issues raised. There may be a discussion on some of the issues or some new issues may be raised. Discussion is an important part of reviews, and many additional potential defects are found during the discussions. All the defects are noted. Effort should *not* be made to suggest methods to remove the defect; that is to be done by the author after the review (or privately after the review meeting). Another important factor to be kept in mind about any review process is the psychological frame of mind of a member of the review committee during the review. It is important that the review process be treated as a constructive engagement and not as a means of attacking the ability of the author. Such an attitude by the members may make the author defensive, which will defeat the purpose of the review. The moderator has to make sure that the review meeting stays in control and is focused on the objective of the meeting.

At the conclusion of the meeting, the moderator produces a summary of the inspection, which lists all defects found that need to be addressed. The authors have to address all the issues raised. Many of them will be defects and will require rework to address them. The moderator has to ensure that all the issues listed have been satisfactorily addressed. The moderator also has to state in the report whether there should be another review after the rework is complete. If the defects detected and the issues raised are serious, then another meeting should be convened after the rework is done. If no further meeting needs to be convened, then it is the responsibility of the moderator to ensure that the rework has addressed all issues mentioned in the report. This process of review is shown in Figure 4.6.

Proper execution of reviews is critical to success. Reviews should be done at defined points during product development, and time must be allocated in the management plans to accommodate review-related activities, particularly the rework. Reviews should not last too long, as efficiency falls once the participants get tired. A limit of two hours is considered reasonable.

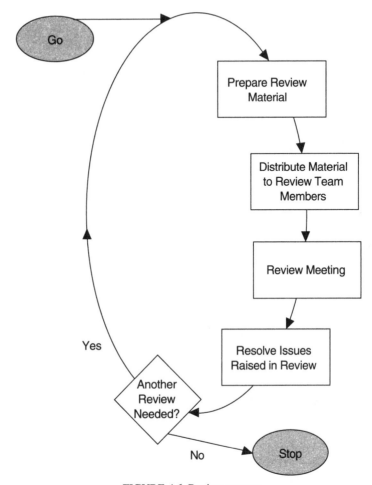

FIGURE 4.6. Review process.

Inspection Benefits and Costs

Inspections have been in use for more than two decades now. Considerable data now exists to show their effectiveness. There are books that deal exclusively with the topic of software inspections [GG94]. An excellent concise description of inspections is given in [Hum89]. There is a general agreement that reviews are an effective means to improve quality and productivity. The book [GG94] gives a lot of data from various reports in support of this. We now discuss some of these data as reported in [GG94].

In the original article of Fagan [Fag76], an increase of 23% in coding productivity and a 25% reduction in schedules were reported. The IBM Federal Systems Division found that the overall productivity in projects that used inspection was more than twice than in projects that did not use formal inspections. Some data suggests that 50 to 80% of the defects can be detected through inspections (i.e., before testing begins). The goal of the IBM Federal Systems Division is to detect 85% of all defects before testing begins. Clearly, if such a high percentage of defects can be detected in the early stages, it will substantially reduce the cost of testing and rework. In a project, it was found that if test cases are inspected, as much as 85% of the effort needed for unit testing may be saved (e.g., by removing test cases that do not add value). In one case, it was found that inspections detected more than 3500 defects while testing and field experience showed only about 125 defects. Productivity increases of 30 to 100% through reviews have been reported. A lot more data about direct benefits of reviews is given in [GG94].

Inspections have other side benefits. It provides a good means for the project management to monitor the quality and progress of the project. Although frequently, maintenance is not included as a part of development, a major benefit of inspections will be in maintenance. Early detection of defects will ensure that the structure of the software is not compromised through "quick fixes" that are inevitable if errors are detected late. Furthermore, some of the desired qualities, like coupling and cohesion, can be checked much more easily through reviews. These together will contribute to making the task of the maintainer much easier. Another major benefit of inspections is that it improves the capability of people. Through getting their products reviewed and through reviewing others' products, people learn from each other and learn about the type of errors they and others are making. This, in the long run, leads to people producing products with lower error rates.

Although inspections are effective, their effectiveness clearly depends on their implementation. For example, inspections are most effective if the rate of inspection is "reasonable." If the rate is very fast (i.e., too much material covered in one review), it tends to reveal too few errors. If the rate is too slow, the cost increases. Hence, it is important to have a reasonable rate for review. A review rate of a few pages of document per hour is considered reasonable by some. However, it might be best to determine the optimum rate for an organization through experimentation. The effect of rate on review effectiveness discussed in [Hum89] indicates that the optimum rate is between 0.2 and 0.4 KDLOC per hour for FORTRAN programs.

Now let us look at the cost of inspections. The major cost of inspections is the time spent by the review team members conducting the inspection. It has been estimated that the cost of the review can be 5 to 10% of the total project cost. However, this is the percentage of the cost of the project that has used reviews (which is likely to be much less than the cost if there were no inspections). So it should not be taken to mean that the project cost has gone up. However, there are actual costs involved in initiating reviews in an organization. These include costs of training, mock reviews, and preparing people to accept inspections. And, as with many technologies, inspections do not start showing big gains right from start. In fact, at the start, inspections may not provide any benefit and might only add to the cost. As people get better at conducting inspections, the benefits will increase. The big gains mentioned earlier are mostly in organizations that are quite advanced in their implementation of inspections and have a lot of experience through which they have fine-tuned their inspection process.

In summary, reviews have been found to be extremely effective for detecting defects, improving productivity, and lowering costs. They provide good checkpoints for the management to study the progress of a particular project. Reviews are also a good tool for ensuring quality control. In short, they have been found to be extremely useful by a diverse set of people and have found their way into standard management and quality control practices of many institutions. Their use continues to grow.

4.6 Project Monitoring Plans

A good plan is useless unless it is properly executed. Consequently, the major management activity during the project is to ensure that the plan is properly executed, and when needed, to modify plans appropriately. Project assessment will be straightforward if everything went according to plan and no changes occurred in the requirements. However, on large projects, deviations from the original plan and changes to requirements are both to be expected. In these cases the plan should be modified. Modifications are also needed as more information about the project becomes available or due to personnel turnover.

The project control phase of the management activity is the longest. For this kind of routine management activity, lasting for a long period of time, proper project monitoring can play a significant role in aiding project management. However, all the methods management intends to use to monitor the project should be planned before, during the planning phase, so that management is prepared to handle the changes and deviations from the plan and can respond quickly. In this section we will discuss some methods for monitoring a project.

4.6.1 Time Sheets

Once project development commences, the management has to track the progress of the project and the expenditure incurred on the project. Progress can be monitored by using the schedule and milestones laid down in the plan. The earned value method, discussed later, can also be used.

The most common method of keeping track of expenditures is by the use of a time sheet. The time sheet records how much time different project members are spending on the different identified activities in the project.

The time sheet is a common mechanism for collecting raw data. Time sheets can be filled daily or weekly. The data obtained from the time sheets can be used to obtain information regarding the overall expenditure and its breakup among different tasks and different phases at any given time. For example, the effort distribution with phases (of the type discussed in Chapter 1) in a particular organization can be obtained from the time sheets. By assigning codes to projects, tasks within a project, and the nature of the work being done, time sheet processing can easily be automated.

4.6.2   Reviews

We discussed reviews at some length in an earlier section. We will not go into details of reviews here; we'll just comment on a few points regarding the monitoring aspect of reviews. As mentioned earlier, one of the purposes of reviews is to provide information for project control. Reviews provide a definite and clearly defined milestone. It forces the author of a product to complete the product before the review. Having this goal gives some impetus and motivation to complete the product.

For monitoring, as we have discussed, reviews can provide a wealth of information. First, the review schedules can be used to determine how the project is progressing compared to its planned schedule. Then the review reports indicate in which parts of the project the programmers/analysts are having difficulty. With this information, corrective action, such as replacing a junior person with a senior person, can be taken. In addition, review reports provide insight into the quality of the software being produced and the types of errors being detected.

4.6.3   Cost-Schedule-Milestone Graph

A cost-schedule-milestone [Boe81] graph represents the planned cost of different milestones. It also shows the actual cost of achieving the milestones gained so far. By having both the planned cost versus milestones and the actual cost versus milestones on the same graph, the progress of the project can be grasped easily.

The x-axis of this graph is time, where the months in the project schedule are marked. The y-axis represents the cost, in dollars or PMs. Two curves are drawn. One curve is the planned cost and planned schedule, in which each important milestone of the project is marked. This curve can be completed after the project plan is made. The second curve represents the actual cost and actual schedule, and the actual achievement of the milestones is marked. Thus, for each milestone the point representing the time when the milestone is actually achieved and the actual cost of achieving it are marked. A cost-schedule-milestone graph for the example is shown in Figure 4.7.

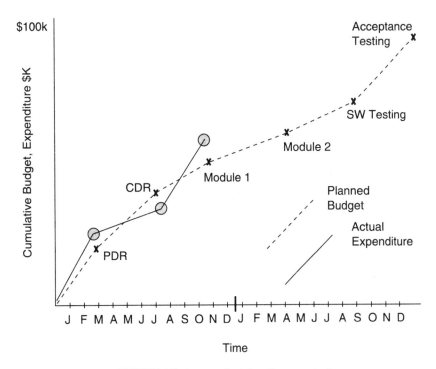

FIGURE 4.7. A cost-schedule-milestone graph.

The chart shown in Figure 4.7 is for a hypothetical project whose cost is estimated to be $100K. Different milestones have been identified and a curve is drawn with these milestones. The milestones in this project are PDR (preliminary design review), CDR (critical design review), Module 1 completion, Module 2 completion, integration testing, and acceptance testing. For each of these milestones some budget has been allocated based on the estimates. The planned budget is shown by a dotted line. The actual expenditure is shown with a bold line. This chart shows that only two milestones have been achieved, PDR and CDR, and though the project was within budget when PDR was complete, it is now slightly over budget.

4.6.4   Earned Value Method

The system design usually involves a small group of (senior) people. Having a large number of people at the system design stage is likely to result in a not-very-cohesive design. After the system design is complete, a large number of programmers whose job is to do the detailed design, coding, and testing may enter the project. During these activities, proper monitoring of people, progress of the different components, and progress of the overall project are important.

An effective method of monitoring the progress of a project (particularly the phases after system design) is the earned value method. The earned value method uses a *Summary Task Planning Sheet (STPS)* [Boe81]. The STPS is essentially a Gantt chart, with each task (relating to an independently assignable module) having an entry in the chart. Each task has the following milestones marked in STPS: detailed design, coding, testing, and integration.

Each milestone of a task is assigned an *earned value*, which is the value (in dollars or person-months) that will be "earned" on completion of this milestone. The sum of the assigned values for all the milestones for a task is equal to the total cost assigned to this task (or the total estimated effort required for this task).

At any given time, the total effort (or cost) spent on a particular task can be determined from the time sheets. The total value earned can be determined by adding the earned value of all the completed milestones of that task. By comparing the earned value with the total cost spent, the project manager can determine how far the project is deviating from the initial estimates and then take the necessary actions.

It should be pointed out that, in general, the earned value will be somewhat less than the actual effort spent on a task, because this method only attaches value to the completed milestones. The work in progress does not get adequately represented in the earned value.

The STPS usually has much more detail than is needed by project management. The earned value aspect can be summarized in an *earned value summary report*. This report summarizes the earned value for each task, the actual effort spent on that task, and how these compare for a given point in time. The summary report can be produced monthly or biweekly.

4.6.5   Unit Development Folder

The project plan produced after the requirements is a macro-level plan. Even if this plan is prepared meticulously and accurately, if proper control is not exercised at the micro level (at the level of each programmer and each module), it will be impossible to implement the project plan.

A major problem in tracking micro-level progress is getting accurate information about the status of a module. Often, a manager relies on the person implementing the module to assess the progress. This estimate by individuals about what percentage of work is complete is often not very reliable and can produce the "90% syndrome" [Boe81].

What happens in the 90% syndrome is that if an individual programmer is asked how much work he has completed, the answer after some time is 90%, and it stays around this percentage for a long time. Essentially, an individual programmer's overconfidence results in under-estimating the effort needed toward the end.

The unit development folder (UDF) [Ing86] has been used successfully to counter the 90% syndrome. It is sometimes also called the *programmers' notebook*. The UDF contains the plan, progress, and all documentation related to the development of a program unit. A unit of software is one that performs a specific function, is amenable to development by one person, is at a level to which the requirements can be traced, and can be tested independently. A unit could be a module, a procedure, or a collection of such modules.

A UDF is typically established after the system design phase, when tasks are distributed among programmers. There is a UDF for each unit, and initially it contains all specifications of that unit, as obtained from the requirements and system design. It is given to the programmer responsible for the development of the unit. All documentation produced for this unit goes in the UDF. This includes the detailed design for the unit, the unit test plan, and the unit test results. The documents from different UDFs are finally merged together to form the system documentation about detailed design, test report, and so forth.

An important element of the UDF is the schedule and progress report of the unit. The overall schedule for the unit is determined from the project plan and is given to the programmer responsible for the unit. The programmer then breaks up the allotted time and produces a detailed schedule for the development of the unit, with intermediate milestones for detailed design, coding, test plan, unit testing, and the test report. As each of these milestones is achieved, the programmer gets it certified from the manager and writes the milestone completion date.

The basic idea here is to force the programmer to identify intermediate milestones in the task. The achievement of these milestones is clearly defined and is not subjective. This prevents the programmer from giving the subjective opinion that the work is "90% done."

The advantages of the programmer notebook are that it provides a single place for collecting all the documentation for a unit, it provides an orderly and consistent approach for the development of a unit, and it provides better management and visibility of the progress in a unit's development.

4.7 Risk Management

Any large project involves certain risks, and that is true of software projects. Risk management is an emerging area that aims to address the problem of identifying and managing the risks associated with a software project.

Risk in a project is the possibility that the defined goals are not met. The basic motivation of having risk management is to avoid disasters or heavy losses. The current interest in risk management is due to the fact that the history of software development projects is full of major and minor failures. A large percentage of projects have run considerably overbudget and behind schedule, and many of them have been abandoned midway. It is now argued that many of these failures were due to the fact that the risks were not identified and managed properly.

Risk management is an important area, particularly for large projects. Like any management activity, proper planning of that activity is central to success. Here we discuss various aspects of risk management and planning.

4.7.1   Risk Management Overview

Risk is defined as an exposure to the chance of injury or loss [Kon94]. That is, risk implies that there is a possibility that something negative may happen. In the context of software projects, negative implies that there is an adverse effect on cost, quality, or schedule. *Risk management* is the area that tries to ensure that the impact of risks on cost, quality, and schedule is minimal. Like configuration management, which minimizes the impact of change, risk management minimizes the impact of risks. However, risk management is generally done by the project management. For this reason we have not considered risk management as a separate process (though it can validly be considered one) but have considered such activities as part of project management.

Risk management can be considered as dealing with the possibility and actual occurrence of those events that are not "regular" or commonly expected. The commonly expected events, such as people going on leave or some requirements changing, are handled by normal project management. So, in a sense, risk management begins where normal project management ends. It deals with events that are infrequent, somewhat out of the control of the project management, and are large enough (i.e., can have a major impact on the project) to justify special attention [Kon94].

Most projects have risk. The idea of risk management is to minimize the possibility of risks materializing, if possible, or to minimize the effect of risk actually materializing. For example, when constructing a building, there is a risk that the building may later collapse due to an earthquake. That is, the possibility of an earthquake is a risk. If the building is a large residential complex, then the potential cost in case the earthquake risk materializes can be enormous. This risk can be reduced by shifting to a zone that is not earthquake-prone. Alternatively, if this is not acceptable, then the effects of this risk materializing are minimized by suitably constructing the building (the approach taken in Japan and California). At the same time, if a small dumping ground is to be constructed, no such approach might be followed, as the financial and other impact of an actual earthquake on such a building is so low that it does not warrant special measures.

It should be clear that risk management has to deal with identifying the undesirable events that can occur, the probability of their occurring, and the loss if an undesirable event does occur. Once this is known, strategies can be formulated for either

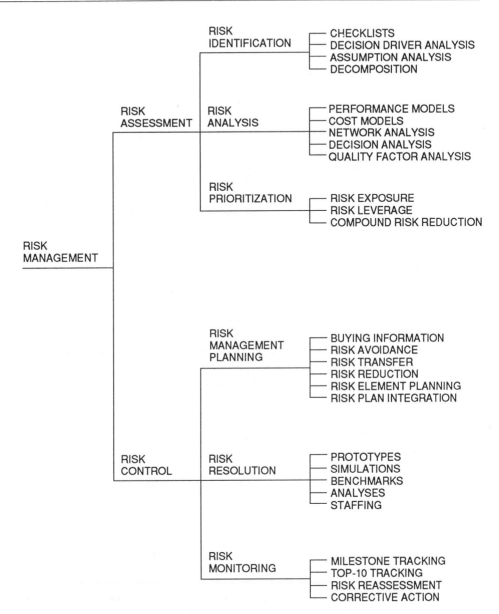

FIGURE 4.8. Risk management activities.

reducing the probability of the risk materializing or reducing the effect of risk materializing. So the risk management revolves around *risk assessment* and *risk control*. For each of these major activities, some subactivities have to be performed. A breakdown of these activities is given in Figure 4.8 [Boe89].

4.7.2 Risk Assessment

Risk assessment is an activity that must be undertaken during project planning. This involves identifying the risks, analyzing them, and prioritizing them on the basis of the analysis. The major planning activity in risk management is assessment and consequent planning for risk control. Due to the nature of a software project, uncertainties are most near the beginning of the project (just as for cost estimation). As the project nears its end, risks can be assessed more precisely. Due to this, although risk assessment should be done throughout the project, it is most needed in the starting phases of the project. In addition, identifying the risks early provides the management with a lot of time to effectively handle the risks.

At a very high level, the software risks can be broadly divided into three categories. These are:

- Cost risk
- Performance risk
- Schedule risk

Cost risk is the degree of uncertainty associated with budgets and outlays for the project and its impact on the project. Performance risk is the possibility that the system will be unable to deliver all or some of the anticipated benefits or will not perform according to the requirements. Here performance includes quality. Schedule risk is the degree of uncertainty associated with the project schedule or the ability of the project to achieve the specified milestones.

The goal of risk assessment is to prioritize the risks so that risk management can focus attention and resources on the more risky items. *Risk identification* is the first step in risk assessment, which identifies all the different risks for a particular project. These risks are project-dependent, and their identification is clearly necessary before any risk management can be done for the project.

Based on surveys of experienced project managers, Boehm [Boe89] has produced a list of the top-10 risk items likely to compromise the success of a software project. Though risks in a project are specific to the project, this list forms a good starting point for identifying such risks. Figure 4.9 shows these top-10 items along with the techniques preferred by management for managing these risks.

The top-ranked risk item is personnel shortfalls. This involves just having fewer people than necessary or not having people with specific skills that a project might require. Some of the ways to manage this risk is to get the top talent possible and to match the needs of the project with the skills of the available personnel. Adequate training, along with having some key personnel for critical areas of the project, will also reduce this risk.

The second item, unrealistic schedules and budgets, happens very frequently due to business and other reasons. It is very common that high-level management

RISK ITEM	RISK MANAGEMENT TECHNIQUES
1. PERSONNEL SHORTFALLS	STAFFING WITH TOP TALENT; JOB MATCHING; TEAMBUILDING; KEY-PERSONNEL AGREEMENTS; TRAINING; PRESCHEDULING KEY PEOPLE
2. UNREALISTIC SCHEDULES AND BUDGETS	DETAILED MULTISOURCE COST AND SCHEDULE ESTIMATION; DESIGN TO COST; INCREMENTAL DEVELOPMENT; SOFTWARE REUSE; REQUIREMENTS SCRUBBING
3. DEVELOPING THE WRONG SOFTWARE FUNCTIONS	ORGANIZATION ANALYSIS; MISSION ANALYSIS; OPS-CONCEPT FORMULATION; USER SURVEYS; PROTOTYPING; EARLY USERS' MANUALS
4. DEVELOPING THE WRONG USER INTERFACE	PROTOTYPING; SCENARIOS; TASK ANALYSIS; USER CHARACTERIZATION (FUNCTIONALITY, STYLE, WORKLOAD)
5. GOLD PLATING	REQUIREMENTS SCRUBBING; PROTOTYPING; COST-BENEFIT ANALYSIS; DESIGN TO COST
6. CONTINUING STREAM OF REQUIREMENTS CHANGES	HIGH CHANGE THRESHOLD; INFORMATION HIDING; INCREMENTAL DEVELOPMENT (DEFER CHANGES TO LATER INCREMENTS)
7. SHORTFALLS IN EXTERNALLY FURNISHED COMPONENTS	BENCHMARKING; INSPECTIONS; REFERENCE CHECKING; COMPATIBILITY ANALYSIS
8. SHORTFALLS IN EXTERNALLY PERFORMED TASKS	REFERENCE CHECKING: PREAWARD AUDITS; AWARD-FEE CONTRACTS; COMPETITIVE DESIGN OR PROTOTYPING; TEAMBUILDING
9. REAL-TIME PERFORMANCE SHORTFALLS	SIMULATION; BENCHMARKING; MODELING; PROTOTYPING; INSTRUMENTATION; TUNING
10. STRAINING COMPUTER SCIENCE CAPABILITIES	TECHNICAL ANALYSIS; COST-BENEFIT ANALYSIS; PROTOTYPING; REFERENCE CHECKING

FIGURE 4.9. Top-10 risk items and techniques for managing them.

imposes a schedule for a software project that is not based on the characteristics of the project and is unrealistic. This risk applies to all projects. Project-specific risks in cost and schedule occur due to underestimating the value of some of the cost drivers. Recall that cost models like COCOMO estimate the cost and schedule based on some estimates about size and cost drivers. Even if the size estimate is correct, by incorrectly estimating the value of the cost drivers, the project runs the risk of going overbudget and falling behind schedule. The cost and schedule risks can be approximated by estimating the maximum value of different cost drivers, along with the probability of occurrence and then estimating the possible cost and schedule overruns.

The next few items are related to requirements. Projects run the risk of developing the wrong software if the requirements analysis is not done properly and if development begins too early. Similarly, often improper user interface may be developed. This requires extensive rework of the user interface later or the software benefits are not obtained because users are reluctant to use it. Gold plating refers to adding features in the software that are only marginally useful. This adds unnecessary risk to the project because gold plating consumes resources and time with little return. Some requirement changes are to be expected in any project, but sometimes frequent changes are requested, which is often a reflection of the fact that the client has not yet understood or settled on its own requirements. The effect of requirement changes is substantial in terms of cost, especially if the changes occur when the project has progressed to later phases. Performance shortfalls are critical in real-time systems and poor performance can mean the failure of the project.

If a project depends on externally available components—either to be provided by the client or to be procured as an off-the-shelf component—the project runs some risks. The project might be delayed if the external component is not available on time. The project would also suffer if the quality of the external component is poor or if the component turns out to be incompatible with the other project components or with the environment in which the software is developed or is to operate. If a project relies on technology that is not well developed, it may fail. This is a risk due to straining the computer science capabilities.

Using the checklist of the top-10 risk items is one way to identify risks. This approach is likely to suffice in many projects. The other methods listed in Figure 4.8 are decision driver analysis, assumption analysis, and decomposition. Decision driver analysis involves questioning and analyzing all the major decisions taken for the project. If a decision has been driven by factors other than technical and management reasons, it is likely to be a source of risk in the project. Such decisions may be driven by politics, marketing, or the desire for short-term gain. Optimistic assumptions made about the project also are a source of risk. Some such optimistic assumptions are that nothing will go wrong in the project, no personnel will quit during the project, people will put in extra hours if required, and all external components (hardware or software) will be delivered on time. Identifying such assumptions will point out the source of risks. An effective method for identifying these hidden assumptions is comparing them with past experience. Decomposition implies breaking a large project into clearly defined parts and then analyzing them. Many software systems have the phenomenon that 20% of the modules cause 80% of the project problems. Decomposition will help identify these modules.

Risk identification merely identifies the undesirable events that might take place during the project, i.e., enumerates the "unforeseen" events that might occur. It does not specify the probabilities of these risks materializing nor the impact on the project if the risks indeed materialize. Hence the next tasks are *risk analysis* and *prioritization*.

Not all the items listed earlier can be analyzed with the use of some models; subjective analysis often needs to be done. However, if cost models are used for cost and schedule estimation, then the same models can be used to assess the cost and schedule risk. For example, in the COCOMO cost model, the cost estimate depends on the ratings of the different cost drivers. One possible source of cost risk is underestimating these cost drivers. The other is underestimating the size. Risk analysis can be done by estimating the worst-case value of size and all the cost drivers and then estimating the project cost from these values. This will give us the worst-case analysis. Using the worst-case effort estimate, the worst-case schedule can easily be obtained. A more detailed analysis can be done by considering different cases or a distribution of these drivers.

The other approaches for risk analysis include studying the probability and the outcome of possible decisions (decision analysis), understanding the task dependencies to decide critical activities and the probability and cost of their not being completed on time (network analysis), risks on the various quality factors like reliability and usability (quality factor analysis), and evaluating the performance early through simulation, etc., if there are strong performance constraints on the system (performance analysis). The reader is referred to [Boe89] for further discussion of these topics.

Once the probabilities of risks materializing and losses due to materliazation of different risks have been analyzed, they can be prioritized. One approach for prioritization is through the concept of *risk exposure (RE)* [Boe89], which is sometimes called *risk impact*. RE is defined by the relationship

$$RE = \text{Prob}(UO) * \text{Loss}(UO),$$

where $\text{Prob}(UO)$ is the probability of the risk materializing (i.e., undesirable outcome) and $\text{Loss}(UO)$ is the total loss incurred due to the unsatisfactory outcome. The loss is not only the direct financial loss that might be incurred but also any loss in terms of credibility, future business, and loss of property or life. The RE is the expected value of the loss due to a particular risk. For risk prioritization using RE, the higher the RE, the higher the priority of the risk item.

It is not always possible to use models and prototypes to assess the probabilities of occurrence and of loss associated with particular events. Due to the nonavailability of models, assessing risk probabilities is frequently subjective. A subjective assessment can be done by the estimate of one person or by using a group consensus technique like the Delphi approach [Boe81]. In the Delphi method, a group of people discusses the problem of estimation and finally converges on a consensus estimate.

4.7.3   Risk Control

Whereas risk assessment is a passive activity identifying the risks and their impacts, risk control comprises active measures that are taken by project management to minimize the impact of risks. Though risk assessment is primarily done during project planning as risk assessment in early stages is most important, like cost and schedule estimation, the assessment should be evaluated and changed, if needed, throughout the project.

Like any active task (e.g., configuration management, development), risk control starts with *risk management planning*. Plans are developed for each identified risk that needs to be controlled. Many risks might be combined together for the purposes of planning, if they require similar treatment. This activity, like other other planning activities, is done during the project initiation phase. The risk management plan for a particular risk item need not be elaborate or extensive. A basic risk management plan has five components [Boe89]. These are: (1) why the risk is important and why it should be managed, (2) what should be delivered regarding risk management and when, (3) who is responsible for performing the different risk management activities, (4) how will the risk be abated or the approach be taken, and (5) how many resources are needed.

The main focus of risk management planning is to enumerate the risks to be controlled (based on risk assessment) and specify how to deal with a risk. One obvious strategy is risk avoidance, which entails taking actions that will avoid the risk altogether, like the earlier example of shifting the building site to a zone that is not earthquake-prone. For some risks, avoidance might be possible. Another obvious strategy is risk reduction; if the risk cannot be avoided, perhaps the probability of the risk materializing can be reduced or the loss due to the risk materializing can be reduced. Other strategies were mentioned in Figure 4.8.

The actual elimination or reduction is done in the *risk resolution* step. Risk resolution is essentially implementation of the risk management plan. For example, if the risk avoidance is to be used, the activities that will avoid the risk have to be implemented. Similarly, in plan it might have been decided that the risk can be reduced by prototyping. Then prototyping is done in the risk resolution step and necessary information obtained to reduce the risk. Incidentally, prototyping is a very important technique for reducing risks associated with requirements or reducing risks of the type "perhaps this cannot be done?"

Risk monitoring is the activity of monitoring the status of various risks and their control activities. Like project monitoring, it is performed through the entire duration of the project. Like many monitoring activities, a checklist is useful for monitoring. While monitoring risks, like with monitoring costs and schedules, reassessments might need to be performed, if the real situation differs substantially from the situation predicted earlier based on assessment and planning.

4.8 Summary

A proper project plan is an important ingredient for a successful project. Without proper planning, a large software development project is doomed. Good planning can be done after the requirements for the project are available. The output of the planning phase is the project plan, which forms an additional input to all later phases. The important planning activities are:

- Cost estimation
- Schedule and milestones
- Staffing and personnel plan
- Quality assurance plans
- Configuration management plans
- Project monitoring plans
- Risk management.

Cost estimation is the activity where the overall cost requirement for the project and the breakup of the cost for different phases is estimated. As human resources are the most important for software development, cost estimates are often given in terms of person-months (PM).

For estimating the cost, cost models that estimate the cost as a function of various parameters are used. One well-known model is the COCOMO model. In this model, the initial cost estimate is obtained as a function of the size of the final product. Then the cost estimate is refined based on various properties of the project. The cost for different phases is specified as a fixed percentage of the overall cost and can easily be obtained from the overall cost estimate.

The duration required for the project and for the various activities is an important planning activity. There are models to estimate the duration of a project. In CO-COMO, the overall schedule is obtained in a similar manner as the overall cost. The breakup of this duration into duration for different activities is also done in a manner similar to the method for determining the cost for different phases.

With the overall cost estimate and the overall project duration estimate, the average staff requirement for the project can easily be estimated. For planning, a more detailed staff estimate is usually necessary. This can be obtained from the effort and duration estimate for different tasks and phases.

Once the duration and staff requirement are estimated, a personnel plan can be prepared. This plan defines how many people are needed at different times during the life of the project. It also specifies the team structure.

Quality assurance plans are important for ensuring that the final product is of high quality. The software quality assurance plan specifies the outputs or reports that will be produced during the development and the criterion for accepting them. It identifies all the V&V activities that have to be performed at different stages in the development. The SQAP also schedules these activities.

The configuration management plan is important for large projects that last for a long time. In such projects the code, design, and even the requirements change. Because a change affects many other parts of the system, changes are introduced in a methodical manner by using configuration control. Configuration control planning requires the identification of the configuration items, people who are responsible for configuration control, and the criterion used for evaluating change requests.

For a plan to be successfully implemented it is essential that the project be monitored carefully. This requires that project monitoring plans be prepared. There are a number of ways to monitor the progress, cost, schedule, or quality of the project. These include time sheets, reviews, a cost-schedule-milestone chart, the earned value method, and the unit development folder. The purpose of all these is to provide accurate and objective information management. Some of these techniques also help the programmer better assess his own progress.

The last topic we covered in the chapter is risk management. This is a relatively new area that is gaining importance due to the increasing application of computer systems in increasingly complex environments. Risk is the possibility of loss due to inability of the project to meet the goals. Risk management requires that risks be identified, analyzed, and prioritized. Based on the priorities, plans can be devised to minimize the risks.

Exercises

1. Suppose that the requirements specification phase is divided into two parts: the initial requirements and feasibility study and the detailed requirements specification. Suppose that first part costs about 25% of the total requirement cost. Based on the cost distribution data given earlier, develop a cost estimation model that can be used to predict the cost *after* (a) the feasibility study and (b) the detailed requirements. What are the basic parameters for this cost model? How accurate is this cost model? Is the accuracy better for case (a) or case (b)?

2. A database system is to be developed. After the requirements, its size is estimated to be 10,000 lines of code. Estimate the overall cost using the Watson and Felix model.

3. Consider a project to develop a full-screen editor. The major components identified are (1) screen edit, (2) command language interpreter, (3) file input and output, (4) cursor movement, and (5) screen movement. The sizes for these are estimated to be 4K, 2K, 1K, 2K, and 3K delivered source code

lines. Use the COCOMO model to determine (a) overall cost and schedule estimates (assume values for different cost drivers, with at least three of them being different from 1.0), (b) cost and schedule estimates for different phases, and (c) detailed cost and schedule estimates for the different components.

4. For the preceding example, determine the staff requirement for the different phases. What are the average, maximum, and minimum staff requirements?

5. What are the limitations of the cost estimation models?

6. Suppose each communication path between two people consumes 5% of each person's time. For a project that requires 12 staff-months of programming work, how many people will be needed to finish the project in four months if (a) the democratic team structure is used, and (b) the chief-programmer team structure is used? If the team consists of four persons, what is the difference in the completion time for a team using the democratic structure and a team using the chief-programmer structure?

7. What are the major benefits of reviews?

8. Assume that testing (and bug fixing) effort is proportional to the number of errors detected (regardless of the nature of error). Suppose that testing detects 90% of the total errors in the SW (10% remain undetected). By adding design and code reviews, suppose the cost of the design and coding phases increases by 10% each (from the base distribution given earlier), and 10% of the errors are detected in design reviews and 10% in code reviews. (So, testing now detects only 70% of errors.) What is the impact on the overall cost of reviews?

9. You want to monitor the effort spent on different phases in the project and the time spent on different components. Design a time sheet or form to be filled by the programmers that can be used to get this data. The design should be such that automated processing is possible.

10. Think of two other risks not given in Figure 4.9. Suggest some possible ways to assess and control these.

CASE STUDY PLAN

Here we present a plan for the course scheduling project. The plan covers the entire life cycle of the project. For illustration purposes, derivation of the cost and schedule estimates is shown, although in an actual plan these derivations are not needed. Similarly, at many places commentary and explanations have been included for the purpose of explanation and are not usually part of the plan.

Cost and Schedule Estimates

The size estimates for these in lines of code are:

Input	650
Schedule	650
Output	150
TOTAL	1450 = 1.45 KDLOC

Because this project is somewhat small, COCOMO estimates might be inaccurate. Hence, we use the simple method of determining the effort based on average productivity. Based on experience and capability of programmers (though no data has been formally collected for this), it is felt that for a project of this size the productivity will be of the order of 600 LOC per PM. From this, we get the effort estimate:

$$E = 1.45/.6 = 2.4 \text{ PM.}$$

To get the phase-wise breakup of cost we use the distribution of costs given earlier for COCOMO. The phase-wise cost breakup for the project is

Design	$2.4 * 0.16 = 0.38$ PM
Detailed Design	$.26 * 2.4 = 0.62$ PM
Coding and Testing	$.42 * 2.4 = 1.0$ PM
Integration	$0.16 * 2.4 = 0.38$ PM

To estimate the overall schedule, M, we again use the COCOMO equations and get $M = 2.5 * (2.4)^{0.38} = 3.48$ months. The distribution of the schedule in different activities is (using COCOMO percentages):

Design	0.7 months
Programming	2.2 months
Testing	0.6 months

The project will start in the middle of January and end after 3.5 months at the end of April. The proposed schedule for the project is shown in Table 4.6 in the form of a bar chart.

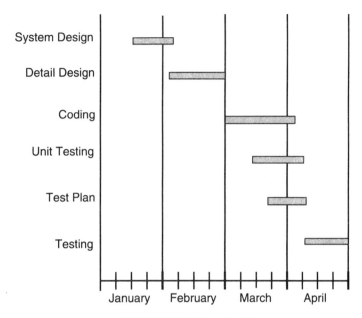

TABLE 4.6. Project schedule.

Personnel Plan and Detailed Schedule

The total coding and unit testing effort is one PM. During this the different modules will be coded and tested. We approximate the effort for the different modules in this phase by dividing one PM in the ratio of the sizes of the modules. From this we get the estimate for coding and unit testing of different modules:

```
Input      .4
Schedule   .4
Output     .2
```

The team consists of two permanent and one floating member. All these team members are students who will devote about one-third of their time to the project. Consequently, the total PM estimate obtained from the personnel plan should be divided by three to obtain the actual person-months cost. The personnel plan is shown in Table 4.7.

From this personnel plan we get the total 7.25. The total effort in person-months here is $7.25/3 = 2.4$ PM, which is the estimate obtained earlier. The effort sanctioned for each module is also close to the estimates obtained above. For example, for the input or schedule module, $1.0/3 = 0.33$ PM has been allotted, while the estimate is 0.4. The sanctioned effort for system design in this plan is 0.5 PM, while the earlier estimate is 0.7. These minor discrepancies exist because of the approximations made.

	January	February	March	April	Total
System Design	2 2	2			1.5
Detail Design		2 2 2	2		2.0
Coding Input Sched. Output			1 1 1 1 1 1 1 1	1 1	1.0 1.0 0.25
Testing				2 2 2	1.5
Total	1.0	2.0	2.25	2.0	7.25

TABLE 4.7. Personnel plan for the project.

A hierarchical team structure similar to the chief programmer team will be used. The group will have a leader, who will allocate tasks to team members. During system and detailed design, only the two permanent members will be involved. During coding and unit testing, the third person might be used, if the leader desires. There will be no librarian in the project, as it is a small project, and the programmers themselves will do the documentation and other library tasks. If necessary, the third member of the team will perform the duties of the librarian.

Configuration Control Plan

In this project, we will only have configuration control for the code. The design will not be under configuration management. The requirements are assumed to be frozen; any change will be negotiated with the management.

The configuration control board (CCB) will consist only of the group leader. A module will be taken for configuration management, only after it has been successfully unit tested and its unit test results have been approved by the group leader. Change requests will be made to the CCB through electronic mail, and the requester will have to justify the request. Requested changes will generally be allowed if the change does not change the interface of the module, and the project is not behind schedule. Changes that will modify the module interface or affect other programmers will, in general, not be approved unless there are good reasons for doing so. In this case, all the concerned parties will be informed of the change through electronic mail.

Quality Assurance Plans

To ensure quality, the following documents (besides this plan and the requirements document) will be produced during the development:

- System design document
- Code
- Unit test report
- System test plan
- System test reports

The following methods will be used for quality control:

- Preliminary design review
- Unit testing
- System test plan review
- System testing

It is felt that because the system is small, a detailed incremental testing is not needed. A two-level testing is used: unit testing followed by system testing. The system test plan, however, will be reviewed before the testing is performed. No code review will be done.

Monitoring Plans

Three basic methods will be used for project monitoring—project logs, biweekly meetings and reviews. Because we do not have a time sheet processing system, each project member will keep a multipurpose log in which he will record the different activities he performs and the date and duration of the activity. The failure and error data obtained during testing will also be recorded in the log. Cross checking of the log data can be done by those events in which more than one person of the team participated. The format of the log entries is:

Date	Time From	Time To	Time In Mts	Activity Type	Comments

Activity type is one of the following: requirement understanding, design (system or detailed), coding, testing, report writing, meetings, debugging (including correcting errors), and others. In the comment field, the errors encountered during testing have to be recorded.

Reviews to be held are defined earlier. In addition to reviews, a biweekly meeting will be held to discuss the progress of the project.

Risk Management

The project has no major hazards associated with it. The only risks it has are the cost and schedule risks. Although analysis can easily be done regarding the schedule risks involved, it is felt that because the team has one part-time member (who is largely under-used), schedule slippage can be easily handled. Similarly, because the costs are low in this small project, it is felt that an analysis of the cost risk is unnecessary.

5

Function-Oriented Design

The design activity begins when the requirements document for the software to be developed is available. This may be the SRS for the complete system, as is the case if the waterfall model is being followed or the requirements for the next "iteration" if the iterative enhancement is being followed or the requirements for the prototype if the prototyping is being followed. While the requirements specification activity is entirely in the problem domain, design is the first step in moving from the problem domain toward the solution domain. Design is essentially the bridge between requirements specification and the final solution for satisfying the requirements.

The term *design* is used in two ways. Used as a verb, it represents the process of design. Used as a noun, it represents the result of the design process, which is the design for the system. The goal of the design process is to produce a model or representation of a system, which can be used later to build that system. The produced model is called the *design of the system*.

The design of a system is essentially a blueprint or a plan for a solution for the system. Here we consider a system to be a set of components with clearly defined behavior that interacts with each other in a fixed defined manner to produce some behavior or services for its environment. A component of a system can be considered a system, with its own components. In a software system, a component is a software module.

The design process for software systems often has two levels. At the first level the focus is on deciding which modules are needed for the system, the specifications of these modules, and how the modules should be interconnected. This is what is called the *system design* or *top-level design*. In the second level, the internal design of the modules, or how the specifications of the module can be satisfied, is decided. This design level is often called *detailed design* or *logic design*. Detailed design essentially expands the system design to contain a more detailed description of the processing logic and data structures so that the design is sufficiently complete for coding.

Because the detailed design is an extension of system design, the system design controls the major structural characteristics of the system. The system design has a major impact on the testability and modifiability of a system, and it impacts its efficiency. Much of the design effort for designing software is spent creating the system design.

A *design methodology* is a systematic approach to creating a design by applying of a set of techniques and guidelines. Most design methodologies focus on the system design. Most current design methodologies essentially offer a set of guidelines that can be used by the developer to design a system. These techniques are not formalized and do not reduce the design activity to a sequence of steps that can be followed by the designer.

The input to the design phase is the specifications for the system to be designed. Hence a reasonable entry criteria can be that the specifications are stable and have been approved, hoping that the approval mechanism will ensure that the specifications are complete, consistent, unambiguous, etc. The output of the top-level design phase is the architectural design or the system design for the software system to be built. This can be produced with or without using a design methodology. A reasonable exit criteria for the phase could be that the design has been verified against the input specifications and has been evaluated and approved for quality.

A design can be object-oriented or function-oriented. In function-oriented design, the design consists of module definitions, with each module supporting a functional abstraction. In object-oriented design, the modules in the design represent data abstraction (these abstractions are discussed in more detail later). In this chapter we discuss the function-oriented methods for design and describe one particular methodology—the structured design methodology—in some detail. In a function-oriented design approach, a system is viewed as a transformation function, transforming the inputs to the desired outputs. The purpose of the design phase is to specify the components for this transformation function, so that each component is also a transformation function. Hence, the basic output of the system design phase, when a function oriented design approach is being followed, is the definition of all the major data structures in the system, all the major modules of the system, and how the modules interact with each other.

In this chapter, before we discuss aspects of function-oriented design, we will discuss some general design principles that are applicable for most design approaches. Then we discuss some concepts specific to function-oriented designs, followed by a notation for expressing function-oriented designs and the description of the structured design methodology. Then we discuss some verification methods for design and some metrics that are applicable to function-oriented designs. As in most chapters, we will end with the case study—the complete design for the case study is given along with some discussion about the application of the design metrics to the case study.

5.1 Design Principles

The design of a system is *correct* if a system built precisely according to the design satisfies the requirements of that system. Clearly, the goal during the design phase is to produce correct designs. However, correctness is not the sole criterion during the design phase, as there can be many correct designs. The goal of the design process is not simply to produce *a* design for the system. Instead, the goal is to find the *best* possible design within the limitations imposed by the requirements and the physical and social environment in which the system will operate.

To evaluate a design, we have to specify some properties and criteria that can be used for evaluation. Ideally, these properties should be as quantitative as possible. In that situation we can mathematically evaluate the "goodness" of a design and use mathematical techniques to formally determine the best design. However, as with many objects in the real world, criteria for quality of software design is often subjective or non-quantifiable. In such a situation, criteria are essentially thumb rules that aid design evaluation.

A design should clearly be verifiable, complete (implements all the specifications), and traceable (all design elements can be traced to some requirements). However, the two most important properties that concern designers are efficiency and simplicity. *Efficiency* of any system is concerned with the proper use of scarce resources by the system. The need for efficiency arises due to cost considerations. If some resources are scarce and expensive, it is desirable that those resources be used efficiently. In computer systems, the resources that are most often considered for efficiency are processor time and memory. An efficient system is one that consumes less processor time and requires less memory. In earlier days, the efficient use of CPU and memory was important due to the high cost of hardware. Now that the hardware costs are small compared to the software costs, for many software systems traditional efficiency concerns now take a back seat compared to other considerations. One of the exceptions is real-time systems, where there are strict execution time constraints.

Simplicity is perhaps the most important quality criteria for software systems. We have seen that maintenance of software is usually quite expensive. Maintainability of software is one of the goals we have established. The design of a system is one of the most important factors affecting the maintainability of a system. During maintenance, the first step a maintainer has to undertake is to understand the system to be maintained. Only after a maintainer has a thorough understanding of the different modules of the system, how they are interconnected, and how modifying one will affect the others should the modification be undertaken. A simple and understandable design will go a long way in making the job of the maintainer easier.

These criteria are not independent, and increasing one may have an unfavorable effect on another. For example, often the "tricks" used to increase efficiency of a system result in making the system more complex. Therefore, design decisions frequently involve trade-offs. It is the designers' job to recognize the trade-offs and achieve the best balance. For our purposes, simplicity is the primary property of interest, and therefore the objective of the design process is to produce designs that are simple to understand.

Creating a simple (and efficient) design of a large system can be an extremely complex task that requires good engineering judgment. As designing is fundamentally a creative activity, it cannot be reduced to a series of steps that can be simply followed, though guidelines can be provided. In this section we will examine some basic guiding principles that can be used to produce the design of a system. Some of these design principles are concerned with providing means to effectively handle the complexity of the design process. Effectively handling the complexity will not only reduce the effort needed for design (i.e., reduce the design cost), but can also reduce the scope of introducing errors during design. The principles discussed here form the basis for most of the design methodologies.

It should be noted that the principles that can be used in design are the same as those used in problem analysis. In fact, the methods are also similar because in both analysis and design we are essentially constructing models. However, there are some fundamental differences. First, in problem analysis, we are constructing a model of the problem domain, while in design we are constructing a model for the solution domain. Second, in problem analysis, the analyst has limited degrees of freedom in selecting the models as the problem is given, and modeling has to represent it. In design, the designer has a great deal of freedom in deciding the models, as the system the designer is modeling does not exist; in fact the designer is creating a model for the system that will be the basis of building the system. That is, in design, the system depends on the model, while in problem analysis the model depends on the system. Finally, as pointed out earlier, the basic aim of modeling in problem analysis is to understand, while the basic aim of modeling in design is to optimize (in our case, simplicity and performance). In other words, though the basic principles and techniques might look similar, the activities of analysis and design are very different.

5.1.1   Problem Partitioning and Hierarchy

When solving a small problem, the entire problem can be tackled at once. The complexity of large problems and the limitations of human minds do not allow large problems to be treated as huge monoliths. For solving larger problems, the basic principle is the time-tested principle of "divide and conquer." Clearly, dividing in such a manner that all the divisions have to be conquered together is not the intent of this wisdom. This principle, if elaborated, would mean "divide into smaller pieces, so that each piece can be conquered separately."

For software design, therefore, the goal is to divide the problem into manageably small pieces that can be solved separately. It is this restriction of being able to solve each part separately that makes dividing into pieces a complex task and that many methodologies for system design aim to address. The basic rationale behind this strategy is the belief that if the pieces of a problem are solvable separately, the cost of solving the entire problem is more than the sum of the cost of solving all the pieces.

However, the different pieces cannot be entirely independent of each other, as they together form the system. The different pieces have to cooperate and communicate to solve the larger problem. This communication adds complexity, which arises due to partitioning and may not have existed in the original problem. As the number of components increases, the cost of partitioning, together with the cost of this added complexity, may become more than the savings achieved by partitioning. It is at this point that no further partitioning needs to be done. The designer has to make the judgment about when to stop partitioning.

As discussed earlier, two of the most important quality criteria for software design are simplicity and understandability. It can be argued that maintenance is minimized if each part in the system can be easily related to the application and each piece can be modified separately. If a piece can be modified separately, we call it *independent* of other pieces. If module A is independent of module B, then we can modify A without introducing any unanticipated side effects in B. Total independence of modules of one system is not possible, but the design process should support as much independence as possible between modules. Dependence between modules in a software system is one of the reasons for high maintenance costs. Clearly, proper partitioning will make the system easier to maintain by making the design easier to understand. Problem partitioning also aids design verification.

Problem partitioning, which is essential for solving a complex problem, leads to hierarchies in the design. That is, the design produced by using problem partitioning can be represented as a hierarchy of components. The relationship between the elements in this hierarchy can vary depending on the method used. For example, the most common is the "whole–part of" relationship. In this, the system consists of some parts, each part consists of subparts, and so on. This relationship can be naturally represented as a hierarchical structure between various system parts. In general, hierarchical structure makes it much easier to comprehend a complex system. Due to this, all design methodologies aim to produce a design that has nice hierarchical structures.

5.1.2   Abstraction

Abstraction is a very powerful concept that is used in all engineering disciplines. It is a tool that permits a designer to consider a component at an abstract level without worrying about the details of the implementation of the component. Any component or system provides some services to its environment. An abstraction of a component describes the external behavior of that component without bothering with the internal details that produce the behavior. Presumably, the abstract definition of a component is much simpler than the component itself.

Abstraction is an indispensable part of the design process and is essential for problem partitioning. Partitioning essentially is the exercise in determining the components of a system. However, these components are not isolated from each other; they interact with each other, and the designer has to specify how a component interacts with other components. To decide how a component interacts with other components, the designer has to know, at the very least, the external behavior of other components. If the designer has to understand the details of the other components to determine their external behavior, we have defeated the purpose of partitioning—isolating a component from others. To allow the designer to concentrate on one component at a time, abstraction of other components is used.

Abstraction is used for existing components as well as components that are being designed. Abstraction of existing components plays an important role in the maintenance phase. To modify a system, the first step is understanding what the system does and how. The process of comprehending an existing system involves identifying the abstractions of subsystems and components from the details of their implementations. Using these abstractions, the behavior of the entire system can be understood. This also helps determine how modifying a component affects the system.

During the design process, abstractions are used in the reverse manner than in the process of understanding a system. During design, the components do not exist, and in the design the designer specifies only the abstract specifications of the different components. The basic goal of system design is to specify the modules in a system and their abstractions. Once the different modules are specified, during the detailed design the designer can concentrate on one module at a time. The task in detailed design and implementation is essentially to implement the modules so that the abstract specifications of each module are satisfied.

There are two common abstraction mechanisms for software systems: *functional abstraction* and *data abstraction*. In *functional abstraction*, a module is specified by the function it performs. For example, a module to compute the log of a value can be abstractly represented by the function log. Similarly, a module to sort an input array can be represented by the specification of sorting. Functional abstraction is the basis of partitioning in function-oriented approaches. That is, when the problem is being partitioned, the overall transformation function for the system is partitioned into smaller functions that comprise the system function. The decomposition of the system is in terms of functional modules.

The second unit for abstraction is *data abstraction*. Any entity in the real world provides some services to the environment to which it belongs. Often the entities provide some fixed predefined services. The case of data entities is similar. Certain operations are required from a data object, depending on the object and the environment in which it is used. Data abstraction supports this view. Data is not treated simply as objects, but is treated as objects with some predefined operations on them. The operations defined on a data object are the only operations that can be performed on those objects. From outside an object, the internals of the object are hidden; only the operations on the object are visible. Data abstraction forms the basis for *object-oriented design*, which is discussed in the next chapter. In using this abstraction, a system is viewed as a set of objects providing some services. Hence, the decomposition of the system is done with respect to the objects the system contains.

5.1.3 Modularity

As mentioned earlier, the real power of partitioning comes if a system is partitioned into modules so that the modules are solvable and modifiable separately. It will be even better if the modules are also separately compilable (then changes in a module will not require recompilation of the whole system). A system is considered *modular* if it consists of discreet components so that each component can be implemented separately, and a change to one component has minimal impact on other components.

Modularity is a clearly a desirable property in a system. Modularity helps in system debugging—isolating the system problem to a component is easier if the system is modular—in system repair—changing a part of the system is easy as it affects few other parts—and in system building—a modular system can be easily built by "putting its modules together."

A software system cannot be made modular by simply chopping it into a set of modules. For modularity, each module needs to support a well-defined abstraction and have a clear interface through which it can interact with other modules. Modularity is where abstraction and partitioning come together. For easily understandable and maintainable systems, modularity is clearly the basic objective; partitioning and abstraction can be viewed as concepts that help achieve modularity.

5.1.4 Top-Down and Bottom-Up Strategies

A system consists of components, which have components of their own; indeed a system is a hierarchy of components. The highest-level component correspond to the total system. To design such a hierarchy there are two possible approaches: top-down and bottom-up. The top-down approach starts from the highest-level component of the hierarchy and proceeds through to lower levels. By contrast, a bottom-up approach starts with the lowest-level component of the hierarchy and proceeds through progressively higher levels to the top-level component.

A top-down design approach starts by identifying the major components of the system, decomposing them into their lower-level components and iterating until the desired level of detail is achieved. Top-down design methods often result in some form of *stepwise refinement*. Starting from an abstract design, in each step the design is refined to a more concrete level, until we reach a level where no more refinement is needed and the design can be implemented directly. The top-down approach has been promulgated by many researchers and has been found to be extremely useful for design. Most design methodologies are based on the top-down approach.

A bottom-up design approach starts with designing the most basic or primitive components and proceeds to higher-level components that use these lower-level components. Bottom-up methods work with *layers of abstraction*. Starting from the very bottom, operations that provide a layer of abstraction are implemented. The operations of this layer are then used to implement more powerful operations and a still higher layer of abstraction, until the stage is reached where the operations supported by the layer are those desired by the system.

A top-down approach is suitable only if the specifications of the system are clearly known and the system development is from scratch. Hence, it is a reasonable approach if a waterfall type of process model is being used. However, if a system is to be built from an existing system, a bottom-up approach is more suitable, as it starts from some existing components. So, for example, if an iterative enhancement type of process is being followed, in later iterations, the bottom-up approach could be more suitable (in the first iteration a top-down approach can be used.)

Pure top-down or pure bottom-up approaches are often not practical. For a bottom-up approach to be successful, we must have a good notion of the top to which the design should be heading. Without a good idea about the operations needed at the higher layers, it is difficult to determine what operations the current layer should support. Top-down approaches require some idea about the feasibility of the components specified during design. The components specified during design should be implementable, which requires some idea about the feasibility of the lower-level parts of a component. A common approach to combine the two approaches is to provide a layer of abstraction for the application domain of interest through libraries of functions, which contains the functions of interest to the application domain. Then use a top-down approach to determine the modules in the system, assuming that the abstract machine available for implementing the system provides the operations supported by the abstraction layer. This approach is frequently used for developing systems. It can even be claimed that it is almost universally used these days, as most developments now make use of the layer of abstraction supported in a system consisting of the library functions provided by operating systems, programming languages, and special-purpose tools.

5.2 Module-Level Concepts

In the previous section we discussed some general design principles. Now we turn our attention to some concepts specific to function-oriented design. Before we discuss these, let us define what we mean by a module. A *module* is a logically separable part of a program. It is a program unit that is discreet and identifiable with respect to compiling and loading. In terms of common programming language constructs, a module can be a macro, a function, a procedure (or subroutine), a process, or a package. In systems using functional abstraction, a module is usually a procedure of function or a collection of these.

To produce modular designs, some criteria must be used to select modules so that the modules support well-defined abstractions and are solvable and modifiable separately. In a system using functional abstraction, coupling and cohesion are two modularization criteria, which are often used together.

5.2.1 Coupling

Two modules are considered independent if one can function completely without the presence of other. Obviously, if two modules are independent, they are solvable and modifiable separately. However, all the modules in a system cannot be independent of each other, as they must interact so that together they produce the desired external behavior of the system. The more connections between modules, the more dependent they are in the sense that more knowledge about one module is required to understand or solve the other module. Hence, the fewer and simpler the connections between modules, the easier it is to understand one without understanding the other. The notion of coupling [SMC74, YC79] attempts to capture this concept of "how strongly" different modules are interconnected.

Coupling between modules is the strength of interconnections between modules or a measure of interdependence among modules. In general, the more we must know about module A in order to understand module B, the more closely connected A is to B. "Highly coupled" modules are joined by strong interconnections, while "loosely coupled" modules have weak interconnections. Independent modules have no interconnections. To solve and modify a module separately, we would like the module to be loosely coupled with other modules. The choice of modules decides the coupling between modules. Because the modules of the software system are created during system design, the coupling between modules is largely decided during system design and cannot be reduced during implementation.

Coupling is an abstract concept and is not easily quantifiable. So, no formulas can be given to determine the coupling between two modules. However, some major factors can be identified as influencing coupling between modules. Among them the most important are the type of connection between modules, the complexity of the interface, and the type of information flow between modules.

Coupling increases with the complexity and obscurity of the interface between modules. To keep coupling low we would like to minimize the number of interfaces per module and the complexity of each interface. An interface of a module is used to pass information to and from other modules. Coupling is reduced if only the defined entry interface of a module is used by other modules (for example, passing information to and from a module exclusively through parameters). Coupling would increase if a module is used by other modules via an indirect and obscure interface, like directly using the internals of a module or using shared variables.

Complexity of the interface is another factor affecting coupling. The more complex each interface is, the higher will be the degree of coupling. For example, complexity of the entry interface of a procedure depends on the number of items being passed as parameters and on the complexity of the items. Some level of complexity of interfaces is required to support the communication needed between modules. However, often more than this minimum is used. For example, if a field of a record is needed by a procedure, often the entire record is passed, rather than just passing that field of the record. By passing the record we are increasing the coupling unnecessarily. Essentially, we should keep the interface of a module as simple and small as possible.

The type of information flow along the interfaces is the third major factor affecting coupling. There are two kinds of information that can flow along an interface: data or control. Passing or receiving control information means that the action of the module will depend on this control information, which makes it more difficult to understand the module and provide its abstraction. Transfer of data information means that a module passes as input some data to another module and gets in return some data as output. This allows a module to be treated as a simple input-output function that performs some transformation on the input data to produce the output data. In general, interfaces with only data communication result in the lowest degree of coupling, followed by interfaces that only transfer control data. Coupling is considered highest if the data is hybrid, that is, some data items and some control items are passed between modules. The effect of these three factors on coupling is summarized in Table 5.1 [SMC74].

5.2.2   Cohesion

We have seen that coupling is reduced when the relationships among elements in different modules are minimized. That is, coupling is reduced when elements in different modules have little or no bonds between them. Another way of achieving

	Interface Complexity	Type of Connection	Type of Communication
Low	Simple obvious	To module by name	Data control
High	Complicated obscure	To internal elements	Hybrid

TABLE 5.1. Factors affecting coupling.

this effect is to strengthen the bond between elements of the same module by maximizing the relationship between elements of the same module. Cohesion is the concept that tries to capture this intra-module [SMC74, YC79]. With cohesion, we are interested in determining how closely the elements of a module are related to each other.

Cohesion of a module represents how tightly bound the internal elements of the module are to one another. Cohesion of a module gives the designer an idea about whether the different elements of a module belong together in the same module. Cohesion and coupling are clearly related. Usually, the greater the cohesion of each module in the system, the lower the coupling between modules is. This correlation is not perfect, but it has been observed in practice. There are several levels of cohesion:

- Coincidental
- Logical
- Temporal
- Procedural
- Communicational
- Sequential
- Functional

Coincidental is the lowest level, and functional is the highest. These levels do not form a linear scale. Functional binding is much stronger than the rest, while the first two are considered much weaker than others. Often, many levels can be applicable when considering cohesion between two elements of a module. In such situations, the highest level is considered. Cohesion of a module is considered the highest level of cohesion applicable to all elements in the module.

Coincidental cohesion occurs when there is no meaningful relationship among the elements of a module. Coincidental cohesion can occur if an existing program is "modularized" by chopping it into pieces and making different pieces modules. If a module is created to save duplicate code by combining some part of code that occurs at many different places, that module is likely to have coincidental cohesion. In this situation, the statements in the module have no relationship with each other, and if one of the modules using the code needs to be modified and this modification includes the common code, it is likely that other modules using the code do not want the code modified. Consequently, the modification of this "common module" may cause other modules to behave incorrectly. The modules using these modules are therefore not modifiable separately and have strong interconnection between them. We can say that, generally speaking, it is poor practice to create a module merely to avoid duplicate code (unless the common code happens to perform some identifiable function, in which case the statements will have some relationship between them) or to chop a module into smaller modules to reduce the module size.

A module has logical cohesion if there is some logical relationship between the elements of a module, and the elements perform functions that fall in the same logical class. A typical example of this kind of cohesion is a module that performs all the inputs or all the outputs. In such a situation, if we want to input or output a particular record, we have to somehow convey this to the module. Often, this will be done by passing some kind of special status flag, which will be used to determine what statements to execute in the module. Besides resulting in hybrid information flow between modules, which is generally the worst form of coupling between modules, such a module will usually have tricky and clumsy code. In general, logically cohesive modules should be avoided, if possible.

Temporal cohesion is the same as logical cohesion, except that the elements are also related in time and are executed together. Modules that perform activities like "initialization," "clean-up," and "termination" are usually temporally bound. Even though the elements in a temporally bound module are logically related, temporal cohesion is higher than logical cohesion, because the elements are all executed together. This avoids the problem of passing the flag, and the code is usually simpler.

A procedurally cohesive module contains elements that belong to a common procedural unit. For example, a loop or a sequence of decision statements in a module may be combined to form a separate module. Procedurally cohesive modules often occur when modular structure is determined from some form of flowchart. Procedural cohesion often cuts across functional lines. A module with only procedural cohesion may contain only part of a complete function or parts of several functions.

A module with communicational cohesion has elements that are related by a reference to the same input or output data. That is, in a communicationally bound module, the elements are together because they operate on the same input or output data. An example of this could be a module to "print and punch record." Communicationally cohesive modules may perform more than one function. However, communicational cohesion is sufficiently high as to be generally acceptable if alternative structures with higher cohesion cannot be easily identified.

When the elements are together in a module because the output of one forms the input to another, we get sequential cohesion. If we have a sequence of elements in which the output of one forms the input to another, sequential cohesion does not provide any guidelines on how to combine them into modules. Different possibilities exist: combine all in one module, put the first half in one and the second half in another, the first third in one and the rest in the other, and so forth. Consequently, a sequentially bound module may contain several functions or parts of different functions. Sequentially cohesive modules bear a close resemblance to the problem structure. However, they are considered to be far from the ideal, which is functional cohesion.

Functional cohesion is the strongest cohesion. In a functionally bound module, all the elements of the module are related to performing a single function. By function, we do not mean simply mathematical functions; modules accomplishing a single goal are also included. Functions like "compute square root" and "sort the array" are clear examples of functionally cohesive modules.

How does one determine the cohesion level of a module? There is no mathematical formula that can be used. We have to use our judgment for this. A useful technique for determining if a module has functional cohesion is to write a sentence that describes, fully and accurately, the function or purpose of the module. The following tests can then be made [SMC74]:

1. If the sentence must be a compound sentence, if it contains a comma, or it has has more than one verb, the module is probably performing more than one function, and it probably has sequential or communicational cohesion.

2. If the sentence contains words relating to time, like "first," "next," "when," and "after" the module probably has sequential or temporal cohesion.

3. If the predicate of the sentence does not contain a single specific object following the verb (such as "edit all data") the module probably has logical cohesion.

4. Words like "initialize," and "cleanup" imply temporal cohesion.

Modules with functional cohesion can always be described by a simple sentence. However, if a description is a compound sentence, it does not mean that the module does not have functional cohesion. Functionally cohesive modules can also be described by compound sentences. If we cannot describe it using a simple sentence, the module is not likely to have functional cohesion.

5.3   Design Notation and Specification

During the design phase there are two things of interest: the design of the system, the producing of which is the basic objective of this phase, and the process of designing itself. It is for the latter that principles and methods are needed. In addition, while designing, a designer needs to record his thoughts and decisions and to represent the design so that he can view it and play with it. For this, design notations are used.

Design notations are largely meant to be used during the process of design and are used to represent design or design decisions. They are meant largely for the designer so that he can quickly represent his decisions in a compact manner that he can evaluate and modify. These notations are frequently graphical.

Once the designer is satisfied with the design he has produced, the design is to be precisely specified in the form of a document. To specify the design, specification languages are used. Producing the design specification is the ultimate objective of the design phase. The purpose of this design document is quite different from that of the design notation. Whereas a design represented using the design notation is largely to be used by the designer, a design specification has to be so precise and complete that it can be used as a basis of further development by other programmers. Generally, design specification uses textual structures, with design notation helping understanding.

Here we first describe a design notation—structure charts—that can be used to represent a function-oriented design. Then we describe a simple design language to specify a design. Though the design document, the final output of the design activity, typically also contains other things like design decisions taken and background, its primary purpose is to document the design itself. We will focus on this aspect only.

5.3.1 Structure Charts

For a function-oriented design, the design can be represented graphically by structure charts. The structure of a program is made up of the modules of that program together with the interconnections between modules. Every computer program has a structure, and given a program its structure can be determined. The structure chart of a program is a graphic representation of its structure. In a structure chart a module is represented by a box with the module name written in the box. An arrow from module A to module B represents that module A invokes module B. B is called the *subordinate* of A, and A is called the *superordinate* of B. The arrow is labeled by the parameters received by B as input and the parameters returned by B as output, with the direction of flow of the input and output parameters represented by small arrows. The parameters can be shown to be data (unfilled circle at the tail of the label) or control (filled circle at the tail). As an example consider the structure of the following program, whose structure is shown in Figure 5.1.

```
main()
{
```

```
        int sum, n, N, a[MAX];
        readnums(a, &N); sort(a, N); scanf(&n);
        sum = add_n(a, n); printf(sum);
}

readnums(a, N)
int a[], *N;
{
    :
}

sort(a, N)
int a[], N;
{
    :
    if (a[i] > a[t]) switch(a[i], a[t]);
    :
}

/* Add the first n numbers of a */
add_n(a, n)
int a[], n;
{
    :
}
```

In general, procedural information is not represented in a structure chart, and the focus is on representing the hierarchy of modules. However, there are situations

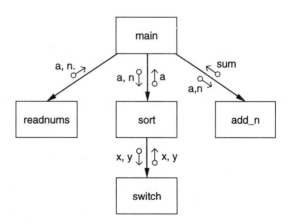

FIGURE 5.1. The structure chart of the sort program.

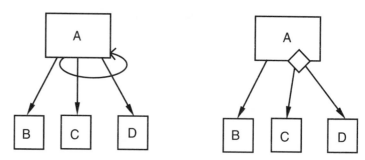

FIGURE 5.2. Iteration and decision representation.

where the designer may wish to communicate certain procedural information explicitly, like major loops and decisions. Such information can also be represented in a structure chart. For example, let us consider a situation where module A has subordinates B, C, and D, and A repeatedly calls the modules C and D. This can be represented by a looping arrow around the arrows joining the subordinates C and D to A, as shown in Figure 5.2. All the subordinate modules activated within a common loop are enclosed in the same looping arrow.

Major decisions can be represented similarly. For example, if the invocation of modules C and D in module A depends on the outcome of some decision, that is represented by a small diamond in the box for A, with the arrows joining C and D coming out of this diamond, as shown in Figure 5.2.

Modules in a system can be categorized into few classes. There are some modules that obtain information from their subordinates and then pass it to their superiordinate. This kind of module is an *input module*. Similarly, there are *output modules*. that take information from their superiordinate and pass it on to its subordinates. As the name suggests, the input and output modules are typically used for input and output of data from and to the environment. The input modules get the data from the sources and get it ready to be processed, and the output modules take the output produced and prepare it for proper presentation to the environment. Then there are modules that exist solely for the sake of transforming data into some other form. Such a module is called a *transform module*. Most of the computational modules typically fall in this category. Finally, there are modules whose primary concern is managing the flow of data to and from different subordinates. Such modules are called *coordinate modules*. The structure chart representation of the different types of modules is shown in Figure 5.3.

A module can perform functions of more than one type of module. For example, the composite module in Figure 5.3 is an input module from the point of view of its superiordinate, as it feeds the data Y to the superiordinate. Internally, A is a coordinate module and views its job as getting data X from one subordinate and passing it to another subordinate, which converts it to Y. Modules in actual systems are often composite modules.

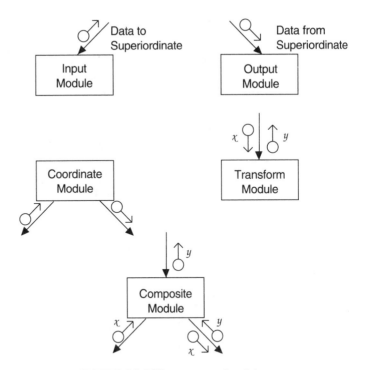

FIGURE 5.3. Different types of modules.

A structure chart is a nice representation mechanism for a design that uses functional abstraction. It shows the modules and their call hierarchy, the interfaces between the modules, and what information passes between modules. It is a convenient and compact notation that is very useful while creating the design. That is, a designer can make effective use of structure charts to represent the model he is creating while he is designing. However, it is not very useful for representing the final design, as it does not give all the information needed about the design. For example, it does not specify the scope, structure of data, specifications of each module, etc. Hence, it is generally not used to convey design to the implementer.

We have seen how to determine the structure of an existing program. But once the program is written, its structure is fixed and little can be done about altering the structure. However, for a given set of requirements many different programs can be written to satisfy the requirements, and each program can have a different structure. That is, although the structure of a given program is fixed, for a given set of requirements, programs with different structures can be obtained. The objective of the design phase using function-oriented method is to control the eventual structure of the system by fixing the structure during design.

5.3.2 Specification

Using some design rules or methodology, a conceptual design of the system can be produced in terms of a structure chart. As seen earlier, in a structure chart each module is represented by a box with a name. The functionality of the module is essentially communicated by the name of the box, and the interface is communicated by the data items labeling the arrows. This is all right while the designer is designing but inadequate when the design is to be communicated to other programmers or archived for future reference. To avoid these problems, the design needs to be formally specified. The design specification is then communicated in the *design document*, which is used as the reference for the design phase for later activities like detailed design and implementation.

As the design document is the means by which the design is communicated, it should contain all information relevant to future phases. First let us decide what a document-specifying system design should contain. A design specification should contain:

- Problem specification
- Major data structures
- Modules and their specifications
- Design decisions

The requirements document specifies the problem in the terminology of the problem domain. Often, before starting design, the requirements are translated into a specification of a problem more suited for design purposes. In this sense, *problem specification* or restatement is the first step in the design process.

During system design, the major data structures for the software are identified; without these, the system modules cannot be meaningfully defined during design. In the design specification, a formal definition of these data structures should be given.

Module specification is the major part of system design specification. All modules in the system should be identified when the system design is complete, and these modules should be specified in the document. During system design only the module specification is obtained, because the internal details of the modules are defined later. To specify a module, the design document must specify (a) the *interface of the module* (all data items, their types, and whether they are for input and/or output), (b) the *abstract behavior* of the module (*what* the module does) by specifying the module's functionality or its input/output behavior, and (c) all other modules used by the module being specified—this information is quite useful in maintaining and understanding the design.

Hence, a design specification will necessarily contain specification of the major data structures and modules in the system. After a design is approved (using some verification mechanism), the modules will have to be implemented in the target language. This requires that the module "headers" for the target language first be created from the design. This translation of the design for the target language can introduce errors if it's done manually. To eliminate these translation errors, if the target language is known (as is generally the case after the requirements have been specified), it is better to have a design specification language whose module specifications can be used almost directly in programming. This not only minimizes the translation errors that may occur, but also reduces the effort required for translating the design to programs. It also adds incentive for designers to properly specify their design, as the design is no longer a "mere" document that will be thrown away after review—it will now be used directly in coding. In the case study, a design specification language close to C has been used. From the design, the module headers for C can easily be created with some simple editing.

To aid the comprehensibility of the design, all major *design decisions* made by the designers during the design process should be explained explicitly. The choices that were available and the reasons for making a particular choice should be explained. This makes a design more *visible* and will help in understanding the design.

5.4 Structured Design Methodology

Creating the software system design is the major concern of the design phase. Many design techniques have been proposed over the years to provide some discipline in handling the complexity of designing large systems. The aim of design methodologies is not to reduce the process of design to a sequence of mechanical steps but to provide guidelines to aid the designer during the design process. Here we describe the structured design methodology [SMC74, YC79] for developing system designs.

Structured design methodology (SDM) views every software system as having some inputs that are converted into the desired outputs by the software system. The software is viewed as a transformation function that transforms the given inputs into the desired outputs, and the central problem of designing software systems is considered to be properly designing this transformation function. Due to this view of software, the structured design methodology is primarily function-oriented and relies heavily on functional abstraction and functional decomposition.

The concept of the structure of a program lies at the heart of the structured design method. During design, structured design methodology aims to control and influence the structure of the final program. The aim is to design a system so that programs implementing the design would have a nice hierarchical structure, with functionally cohesive modules and as few interconnections between modules as possible.

In properly designed systems it is often the case that a module with subordinates does not actually perform much computation. The bulk of actual computation is performed by its subordinates, and the module itself largely coordinates the data flow between the subordinates to get the computation done. The subordinates in turn can get the bulk of their work done by their subordinates until the "atomic" modules, which have no subordinates, are reached. *Factoring* is the process of decomposing a module so that the bulk of its work is done by its subordinates. A system is said to be completely factored if all the actual processing is accomplished by bottom-level atomic modules and if nonatomic modules largely perform the jobs of control and coordination. SDM attempts to achieve a structure that is close to being completely factored.

The overall strategy is to identify the input and output streams and the primary transformations that have to be performed to produce the output. High-level modules are then created to perform these major activities, which are later refined. There are four major steps in this strategy:

1. Restate the problem as a data flow diagram
2. Identify the input and output data elements
3. First-level factoring
4. Factoring of input, output, and transform branches

We will now discuss each of these steps in more detail. The design of the case study using structured design will be given later. For illustrating each step of the methodology as we discuss them, we consider the following problem: there is a text file containing words separated by blanks or new lines. We have to design a software system to determine the number of unique words in the file.

5.4.1   Restate the Problem as a Data Flow Diagram

To use the SD methodology, the first step is to construct the data flow diagram for the problem. We studied data flow diagrams in Chapter 3. However, there is a fundamental difference between the DFDs drawn during requirements analysis and during structured design. In the requirements analysis, a DFD is drawn to model the problem domain. The analyst has little control over the problem, and hence his task is to extract from the problem all the information and then represent it as a DFD.

During design activity, we are no longer modeling the problem domain, but rather are dealing with the solution domain and developing a model for the *eventual system*. That is, the DFD during design represents how the data will flow in the system when it is built. In this modeling, the major transforms or functions in the software are decided, and the DFD shows the major transforms that the software will have and how the data will flow through different transforms. So, drawing a DFD for design is a very creative activity in which the designer visualizes the

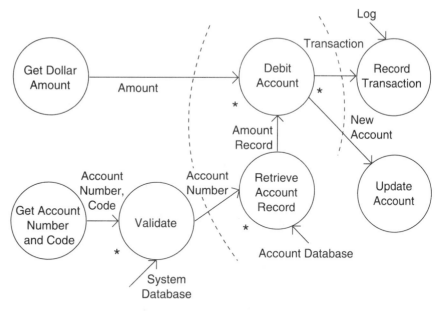

FIGURE 5.4. Data flow diagram of an ATM.

eventual system and its processes and data flows. As the system does not yet exist, the designer has complete freedom in creating a DFD that will solve the problem stated in the SRS. The general rules of drawing a DFD remain the same; we show what transforms are needed in the software and are not concerned with the logic for implementing them. Consider the example of the simple automated teller machine that allows customers to withdraw money. A DFD for this ATM is shown in Figure 5.4.

There are two major streams of input data in this diagram. The first is the account number and the code, and the second is the amount to be debited. The DFD is self-explanatory. Notice the use of * at different places in the DFD. For example, the transform "validate," which verifies if the account number and code are valid, needs not only the account number and code, but also information from the system database to do the validation. And the transform debit account has two outputs, one used for recording the transaction and the other to update the account.

As another example, consider the problem of determining the number of different words in an input file. The data flow diagram for this problem is shown in Figure 5.5

This problem has only one input data stream, the input file, while the desired output is the count of different words in the file. To transform the input to the desired output, the first thing we do is form a list of all the words in the file. It is best to then sort the list, as this will make identifying different words easier. This sorted list is then used to count the number of different words, and the output of

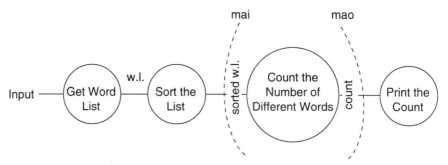

FIGURE 5.5. DFD for the word-counting problem.

this transform is the desired count, which is then printed. This sequence of data transformation is what we have in the data flow diagram.

5.4.2   Identify the Most Abstract Input and Output Data Elements

Most systems have some basic transformations that perform the required operations. However, in most cases the transformation cannot be easily applied to the actual physical input and produce the desired physical output. Instead, the input is first converted into a form on which the transformation can be applied with ease. Similarly, the main transformation modules often produce outputs that have to be converted into the desired physical output. The goal of this second step is to separate the transforms in the data flow diagram that convert the input or output to the desired format from the ones that perform the actual transformations.

For this separation, once the data flow diagram is ready, the next step is to identify the highest abstract level of input and output. *The most abstract input data elements* are those data elements in the data flow diagram that are furthest removed from the physical inputs but can still be considered inputs to the system. The most abstract input data elements often have little resemblance to the actual physical data. These are often the data elements obtained after operations like error checking, data validation, proper formatting, and conversion are complete.

Most abstract input (MAI) data elements are recognized by starting from the physical inputs and traveling toward the outputs in the data flow diagram, until the data elements are reached that can no longer be considered incoming. The aim is to go as far as possible from the physical inputs, without losing the incoming nature of the data element. This process is performed for each input stream. Identifying the most abstract data items represents a value judgment on the part of the designer, but often the choice is obvious.

Similarly, we identify the *most abstract output data elements* (MAO) by starting from the outputs in the data flow diagram and traveling toward the inputs. These are the data elements that are most removed from the actual outputs but can still be considered outgoing. The MAO data elements may also be considered the logical output data items, and the transforms in the data flow diagram after these data items are basically to convert the logical output into a form in which the system is required to produce the output.

There will usually be some transforms left between the most abstract input and output data items. These *central transforms* perform the basic transformation for the system, taking the most abstract input and transforming it into the most abstract output. The purpose of having central transforms deal with the most abstract data items is that the modules implementing these transforms can concentrate on performing the transformation without being concerned with converting the data into proper format, validating the data, and so forth. It is worth noting that if a central transform has two outputs with a + between them, it often indicates the presence of a major decision in the transform (which can be shown in the structure chart).

Consider the data flow diagram shown in Figure 5.5. The arcs in the data flow diagram are the most abstract input and most abstract output. The choice of the most abstract input is obvious. We start following the input. First, the input file is converted into a word list, which is essentially the input in a different form. The sorted word list is still basically the input, as it is still the same list, in a different order. This appears to be the most abstract input because the next data (i.e., count) is not just another form of the input data. The choice of the most abstract output is even more obvious; count is the natural choice (a data that is a form of input will not usually be a candidate for the most abstract output). Thus we have one central transform, count-the-number-of-different-words, which has one input and one output data item.

Consider now the data flow diagram of the automated teller shown in Figure 5.4. The two most abstract inputs are the dollar amount and the validated account number. The validated account number is the most abstract input, rather than the account number read in, as it is still the input—but with a guarantee that the account number is valid. The two abstract outputs are obvious. The abstract inputs and outputs are marked in the data flow diagram.

5.4.3   First-Level Factoring

Having identified the central transforms and the most abstract input and output data items, we are ready to identify some modules for the system. We first specify a main module, whose purpose is to invoke the subordinates. The main module is therefore a coordinate module. For each of the most abstract input data items, an immediate subordinate module to the main module is specified. Each of these modules is an input module, whose purpose is to deliver to the main module the most abstract data item for which it is created.

Similarly, for each most abstract output data item, a subordinate module that is an output module that accepts data from the main module is specified. Each of the

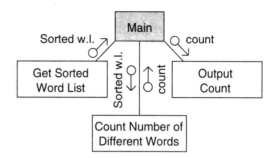

FIGURE 5.6. First-level factoring.

arrows connecting these input and output subordinate modules are labeled with the respective abstract data item flowing in the proper direction.

Finally, for each central transform, a module subordinate to the main one is specified. These modules will be transform modules, whose purpose is to accept data from the main module, and then return the appropriate data back to the main module. The data items coming to a transform module from the main module are on the incoming arcs of the corresponding transform in the data flow diagram. The data items returned are on the outgoing arcs of that transform. Note that here a module is created for a transform, while input/output modules are created for data items. The structure after the first-level factoring of the word-counting problem (its data flow diagram was given earlier) is shown in Figure 5.6.

In this example, there is one input module, which returns the sorted word list to the main module. The output module takes from the main module the value of the count. There is only one central transform in this example, and a module is drawn for that. Note that the data items traveling to and from this transformation module are the same as the data items going in and out of the central transform.

Let us examine the data flow diagram of the ATM. We have already seen that this has two most abstract inputs, two most abstract outputs, and two central transforms. Drawing a module for each of these, we get the structure chart shown in Figure 5.7.

As we can see, the first-level factoring is straightforward, after the most abstract input and output data items are identified in the data flow diagram. The main module is the overall control module, which will form the main program or procedure in the implementation of the design. It is a coordinate module that invokes the input modules to get the most abstract data items, passes these to the appropriate transform modules, and delivers the results of the transform modules to other transform modules until the most abstract data items are obtained. These are then passed to the output modules.

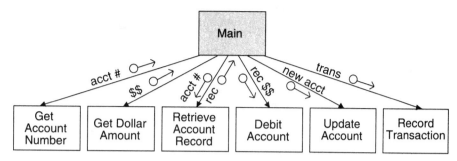

FIGURE 5.7. First-level factoring for ATM.

5.4.4 Factoring the Input, Output, and Transform Branches

The first-level factoring results in a very high-level structure, where each subordinate module has a lot of processing to do. To simplify these modules, they must be factored into subordinate modules that will distribute the work of a module. Each of the input, output, and transformation modules must be considered for factoring. Let us start with the input modules.

The purpose of an input module, as viewed by the main program, is to produce some data. To factor an input module, the transform in the data flow diagram that produced the data item is now treated as a central transform. The process performed for the first-level factoring is repeated here with this new central transform, with the input module being considered the main module. A subordinate input module is created for each input data stream coming into this new central transform, and a subordinate transform module is created for the new central transform. The new input modules now created can then be factored again, until the physical inputs are reached. Factoring of input modules will usually not yield any output subordinate modules.

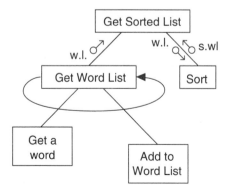

FIGURE 5.8. Factoring the input module.

The factoring of the input module get-sorted-list in the first-level structure is shown in Figure 5.8. The transform producing the input returned by this module (i.e., the sort transform) is treated as a central transform. Its input is the word list. Thus, in the first factoring we have an input module to get the list and a transform module to sort the list. The input module can be factored further, as the module needs to perform two functions, getting a word and then adding it to the list. Note that the looping arrow is used to show the iteration.

The factoring of the output modules is symmetrical to the factoring of the input modules. For an output module we look at the next transform to be applied to the output to bring it closer to the ultimate desired output. This now becomes the central transform, and an output module is created for each data stream going out of this transform. During the factoring of output modules, there will usually be no input modules. In our example, there is only one transform after the most abstract output, so this factoring need not be done.

If the data flow diagram of the problem is sufficiently detailed, factoring of the input and output modules is straightforward. However, there are no such rules for factoring the central transforms. The goal is to determine subtransforms that will together compose the overall transform and then repeat the process for the newly found transforms, until we reach the atomic modules. Factoring the central transform is essentially an exercise in functional decomposition and will depend on the designers' experience and judgment.

One way to factor a transform module is to treat it as a problem in its own right and start with a data flow diagram for it. The inputs to the data flow diagram are the data coming into the module and the outputs are the data being returned by the module. Each transform in this data flow diagram represents a subtransform of this transform. The central transform can be factored by creating a subordinate transform module for each of the transforms in this data flow diagram. This process can be repeated for the new transform modules that are created, until we reach atomic modules. The factoring of the central transform count-the-number-of-different-words is shown in Figure 5.9.

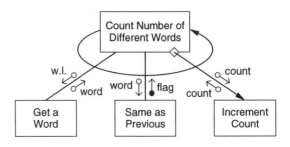

FIGURE 5.9. Factoring the central transform.

This was a relatively simple transform, and we did not need to draw the data flow diagram. To determine the number of words, we have to get a word repeatedly, determine if it is the same as the previous word (for a sorted list, this checking is sufficient to determine if the word is different from other words), and then count the word if it is different. For each of the three different functions, we have a subordinate module, and we get the structure shown in Figure 5.9.

It should be clear that the structure that is obtained depends a good deal on what are the most abstract inputs and most abstract outputs. And as mentioned earlier, determining the most abstract inputs and outputs requires making a judgment. However, if the judgment is different, though the structure changes, it is not affected dramatically. The net effect is that a bubble that appears as a transform module at one level may appear as a transform module at another level. For example, suppose in the word-counting problem we make a judgment that word-list is another form of the basic input but sorted-word-list is not. If we use word-list as the most abstract input, the net result is that the transform module corresponding to the sort bubble shows up as a transform module one level above. That is, now it is a central transform (i.e., subordinate to the main module) rather than a subordinate to the input module "get-sorted-word-list." So, the SDM has the desired property that it is not very sensitive to some variations in the identification of the most abstract input and most abstract output.

5.4.5 Design Heuristics

The design steps mentioned earlier do not reduce the design process to a series of steps that can be followed blindly. The strategy requires the designer to exercise sound judgment and common sense. The basic objective is to make the program structure reflect the problem as closely as possible. With this in mind the structure obtained by the methodology described earlier should be treated as an initial structure, which may need to be modified. Here we mention some heuristics that can be used to modify the structure, if necessary. It must be kept in mind that these are merely pointers to help the designer decide how the structure can be modified. The designer is still the final judge of whether a particular heuristic is useful for a particular application or not.

Module size is often considered an indication of module complexity. In terms of the structure of the system, modules that are very large may not be implementing a single function and can therefore be broken into many modules, each implementing a different function. On the other hand, modules that are too small may not require any additional identity and can be combined with other modules.

However, the decision to split a module or combine different modules should not be based on size alone. Cohesion and coupling of modules should be the primary guiding factors. A module should be split into separate modules only if the cohesion of the original module was low, the resulting modules have a higher degree of cohesion, and the coupling between modules does not increase. Similarly, two or more modules should be combined only if the resulting module has a high degree of cohesion and the coupling of the resulting module is not greater than the coupling of the submodules. Furthermore, a module usually should not be split or combined with another module if it is subordinate to many different modules. As a rule of thumb, the designer should take a hard look at modules that will be larger than about 100 lines of source code or will be less than a couple of lines.

Another parameter that can be considered while "fine-tuning" the structure is the fan-in and fan-out of modules. *Fan-in* of a module is the number of arrows coming in the module, indicating the number of superiordinates of a module. *Fan-out* of a module is the number of arrows going out of that module, indicating the number of subordinates of the module. A very high fan-out is not very desirable, as it means that the module has to control and coordinate too many modules and may therefore be too complex. Fan-out can be reduced by creating a subordinate and making many of the current subordinates subordinate to the newly created module. In general the fan-out should not be increased above five or six.

Whenever possible, the fan-in should be maximized. Of course, this should not be obtained at the cost of increasing the coupling or decreasing the cohesion of modules. For example, implementing different functions into a single module, simply to increase the fan-in, is not a good idea. Fan-in can often be increased by separating out common functions from different modules and creating a module to implement that function.

Another important factor that should be considered is the correlation of the scope of effect and scope of control. The scope of effect of a decision (in a module) is the collection of all the modules that contain any processing that is conditional on that decision or whose invocation is dependent on the outcome of the decision. The scope of control of a module is the module itself and all its subordinates (not just the immediate subordinates). The system is usually simpler when the scope of effect of a decision is a subset of the scope of control of the module in which the decision is located. Ideally, the scope of effect should be limited to the modules that are immediate subordinates of the module in which the decision is located. Violation of this rule of thumb often results in more coupling between modules.

There are some methods that a designer can use to ensure that the scope of effect of a decision is within the scope of control of the module. The decision can be removed from the module and "moved up" in the structure. Alternatively, modules that are in the scope of effect but are not in the scope of control can be moved down the hierarchy so that they fall within the scope of control.

5.4.6 Transaction Analysis

The structured design technique discussed earlier is called *transform analysis*, where most of the transforms in the data flow diagram have a few inputs and a

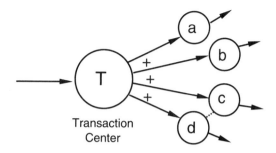

FIGURE 5.10. DFD for transaction analysis.

few outputs. There are situations where a transform splits an input stream into many different substreams, with a different sequence of transforms specified for the different substreams. For example, this is the case with systems where there are many different sets of possible actions and the actions to be performed depend pon the input command specified. In such situations the transform analysis can be supplemented by *transaction analysis.* and the detailed data flow diagram of the transform splitting the input may look like the DFD shown in Figure 5.10.

The module splitting the input is called the *transaction center*; it need not be a central transform and may occur on either the input branch or the output branch of the data flow diagram of the system. One of the standard ways to convert a data flow diagram of the form shown in Figure 5.10 into a structure chart is to have an input module that gets the analyzed transaction and a dispatch module that invokes the modules for the different transactions. This structure is shown in Figure 5.11.

For smaller systems the analysis and the dispatching can be done in the transaction center module itself, giving rise to a flatter structure. For designing systems that

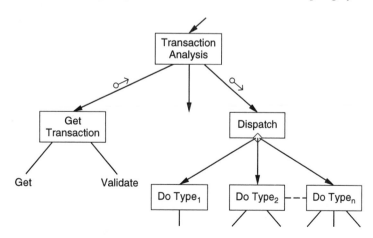

FIGURE 5.11. Factored transaction center.

require transaction analysis, start with a data flow diagram, as in transform analysis, and identify the transform centers. Factor the data flow diagram, as is done in transform analysis. For the modules corresponding to the transform centers, draw the detailed data flow diagram, which will be of the form shown in Figure 5.11. Choose one of the transaction-centered organizations, either one with a separate dispatch and input module or one with all combined in one module. Specify one subordinate module for each transaction. Temptations to combine many similar transactions into one module should be avoided, as it would result in a logically cohesive module. Then each transaction module should be factored, as is done in transform analysis. There are usually many distinct actions that need to be performed for a transaction; they are often specified in the requirements for each transaction. In such cases one subordinate module to the transaction module should be created for each action. Further factoring of action modules into many detailed action modules may be needed. In many transaction-oriented systems, there is a lot of commonality of actions among the different transactions. This commonality should be exploited by sharing the modules at either the action level or the detailed action level.

5.4.7 Discussion

No design methodology reduces design to a series of steps that can be mechanically executed. All design methodologies are, at best, a set of guidelines that, if applied, will most likely give a design that will satisfy the design objectives. The basic objective is to produce a design that is modular and simple. One way to achieve modularity is to have a design that has highly cohesive modules with low coupling between different modules. In other words, the basic objective of the design activity using a function-oriented approach is to create an architecture, that, if implemented, will satisfy the SRS, and that contains cohesive modules that have low coupling with others. Structured design methodology is an approach for creating a design that is likely to satisfy this objective. Now that we have studied the methodology, let us see how it actually achieves this goal.

The basic principle behind the SDM, as with most other methodologies, is problem partitioning, in which the problem is partitioned into subproblems that can be solved separately. In SDM, at the very basic level, this is done by partitioning the system into subsystems that deal with input, subsystems that deal with output, and subsystems that deal with data transformation.

The rationale behind this partitioning is that in many systems, particularly data processing systems, a good part of the system code deals with managing the inputs and outputs. And the components dealing with inputs have to deal with issues of screens, reading data, formats, errors, exceptions, completeness of information, structure of the information, etc. Similarly, the modules dealing with output have to prepare the output in presentation formats, make charts, produce reports, etc.

Hence, for many systems, it is indeed the case that a good part of the software has to deal with inputs and outputs. The actual transformation in the system is frequently not very complex—it is dealing with data and getting it in proper form for performing the transformation or producing the output in the desired form that requires considerable processing.

Structured design methodology clearly separates the system at the very top level into various subsystems, one for managing each major input, one for managing each major output, and one for each major transformation. The modules performing the transformation deal with data at an abstract level, that is, in the form that is most convenient for processing. Due to this, these modules can focus on the conceptual problem of how to perform the transformation without bothering with how to obtain "clean" inputs or how to "present" the output. And these subsystems are quite independent of each other, interacting only through the main module. Hence, this partitioning leads to independent subsystems that do not interact directly, and hence can be designed and developed separately.

This partitioning is at the heart of SDM. In the SDM itself, this partitioning is obtained by starting with a data flow diagram. However, the basic idea of the SDM can be effectively used even if one wants to go directly to the first structure (without going through a DFD).

Besides this central idea, another basic idea behind the SDM is that processing of an input subsystem should be done in a progressive manner, starting from the raw input and progressively applying transformations to eventually reach the most abstract input level (what this input subsystem has to produce). Similar is the case with the structure for the subsystems dealing with outputs. The basic idea here is to separate the different transformations performed on the input before it is in a form ready to be "consumed." And if the SDM is followed carefully, this leads to a "thin and tall" tree as a structure for the input or output subsystem. For example, if an input goes through a series of bubbles in the DFD before it is considered most abstract, the structure for this will be a tree with each node having two subordinates—one obtaining the input data at its level of abstraction and the other a transform module that is used to transform the data to the next abstract level (which is passed to the superordinate). Similar effect can also be obtained by the main input module having one input module and then a series of transform modules, each performing one transform. In other words, the basic idea in SDM for processing an input is to partition the processing of an input into a series of transforms. As long as this approach is followed, it is not terribly important how the structure for the input subsystem is obtained.

These ideas that the methodology uses to partition the problem into smaller modules lead to a structure in which different modules can be solved separately and the connections between modules are minimized (i.e., the coupling is reduced)—most connections between modules go through some coordinate modules. These ideas of structuring are sound and lead to a modular structure. It is important that these fundamental ideas behind the SDM be kept in mind when using this approach. It may not be so important to follow SDM down to the lowest detail. This is how experienced designers use most methodologies; the detailed steps of the methodology are not necessarily followed, but the philosophy is. Many experienced designers do not start with a detailed DFD when using the SDM; they prefer to work directly with the structure or with a very high-level DFD. But they do use these principles when creating the structure. Such an approach is recommended only when one has some experience with the SDM.

5.5   Verification

The output of the system design phase, like the output of other phases in the development process, should be verified before proceeding with the activities of the next phase. Unless the design is specified in a formal, executable language, the design cannot be executed for verification. Other means for verification have to be used. The most common approach for verification is design reviews or inspections (although sometimes these terms mean different things, we will not distinguish between the two). We will discuss this approach here.

5.5.1   Design Reviews

The purpose of design reviews is to ensure that the design satisfies the requirements and is of "good quality." If errors are made during the design process, they will ultimately reflect themselves in the code and the final system. As the cost of removing faults caused by errors that occur during design increases with the delay in detecting the errors, it is best if design errors are detected early, before they manifest themselves in the system. Detecting errors in design is the aim of design reviews.

The system design review process is similar to the other reviews, in that a group of people get together to discuss the design with the aim of revealing design errors or undesirable properties. The review group must include a member of both the system design team and the detailed design team, the author of the requirements document, the author responsible for maintaining the design document, and an independent software quality engineer.

The review can be held in the same manner as the requirement review. Each member studies the design before the meeting, and with the aid of a checklist, marks items that the reviewer feels are incorrect or need clarification. The member asks questions and the chief designer tries to explain the situation. Discussion ensues, and during its course design errors are revealed.

As with any review, it should be kept in mind that the aim of the meeting is to uncover design errors not to try to fix them; fixing is done later. Also, the psychological frame of mind should be healthy, and the designer should not be put in a defensive position. The meeting ends with a list of action items, which are later acted on by the design team. Further reviews may be organized, if needed.

The number of ways in which errors can come in a design is limited only by the creativity of the designer. However, there are some forms of errors that are more often observed. Here we mention some of these [Dun84]. Perhaps the most significant design error is omission or misinterpretation of specified requirements. Clearly, if the system designer has misinterpreted or not accounted for some requirement it will be reflected later as a fault in the system. Sometimes, this design error is caused by ambiguities in the requirements.

There are some other quality factors that are not strictly design errors but that have implications on the reliability and maintainability of the system. An example of this is weak modularity (that is, weak cohesion and/or strong coupling). During reviews, elements of design that are not conducive to modification and expansion or elements that fail to conform to design standards should also be considered "errors."

A Sample Checklist: The use of checklists can be extremely useful for any review. The checklist can be used by each member during private study of the design and during the review meeting. For best results the checklist should be tailored to the project at hand, to uncover problem-specific errors. Here we list a few general items that can be used to construct a checklist for a design review [Dun84]:

- Is each of the functional requirements taken into account?
- Are there analyses to demonstrate that performance requirements can be met?
- Are all assumptions explicitly stated, and are they acceptable?
- Are there any limitations or constraints on the design beyond those in the requirements?
- Are external specifications of each module completely specified?
- Have exceptional conditions been handled?
- Are all the data formats consistent with the requirements?
- Are the operator and user interfaces properly addressed?
- Is the design modular, and does it conform to local standards?
- Are the sizes of data structures estimated? Are provisions made to guard against overflow?

5.5.2   Automated Cross-Checking

One of the important issues during system design verification is whether the design is internally consistent. For example, those modules used in a module that is defined in the system design must also be defined in the design. One should also check whether the interface of a module is consistent with the way in which other modules use it. Other internal consistency issues can be consistent use of data structures and whether data usage is consistent with declaration. These consistency issues can be checked during design review and is usually the place where they are checked if no automated help is available.

However, if the design is expressed in a language designed for machine processing, most consistency checking can be automated. For example, if a language like PDL (described in a later chapter) is used, the design can be "compiled" to check for consistency. Similarly, the method used to express the system design of the case study later in this chapter can be formalized to make it suitable for machine processing. The basic requirement is that the data and module definitions be given in a defined format that is suitable for checking.

5.6 Metrics

We have already seen that the basic purpose of metrics is to provide quantitative data to the management process, which is useful for effective monitoring and control. For this purpose, some quantitative information in the form of metrics flows from each step in the development process to the management process. The first question we must address is what type of metrics from the system design phase are useful to the management process.

The general process metrics of interest from each major step are the cost or total effort spent in the activity, the schedule, and the number and distribution of errors detected by the reviews. The cost and schedule metrics are largely needed for tracking if the project is progressing according to the plan, and if not, what actions should be performed by the project management. These are typically tracked throughout the phase, though at the end of a defined phase, its effect on the overall project schedule and cost can be better understood. If the cost and schedule of the phase is different from what was specified in the plan, this implies that either the project is not being managed properly and hence there are cost and schedule overruns or that the earlier estimates were incorrect. In the first case, closer monitoring and tighter control results. In the second case, cost and schedule are estimated again after the design, and if the revised estimates of cost and schedule are different from earlier estimates, a renegotiation of the project and modification of the plan results.

Quality is monitored generally through reviews. As discussed in Chapter 3, if the process is under statistical control, one can expect density and distribution of errors found by reviews in the design of this project to be similar to what was found in earlier projects. Using the past history about design reviews (i.e., the model that has been built to predict the density and distribution of errors) and the current review data, the quality of the design can be estimated. At least, it can be ensured that the design of this project is as good as the design of earlier projects done using the existing process.

Size is always a product metric of interest, as size is the single most influential factor deciding the cost of the project. As the actual size of the project is known only when the project ends, at early stages the project size is only an estimate. As we saw in Figure 4.1, our ability to estimate size becomes more accurate as development proceeds. Hence, after design, size (and cost) re-estimation are typically done by project management. After design, as all the modules in the system and major data structures are known, the size of the final system can be estimated quite accurately.

For estimating the size, the *total number of modules* is an important metric. This can be easily obtained from the design. By using an average size of a module, from this metric the final size in LOC can be estimated. Alternatively, the size of each module can be estimated, and then the total size of the system will be estimated as the sum of all the estimates. As a module is a small, clearly specified programming unit, estimating the size of a module is relatively easy.

Besides the size metric, the other product metric of interest at design time is design quality. Before we can discuss metrics for quality, we must agree on what is a "good" design. We said earlier that simplicity is the most important design quality attribute, as it directly affects the testability and maintainability of the software. Complexity metrics are frequently used to quantify simplicity.

A possible use of complexity metrics at design time is to improve the design by reducing the complexity of the modules that have been found to be most complex. This will directly improve the testability and maintainability. If the complexity cannot be reduced because it is inherent in the problem, complexity metrics can be used to highlight the more complex modules. As complex modules are generally more error-prone, this feedback can be used by project management to ensure that strict quality assurance is performed on these modules as they evolve. Overall, complexity metrics are of great interest at design time and they can be used to evaluate the quality of design, improve the design, and improve quality assurance of the project. We will describe some of the metrics that have been proposed to quantify the complexity of design and some empirical evidence of their use.

5.6.1 Network Metrics

Network metrics for design focus on the structure chart (mostly the call graph component of the structure chart) and define some metrics of how "good" the structure or network is in an effort to quantify the complexity of the call graph. As coupling of a module increases if it is called by more modules, a good structure is considered one that has exactly one caller. That is, the call graph structure is simplest if it is a pure tree. The more the structure chart deviates from a tree, the more complex the system. Deviation of the tree is then defined as the *graph impurity* of the design [YW78]. Graph impurity can be defined as

$$\text{Graph impurity} = n - e - 1$$

where n is the number of nodes in the structure chart and e is the number of edges. As in a pure tree the total number of nodes is one more than the number of edges, the graph impurity for a tree is 0. Each time a module has a fan-in of more than one, the graph impurity increases. This is the major drawback of this approach; it ignores the common use of some routines like library or support routines. In the design evaluation tool that we use (described later), we do not consider the lowest-level nodes for graph impurity because we believe that most often the lowest-level modules are the ones that are used by many different modules, particularly if the structure chart was factored. Library routines are also at the lowest level of the structure chart (even if they have a structure of their own, it does not show in the structure chart of the application using the routine).

Other network metrics have also been defined. For most of these metrics, significant correlations with properties of interest have not been established. Hence, their use is limited to getting some idea about the structure of the design.

5.6.2   Stability Metrics

We know that maintainability of software is a highly desired quality attribute. Maintenance activity is hard and error-prone as changes in one module require changes in other modules to maintain consistency, which require further changes, and so on. It is clearly desirable to minimize this ripple effect of performing a change, which is largely determined by the structure of the software. *Stability* of a design is a metric that tries to quantify the resistance of a design to the potential ripple effects that are caused by changes in modules [YC85]. The higher the stability of a program design, the better the maintainability of the program. Here we define the stability metric as defined in [YC85].

At the lowest level, stability is defined for a module. From this, the stability of the whole system design can be obtained. The aim is to define a measure so that the higher the measure the less the ripple effect on other modules that in some way are related to this module. The modules that can be affected by change in a module are the modules that invoke the module or share global data (or files) with the module. Any other module will clearly not be affected by change in a module. The potential ripple effect is defined as the total number of assumptions made by other modules regarding the module being changed. Hence, counting the number of assumptions made by other modules is central to determining the stability of a module.

As at design time only the interfaces of modules are known and not their internals, for calculating design stability only the assumptions made about the interfaces need be considered. The interface of a module consists of all elements through which this module can be affected by other modules, i.e., through which this module can be coupled with other modules. Hence, it consists of the parameters of the modules and the global data the module uses. Once the interface is identified, the structure of each element of the interface is examined to determine all the *minimal* entities in this element for which assumptions can be made. The minimal entities generally are the constituents of the interface element. For example, a record is broken into its respective fields as a calling module can make assumptions about a particular field.

For each minimal entity at least two categories of assumptions can be made—about the type of the entity and about the value of the entity. (The assumption about the type is typically checked by a compiler if the programming language supports strong typing.) Each minimal entity in the interface is considered as contributing one assumption in each category. A structured type is considered as contributing one more assumption about its structure in addition to the assumptions its minimal elements contribute. The procedure for determining the stability of a module x and the stability of the program can be broken into a series of steps [YC85]:

Step 1: From the design, analyze the module x and all the modules that call x or share some file or data structure with x, and obtain the following sets.

J_x = {modules that invoke x}

J_x' = {modules invoked by x}

R_{xy} = {passed parameters returned from x to y, $y \in J_x$}

R_{xy}' = {parameters passed from x to y, $y \in J_x'$}

GR_x = {Global data referenced in x}

GD_x = {Global data defined in x}

Note that determining GR_x and GD_x is not always possible when pointers and indirect referencing are used. In that case, a conservative estimate is to be used. From these, for each global data item i, define the set G_i as

$G_i = \{x | i \in GR_x \cup GD_x\}.$

The set G_i represents the set of modules where the global data i is either referenced or defined. Where it is not possible to compute G accurately, the worst case should be taken.

Step 2: For each module x, determine the number of assumptions made by a caller module y about elements in R_{xy} (parameters returned from module x to y) through these steps:

1. Initialize assumption count to 0.

2. If i is a structured data element, decompose it into base types, and increment the assumption count by 1; else consider i minimal.

3. Decompose base types, and if they are structured, increment the count by 1.

4. For each minimal entity i, if module y makes some assumption about the value of i, increment the count by 2; else increment by 1.

Let TP_{xy} represent the total number of assumptions made by a module y about parameters in R_{xy}.

Step 3: Determine TP'_{xy}, the total number of assumptions made by a module y called by the module x about elements in R'_{xy} (parameters passed from module x to y). The method for computation is the same as in the previous step.

Step 4: For each data element $i \in GD_x$ (i.e., the global data elements modified by the module x), determine the total number of assumptions made by other modules about i. These will be the modules other than x that use or modify i, i.e., the set of modules to be considered is $\{G_i - \{x\}\}$. The counting method of step 2 is used. Let TG_x be the total number of assumptions made by other modules about the elements in GD_x.

Step 5: For a module x, the design logical ripple effect (DLRE) is defined as:

$$\text{DLRE}_x = TG_x + \sum_{y \in J_x} TP_{xy} + \sum_{y \in J'_x} TP'_{xy}.$$

DLRE_x is the total number of assumptions made by other modules that interact with x through either parameters or global data. The design stability (DS) of a module x is then defined as

$$\text{DS}_x = 1/(1 + \text{DLRE}_x).$$

Step 6: The program design stability (PDS) is computed as

$$\text{PDS} = 1 \left/ \left(1 + \sum_x \text{DLRE}_x\right)\right..$$

By following this sequence of steps, the design stability of each module and the overall program can be computed. The stability metric, in a sense, is trying to capture the notion of coupling of a module with other modules. The stability metrics can be used to compare alternative designs—the larger the stability, the more maintainable the program. It can also be used to identify modules that are not very stable and that are highly coupled with other modules with a potential of high ripple effect. Changes to these modules will not be easy, hence a redesign can be considered to enhance the stability. Only a limited validation has been done for this metric. Some validation has been given in [YC85], showing that if good programming practices of data encapsulation, etc. are followed, which are generally recognized as enhancing maintainability, then higher program stability results.

Another stability metric was described in [Mye79]. In this formulation, the effect of a change in a module i on another module j is represented as a probability.

For the entire system, the effect of change is captured by the probability of change metrics C. An element $C[i, j]$ of the matrix represents the probability that a change in module i will result in a change in module j. With this matrix the ripple effect of a change in a module can also be easily computed. This can then be used to model the stability of the system. The main problem with this metric is to estimate the elements of the matrix.

5.6.3 Information Flow Metrics

The network metrics of graph impurity had the basis that as the graph impurity increases, the coupling increases. However, it is not a very good approximation for coupling, as coupling of a module increases with the complexity of the interface and the total number of modules a module is coupled with, whether it is the caller or the callee. So, if we want a metric that is better at quantifying coupling between modules, it should handle these. The information flow metrics attempt to define the complexity in terms of the total information flowing through a module, in an effort to quantify coupling.

The earliest work on information flow metrics was done by Henry and Kafura [HK81, HK84]. In their metric, the complexity of a module is considered as depending on the intramodule complexity and the intermodule complexity. The intramodule complexity is approximated by the size of the module in lines of code (which is actually the estimated size at design time). The intermodule complexity of a module depends on the total information flowing in the module (*inflow*) and the total information flowing out of the module (*outflow*). The inflow of a module is the total number of abstract data elements flowing in the module (i.e., whose values are used by the module), and the outflow is the total number of abstract data elements that are flowing out of the module (i.e., whose values are defined by this module and used by other modules). The module design complexity, D_c, is defined as

$$D_c = \text{size} * (\text{inflow} * \text{outflow})^2.$$

The term (inflow $*$ outflow) refers to the total number of combinations of input source and output destination. This term is squared, as the interconnection between the modules is considered a more important factor (compared to the internal complexity) determining the complexity of a module. This is based on the common experience that the modules with more interconnections are harder to test or modify compared to other similar-size modules with fewer interconnections.

The metric defined earlier defines the complexity of a module purely in terms of the total amount of data flowing in and out of the module and the module size. A variant of this was proposed based on the hypothesis that the module complexity depends not only on the information flowing in and out, but also on the number of modules to or from which it is flowing. The module size is considered an insignificant factor, and complexity D_c for a module is defined as [ZZ93]:

$$D_c = \text{fan\_in} * \text{fan\_out} + \text{inflow} * \text{outflow}$$

where fan_in represents the number of modules that call this module and fan_out is the number of modules this module calls.

The main question that arises is how good these metrics are. For "good," we will have to define their purpose, or how we want to use them. Just having a number signifying the complexity is, in itself, of little use, unless it can be used to make some judgement about cost or quality. One way to use the information about complexity could be to identify the complex modules, as these modules are likely to be more error prone and form "hot spots" later, if they are left as is. Once these modules are identified, the design can be evaluated to see if the complexity is inherent in the problem or if the design can be changed to reduce the complexity.

To identify modules that are "extra complex," we will have to define what complexity number is normal. Having a threshold complexity above which a module is considered complex assumes the existence of a globally accepted threshold value. This may not be possible, as designs in different problem domains produce different types of modules. Another alternative is to consider a module against other modules in the current design only, instead of comparing the modules against a prespecified standard. That is, evaluate the complexity of the modules in the design and highlight modules that are, relatively speaking, more complex. In this approach, the criteria for marking a module complex is also determined from the current design.

One such method for highlighting the modules was suggested in [ZZ93]. Let $avg\_complexity$ be the average complexity of the modules in the design being evaluated, and let $std\_deviation$ be the standard deviation in the design complexity of the modules of the system. The proposed method classifies the modules in three catagories: error-prone, complex, and normal. If D_c is the complexity of a module, it can be classified as follows:

Error-prone	If $D_c >$ avg_complexity + std_deviation
Complex	If avg_complexity $< D_c <$ avg_complexity + std_deviation
Normal	Otherwise

Note that this definition of error-prone and complex is independent of the metric definition used to compute the complexity of modules. With this approach, a design can be evaluated by itself, not for overall design quality, but to draw attention to the error-prone and complex modules. This information can then be used to redesign the system to reduce the complexity of these modules (which also results in overall complexity reduction). This approach has been found to be very effective in identifying error-prone modules [ZZ93, MJ95]. In evaluations of some completed projects, it has been shown that error-prone and complex modules together highlight the modules in which most errors occurred [ZZ93, MJ95]. This suggests that for a project, modules thus highlighted during design time point to modules that will be "hot spots" if the design is not improved by reducing their complexity. Another use of this is that even if the complexity of these modules is not reduced (perhaps because the complexity is intrinsic in the problem), identification of error-prone modules can help in quality assurance later; these modules can be required to undergo more rigorous quality assurance.

In some cases it is found that there are some modules with extreme values that adversely affect the threshold defined through average and standard deviation. In such situations, some of the error-prone modules may not be highlighted. To take care of this, an *x-less* approach can be followed in which the top *x* modules with the highest complexity can be eliminated for the purpose of computation of average and standard deviation [ZZ93]. However, how many, if any, modules to ignore is a subjective judgment that must be left to the designer. In some cases, the *x-less* approach shows better results than the earlier approach.

It should be pointed out that this approach cannot be repeatedly applied as the design evolves. That is, once the modules have been highlighted by this approach and the design modified, using this approach to highlight modules again on the modified design will not yield good results. There is always an average and standard deviation, so as the design is improved and made less complex, using average and standard deviation to separate modules as complex and error-prone will be misleading. For example, if after the design has been modified to reduce the complexity of the error-prone or complex modules, the design might be such that complexity of most modules is similar. In this situation, this approach will highlight all those modules whose complexity is more than the average, even though all modules are close to average complexity, which is clearly misleading. Hence, this approach should be used only for evaluating the first few designs of a system.

5.7 Summary

The *design* of a system is a plan for a solution such that if the plan is implemented, the implemented system will satisfy the requirements of the system. The goal of the *design process* is to find the best possible design. The most important criteria to judge a design are *verifiability, reliability*, and *maintainability*. The design activity is a two-level process. The first level produces the *system design* which defines the components needed for the system, and how the components interact with each other. The *detailed design* refines the system design, by providing more description of the processing logic of components and data structures, so that the design can be easily implemented. A design methodology is a systematic approach to creating a design. Most design methodologies concentrate on system design.

Problem partitioning is a basic principle for guiding the design process. The goal is to effectively handle the complexity of designing large systems by partitioning the problem into separate pieces so that each piece can be solved separately. Problem partitioning depends on the effective use of *abstraction*. Abstraction of a component is a view of the component that extracts the essential information relevant to the particular purpose and ignores the rest of the information. It allows a module to be specified by its external behavior only. Abstraction permits a designer to concentrate on one component at a time by using the abstraction of other components to decide the interaction between components.

Modularity is a means of problem partitioning in software design. A system is considered modular if each component has a well-defined abstraction and if change in one component has minimal impact on other components. Two criteria used for deciding the modules during design are *coupling* and *cohesion*. Coupling is a measure of interdependence between modules, while cohesion is a measure of the strength with which the different elements of a module are related. There are different levels of cohesion, functional and type cohesion being the highest levels and incidental being the lowest. In general, other properties being equal, coupling should be minimized and cohesion maximized.

The structured design method is one of the best known methods for developing the design of a software system. This method creates a structure chart that can be used to implement the system. The goal is to produce a structure where the modules have minimum dependence on each other (low coupling) and a high level of cohesion. The basic methodology has four steps: (1) restate the problem as a data flow graph; (2) identify the most abstract input and output data elements; (3) perform first-level factoring, which is done by specifying an input module for each of the most abstract inputs, an output module for each of the most abstract outputs, and a transform module for each of the central transforms; and (4) factor each of the input, output, and transform modules.

The methodology does not reduce the problem of design to a series of steps that can be followed blindly. The essential goal is to get a clear hierarchical structure. A number of design heuristics can be used to improve the structure resulting from the application of the basic methodology. The basic guiding principles are simplicity, high cohesion, and low coupling.

Every phase in the waterfall model must end with verification of the output produced in that phase. In the system design phase the output is the *system design document*, which contains the major data structures and the module definitions. The most common method for verification is *design reviews*, in which a team of persons reviews the design. If a design language is used for design specification and if tools are available to process designs expressed in that language, then some amount of consistency checking can be done automatically by these tools.

There are a number of metrics that can be used to evaluate function-oriented designs. Network metrics evaluate the structure chart and consider deviation from the tree as the metric signifying the quality of design. The stability metric we discussed tries to quantify how resistant the design is to the ripple effects caused by changes by explicitly counting the number of assumptions modules make about each other. The information flow complexity metrics define design complexity based on the internal complexity of the module and the number of connections between modules. We have used information flow complexity for the evaluation of the design of the case study, using a tool for metrics extraction. The tool is available to the readers from the home page of the book.

Exercises

1. Consider a program containing many modules. If a global variable x must be used to share data between two modules A and B, how would you design the modules to minimize coupling?

2. List a set of poor programming practices, based on the criteria of coupling and cohesion.

3. What is the cohesion of the following module? How would you change the module to increase cohesion?

    ```
    procedure file (file_ptr, file_name, op_name);
    begin
        case op_name of
            "open": perform activities for opening the file.
            "close": perform activities for opening the file.
            "print": print the file
        end case
    end
    ```

4. If some existing modules are to be re-used in building a new system, will you use a top-down or bottom-up approach? Why?

5. If a module has logical cohesion, what kind of coupling is this module likely to have with others?

6. What is the difference between a flow chart and a structure chart?

7. Draw the structure chart for the following program:

    ```
    main();
    {    int x, y;
         x = 0; y = 0;
         a(); b(); }
    a()
    {    x = x+y; y = y+5; }
    b()
    {    x = x+5; y = y+x; a(); }
    ```
    How would you modify this program to improve the modularity?

8. If a '+' or a '*' is present between two output streams from a transform in a data flow graph, state some specific property about the module for that transform.

9. Use the structured design methodology to produce a design for the following:

   (a) A system to convert ASCII to EBSDIC.

   (b) A system to analyze your diet when given your daily intake (and some data files about different types of food and recommended intakes).

   (c) A system to do student registration in the manner it is done at your college.

   (d) A system to manage the inventory at a hardware store.

   (e) A system for a drug store that will manage inventory, keep track of expiration dates, and track allergy records of patients to avoid issuing medicines that might be harmful.

   (f) A system that acts as a calculator with only basic arithmetic functions.

10. Is this statement true: "If we follow the structured design methodology (without applying any heuristics), the resulting structure will always have one transform module for each bubble in the data flow graph"? Explain your answer.

11. Given a structure with high fan-out, how would you convert it to a structure with a low fan-out?

12. What are the major metrics that can be used to evaluate system design? Which of these can be used to better approximate the size of the final system, and how?

13. What are the major methods for verifying a design? If the design is expressed in a formal language, can an automated tool help in verification, and in what manner?

14. Design an experiment to study whether the information flow metrics and stability metrics are correlated.

15. If you have all the metrics data available for design, how will you use this data? Specify your objectives, the metrics you will use, how you will interpret the value, and what possible actions you will take based on the interpretation.

CASE STUDY

Structured Design

Data Flow Diagram: This is the first step in the structured design method. In our case study, there are two inputs: file1 and file2. Three outputs are required: the time table, the conflict table, and the explanations for the schedule. A high-level data flow diagram of this problem is given in Figure 5.12.

The diagram is fairly clear. First we get from file1 the information about classrooms, lecture times, and courses, and we validate their format. The validated input from file1 is used for cross-validating information in file2. After validating the file2 input, we get an array of valid course records (with preferences, etc.) that must be scheduled. Because PG courses have to be scheduled before UG courses, these course records are separated into different groups: PG courses with preferences, UG courses with preferences, PG courses with no preference, and UG courses with no preference. This separated course list is the input to the schedule transform, the output of which is the three desired outputs.

The most abstract input and most abstract output are fairly obvious here. The "separated course schedule" is the most abstract input and the three outputs of the schedule transform are the most abstract outputs. There is only one central transform: schedule.

First-Level Factoring: The first-level structure chart can easily be obtained and is shown in Figure 5.13. In the structure chart, instead of having one output module for each of the three outputs, as is shown in the data flow diagram, we have only one output module, which then invokes three output modules for the different outputs.

Factoring the Input and Output Modules: The output module does not need any factoring. According to the design methodology, the input module get_validated_ input will have one input module to get the array of validated course records and one transform module to separate into course groups. This input module can then be further factored into three input modules to get different validated inputs from file1, one input module to get data from file2, and one module for validating the file2 data. Because the data from file1 is also needed for the central transform, we modify the structure of the input branch. The structure chart for the input branch is shown in Figure 5.14.

Factoring the Central Transform: Now the central transform has to be factored. According to the requirements, PG courses have to be given preference over UG courses, and the highest priority of each course must be satisfied. This means that the courses with no priority should be scheduled after the courses with priority. Hence, we have four major subordinate modules to the central transform: schedule PG courses with preferences, schedule UG courses with preferences, schedule PG

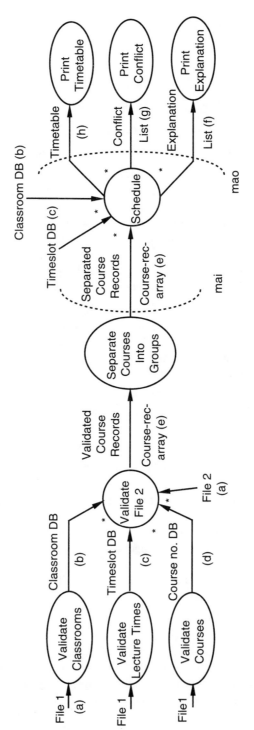

FIGURE 5.12. Data flow diagram for the case study.

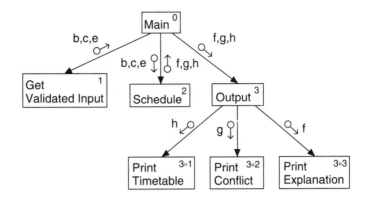

FIGURE 5.13. First level factoring.

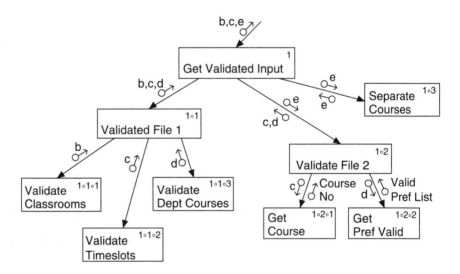

FIGURE 5.14. Factoring of the input branch.

courses with no preferences, and schedule UG courses with no preferences. The structure of the central transform is shown in Figure 5.15.

These can then be combined into a structure chart for the system. The overall structure chart is shown in Figure 5.16. This structure chart gives an overall view of the strategy for structuring the programs. Further details about each module will evolve during detailed design and coding.

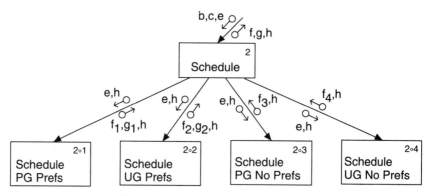

FIGURE 5.15. Factoring the central transform.

Design Analysis

Requirements Tracing

Here we list each major requirement and then list the modules in the structure chart that implement that requirement. The tracing shows that each requirement has been handled in the design:

1. No more than one course should be scheduled at the same time in the same room: sched_pg_pref, sched_ug_pref, sched_pg_no_pref, sched_ug_no_pref

2. The class capacity should be more than the expected enrollment of the course: sched_pg_pref, sched_ug_pref, sched_pg_no_pref, sched_ug_no_pref

3. Preference is given to PG courses over UG courses for scheduling: sched_pg_pref, sched_ug_pref, sched_pg_no_pref, sched_ug_no_pref

4. The courses should be scheduled so that the highest possible priority of an instructor is given: sched_pg_pref, sched_ug_pref, sched_pg_no_pref, sched_ug_no_pref
   If no priority is specified, any room and time can be assigned: sched_pg_no_pref, sched_ug_no_pref

5. If any priority is incorrect, it is to be discarded: get_pre_valid

6. No two PG courses should be scheduled at the same time: sched_pg_pref, sched_pg_no_pref

7. If no preference is specified for a course, the course should be scheduled in any manner that does not violate the preceding constraints: sched_pg_no_pref, sched_ug_no_pref

8. The validity of the data in input_file1 should be checked where possible: validate_file1 and its subordinates.

9. The data in input file2 should be checked for validity against the data provided in input file1: validate_file2

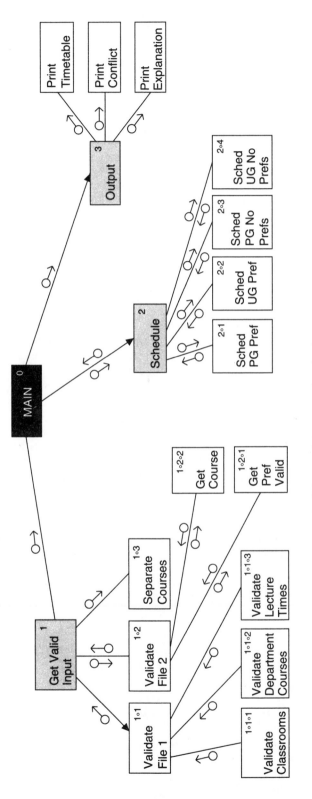

FIGURE 5.16. Structure chart for the system.

Analysis Using Information Flow Metrics

Based on the structure chart, the design of the system was first specified completely: this required formally specifying the data structures and all the modules. For each module, we specified the purpose of the module, its interface, the modules it invokes, and the estimated size of the module (in LOC). This formed the first version of the design document.

The first thing that could be noted was that when specifying a complete design from the structure chart, the design usually expands. For example, we found that for supporting the module for scheduling the UG courses with preferences (SchedUg-Prefs) a lot more needs to be done. The reason is as follows. The UG courses with preferences are scheduled before PG courses with no preferences. However, PG courses are to be given preferences and no two PG courses can be scheduled in the same time slot. Hence, a UG course should not be allotted a slot that makes a PG course "unschedulable." This requires that "safety" of a room and time for a UG course should be checked before allocation.

For this, another data structure was specified. Essentially, a three-dimensional linked list was defined, which contained for each PG course the list of time slots for which it could be allotted, and for each time slot a list of all rooms where it could be allotted was maintained. This structure can be used for checking the safety—an allocation should not make a PG course unschedulable. In addition to this, a lot of utility routines needed to be defined to support the other functions, e.g., sort_rooms(), get_index(), and chk_fmt_course_no().

The complete first version of the design is not given here, but it can be obtained from the home page of the book (the addresss is given in the Preface). Here, we specify just the portions that are different from the final version of the design, which is given later. The basic difference was in how UG courses with preferences were scheduled. The data structures and the relevant modules for this portion are given here. If the reader wants, the final design document, given later in this chapter, can be used to understand the first version by "replacing" appropriate portions related to checking of safety by the portions given here.

The specification language is simple and clear from the design fragment given here and the complete design given later. It is essentially oriented toward C and is such that the design can easily be converted to module headers for C programs with some simple editing.

```
/**************************************************************************/
/* Following are for reserving slots for PgNoPrefs courses. A 3-D linked list
 * is maintained. For each PgNoPref course (in the list of all courses), list
 * of time slots is kept. For each time slot, list of possible rooms is kept.
 * Using this structure, before allotting a UgPref course, it can be checked
 * if by allotting it we are making a PgNoPref course unallottable. If that
 * is the case, that allotment for the UG course is not done */
```

```
typedef struct R_Node /* list of indices into class room_db; contains rooms
                  with capacity greater than enrol of PgNoPref course */
{
     int r_index;
     struct R_Node  *next;
}r_node;

typedef struct T_Slot_Node  /* list of possible time slots for pg_no_prefs */
{
     int time_slot;
     r_node *roomlist;
     struct T_Slot_Node *next;
}t_slot_node;

typedef struct Pg_Res_Node                 /* list of pg_no_pref courses */
{
     int pgcourse;
     t_slot_node *time_slots;
     struct Pg_Res_Node *next;
}pg_res_node;

/*---------------------------------------------*/

/* Schedule UG courses with preferences. This is not straightforward. Before
 * alloting a <timeslot, classroom>, it has to check if this allotment is "safe,"
 * i.e., the schedulability of PG courses with no prefs is not disturbed.
 * Does so by "simulating" scheduling of pg_no_pref courses - an allotment
 * is safe if the same no. can be still be scheduled after this allotment */

sched_ug_pref(IN:SchCourses,PgAlloc, OUT:ConflLst,ExplnLst, IN_OUT:TimeTable)
course *SchCourses;
int *PgAlloc;
error *ConflLst;
error *ExplnLst;
int **TimeTable;
{
    SUBORDINATES :get_room(),is_safe_allotment(),
                    initialize_pg_reserve(), update_pg_reserve();

    SIZE:100
}


/* Initializes the 3-D linked data structure - pg_reserve */
initialize_pg_reserve(IN:PgAlloc, SchCourses, OUT:pg_reserve)
int PgAlloc[];
```

```
course SchCourses[];
pg_res_node pg_reserve;
{
    SUBORDINATES :get_room();
    SIZE:50
}


/* Updates the PG reserve after a UG course with preference is allotted */
update_pg_reserve(IN:time,roomno,IN_OUT:pg_reserve)
int time,roomno;
pg_res_node pg_reserve;
{
    SUBORDINATES :
    SIZE:50
}



/* Checks if an allotment for a UG course with preference is safe, i.e.
 * the schedulability of PG courses with no preferences is not affected */

int is_safe_allotment(IN:time_slot,roomno,pg_reserve)
int time_slot,roomno;
pg_res_node pg_reserve;
{
    SUBORDINATES :
    SIZE: 80
}


/****************************************************************************/
```

The complete first version design was then analyzed using information flow metrics described earlier in the chapter. We followed the approach of comparing modules of the design among themselves and then highlight the "error-prone" and "complex modules" (as described earlier). In the case study we used the metric where complexity of a module is defined as $D_c = fan\_in * fan\_out + inflow * outflow$. The definition of error-prone and complex is as given earlier, except that we also use size for classification; the size of the module must also be above average or above (average + standard deviation) for it to be classified as complex or error prone. A locally developed tool called dmetric was used to extract the information flow metrics. (The tool is available to the readers from the home page.) The overall metrics for the design and the metrics for the modules highlighted by the tool are given here.

```
-----------------------------------------------------------------
OVERALL METRICS
-----------------------------------------------------------------
#modules: 35  Total size: 1330    Avg. size: 38   Std.Deviation: 27
```

```
Total complexity: 595        Avg. complexity: 17   Std.Deviation: 33

Deviation of the structure chart from a tree  = 0
(without considering leaves)


------------------------------------------------------------------------

 ERROR-PRONE MODULES
------------------------------------------------------------------------

8) sched_ug_pref
     call_in: 1   call_out: 4   inflow: 5   outflow:13   size:100
     design complexity:   69


------------------------------------------------------------------------

 COMPLEX  MODULES
------------------------------------------------------------------------

5) validate_file2
     call_in: 1   call_out: 4   inflow: 4   outflow: 8   size:100
     design complexity:   36

7) sched_pg_pref
     call_in: 1   call_out: 1   inflow: 1   outflow: 6   size:75
     design complexity:    7

13) is_safe_allotment
     call_in: 1   call_out: 0   inflow: 3   outflow: 1   size:80
     design complexity:    3

15) validate_classrooms
     call_in: 1   call_out: 5   inflow: 3   outflow: 7   size:80
     design complexity:   26

16) validate_dept_courses
     call_in: 1   call_out: 3   inflow: 2   outflow: 5   size:75
     design complexity:   13

17) validate_lec_times
     call_in: 1   call_out: 3   inflow: 2   outflow: 5   size:70
     design complexity:   13
------------------------------------------------------------------------
```

This data flow analysis clearly points out that the module to schedule UG courses with preferences is the most complex, with a complexity considerably higher than the average. It also shows that the overall structure is a tree (with a 0 deviation). Hence, we considered the structure to be all right. Based on this analysis, parts of the design dealing with scheduling of UG courses was re-examined in an effort to reduce complexity.

During analysis we observed that much of the complexity was due to the 3-D linked data structure being used for determining safety. Through discussions, we then developed a different approach for determining safety. The idea was that instead of using a separate data structure, before allocating a UG course, we will "simulate" the scheduling of the PgNoPref courses, using the regular function for scheduling these courses. If the number of courses the function sched_pg_no_prefs() returns is the same before and after the planned UG course scheduling, then the current allocation is safe. For this approach, we just have to make sure that is_safe_allotment() invokes sched_pg_no_prefs() with temporary data structures such that the actual timetable is not affected during this "simulation." The design was then modified to incorporate this approach. On analyzing the complexity again, we found that this approach reduced the complexity of the sched_ug_pref() module significantly and the complexity of this module was now similar to complexity of other modules. Overall, we considered the modified design satisfactory. The final design is given soon; it can also be obtained from the home page.

This demonstrates how highlighting of "hot spots" can be used to focus the attention of the designer or analysts and to improve the quality of the design. Note that this is done before the coding has started, which makes it very efficient from the point of view of cost. For example, if the same decision of changing the method of determining safety was taken after the code was developed, it would require that some parts of the old code be discarded, new code developed, and the design document changed to reflect the new design. All this will require considerably more effort than what was spent to change the design. Metrics-based analysis can also be used for monitoring by the project management; a quick look at the results of complexity and structure analysis will reveal if the structure and complexity are "acceptable" or if the design needs improvement.

Design Specification

```
/*  Revised version. Last modification 24 Feb 1995    */

/* This software is for scheduling a set of courses offered by the Computer
 * Science Department - requirements of which are given in the SRS.
 * The design was done using structured design methodology, and the structure
 * chart is given elsewhere. This design document specifies the design formally.
 * It contains all descriptions of the major data structures and the modules
 * that are needed to implement a solution. This design was analyzed using
 * the dmetric tool for analyzing information flow complexity and was
 * found to be acceptable */

/******************************************************************/
/* DATA DEFINITIONS        */
/******************************************************************/
```

```
typedef char courseno[MAX_COURSENO_SIZE];
typedef char timeslot[MAX_TIMESLOT_SIZE];

typedef struct {
     int room_no;
     int capacity;
} room;

typedef struct LstNode {  /* A general linked list of integers */
   int index;      /* typically index in some DB will be kept */
   struct LstNode *next;
} lstnode;

typedef struct {      /* information about a course to be scheduled */
     int cnum;                /* index in CourseDB of this course */
     int enrol;               /* expected enrollment */
     lstnode *prefs; /* list of prefs, kept as index in timeslotDB */
} course;

typedef struct {              /* to produce conflict or explanation info */
     int err_code;
     int cnum;              /* course no. for which error found */
     int roomno;            /* room no. may be needed in some error message */
     lstnode *prefs;        /* lst of prefs (time slots) */
} error;


/*--------------------------------------------------*/

FILE *file1,*file2; /* input files */

courseno CourseDB[MAX_COURSES];     /* List of valid courses */
room ClassroomDB[MAX_ROOMS]; /* List of valid classrooms */
timeslot TimeslotDB[MAX_TIMES];     /* List of valid time slots */
course SchCourses[MAX_COURSES]; /* List of courses to be scheduled */

int TimeTable[MAX_ROOMS][MAX_TIMES]; /* rows are indices in ClassroomDB;
                        ●       columns in TimeslotDB */

int PgAlloc[MAX_TIMES]; /* Time slots occupied by PG courses. An entry is -ve
                  if not allocated to a PG course, +ve otherwise. Used
                             for checking  conflicts while schduling PG courses*/

error ExplnLst[MAX_COURSES]; /* expln for each unschedulable pref */
error ConflLst[MAX_COURSES]; /* expln for unschedulable courses */
```

```
/******************************************************************/
/*    MODULE SPECIFICATIONS    */
/******************************************************************/

main(IN:file1,file2)
char *file1, *file2;
{
    SUBORDINATES : get_validated_input(),schedule(),print_output();
    SIZE: 10
}


/******************************************************************/

/* This module validates the contents of file1 and file2 and produces
 * lists for valid courses, classrooms, time slots, and courses to be
 * scheduled. If errors are found in the input file format, it exits if
 * scheduling is not possible, else ignores the erroneous data */

get_validated_input(IN:fd1,fd2, OUT:TimeslotDB,ClassroomDB,CourseDB,SchCourses)
FILE *fd1,*fd2;
timeslot *TimeslotDB;
room *ClassroomDB;
courseno *CourseDB;
course *SchCourses;
{
    SUBORDINATES :validate_file1(),validate_file2(),separate_courses();
    SIZE: 20
}


/*----------------------------------------------*/

/* Top-level module to schedule courses. Besides timetable, it
 * gives explanation for courses/prefs that could not be satisfied */

schedule(IN:ClassroomDB,TimeslotDB,CourseDB,SchCourses,
         OUT:TimeTable,ConflLst,ExplnLst)
room *ClassroomDB;
timeslot *TimeslotDB;
courseno *CourseDB;
course *SchCourses;
int **TimeTable;
error *ConflLst;
error *ExplnLst;
{
    SUBORDINATES : sched_pg_pref(), sched_ug_pref(),
                   sched_ug_no_pref(), sched_pg_no_pref();
```

```
    SIZE:10
}

/*---------------------------------------------*/

/* Top-level Print module to  produce all outputs */

print_output(IN:TimeTable,ExplnLst,ConflLst)
int **TimeTable;
error *ConflLst;
error *ExplnLst;
{
    SUBORDINATES :print_TimeTable(), print_explanation(), print_conflict();
    SIZE:10
}

/******************************************************************/

validate_file1(IN:fd,OUT:ClassroomDB,CourseDB,TimeslotDB)
FILE *fd;
room *ClassroomDB;
char *CourseDB;
char *TimeslotDB;
{
    SUBORDINATES :validate_classrooms(), validate_dept_courses(),
        validate_lec_times();
    SIZE: 10
}

/*---------------------------------------------*/

validate_file2(IN:fd, OUT:SchCourses)
FILE *fd;
course *SchCourses;
{
    SUBORDINATES :get_course_index(),chk_dup_sched_course(),
                      get_next_line(),form_pref_list();

    SIZE: 100
}

/*---------------------------------------------*/

/* Rearrange courses in this order:  PG courses with preferences, UG courses
 * with prefs, PG courses with no prefs, UG courses with no prefs */

separate_courses(IN:CourseDB,IN_OUT:SchCourses)
```

```
char *CourseDB;
course *SchCourses;
{
    SUBORDINATES :
    SIZE:60
}


/*-------------------------------------------*/


/* Schedules PG courses with prefs - allots highest possible preference
 * (records in PgAlloc also). For prefs it cannot satisfy, makes entry in ExplnLst.
 * If cannot schedule a course, makes entry in ConflLst */


sched_pg_pref(IN:SchCourses,OUT:TimeTable,ExplnLst,ConflLst,PgAlloc)
course *SchCourses;
int **TimeTable;
error *ExplnLst;
error *ConflLst;
int *PgAlloc;
{
    SUBORDINATES :get_room();
    SIZE:75
}


/*-------------------------------------------*/


/* Schedule UG courses with preferences. This is not straightforward.
 * Before alloting a <timeslot, classroom>, it has to check if this allotment
 * is "safe," i.e., the schedulability of PG courses with no prefs is not disturbed.
 * It does so by first "simulating" a scheduling of pg_no_pref courses - an allotment
 * is safe if the same no. can be still be scheduled after this allocation */


sched_ug_pref(IN:SchCourses,PgAlloc, OUT:ConflLst,ExplnLst, IN_OUT:TimeTable)
course *SchCourses;
int *PgAlloc;
error *ConflLst;
error *ExplnLst;
int **TimeTable;
{
    SUBORDINATES :get_room(),PgNoPrefSchlable(),is_safe_allotment();

    SIZE:100
}


/*-------------------------------------------*/


/* Schedule PG courses with no prefs. Returns the number of courses scheduled */
int sched_pg_no_pref(IN:SchCourses,PgAlloc, OUT:ConflLst,TimeTable)
```

```
course *SchCourses;
error *ConflLst;
int *PgAlloc;
int **TimeTable;
{

    SUBORDINATES :get_room();
    SIZE:50
}

/*---------------------------------------------*/

sched_ug_no_pref(IN:SchCourses, OUT:ConflLst, IN_OUT:TimeTable)
course *SchCourses;
int **TimeTable;
error *ConflLst;
{
    SUBORDINATES :get_room();
    SIZE:40
}

/************************************************************************/

/* Checks if an allotment for a UG course with preference is safe, i.e.
 * the schedulability of PG courses with no preferences is not affected */

int is_safe_allotment(IN:time_slot,roomno,SchedPgNoPrefs,TimeTable,PgAlloc,SchCourses)
int time_slot,roomno;
int SchedPgNoPrefs; /* initially  schedulable pg_no_pref courses */
int **TimeTable;
int *PgAlloc;
course *SchCourses;
{
    SUBORDINATES : PgNoPrefSchlable();
    SIZE:50
}


/*---------------------------------------------*/

/* Returns the number of schedulable pg_no_pref courses without modifying
 * the timetable and PgAlloc */

int PgNoPrefSchlable(IN:TimeTable,PgAlloc,SchCourse)
int TimeTable[][MAX_TIMES];
int *PgAlloc;
course *SchCourse;
```

```
{
   SUBORDINATES : sched_pg_no_pref();
   SIZE : 15

}


/**********************************************************************/

/* Get validated classroom info and build ClassroomDB.  If any error, continue
 * parsing, ignoring that room no. Room records sorted in increasing capacity */

validate_classrooms(IN:fd,OUT:ClassroomDB)
FILE *fd;
room *ClassroomDB;
{
    SUBORDINATES :get_next_line(),chk_fmt_room_no(),
  chk_range_cap(),chk_dup_room(),sort_rooms();
    SIZE:80
}

/*--------------------------------------------*/

/* Get validated list of courses from File 1*/
validate_dept_courses(IN:fd,OUT:CourseDB)
FILE *fd;
char *CourseDB;
{
    SUBORDINATES :get_next_line(),chk_dup_course(),chk_fmt_course_no();
    SIZE:75
}

/*--------------------------------------------*/

/* Get validated time slots from File 1*/
validate_lec_times(IN:fd,OUT:TimeslotDB)
FILE *fd;
timeslot *TimeslotDB;
{
    SUBORDINATES :get_next_line(),chk_fmt_time_slot(),
  chk_dup_slot();
    SIZE:70
}

/*--------------------------------------------*/

 /* Forms a list of validated preferences in the given order  */
form_pref_list(IN:line,TimeslotDB,OUT:pref_list)
char *line;
```

```
timeslot *TimeslotDB;
lstnode *pref_list;
{
    SUBORDINATES :
    SIZE: 45
}



/*******************************************************************/


print_TimeTable(IN:TimeslotDB,ClassroomDB,CourseDB,TimeTable)
timeslot *TimeslotDB;
room *ClassroomDB;
courseno *CourseDB;
int **TimeTable;
{
    SUBORDINATES :
    SIZE:40
}

/*---------------------------------------------*/

/* Print the reasons why higher prefs for a course could not be honored */
print_explanation(IN:ExplnLst,CourseDB,TimeslotDB,TimeTable,ClassroomDB)
error *ExplnLst;
courseno *CourseDB;
timeslot *TimeslotDB;
room *ClassroomDB;
{
    SUBORDINATES :
    SIZE:50
}

/*---------------------------------------------*/

/* Print the list of courses that are not scheduled in the final table
 * and specify the conflicts that prevented their scheduling */

print_conflict(IN:ConflLst,CourseDB)
error *ConflLst;
courseno *CourseDB;
{
    SUBORDINATES :
    SIZE:50
}
```

```
/***********************************************************************
 *                    Utility Routines                                *
 ***********************************************************************/


/* Check if capacity of a room is in the range [10 ... 300] */
int chk_range_cap(IN:cap)
int cap;
{ SUBORDINATES : SIZE:10 }


/* Sort the room records in increasing order of capacity */
sort_rooms(IN_OUT:ClassroomDB)
room ClassroomDB;
{ SUBORDINATES : SIZE:20 }


/* Checks if the room_no given already exists in the ClassroomDB */
int chk_dup_room(IN:ClassroomDB,room_no)
room *ClassroomDB;
char *room_no;
{ SUBORDINATES : SIZE:20 }


/* Check whether this course_no already exists in the CourseDB */
int chk_dup_course(IN:CourseDB,course_no)
courseno *CourseDB;
char *course_no;
{ SUBORDINATES : SIZE:20 }


/* check whether this time slot is a duplicate */
int chk_dup_slot(IN:TimeslotDB,time_slot)
timeslot *TimeslotDB;
char *time_slot;
{ SUBORDINATES : SIZE:20 }


/* Returns the index of the course number in CourseDB */
get_course_index(IN:course_no,CourseDB, OUT:course_index)
int course_index;
char *course_no;
courseno *CourseDB;
{ SUBORDINATES : SIZE:15 }


/* checks if a course number is a duplicate */
int duplicate_course(IN:CourseDB,cnum)
courseno *CourseDB;
char *cnum;
{ SUBORDINATES : SIZE:20 }


/* returns the index of the smallest room that can accommodate the course */
int get_room(IN:ClassroomDB,enrol)
```

```
room *ClassroomDB;
int enrol;
{ SUBORDINATES : SIZE:15 }


/* returns first nonempty line from the input file */
get_next_line(IN:fd,OUT:line)
FILE *fd;
char *line;
{ SUBORDINATES : SIZE : 25 }


/* checks the format of the room number */
int chk_fmt_room_no(IN:room_no)
char *room_no;
{ SUBORDINATES : SIZE: 25 }


/* checks the format of the given course number */
int chk_fmt_course_no(IN:course_no)
char *course_no;
{ SUBORDINATES : SIZE : 25 }


/* checks the format of the given time slot */
int chk_fmt_time_slot(IN:time_slot)
char *time_slot;
{ SUBORDINATES : SIZE : 25 }


/* checks whether given SchCourses_index is a duplicate occurrence */
int chk_dup_sched_course(IN:SchCourses,SchCourses_index)
course SchCourses;
int SchCourses_index;
{ SUBORDINATES : SIZE : 25 }
```

6

Object-Oriented Design

In Chapter 5, we mentioned that one of the general principles for designing is abstraction, and that abstraction in software generally takes two forms—functional abstraction and data abstraction. The structured design methodology that we discussed uses functional abstraction. It is essentially a top-down functional refinement technique that identifies the hierarchy of modules, with each module supporting some functional abstraction so that the hierarchy implements the overall functional specifications of the system. The system components that the SDM identifies are modules supporting functional abstraction.

In this chapter we discuss a different approach for system design based on data abstraction. In this approach, called object-oriented (OO) design, the basic system component is a module that supports data abstraction. The goal of design is to identify the objects that the system contains and the relationships and interactions between the objects so that the system implements the specifications.

Object-oriented approaches are getting a lot of attention these days. Many claims have been made in support of object-oriented approaches. One main claimed advantage of using object orientation is that an OO model closely represents the problem domain, which makes it easier to produce and understand designs. In addition, as requirements change, the objects in a system are less immune to these changes, thereby permitting changes more easily. Due to inheritance and close association of objects in design to problem domain entities, it is also believed that OO designs will encourage more re-use, i.e., new applications can use existing modules more effectively, thereby reducing development cost and cycle time. Reuse is considered one of the major advantages of object orientation as one of the by-products of using this paradigm properly is that it allows the building of object libraries that can be used later by other software developers. For this advanced topic of re-use in object-oriented software, the reader is referred to [G+94] which discusses how patterns can be used to enhance re-use. Finally, the object-oriented approach is believed to be more natural, which provides nice structures for thinking and abstracting and leads to modular designs. It should, however, be pointed out there is currently little empirical evidence to support (or contradict) these claims. Regardless of lack of empirical evidence, these claims are believed by many and use of object-oriented approaches is growing very rapidly.

The object-oriented design approach is fundamentally different from the function-oriented design approaches primarily due to the different abstraction that is used. It requires a different way of thinking and partitioning. It can be said that thinking in object-oriented terms is most important for producing truly object-oriented designs.

In this chapter, we will discuss some important concepts that form the basis of object-oriented design (OOD). Then we'll define the notation that can be used while doing an object-oriented design and a method of specifying the design produced. Then we describe one OOD methodology. Though methodologies are useful, the most important issue while doing any activity that needs creativity is to understand the final objective (i.e., what needs to be done), the guiding principles for performing the activity, and methods for evaluating the output. Therefore, though many OOD methodologies have been proposed that differ somewhat from each other, we will discuss only one. Then we'll discuss some metrics that are applicable on OOD and that can be used to evaluate the quality of design. We do not discuss verification methods, as the design verification methods discussed in the previous chapter are general methods that can be used regardless of the approach used for producing the design. Finally, as with other chapters, we'll end by doing the OO design of the case study and giving the complete specification of the OOD for the case study. Before we discuss OO design, let us understand the relationship between OO analysis and OO design.

6.1   OO Analysis and OO Design

Pure object-oriented development requires that object-oriented techniques be used during the analysis, design, and implementation of the system. However, much of the focus of the object-oriented approach to software development has been on OOA and OOD. Various methods have been proposed for OOA and OOD, many of which propose a combined analysis and design technique. We will refer to a combined method as *OOAD*. For properties of the various techniques that have been proposed, the reader is referred to [MP92]. When object orientation is used in analysis as well as design, the boundary between OOA and OOD is blurred. This is particularly true in methods that combine analysis and design. One reason for this blurring is the similarity of basic constructs (i.e., objects and classes) that are used in OOA and OOD. Though there is no agreement about what parts of the

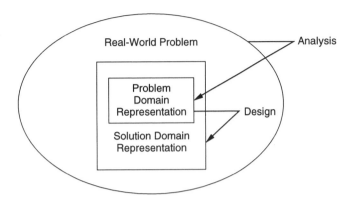

FIGURE 6.1. Relationship between OOA and OOD.

object-oriented development process belong to analysis and what parts to design, there is some general agreement about the domains of the two activities.

The fundamental difference between OOA and OOD is that the former models the problem domain, leading to an understanding and specification of the problem, while the latter models the solution to the problem. That is, analysis deals with the problem domain, while design deals with the solution domain. However, in OOAD it is believed that the problem domain representation created by OOA is generally subsumed in the solution domain representation. That is, the solution domain representation, created by OOD, generally contains much of the representation created by OOA, and more. This is shown in Figure 6.1 [MP92].

As the objective of both OOA and OOD is to model some domain, frequently the OOA and OOD processes (i.e., the methodologies) and the representations look quite similar. This contributes to the blurring of the boundaries between analysis and design. It is often not clear where analysis ends and design begins. The separating line is a matter of perception, and different people have different views on it. The lack of clear separation between analysis and design can also be considered one of the strong points of the object-oriented approach—the transition from analysis to design is "seamless." This is also the main reason OOAD methods—where analysis and design are both performed—have been proposed.

Despite the difference in perceptions on the boundary between OOA and OOD, one thing is clear. The main difference between OOA and OOD, due to the different domains of modeling, is in the type of objects that come out of the analysis and design processes. The objects during OOA focus on the problem domain and generally represent some things or concepts in the problem. These objects are sometimes called *semantic objects* as they have a meaning in the problem domain [MP92]. The solution domain, on the other hand, consists of semantic objects as well as other objects. During design, as the focus is on finding and defining a solution, the semantic objects identified during OOA may be refined and extended from the point of view of implementation, and other objects are added that are specific to the solution domain. The solution domain objects include *interface, application*, and *utility* objects [MP92]. The interface objects deal with the user interface, which is not directly a part of the problem domain but represents some aspect of the solution desired by the user. The application objects specify the control mechanisms for the proposed solution. They are driver objects that are specific to the application needs. Utility objects are those needed to support the services of the semantic objects or to implement them efficiently (e.g., queues, trees, and tables). These objects are frequently general-purpose objects and are not application-dependent.

The basic goal of the analysis and design activities is to produce the object design for the system, frequently represented by object diagrams. However, the system has to support some functionality and behavior. Hence, in addition to concentrating on the static structure of the problem or solution domains, the dynamic behavior of the system has to be studied to make sure that the final design supports the desired dynamic behaviors. Due to this, some dynamic modeling of the system is desired before the design is complete. Whether this type of modeling is part of analysis or design, i.e., where in the overall OOAD process the boundary between analysis and design is, is not generally agreed on.

We take the view that analysis should focus mostly on the structure of the system, while the impact of the dynamics of the system on the structure should be studied during the design. So, design should deal with both the static structure and dynamic behavior. It is this view that is reflected in the design methodology we discuss later in the chapter.

For a design to fully represent the solution to the problem, the functional requirements (i.e., what functional capabilities the system must have) must also be taken into account. The object model is not a suitable vehicle to model the functional aspects of the system. Integration of different views or models of a system into a coherent object-oriented design is a problem that has not yet been satisfactorily resolved. An early approach was proposed in [Jal89a] to integrate object and functional views of a solution. In this chapter, we will discuss the object modeling technique (OMT), which tries to integrate the object, functional, and dynamic models of a system [R+91].

6.2   Concepts

Here we discuss the main concepts behind object-oriented design. Though all these concepts were also used during object-oriented analysis, they are discussed in more concrete terms here, as a design deals with the solution domain and is therefore closer to the final implementation, whereas analysis deals with the problem domain and does not have to be concerned with implementation issues. In design, a model is built for the (eventual) implementation. As a consequence, implementation issues drive the modeling process during design, while in analysis, comprehension and representation issues drive the process. This also results in OOA sometimes using primitives that are somewhat richer than the ones used in OOD, as the OOD primitives tend to be closely associated with the features of the programming language to be used for implementing the design. The models built during object-oriented analysis form the starting point of object-oriented design, and the model built by OOD forms the basis for object-oriented implementation.

The ultimate goal of object-oriented design, like function-oriented design, is to design modular systems so that each module is easy to comprehend and change separately. However, unlike the function-oriented approaches that use functional abstraction to support modularity, in object-oriented design, data abstraction is used. And this fundamental difference shows up in various ways in the architecture of the system.

6.2.1   Classes and Objects

Classes and objects are the basic building blocks of an OOD, just like functions (and procedures) are for a function-oriented design. During design, we are not dealing just with abstractions of real-world objects (as is the case with analysis), but we are also dealing with abstract software objects. During analysis, we viewed an object as an entity in the problem domain that had clearly defined boundaries and behavior. During design, this has to be extended to accommodate software objects.

Encapsulation

In general, we consider objects entities that provide some services to be used by a client, which could be another object, program, or a user. The basic property of an object is *encapsulation*: it encapsulates the data and information it contains and supports a well-defined abstraction. For this, an object provides some well-defined services its clients can use, with the additional constraint that a client can access the object only through these services. This encapsulation of information along with the implementation of the operations performed on the information such that from outside an object can be characterized by the set of services it provides is a key concept in object orientation. The set of services that can be requested from outside the object forms the *interface* of the object. An object may have operations defined only for internal use that cannot be used from outside. Such operations do not form part of the interface. The interface defines all ways in which an object can be used from outside.

For example, consider an object `directory` of telephone numbers that has add-name(), change-number(), and find-number() operations as part of the interface. These are the operations that can be invoked from outside on the object `directory`.

It may also have internal operations like hash() and insert() that are used to support the operations in the interface but do not form part of the interface. These operations can only be invoked from within the object directory (i.e., by the operations defined on the object). Note that objects of other classes may also have the same interface (see the discussion on inheritance later).

A major advantage of encapsulation is that access to the encapsulated data is limited to the operations defined on the data. Hence, it becomes much easier to ensure that the integrity of data is preserved, something very hard to do if any program from outside can directly manipulate the data structures of an object. This is an extremely desirable property when building large systems, without which things can be very chaotic. In function-oriented systems, this is usually supported through self-discipline by providing access functions to some data and requiring or suggesting that other programs access the information through the access functions. In OO languages, this is enforced by the language, and no program from outside can directly access the encapsulated data.

Encapsulation, leading to the separation of the interface and its implementation, has another major consequence. As long as the interface is preserved, implementation of an object can be changed without affecting any user of the object. For example, consider the directory object discussed earlier. Suppose the object uses an array of words to implement the operations defined on directory. Later, if the implementation is changed from the array to a B-tree or by using hashing, only the internals of the object need to be changed (i.e., the data definitions and the implementation of the operations). From the outside, the directory object can continue to be used in the same manner as before, because its interface is not changed.

State, Behavior, and Identity

An object has state, behavior, and identity [Boo94]. The encapsulated data for an object defines the *state* of the object. An important property of objects is that this state *persists*, in contrast to the data defined in a function or procedure, which is generally lost once the function stops being active (finishes its current execution). In an object, the state is preserved and it persists through the life of the object, i.e., unless the object is actively destroyed.

The various components of the information an object encapsulates can be viewed as "attributes" of the object. That is, an object can be viewed as having various attributes, whose values (together with the information about the relationship of the object to the other objects) form the state of the object. The relationship between attributes and encapsulated data is that the former is in terms of concepts that may have some meaning in the problem domain: they essentially represent the abstract information being modeled by the components of the data structures.

The state and services of an object together define its *behavior*. We can say that the behavior of an object is how an object reacts in terms of state changes when it is acted on, and how it acts upon other objects by requesting services and operations [Boo94]. Generally, for an object, the defined operations together specify the behavior of the object. However, it should be pointed out that although the operations specify the behavior, the actual behavior also depends on the state of the object as an operation acts on the state and the sequence of actions it performs can depend on the state. A side effect of performing an operation may be that the state of the object is modified. As operations are the only means by which some activity can be performed by the object, it should also be clear that the current state of an object represents the sequence of operations that have been performed on it.

Finally, an object has *identity*. Identity is the property of an object that distinguishes it from all other objects [Boo94]. In most programming languages, variable names are used to distinguish objects from each other. So, for example, one can declare objects s1, s2, ... of class type `Stack`. Each of these variables s1, s2, ... will refer to a unique stack having a state of its own (which depends on the operations performed on the stack represented by the variable).

Classes

Objects represent the basic run-time entities in an OO system; they occupy space in memory that keeps its state and is operated on by the defined operations on the object. A *class*, on the other hand, defines a possible set of objects. We have seen that objects have some attributes, whose values constitute much of the state of an object. What attributes an object has are defined by the class of the object. Similarly, the operations allowed on an object or the services it provides, are defined by the class of the object. But a class is merely a definition that does not create any objects and cannot hold any values. When objects of a class are created, memory for the objects is allocated.

A class can be considered template that specifies the properties for objects of the class. Classes have [SR90]:

1. An interface that defines which parts of an object of a class can be accessed from outside and how.
2. A class body that implements the operations in the interface.
3. Instance variables that contain the state of an object of that class.

Each object, when it is created, gets a private copy of the instance variables, and when an operation defined on the class is performed on the object, it is performed on the state of the particular object.

The relationship between a class and objects of that class is similar to the relationship between a type and elements of that type. A class represents a set of objects that share a common structure and a common behavior, whereas an object is an instance of a class. The interface of the objects of a class—the behavior and the state space (i.e., the states an object can take)—are all specified by the class. The class specifies the operations that can be performed on the objects of that class and the interface of each of the operations.

Note that classes can be viewed as an *abstract data type (ADT)*. Abtract data types were promulgated in the 1970s, and a considerable amount of work has been done on specification and implementation of ADTs. The major differences between ADTs and class are inheritance and polymorphism (discussed later). Classes without inheritance are essentially ADTs, but with inheritance, which is considered a central property of object orientation, their semantics are richer than that of an ADT.

Not all operations defined on a class can be invoked on objects of that class from outside the object—some operations are defined that are entirely for internal use. The case for data declarations within the class is similar. Although generally it is fully encapsulated, in some languages it is possible to have some data visible from outside. However, this distinction of what is visible from outside has to be enforced by the language. Using the C++ classification, the data and operations of a class (sometimes collectively referred to as *features*) can be declared as one of three types:

- *Public.* These are (data or operation) declarations that are accessible from outside the class to anyone who can access an object of this class.
- *Protected.* These are declarations that are accessible from within the class itself and from within subclasses (actually also to those classes that are declared as friends).
- *Private.* These are declarations that are accessible only from within the class itself (and to those classes that are declared as friends).

Different programming languages provide different access restrictions, but public and private separation are generally needed. At least one operation is needed to create (and initialize) an object and one is needed to destroy an object. The operation creating and initializing objects is called *constructor*, and the operation destroying objects is called *destructor*. The remaining operations can be broadly divided into two categories: modifiers and value-ops. Modifiers are operations that modify the state of the object, while value-ops are operations that access the object state but do not alter it. The operations defined on a class are also called *methods* of that class.

When a client requests some operations on an object, the request is actually bound to a method defined on the class of the object. Then that method is executed, using the state of the object on which the operation is to be executed. In other words, the object itself provides the state while the class provides the actual procedure for performing the operation on the object.

```
class List{
  private:
  // data definitions to implement bag
  int list[MAX];
  int size;

  public:
    List() {size = 0};
    add (number); // add a number
    int ispresent (number); //check if number is present
    int delete (number); // delete a number, if present
}
```

FIGURE 6.2. Class List of numbers.

An Example

An example will illustrate these concepts. Suppose we need to have an object that represents a list of integers. The list consists of the numbers we put in it. We want it to be such that we can check if a number exists, and add or remove a number. In C++, the class definition List (to be used for obtaining the object list) could be something like Figure 6.2.

With this definition, a particular list, list, can be created by declaring List list. We can declare as many objects of the type List as we want. Whenever an object is declared of the type List, the constructor operator List() is executed, which sets the size of that list to 0. In C++, the operator with the same name as the name of the class is the constructor operator invoked to initialize the object whenever the object is created by declaration. We can add a number n to this bag by invoking list.add(n). The history of whatever numbers we add to list is preserved within the list (in its private data members). Much later, when we want to check if a number is present, it will return that the number is present if at any time in the past the number was added to list and it has not been deleted.

Note that the fact that the list is implemented as an array and a size pointer is not visible from outside. Other programs use lists by declaring objects of the type List and then performing operations on them. If at a later time, due to efficiency reasons we want to change the implementation of List to use a binary search tree, we will have to change the data structures and the code of the operations. However, no change needs to be made to the programs that declare and use various lists.

In C++, the interface of the object is whatever is defined as *public*. Generally, it will contain only the operations. The declarations in the private part can only be used from within the object; they cannot be accessed from outside. If some function is declared as private, then that function cannot be invoked from outside; it can only be used by the other operations defined on the class. The code for a function defined in a class can either be given with the definition of the function interface (as was done with the constructor List()) or defined elsewhere. If it is defined elsewhere, the definition has to be prefixed with the class name. For example, the function add(n) will be declared as List::add(int n).

6.2.2   Relationships Among Objects

An object, as a stand-alone entity, has very limited capabilities—it can only provide the services defined on it. Any complex system will be composed of many objects of different classes, and these objects will interact with each other so that the overall system objectives are met. In object-oriented systems, an object interacts with another by sending a *message* to the object to perform some service it provides. On receiving the message, the object invokes the requested service or the method and sends the result, if needed. Frequently, the object providing the service is called the *server* and the object requesting the service is called the *client*. This form of client-server interaction is a direct fall out of encapsulation and abstraction supported by objects.

If an object invokes some services in other objects, we can say that the two objects are *related* in some way to each other. All objects in a system are not related to all other objects. In fact, in most programming languages, an object cannot even access all objects, but can access only those objects that have been explicitly programmed or located for this purpose. During design, which objects are related has to be clearly defined so that the system can be properly implemented.

If an object uses some services of another object, there is an *association* between the two objects. This association is also called a *link*—a link exists from one object to another if the object uses some services of the other object. Links frequently show up as pointers when programming. A link captures the fact that a message is flowing from one object to another. However, when a link exists, though the message flows in the direction of the link, information can flow in both directions (e.g., the server may return some results).

With associations comes the issue of visibility, that is, which object is visible to which. This is an issue that is very pertinent for implementation and therefore comes up during design. However, this is not an important issue during analysis and is therefore rarely dealt with during OOA. The basic issue here is that if there is a link from object A to object B, for A to be able to send a message to B, B must be visible to A in the final program. There are different ways to provide this visibility. Some of the important possibilities are [Boo94]:

- The supplier object is global to the client.
- The supplier object is a parameter to some operation of the client that sends the message.
- The supplier object is a part of the client object.
- The supplier object is locally declared in some operation.

Each of these has some consequences. For example, if the supplier object is a global object to the client, then the scoping of languages may make the client visible to many other objects. This is, in general, not very desirable, and should be done only when there is common information that many different classes need. If the supplier object is a parameter of a method, then the intention is to show that the object belongs elsewhere, and this object may access it only through this method. If the supplier object is a part of the client, it means that the supplier object is declared as a data member of this class. This implies that when the life of the client object finishes, the supplier object is also destroyed. This clearly can have implications on sharing of objects and services. Overall, how an object is made visible to an object that needs to access it is an important design issue to be kept in mind when designing associations.

If the supplier object is declared in the client object, there are different ways to implement associations. It can be implemented by a pointer in one of the objects (generally the client object) to the other object. The problem with this approach comes if the link is to be traversed in the reverse direction from the object to which it is pointed. For this, a search needs to be performed on all existing objects of the class with which this class has an association to find which object has the pointer to this object. Hence, this method of implementation should be used only if it is clear that the application is such that the reverse traversal of the link will never be needed.

Another way of implementing the association is by making the link bi-directional, which is what links generally mean in modeling. This can be done by keeping a pointer to the other object in each of the two objects. This is more expensive in terms of storage, but it solves the problem. However, care must be taken to see that the links are consistent; whenever one of the pointers is modified, the other pointer needs to be modified accordingly.

Yet another way of implementing association is to create a new object, whose only duty is to keep track of the links between objects. This approach separates the link maintenance job from the two objects. This is useful when there are many links. Each object will register its link with this special-purpose object.

Links between objects capture the client/server type of relationship. Another type of relationship between objects is *aggregation*, which reflects the whole/part-of relationship. Though not necessary, aggregation generally implies containment. That is, if an object A is an aggregation of objects B and C, then objects B and C will generally be within object A (though there are situations where the conceptual relationship of aggregation may not get reflected as actual containment of objects). The main implication of this is that a contained object cannot survive without its containing object. With links, that is not the case. An example of aggregation in C++ notation is shown next:

```
class Disk {
  private:
    Track *tracks;
    disk information
      :
};
class Track {
  private:
    Sector sectors[MAX];
      :
};
Class Sector {
  private:
      :
}
```

In this example, a class of type Disk is declared, which specifies that any object of this type will have within it a pointer to another object of class Track, and this pointer is private information of the object that cannot be accessed from outside the object. The definition of the class Track states that each object of this type will have an array of elements of class Sector within it as private data members. The example captures the fact that a disk consists of many tracks, and each track contains many sectors. As shown by class definitions, aggregation can be implemented by declaring the parts as objects within the class, as is done while defining the class Track. Or it can be implemented as a pointer to the part, as is done while defining Disk. The latter method is also used for defining aggregation; hence representing aggregation is used only for efficiency reasons or if the object is to be accessed by many other objects outside the container object.

6.2.3   Inheritance and Polymorphism

Inheritance is a concept unique to object orientation. Some of the other concepts, such as information hiding, can be supported by non-object-oriented languages through self-discipline, but inheritance cannot generally be supported by such languages. It is also the concept central to many of the arguments claiming that software reuse can be better supported with object orientation.

Inheritance is a relation between classes that allows for definition and implementation of one class based on the definition of existing classes [KG90]. Let us try to understand this better. When a class B inherits from another class A, B is referred to as the *subclass* or the *derived class* and A is referred to as the *superclass* or the *base class*. In general, a subclass B will have two parts: a derived part and an incremental part [KG90]. The derived part is the part inherited from A and the

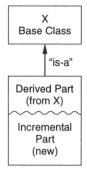

Y - Derived class

FIGURE 6.3. Inheritance.

incremental part is the new code and definitions that have been specifically added for B. This is shown in Figure 6.3 [KG90]. Objects of type B have the derived part as well as the incremental part. Hence, by defining only the incremental part and inheriting the derived part from an existing class, we can define objects that contain both.

Inheritance is often called an "is a" relation, implying that an object of type B is also an instance of type A. That is, an instance of a subclass, though more than an instance of the superclass, is also an instance of the superclass.

In general, an inherited feature of A may be redefined in various forms in B. This redefinition may change the visibility of the operation (e.g., a public operation of A may be made private in B), changed (e.g., by defining a different sequence of instructions for this operation), renamed, voided, and so on.

The inheritance relation between classes forms a hierarchy. As inheritance represents an "is a" relation, it is important that the hierarchy represent a structure present in the application domain and is not created simply to reuse some parts of an existing class. That is, the hierarchy should be such that an object of a class is also an object of all its superclasses in the problem domain.

The power of inheritance lies in the fact that all common features of the subclasses can be accumulated in the superclass. In other words, a feature is placed in the higher level of abstractions. Once this is done, such features can be inherited from the parent class and used in the subclass directly. This implies that if there are many abstract class definitions available, when a new class is needed, it is possible that the new class is a specialization of one or more of the existing classes. In that case, the existing class can be tailored through inheritance to define the new class.

Inheritance promotes reuse by defining the common operations of the subclasses in a superclass. However, inheritance makes the subclasses dependent on the superclass, and a change in the superclass will directly affect the subclasses that inherit

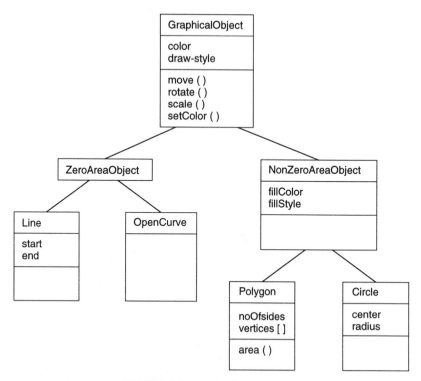

FIGURE 6.4. An inheritance example.

from it. As classes may change as design is refined, with each change in a class, its impact on the subclasses will also have to be analyzed. This also has an impact on the testing of classes. We will discuss the issue of testing later in the book.

Let us illustrate inheritance through the use of an example. Consider a graphics package that has the class GraphicalObject representing all graphical objects. A graphical object can have a zero area or a non-zero area, giving two subclasses ZeroAreaObject and NonZeroAreaObject. Line and Curve are two specific object classes of the first category, and Polygon and Circle are two specific object classes of the latter category. This hierarchy of classes is shown in Figure 6.4.

As we can see, the GraphicalObject has attributes of color and draw-style (which represents the style of drawing the figure)—both of which each graphical object has. It has many operations defined on it—move(), rotate(), scale(), etc.—the ones that are needed for every object by the graphics package. Note, however, that even though operations like rotate() and scale() are defined for an object, they are totally conceptual in that their exact specification depends on the nature of the object (e.g., rotate() on a circle has to do different things than rotate() on a line). Hence, these operations have to be defined for each object. In C++, such operations that are declared in a superclass and redefined in a subclass are declared as virtual in the superclass. (This helps in implementing dynamic binding of the operations; see discussion later.) If an operation specified in a class is always redefined in its subclass, then the operation can be defined as *pure virtual* (in C++, this is done by equating it to 0), implying that the operation has no body. The implication of existence of these operations is that no objects of this class can be created, as some of the operations declared in the class are not defined and hence cannot be performed. Such a class is sometimes called an *abstract base class*. The C++ class skeletons for this hierarchy are shown next:

```
class GraphicalObject {
  protected:
    unsigned int color;
    unsigned int draw_style;
  public:
    virtual void move( Point &newLocation );
    virtual void rotate( double angle );
    virtual void scale( double XScale , double YScale);
    void setColor( unsigned int col );
    void setDrawStyle( unsigned int style );
};

class ZeroAreaObject: public GraphicalObject {};

class NonZeroAreaObject: public  GraphicalObject {
  protected:
    unsigned int fillColor;
    unsigned int fillStyle;
  public:
    virtual fill();
};

class Line: public ZeroAreaObject {
  private:
    Point start, end;
  public:
    int length();
    Point &midPoint();
    // Inherited virtual features are given definition here
    void move( Point &newLocation );
    void rotate( double angle );
    void scale( double XScale , double YScale );
};
```

```
class OpenCurve: public ZeroAreaObject {
  private:
    Point *controlPoints;
  public:
    // Inherited virtual features are given definition here
};

class Polygon: public NonZeroAreaObject {
  private:
    Point *vertices;
    unsigned int noOfSides;
  public:
    double area();
    // Inherited virtual features are defined here
};

class Circle: public NonZeroAreaObject {
  private:
    Point centre;
    unsigned int radius;
  public:
    double area();
    // Inherited virtual features are defined here
};
```

Inheritance can be broadly classified as being of two types: strict inheritance and nonstrict inheritance [SR90]. In *strict inheritance* a subclass takes all the features from the parent class and adds additional features to specialize it. That is, all data members and operations available in the base class are also available in the derived class. This form supports the "is-a" relation and is the easiest form of inheritance. *Nonstrict inheritance* occurs when the subclass does not have all the features of the parent class or some features have been redefined. This form of inheritance has consequences in the dynamic behavior and complicates testing.

A class hierarchy need not be a simple tree structure. It may be a graph, which implies that a class may inherit from multiple classes. This type of inheritance, when a subclass inherits from many superclasses, is called *multiple inheritance*. Consider part of the class hierarchy of logic gates for a system for simulating digital logic of circuits as shown in Figure 6.5. In this example, there are separate classes to represent And gates, Nor gates, and Or gates. The class for representing Nand gates inherits from both the class for And gates and the class for Not gates. That is, all the definitions (instances and operations) that have been declared as public (or protected) in the classes NotGate and AndGate are available for use to the class NandGate. Similarly, the class NorGate inherits from the OrGate and NotGate. Like in regular inheritance, a subclass can redefine any feature if it desires.

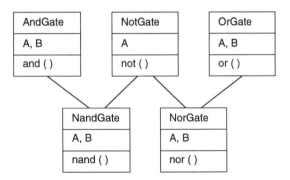

FIGURE 6.5. Multiple inheritance.

Multiple inheritance brings in some new issues. First, some features of two-parent classes may have the same name. So, for example, there may be an operation $O()$ in class A and class B. If a class C inherits from class A and class B, then when $O()$ is invoked from an object of class C, if $O()$ is not defined locally within C, it is not clear from where the definition of $O()$ should be taken—from class A or from class B. This ambiguity does not arise if there is no multiple inheritance; the operation of the closest ancestor in which $O()$ is defined is executed. Different language mechanisms or rules can be used to resolve this ambiguity. In C++, when such an ambiguity arises, the programmer has to resolve it by explicitly specifying the superclass from which the definition of the feature is to be taken.

Multiple inheritance also brings in the possibility of *repeated inheritance*, where a class inherits more than once from the same class [SR90]. For example, consider the situation shown in Figure 6.6 where classes B and C inherit from class A and class D inherits from both B and C. A situation like this means that effectively class D is inheriting twice from A—once through B and once through C. This form of inheritance is even more complex, as features of A may have been renamed in B and C, and can lead to run-time errors.

Due to the complexity that comes with multiple inheritance and its variations and the possibility of confusion that comes with them, it is generally advisable to avoid their usage.

Inheritance brings in *polymorphism*, a general concept widely used in type theory, that deals with the ability of an object to be of different types. In OOD, polymorphism comes in the form that a reference in an OO program can refer to objects of different types at different times. Here we are not talking about "type coercion," which is allowed in languages like C; these are features that can be avoided if desired. In object-oriented systems, with inheritance, polymorphism cannot be avoided—it must be supported. The reason is the "is a" relation supported by inheritance—an object x declared to be of class B is also an object of any class A

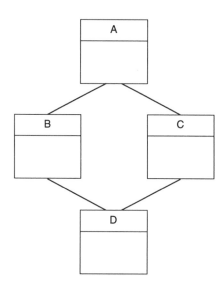

FIGURE 6.6. Repeated inheritance.

that is the superclass of B. Hence, anywhere an instance of A is expected, x can be used.

With polymorphism, an entity has a static type and a dynamic type [KG90]. The static type of an object is the type of which the object is declared in the program text, and it remains unchanged. The dynamic type of an entity, on the other hand, can change from time to time and is known only at reference time. Once an entity is declared, at compile time the set of types that this entity belongs to can be determined from the inheritance hierarchy that has been defined. The dynamic type of the object will be one of this set, but the actual dynamic type will be defined at the time of reference of the object. In the preceding example, the static type of x is B. Initially, its dynamic type is also B. Suppose an object y is declared of type A, and in some sequence of instructions there is an instruction $x := y$. Due to the "is a" relation between A and B, this is a valid statement. After this statement is executed, the dynamic type of x will change to A (though its static type remains B). This type of polymorphism is called *object polymorphism* [SR90], in which wherever an object of a superclass can be used, objects of subclasses can be used.

This type of polymorphism requires *dynamic binding* of operations, which brings in *feature polymorphism*. Dynamic binding means that the code associated with a given procedure call is not known until the moment of the call [KG90]. Let us illustrate with an example. Suppose x is a polymorphic reference whose static type is B but whose dynamic type could be either A or B. Suppose that an operation O is defined in the class A, which is redefined in the class B. Now when the operation O is invoked on x, it is not known statically what code will be executed. That is, the code to be executed for the statement $x.O$ is decided at run time, depending on the dynamic type of x—if the dynamic type is A, the code for the operation O in class A will be executed; if the dynamic type is B, the code for operation O in class B will be executed. This dynamic binding can be used quite effectively during application development to reduce the size of the code. For example, take the case of the graphical object hierarchy discussed earlier. In an application, suppose the elements of a figure are stored in an array A (of `GraphicalObject` type). Suppose element 1 of this array is a line, element 2 is a circle, and so on. Now if we want to rotate each object in the figure, we simply loop over the array performing `A[i].rotate()`. For each A[i], the appropriate rotate function will be executed. That is, which function A[i].rotate() refers to is decided at run time, depending on the dynamic type of object A[i].

This feature polymorphism, which is essentially overloading of the feature (i.e., a feature can mean different things in different contexts and its exact meaning is determined only at run time) causes no problem in strict inheritance because all features of a superclass are available in the subclasses. But in nonstrict inheritance, it can cause problems, because a child may lose a feature. Because the binding of the feature is determined at run time, this can cause a run-time error as a situation may arise where the object is bound to the superclass in which the feature is not present.

6.2.4 Design Concepts

So far we have discussed general concepts of object orientation and some key properties of the basic building blocks for OOD. Now let us look at some concepts for creating good OO design. Like in functional designs, just understanding the basic building blocks is not sufficient to create designs that are simple to understand and maintain. While designing, there are always many options available, and deciding which option to select requires some guidelines for distinguishing a "good" design from a "bad" design. Here we discuss some of the features a good design should have [KG90]. The basic objective of any design process is to produce modular designs so that each module can be understood and modified separately. In an OOD, the basic modules are classes, and proper design of classes is the central concern of an OOD methodology. Here we discuss some desirable properties that classes in a good design should have.

Information Hiding. A class supports information hiding by hiding the data in the class and only providing some specified operations on this data. The implementation of these operations is also hidden. This separation of class interface and class implementation naturally supports information hiding. However, many languages provide methods by which information hiding can be violated. For example, in C++, `friends` of a class can directly access the private members of a class. Furthermore, any part of the encapsulated information can be made available to outside by making it `public`. Use of such constructs violate the information-hiding principle, presumably to provide shortcuts to the designer or programmer. Information hiding requires that such violations do occur.

Coupling. The basic idea behind coupling is the same as in Chapter 5—two objects are coupled if at least one of them acts on the other and at least one of them is affected by the other. In other words, if two objects interact, they are coupled. Interaction between classes comes due to the relationships between them. For example, if an instance of class A is declared within class B, then each instance of class B will contain an instance of class A, and hence objects of class B can invoke operations on the instance of class A contained in the object. Hence, in this case the two classes are coupled. There are various other ways in which objects may be coupled. In general we can say that if any method of an object uses methods or instance variables of another object, then the two objects are coupled [CK94]. Two classes are coupled if methods declared in one class use methods or instance variables of the other class. Like in function-oriented design, the objective of the design activity should be to keep the coupling between objects or classes to a minimum, as the higher the coupling the harder it will be to understand and modify classes separately. In other words, during design, the connections between the objects should be minimized.

Cohesion. Cohesion is the property that specifies how tightly bound the elements of a module are. It is desirable to have each class highly cohesive—all the elements are together to support a well-defined abstraction. A class is naturally a cohesive entity, as all its data and operations are packaged together for a purpose. However, if a class does not support a well-defined abstraction or does not represent some concept or entity in the problem domain, then its cohesion weakens. For strong cohesion, each data defined within the class and all the operations on the class should naturally belong to the concept being modeled by the class. Adding functions that do not naturally belong to the concept to be modeled or adding further information to create "large" objects that do too many things or support multiple concepts weaken the cohesion.

Cohesion can be modeled by the degree of similarity between methods of the same class [CK94]. The degree of similarity between two methods of a class is the intersection of the sets of instance variables of the class the two methods access. The higher the degree of similarity between methods, the more cohesive a class is. In other words, if the different methods of the class operate on the same set of instance variables of the class, the class is cohesive.

Reuse. The object-oriented paradigm provides strong support for software reuse. In fact, this is one of the basic reasons for the increased interest in object orientation. There are basically two ways in which reuse is supported in OO. The first is through class definition—every time a new object of a class is defined, we reuse all the code and declarations of that class. However, this type of reuse can be supported in the function-oriented approach also. The other type of reuse, which is particular to object orientation, is through inheritance.

When a class is declared as a subclass of an existing class, it inherits all the declarations and definitions of the superclass. Furthermore, the inheritance mechanism allows the existing class to be specialized by redefining some of the existing operations or by adding new operations to suit the existing purpose. One can imagine that if there is a large library of class definitions available, it is quite likely that when a new class is desired, some existing class will be very "close," though not exactly the same, to what is desired. With inheritance, such a class definition can be used to define the new class—all the features of the existing class that are desired for the new class are kept as it, the others are redefined, or new services are added. By this, all the parts of the existing class that can be reused are used in the new class definition. It is important to note that in this reuse, the class definition of the existing class is not modified. This is what makes reuse potentially very useful compared to the approach followed in function-oriented systems, where an existing function close to the desired function is actually modified to support the desired functionality. This requires that classes be designed properly to enable reuse [JF88]. We will not go into more detail of software reuse and the impact of object orientation on it, as this is an advanced topic beyond our scope. Some guidelines for designing reusable classes are, however, discussed later based on the work in [JF88].

It should be pointed out that the use of inheritance actually increases coupling between classes—with inheritance the two classes are tightly coupled. In general, modularity is also diluted due to this dependence between classes—any change in the definition of a class can impact all its subclasses. So it is imperative that inheritance is used with care. It should only be used when it supports a clear hierarchy that can be easily identified in the problem or the solution domain and when the class definitions are stable. Inheritance is useful if the benefits it provides in terms of representation and reuse outweigh the cost of increased coupling that comes with inheritance.

Some Guidelines. In an OO design, class definitions make up the bulk of the system definition. Therefore, the design of classes has a major impact on the overall quality of the design. Here we present a set of guidelines for class design that can be used to produce "good quality" classes [KG90], or reusable classes [JF88]. Most of these rules, and their intent, are self-explanatory and based on the preceding discussion.

1. The public interface of a class should only contain the operations defined on the class. That is, the data definitions should not be a part of the public interface.

2. Only the operations that form the interface for a class, that is, the ones needed by the users of the class, should be the public members of the class.

3. An instance of a class should not send messages directly to components of another class. That is, if there is a class C defined inside a class B, then objects of a class A should not directly perform operations on objects of class C (though many languages will permit it).

4. Each operation defined on a class should be such that it either modifies or accesses some data defined in the class.

5. A class should be dependent on as few classes as possible.

6. The interaction between two classes should be explicit. That is, global objects should be avoided, and any objects needed by an object should be explicitly passed as a parameter or accessed through other explicitly defined means.

7. Each subclass should be developed as a specialization of the superclass with the public interface of the superclass becoming part of the public interface of the subclass.

8. The inheritance hierarchy should model some hierarchy that naturally exists, and the class definition at each level should represent some concept. The top of the hierarchy should be an abstract class.

9. Inside a class, case analysis on object type should be avoided. If this is needed, it should be done by sending messages.

10. The number of arguments and the size of methods should be kept small.

6.3   Design Notation and Specification

Frequently, design approaches use some graphical notation to represent the design. This notation is generally independent of the methodology (even though they are typically proposed together). Notations are compact pictorial representations of a design, and they are particularly useful in the process of design, i.e., while the designer is designing the system. However, for finally specifying the design (say, in a design document), the design notations are generally not sufficient. Also, converting them to code (or detailed design) is not convenient. So, frequently, in formal design representations, textual forms are used, which are essentially skeletons of the final programs without the logic in them. Here, we briefly discuss the notation used for creating an object-oriented design and specification language that can be used for specifying a design.

The notation is similar to the notation used in OO analysis. As classes form the main component of an OOD, class representation is the basic unit of the notation. A class is represented as a rectangle with three parts—the first part gives its name, the second part gives its attributes, and the third part gives the methods it has. Association between objects of classes is represented by drawing a line between the two class representations. An association may also be given a name (and can have attributes of its own). Multiplicity in an association is expressed by putting a solid ball adjacent to the class for which multiple objects may be related through the relation represented by the association. Aggregation is represented with a diamond attached to the "container" class, and inheritance is shown by a triangle connecting the superclass and all the subclasses. In addition to these, we have a template class,

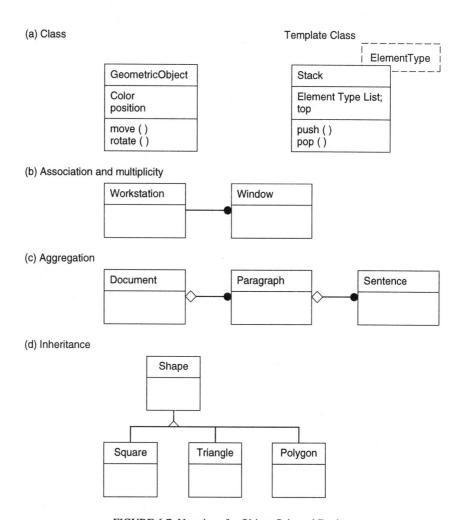

FIGURE 6.7. Notations for Object-Oriented Design.

which represents the "generic classes," where the type of the major attribute of the class is not defined; it is given a symbolic name and the actual type is specified when objects of the type are defined. For example, we may define a template class Stack, whose element type is ElmentType. So, whether it is a stack of integers, characters, or strings is not specified. The type of the element of the stack is specified when an object of the type Stack is created. The notations for all these are shown in Figure 6.7.

The final design for a system will be composed of several of these elements. As is generally the case with any creative activity, design is an iterative process where we start with some structure and refine and enhance it until the designer is satisfied.

For this iterative process, pictorial representations are quite handy. As mentioned earlier, to represent the final design, textual specifications are frequently used. In the design specification, most of the modules and their interfaces are specified. It is most efficient if the specification language is close to the target language in which the final software is to be implemented. In this case, translating from design to code becomes easier, and errors that may be introduced during the translation are reduced.

The final design specification needs to specify all the classes, their relationships, global data structures, and the main parts of the main program. With this design specification, if it is in a language that is consistent with the target implementation language, then during coding, only further details need to be filled. In our design specification language, the classes are defined using C++ class structures, though the logic of the methods is not specified. That is, all the major instance variables and all the operations are specified, together with their visibility restrictions (i.e., whether private, restricted, or public). All the objects defined in the main program or as global are specified and a brief description of the main program is given. This forms the complete design specification, which can be used for specification and further implementation.

6.4   Design Methodology

Many design and analysis methodologies have been proposed. Some of the major ones are [Boo94, CY91, Jac92, R+91]. As we stated earlier, a methodology basically uses the concepts (of OO in this case) to provide guidelines and notation for the design activity. Though methodologies are useful, they do not reduce the activity of design to a sequence of steps that can be followed mechanically. Due to this, the overall approach and the principles behind them are often more useful than the details of the methodologies. Due to this, the particular methodology used often has a limited impact. In fact, most experienced designers tailor the methodology to suit their way of thinking and working. We will discuss only one particular methodology here, as at an abstract level most methodologies start to seem very similar and vary mostly in details.

For any large system, the problem has to first be partitioned into subsystems, so that each subsystem can be separately designed. Sometimes, this high-level partitioning will be evident from the subsystems that exist in the problem domain. At other times, this partitioning will have to be done by the designer. This partitioning of a problem into components is what is sometimes called the *complexity management component* of a design methodology [MP92]. This complexity management is important from the design and presentation viewpoints—it is hard to create a design for a large system as a whole, and it is hard to represent the design of a large system for presentation and evaluation purposes. Most analysis and design techniques do not address this problem in any detail and suggest some general guidelines for it. Combining objects into a subject, as discussed briefly during object-oriented analysis, is one such guideline proposed by [CY90]. In the OMT methodology, which we will discuss here, it is suggested that the system be broken into subsystems by considering a system as layers or partitions. However, no detailed guidelines are given for this partitioning. We assume that using the general principles of problem partitioning and the concepts of layering and refinement, a system is broken into high-level subsystems. The problem we address is how to produce an object-oriented design for a subsystem, which can be viewed as a system in its own right and will be referred to as the system in the rest of the chapter.

As we discussed earlier, the OO design of a system consists of specification of all the classes and objects that will exist in the system implementation, together with a main function that provides the very high-level flow of control in the system. The main function is frequently not very significant in systems modeled using object orientation, because most of the work is done by objects themselves and the primary objective of the design activity is to produce the object design, in which all the classes are completely specified. That is, for each class, the attributes, methods, and associations are clearly identified. A complete object design should be such that in the implementation phase only further details about methods need to be added. A few low-level objects may be added later, but most of the classes and objects and their relationships are identified during design.

In OO design, the OO analysis forms the starting step. Using the model produced during analysis, a detailed model of the final system is built. As we discussed earlier, in an object-oriented approach, the separation between analysis and design is not very clear and depends on the perception. We will follow what we defined in Chapter 3 regarding what constitutes the output of an OOA—an object model of the problem. The OMT methodology that we discuss for design considers dynamic modeling and functional modeling parts of the analysis [R+91]. As these two models have little impact on the object model produced in OOA or on the SRS, we view these modeling as part of the design activity. Hence, performing the object modeling can be viewed as the first step of design. With this point of view, the design methodology for producing an OO design consists of the following sequence of steps:

- Produce the object model.
- Produce the dynamic model and use it to define operations on classes.
- Produce the functional model and use it to define operations on classes.
- Define algorithms for implementing major operations, and from them identify internal classes and operations.
- Optimize and package.

We discussed object modeling in Chapter 3, along with a methodology for performing the modeling. Any other methodology for object modeling can be followed, as long as the output of the modeling activity is the object diagram representing the problem structure. Hence, the first step of the design is generally performed during the requirements phase when the problem is being modeled for producing the SRS. Briefly, during analysis, the basic goal is to produce an object model of the problem domain. This requires identification of object types in the problem domain, the structures between classes (both inheritance and aggregation), attributes of the different classes, associations between the different classes, and the services each class needs to provide to support the system. For further details, the reader should refer to Chapter 3.

6.4.1   Dynamic Modeling

Object modeling tries to model the static structure of the system, and the object diagram produced from modeling represents the structure graphically. The object model produced during modeling forms the starting point for object design. However, just modeling the static structure is not sufficient for designing the system, as the desired effect of the events on the system state will also impact the final structure of the system. After all, the state of the system is the state of its objects, and the state of an object changes through the execution of its operations. So, a better understanding of the dynamic behavior of the system will help in further refining the object design.

The dynamic model of a system aims to specify how the state of various objects changes when events occur. An event is something that happens at some time instance. For an object, an event is essentially a request for an operation. An event typically is an occurrence of something and has no time duration associated with it. Each event has an initiator and a responder. Events can be internal to the system, in which case the event initiator and the event responder are both within the system. An event can be an external event, in which case the event initiator is outside the system (e.g., the user or a sensor). Events of the same type can be grouped into *event classes*.

A *scenario* is a sequence of events that occur in a particular execution of the system [R+91]. A scenario may describe all the events that occur in the system or may limit itself to the events associated with a group of objects. A scenario can be described textually by enumerating the sequence of events, or it can be shown as an event trace diagram, in which events between objects are shown (external events are shown to be emanating from an external object). From the scenarios, the different events being performed on different objects can be identified, which are then used to identify services on objects. The different scenarios together can completely characterize the behavior of the system. If the object design is such that it can support all the scenarios, we can be sure that the desired dynamic behavior of the system can be supported by the design. This is the basic reason for performing dynamic modeling. Use of scenarios is a central concept in object-oriented approaches. In the methodology proposed in [Jac92], these are called *use cases*, and they are used heavily. A use case specifies the interaction of *actors* (which are outside the system to be designed but interact with the system) with the system in natural English. Scenarios and their modeling are also used in [Boo94]. The major steps in dynamic modeling are [R⁺91]:

1. Prepare scenarios of typical interaction sequences.
2. For each scenario, identify events between objects and prepare event traces.
3. Build state diagrams.
4. Match events between objects to verify consistency.

It is best to start dynamic modeling by looking at scenarios being triggered by external events. The scenarios should not necessarily cover all possibilities, but the major ones should be considered. Such scenarios will not exist or will be trivial in batch processing systems but are significant in interactive systems. First scenarios for "normal" cases should be prepared, then scenarios for "exceptional" cases should be prepared. For example, in the system for a restaurant that we discussed in Chapter 3, the "normal" scenario could be:

> Menu is given to the customer; customer reads the menu.
> Order of the customer is taken.
> Order is sent to the kitchen.
> Dishes are prepared and meal served.
> Bill is produced for this order for the customer.
> Customer is given the bill; customer pays the money.
> Customer is given the receipt.

An "exception" scenario could be if the ordered item was not available or if the customer cancels his order. From each scenario, events have to be identified. Events are interactions with the outside world and object-to-object interactions. All the events that have the same effect on the flow of control in the system are grouped as a single event type. Note that two events may be of the same event type even though the value of their parameters is different. Each event type is then allocated to the object classes that initiate it and that service the event. With this done, a scenario can be represented as an event trace diagram showing the events that will take place on the different objects if the execution corresponding to the scenario takes place. The objects related to the event and the temporal order of occurrence of events is also represented in the event trace diagram. Note that to represent a scenario that shows the interaction with objects in the environment of the system, these external objects also have to be shown in the diagram to completely represent the scenario. A possible event trace diagram of the preceding scenario is given in Figure 6.8.

Once scenarios are constructed, various events on objects that are needed to support executions corresponding to the various scenarios are known. The effect of these events on individual objects can be shown as an object diagram. The object diagram

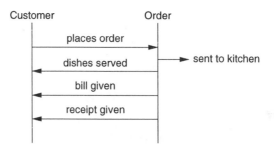

FIGURE 6.8. The event trace diagram.

is a finite state machine with states representing the different states of the object and events causing the state transitions. Once the state diagrams are built, each scenario corresponds to a path in the state diagram. The state diagrams help understand the behavior of objects under different state conditions and different events (i.e., invocation of operations).

The main reason for performing dynamic modeling is that scenarios and event trace diagrams extend the initial design based on the object model produced during analysis. Generally speaking, for each event in the event trace diagrams, there will be an operation on the object on which the event is invoked. So, by using the scenarios and event traces we can further refine our view of the objects and add operations that are needed to support some scenarios but may not have been identified during object modeling. For example, from the event trace diagram in Figure 6.8, we can see that "place order" and "generate bill" will be two operations required on the object order if the scenario is to be supported.

Scenarios and their impact on design are commonly accepted methods during object-oriented design. Many design approaches use the concept of scenarios in one form or another. Scenarios help understand the interplay between different objects in the system and help determine the interface of the different objects. Explicit specification of the scenarios also help clarify the specifications of the system. As they are generally developed from the external point of view, they capture how the system is to be used by the environment and the users, thereby helping clearly specify the system interface and behavior. We did not go into detail of the state modeling of the objects, as the role of state modeling is more to understand an object better, which will undoubtedly help in implementing the class, but has a limited role in understanding the object interfaces and the relationship between objects. The state diagrams for objects can be viewed as a tool to do detailed design for the class for that object, giving the flow of control in a pictorial form. Though OMT treats state modeling as an essential component of modeling, it does not specify clearly how it affects the object design. Furthermore, other methodologies (e.g., [Jac92]) do not consider state modeling of objects an integral component of design. For these reasons, we believe that the state transition diagram is of limited use during system design but may be more useful during detailed design.

6.4.2 Functional Modeling

The functional model describes the computations that take place within a system. It is the third dimension in modeling—object modeling looks at the static structure of the system, dynamic modeling looks at the events in the system, and functional modeling looks at the functionality of the system. In other words, the functional model of a system specifies what happens in the system, the dynamic model specifies when it happens, and the object model specifies what it happens to [R+91].

A functional model of a system specifies how the output values are computed in the system from the input values, without considering the control aspects of the computation. This represents the functional view of the system—the mapping from inputs to outputs and the various steps involved in the mapping. Generally, when the transformation from the inputs to outputs is complex, consisting of many steps, the functional modeling is likely to be useful. In systems where the transformation of inputs to outputs is not complex, the functional model is likely to be straightforward.

As we have seen, the functional model of a system (either the problem domain or the solution domain) can be represented by a data flow diagram (DFD). We have used DFDs in problem modeling, and the structured design methodology, discussed in Chapter 5, uses DFDs to represent the model for the proposed solution (which is then converted into a structure chart). We will not discuss methods for producing the DFD of a system; the rules for doing so have been discussed in earlier chapters. DFDs model a system in terms of data flows, processes, and data stores to represent the flow of data within the system. Data flows represent the various forms the data takes before becoming the desired output form, whereas the processes represent the transformation functions responsible for transforming one form of data to another. Eventually, through the network of processes, the input data is transformed into the desired output data. Data stores are essentially files or objects that passively store data.

Once the functional model of the system is finished using DFDs, its role in the OO design has to be defined. Just as with dynamic modeling, the basic purpose of doing functional modeling, when the goal is to obtain an object oriented design for the system, is to use the model to make sure that the object model can perform the transformations required from the system. As processes represent operations and in an object-oriented system, most of the processing is done by operations on objects, all processes should show up as operations on objects. Some operations might appear as single operations on an object; others might appear as multiple operations on different objects, depending on the level of abstraction of the DFD. If the DFD is sufficiently detailed, most processes will occur as operations on objects.

The DFD also specifies the abstract signature of the operations by identifying the inputs and outputs.

6.4.3   Defining Internal Classes and Operations

The objects identified so far are the objects that come from the problem domain. The methods identified on the objects are the ones needed to satisfy all the interactions with the environment and the user and to support the desired functionality. However, the final object design is a blueprint for implementation. Hence, implementation issues have to be considered. While considering implementation issues, algorithm and optimization issues arise. These issues are handled in this step.

First, each object is critically evaluated to see if it is needed in its present form in the final implementation. Some of the objects might be discarded if the designer feels they are not needed during implementation.

Then the implementation of operations on the objects is considered. For this, rough algorithms for implementation might be considered. While doing this, a complex operation may get defined in terms of lower-level operations on simpler objects. In other words, effective implementation of operations may require heavy interaction with some data structures and the data structure to be considered an object in its own right. These objects that are identified while considering implementation concerns are largely support objects that may be needed to store intermediate results or to model some aspects of the object whose operation is to be implemented. The classes for these objects are called *container classes*. In [Jal89a] they were called *nested objects*. However, some of these classes might be needed for implementation of methods of different classes and hence need not be defined as local to a class.

Once the implementation of each class and each operation on the class has been considered and it has been satisfied that they can be implemented, the system design is complete. The detailed design might also uncover some very low-level objects, but most such objects should be identified during system design.

6.4.4   Optimize and Package

In the design methodology used, the basic structure of the design was created during analysis. As analysis is concerned with capturing and representing various aspects of the problem, some inefficiencies may have crept in. In this final step, the issue of efficiency is considered, keeping in mind that the final structures should not deviate too much from the logical structure produced by analysis, as the more the deviation, the harder it will be to understand a design. Some of the design optimization issues are discussed next [R+91].

Adding Redundant Associations. The association in the initial design may make it very inefficient to perform some operations. In some cases, these operations can be made more efficient by adding more associations. Consider the example where a Company has a relationship to a person (a company employs many persons) [R+91]. A person may have an attribute languages-spoken, which lists the languages the person can speak. If the company sometimes needs to determine all its employees who know a specific language, it has to access each employee object to perform this operation. This operation can be made more efficient by adding an index in the Company object for different languages, thereby adding a new relationship between the two types of objects. This association is largely for efficiency. For such situations, the designer must consider each operation and determine how many objects in an association are accessed and how many are actually selected. If the hit ratio is low, indexes can be considered.

Saving Derived Attributes. A derived attribute is one whose value can be determined from the values of other attributes. As such an attribute is not independent, it may not have been specified in the initial design. However, if it is needed very often or if its computation is complex, its value can be computed and stored once and then accessed later. This may require new objects to be created for the derived attributes. However, it should be kept in mind that by doing this the consistency between derived attributes and base attributes will have to be maintained and any changes to the base attributes may have to be reflected in the derived attributes.

Use of Generic Types. A language like C++ allows "generic" classes to be declared where the base type or the type of some attribute is kept "generic" and the actual type is specified only when the object is actually defined. (The approach of C++ does not support true generic types, and this type of definition is actually handled by the compiler.) By using generic types, the code size can be reduced. For example, if a list is to be used in different contexts, a generic list can be defined and then instantiated for an integer, real, and char types.

Adjustment of Inheritance. Sometimes the same or similar operations are defined in various classes in a class hierarchy. By making the operation slightly more general (by extending interface or its functionality), it can be made a common operation that can be "pushed" up the hierarchy. The designer should consider such possibilities. Note that even if the same operation has to be used in only some of the derived classes, but in other derived classes the logic is different for the operation, inheritance can still be used effectively. The operation can be pushed to the base class and then redefined in those classes where its logic is different.

Another way to increase the use of inheritance, which promotes reuse, is to see if abstract classes can be defined for a set of existing classes and then the existing classes considered as a derived class of that. This will require identifying common behavior and properties among various classes and abstracting out a meaningful common superclass. Note that this is useful only if the abstract superclass is meaningful and the class hierarchy is "natural." A superclass should not be created simply to pack the common features on some classes together in a class.

Besides these, the general design principles discussed earlier should be applied to improve the design—to make it more compact, efficient, and modular. Often these goals will conflict. In that case, the designer has to use his judgment about which way to go. In general, as we stated in Chapter 5, we take the view that understandability and modularity should be given preference over efficiency and compactness.

6.4.5 Examples

Before we apply the methodology on some examples, it should be remembered again that no design methodology reduces the activity of producing a design to a series of steps that can be mechanically executed; each step requires some amount of engineering judgment. Furthermore, the design produced by following a methodology should not be considered the final design. The design can and should be modified using the design principles and the ultimate objectives of the project in mind. Methodologies are essentially guidelines to help the designer in the design activity; they are not hard-and-fast rules. The examples we do here are relatively small, and all aspects of the methodology do not get reflected in them. However, the design of the case study, given at the end of the chapter, will provide a more substantial example for design.

The Word-Counting Problem

Let us first consider the word counting problem discussed in Chapter 5 (for which the structured design was done). The initial analysis clearly shows that there is a File object, which is an aggregation of many Word objects. Further, one can consider that there is a Counter object, which keeps track of the number of different words. It is a matter of preference and opinion whether Counter should be an object, or counting should be implemented as an operation. If counting is treated as an operation, the question will be to which object it belongs. As it does not belong "naturally" to either the class Word nor the class File, it will have to be "forced" into one of the classes. For this reason, we have kept Counter as a separate object. The basic problem statement finds only these three objects. However, further analysis for services reveals that some history mechanism is needed to check if the word is unique. The object model obtained after doing object modeling is shown in Figure 6.9.

Now let us consider the dynamic modeling for this problem. This is essentially a batch processing problem, where a file is given as input and some output is given by the system. Hence, the scenarios for this problem are straightforward. For example, the scenario for the "normal" case can be:

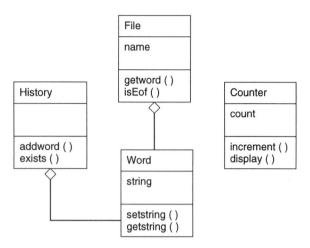

FIGURE 6.9. Object model for the word counting problem.

System prompts for the file name; user enters the file name.
System checks for existence of the file.
System reads the words from the file.
System prints the count.

From this simple scenario, no new operations are uncovered, and our object diagram stays unchanged. Now we consider the functional model. One possible functional model is shown in Figure 6.10. The model reinforces the need for some object where the history of what words have been seen is recorded. This object is used to check the uniqueness of the words. It also shows that various operations like increment(), isunique(), and addToHistory() are needed. These operations can either appear as operations in classes or they will have to be implemented in the main program. In this example, most of these processes are reflected as operations on classes and are already incorporated in the object model.

Now we are at the last two steps of design methodology, where implementation and optimization concerns are used to enhance the object model. First decision we take is that the history mechanism will be implemented by a binary search tree. Hence, instead of the object History, we have a different object Btree. Then, for the class Word, various operations are needed to compare different words. Operations are also needed to set the string value for a word and retrieve it. The final object model is similar in structure to the one shown in Figure 6.9, except for these changes.

The final step of the design activity is to specify this design using some design specification language. This is not a part of the design methodology, but it is an essential step, as the design specification is what forms the major part of the design document. The design specification, as mentioned earlier, should specify all the classes that are in the design, all methods of the classes along with their interfaces

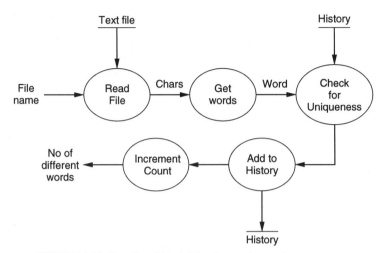

FIGURE 6.10. Functional Model for the word counting problem.

(including which other methods of other objects they invoke), and the basic steps in the main program. We use C++ class structures for our specification. The final specification of this problem is given next. This specification can be reviewed for design verification and can be used as a basis of implementing the design (in C++).

```
class Word  {
  private :
    char *string; // string representing the word
  public:
    bool operator == ( Word ); // Checks for equality
    bool operator < ( Word );
    bool operator > ( Word );
    Word operator = ( Word ); // The assignment operator
    void setWord ( char * ); // Sets the string for the word
    char *getWord (); // gets the string for the word
};

class File {
  private:
    FILE inFile;
    char *fileName;
  public:
    Word getWord (); // get a word; Invokes operations of Word
    bool isEof (); // Checks for end of file
    void fileOpen ( char * );
};

class Counter {
  private:
```

```
      int counter;
   public:
      void increment ();
      void display ();
};

class Btree: GENERIC in <ELEMENT_TYPE>  {
   private:
      ELEMENT_TYPE element;
      Btree < ELEMENT_TYPE > *left;
      Btree < ELEMENT_TYPE > *right;
   public:
      void insert( ELEMENT_TYPE ); // to insert an element
      bool lookup( ELEMENT_TYPE ); // to check if an element exists
};

main (int argc, char *argv[]) {
   FILE file;
   Word word;
   Counter counter;
   Btree <Word> btree;

//    Reads the file word-by-word until EOF
//    For each word, if word does not exist in btree, add it
//    to btree and increment counter
//    In the end, display the counter
}
```

As we can see, all the class definitions complete with data members and operations and all the major object declarations (in this case only in main()) are given in the design specification. Only the implementation of the methods and main() are not provided. In this example, most of the interaction between the objects is taking place through main(). If objects send messages, then in the design specification approach we use, the messages can be mentioned as comments for the methods that send them. This design was later converted to C++. The conversion to code required only minor additions and modifications to the design. The final code was about 240 lines of C++ code (counting noncomment and nonblank lines only).

Rate of Returns Problem

Let us consider a slightly larger problem: of determining the rate of returns on investments. An investor has made investments in some companies. For each investment, in a file, the name of the company, all the money he has invested (in the initial purchase as well as in subsequent purchases), and all the money he has withdrawn (through sale of shares or dividends) are given, along with the dates of each transaction. The current value of the investment is given at the end, along with the date. The goal is to find the rate of return the investor is getting for each investment, as well as the rate of return for the entire portfolio. In addition, the amounts he has invested initially, amounts he has invested subsequently, amounts he has withdrawn, and the current value of the portfolio also is to be output.

This is a practical problem that is frequently needed by investors. The computation of rate of return is not straightforward and cannot be easily done through spread sheets. Hence, such a software can be of practical use. Besides the basic functionality given earlier, the software needs to be robust and catch errors that can be caught in the input data.

We start with the analysis of the problem. Initial analysis clearly shows that there are a few object classes of interest—Portfolio, Investment, and Transaction. A portfolio consists of many investments, and an investment consists of many transactions. Hence, the class Portfolio is an aggregation of many Investments, and an Investment s an aggregation of many Transactions. A transaction can be of Withdrawal type or Deposit type, resulting in a class hierarchy, with Investment being the superclass and Withdrawal and Deposit subclasses.

For an object of class Investment, the major operation we need to perform is to find the rate of return. For the class Portfolio we need to have operations to compute rate of return, total initial investment, total withdrawal, and total current value of the portfolio. Hence, we need operations for these. The object model obtained from analysis of the problem is shown in Figure 6.11.

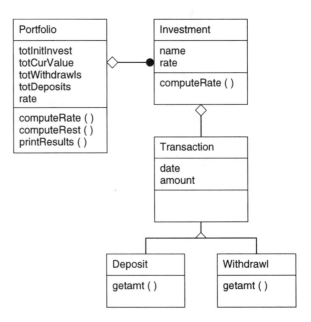

FIGURE 6.11. Object model for rate of return problem.

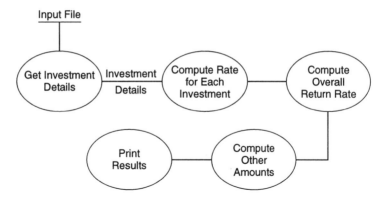

FIGURE 6.12. Functional model for the rate of return problem.

In this problem, as the interaction with the environment is not much, the dynamic model is not significant. Hence, we omit the dynamic modeling for this problem. A possible functional model is given in Figure 6.12. The object model is then enhanced to make sure that each of the processes of the functional model is reflected as operations on various objects. As we can see, most of the processes already exist as operations.

Now we have to perform the last two steps of the design methodology, where implementation and optimization concerns are used to enhance the object model. While considering the implementation of computation of total initial investment, computation of overall return rate, overall withdrawals and so on, we notice that for all of these, appropriate data from each investment is needed. Hence, to the class Investments, appropriate operations need to be added. Further, we note that all the computations for total initial investment, total current value, and so on are all done together, and each of these is essentially adding values from various investments. Hence, we combine them in a single operation in Portfolio and a corresponding single operation in Investment. Studying the class hierarchy, we observe that the only difference in the two subclasses Withdrawal and Deposit is that in one case the amount is subtracted and in the other it is added. In such a situation, the two types can be easily considered a single type by keeping the amount as negative for a withdrawal and positive for a deposit. So we remove the subclasses, thereby simplifying the design and implementation. Instead of giving the object diagram for the final design, we provide the final design specification:

```
class Transaction {
  private:
    int amount; // money amount for the transaction
    int month; // month of the transaction
    int year; // year of the transaction
  public:
    getAmount();
```

```
        getMonth();
        getYear();
        Transaction(amount, month, year); // sets values
};

class Investment {
  private:
    char *investmentName; // Name of the company
    Transaction *transactArray; // List of transactions
    int noOfTransacts; // Total number of transactions
    float rateOfReturn; // rate of return
  public:
    getTransactDetails();  // Set details of transactions
    computeRate();
    float getRate(); // Return the rate of the returns
    compute(initVal, totWithdrawls, totCurVal, totDeposits);
      // Returns these values for this investment
};

class Portfolio {
  private:
    Investment *investArray; // List of investments
    int noOfInvestments; // Total number of investments
    int totalInitInvest;
    int totalDeposits;
    int totalCurVal;
    int totalWithdrawl;
    float RateOfReturns; // Overall rate of returns
  public:
    getInvestDetails( char * fname ); // Parse the input file
    computeRate(); // Compute rates of return
    compute(); // Compute other totals
    printResults(); // Print return rates, total values, etc.
};

main(argc, argv)
{
  Portfolio pf;

  pf.getInvestDetails (argv[1]);
  pf.computeRate ();
  pf.compute ();
  pf.printResults();
}
```

The design is self-explanatory. This design was later converted in C++ code, and we
found that only minor implementation details got added during the implementation,
showing the correctness and completeness of the design. The final size of the

program was about 470 lines of C++ code (counting noncomment and nonblank lines only).

6.5 Metrics

We have already seen that the basic paradigm behind OOD is fundamentally different from the paradigm of function-oriented design. This has brought in a different building block and concepts related to this building block. The definition of modularity has also changed for this new building block, and new methodologies have been proposed for creating designs using this paradigm. It is, therefore, natural to expect that a new set of metrics will be required to evaluate an OO design. However, as the enhanced interest in OO is a relatively recent phenomenon, only a few attempts have been made to propose metrics for object-oriented software [AC94, CK94, LH93]. As these metrics proposals are very recent, none of the proposed metrics have been widely validated to show how they can be used in improving cost or quality, our two major objectives.

Here we present some metrics that have been proposed for evaluating the complexity of an OOD. As design of classes is the central issue in OOD and the major output of any OOD methodology is the class definition, these metrics focus on evaluating classes. Note that for measuring the size of a system, conventional approaches, which measure the size in LOC or function points, can be used, even if OO is used for design. It is the metrics for evaluating the quality or complexity of the design that need to be redefined for OOD. The metrics discussed were proposed in [CK94], and the discussion is based on this work. The results of an experiment described in [BBM95] for validating these metrics and the metrics data presented in [CK94] are used to discuss the role of these metrics.

Weighted Methods per Class (WMC)

The effort in developing a class will in some sense will be determined by the number of methods the class has and the complexity of the methods. Hence, a complexity metric that combines the number of methods and the complexity of methods can be useful in estimating the overall complexity of the class. The weighted methods per class (WMC) metric does precisely this.

Suppose a class C has methods $M_1, M_2, \ldots, M_n$ defined on it. Let the complexity of the method M_i be c_i. As a method is like a regular function or procedure, any complexity metric that is applicable for functions can be used to define c_i (e.g., estimated size, interface complexity, and data flow complexity). The WMC is defined as:

$$\text{WMC} = \sum_{i=1}^{i=n} c_i.$$

If the complexity of each method is considered 1, WMC gives the total number of methods in the class.

The data given in [BBM95, CK94], which is based on evaluation of some existing programs, shows that in most cases, the classes tend to have only a small number of methods, implying that most classes are simple and provide some specific abstraction and operations. Only a few classes have many methods defined on them. The analysis in [BBM95] showed that the WMC metric has a reasonable correlation with fault-proneness of a class. As can be expected, the larger the WMC of a class the better the chances that the class is fault-prone.

Depth of Inheritance Tree (DIT)

Inheritance is, as we have mentioned, one of the unique features of the object-oriented paradigm. As we have said before, inheritance is one of the main mechanisms for reuse in OOD—the deeper a particular class is in a class hierarchy, the more methods it has available for reuse, thereby providing a larger reuse potential. At the same time, as we have mentioned, inheritance increases coupling, which makes changing a class harder. In other words, a class deep in the hierarchy has a lot of methods it can inherit, which makes it difficult to predict its behavior. For both these reasons, it is useful to have some metric to quantify inheritance. The depth of inheritance tree (DIT) is one such metric.

The DIT of a class C in an inheritance hierarchy is the depth from the root class in the inheritance tree. In other words, it is the length of the shortest path from the root of the tree to the node representing C or number of ancestors C has. In case of multiple inheritance, the DIT metric is the maximum length from a root to C.

The data in [BBM95, CK94] suggests that most classes in applications tend to be close to the root, with the maximum DIT metric value (in the applications studied) being around 10. Most the classes have a DIT of 0 (that is, they are the root). This seems to suggest that the designers tend to keep the number of abstraction levels (reflected by the levels in the inheritance tree) small, presumably to aid understanding. In other words, designers (of the systems evaluated) might be giving up on reusability in favor of comprehensibility. The experiments in [BBM95] show that DIT is very significant in predicting defect-proneness of a class: the higher the DIT the higher is the probability that the class is defect-prone.

Number of Children (NOC)

The number of children (NOC) metric value of a class C is the number of immediate subclasses of C. This metric can be used to evaluate the degree of reuse, as a higher NOC number reflects reuse of the definitions in the superclass by a larger number of subclasses. It also gives an idea of the direct influence of a class on other elements of a design—the larger the influence of a class, the more important that the class is correctly designed. In the empirical observations, it was found that classes generally had a small NOC metric value, with a vast majority of classes having no children (i.e., NOC is 0). This suggests that in the systems analyzed, inheritance was not used very heavily. However, the data in [BBM95] seems to suggest that the larger the NOC, the lower the probability of detecting defects in a class. That is, the higher NOC classes are less defect-prone. The reasons for this are not very clear or definite.

Coupling between Classes (CBC)

As discussed earlier in this chapter and in Chapter 5, coupling between modules of a system, in general, reduce modularity and make module modification harder. In OOD, as the basic module is a class, it is desirable to reduce the coupling between classes. The less coupling of a class with other classes, the more independent the class, and hence it will be more easily modifiable. Coupling between classes (CBC) is a metric that tries to quantify coupling that exists between classes.

The CBC value for a class C is the total number of other classes to which the class is coupled. Two classes are considered coupled if methods of one class use methods or instance variables defined in the other class. In general, whether two classes are coupled can easily be determined by looking at the code and the definitions of all the methods of the two classes. However, note that there are indirect forms of coupling (through pointers, etc.) that are hard to identify by evaluating the code.

The experimental data indicates that most of the classes are self-contained and have a CBC value of 0, that is, they are not coupled with any other class, including superclasses [CK94]. Some types of classes, for example the ones that deal with managing interfaces (called interface objects earlier), generally tend to have higher CBC values. The data in [BBM95] found that CBC is significant in predicting the fault-proneness of classes, particularly those that deal with user interfaces.

Response for a Class (RFC)

Although the CBC for a class captures the number of other classes to which this class is coupled, it does not quantify the "strength" of interconnection. In other words, it does not explain the degree of connection of methods of a class with other classes. Response for a class (RFC) tries to quantify this by capturing the total number of methods that can be invoked from an object of this class.

The RFC value for a class C is the cardinality of the response set for a class. The response set of a class C is the set of all methods that can be invoked if a message is sent to an object of this class. This includes all the methods of C and of other classes to which any method of C sends a message. It is clear that even if the CBC value of a class is 1 (that is, it is coupled with only one class), the RFC value may be quite high, indicating that the "volume" of interaction between the two classes is very high. It should be clear that it is likely to be harder to test classes that have higher RFC values.

The experimental data found that most classes tend to invoke a small number of methods of other classes. Again, classes for interface objects tend to have higher RFC values. The data in [BBM95] found that RFC is very significant in predicting the fault-proneness of a class—the higher the RFC value the larger the probability that the class is defect-prone.

Lack of Cohesion in Methods (LCOM)

This last metric in the suite of metrics proposed in [CK94] tries to quantify cohesion of classes. As we have seen, along with low coupling between modules, high cohesion is a highly desirable property for modularity. For classes, cohesion captures how closely bound the different methods of the class are. One way to quantify this is given by the LCOM metric.

Two methods of a class C can be considered "cohesive" if the set of instance variables of C that they access have some elements in common. That is, if I_1 and I_2 are the set of instance variables accessed by the methods M_1 and M_2, respectively, then M_1 and M_2 are similar if $I_1 \cap I_2 \neq \phi$. Let Q be the set of all cohesive pairs of methods, that is, all (M_i, M_j) such that I_i and I_j have a non-null intersection. Let P be the set of all noncohesive pairs of methods, that is, pairs such that the intersection of sets of instance variables they access is null. Then LCOM is defined as

$$\text{LCOM} = |P| - |Q|, \text{ if } |P| > |Q| \quad 0 \quad \text{otherwise.}$$

If there are n methods in a class C, then there are $n(n-1)$ pairs, and LCOM is the number of pairs that are noncohesive minus the number of pairs that are cohesive. The larger the number of cohesive methods, the more cohesive the class will be, and the LCOM metric will be lower. A high LCOM value may indicate that the methods are trying to do different things and operate on different data entities, which may suggest that the class supports multiple abstractions, rather than one abstraction. If this is validated, the class can be partitioned into different classes. The data in [BBM95] found little significance of this metric in predicting the fault-proneness of a class.

In [BBM95], the first five metrics, which were found to be significant in predicting the fault-proneness of classes, were combined to predict the fault-proneness of classes. The experiments showed that the first five metrics, when combined (in this case the coefficients for combination were determined by multivariate analysis of the fault and metric data) are very effective in predicting fault-prone classes. In their experiment, out of a total of 58 faulty classes, 48 classes were correctly predicted as fault-prone. The prediction missed 10 classes and predicted 32 extra classes as fault-prone, although they were not so.

6.6 Summary

In Chapter 5 we studied how a software system can be designed using functional abstraction as the basic unit. In this chapter, we looked at how a system can be designed using *objects* as the basic unit. The fundamental difference in this approach from functional approaches is that an object encapsulates state and provides some predefined operations on that state. That is, state (or data) and operations (i.e., functions) are considered together, whereas in the function-oriented approach the two are kept separate.

When using an object-oriented approach, an object is the basic design unit. That is, the goal of design is to partition the system into objects rather than partition it into functions. For objects, during design, the class for the objects is identified. A *class* represents the type for the object and defines the possible state space for the objects of that class and the operations that can be performed on the objects. An object is an instance of a class and has state, behavior, and identity.

Objects in a system do not exist in isolation but are related to each other. One of the goals of design is to identify the relationship between the objects. This relationship is generally either an *association* or an *aggregation*. An association is a general relationship between objects of two classes, implying that objects of a class invoke operations on the objects of the other class. Aggregation captures the "whole–part of" relationship, implying that the part objects belong to the container object.

A key property of object-oriented systems is *inheritance*, that allows the definition of a class in terms of some existing classes. The new class inherits features from some existing classes, thereby promoting reuse. The class that inherits is called the subclass or the derived class, while the parent class is called the superclass or the base class. With inheritance, all the features of a base class can be made accessible to the derived class. The derived class can add features or redefine them, thereby creating a specialized class. The inheritance relationship results in creation of class hierarchies, use of which is fundamental to object-oriented approaches. Generally, single inheritance suffices where a derived class has exactly one base class. Multiple inheritance is the situation where a class may derive features from various base classes. This form of inheritance brings in some new issues.

Hence, an object-oriented design is one where the final system is represented in terms of object classes, relationships between objects, and relationships between classes. To ensure that the design is modular, some general properties should be satisfied. The main desirable properties are information hiding, low coupling, and high cohesion, where coupling and cohesion are defined in terms of classes. Reuse through inheritance is another important issue, although how to use it is not straightforward, as reuse frequently conflicts with the desire for low coupling. Some other guidelines for design have been given.

Although the basic concepts and principles to use for design and the basic means to evaluate the quality of a design are sufficient to ensure that proper designs are obtained, some help is also needed in how to create a design. Design methodologies help here by providing some guidelines of how to create a design. We discussed the object modeling technique (OMT) for design. The technique actually focuses on modeling. However, the boundary between analysis and design is generally not clear in object-oriented approaches. We consider that modeling is the starting step for design and have thus represented OMT as a design technique. Two examples of creating object-oriented designs using OMT were given.

Finally, we discussed some metrics that can be used to study the complexity of an object-oriented design. We presented one suite of metrics that were proposed, along with some data regarding their validation. The metric weighted methods per class is defined as the sum of complexities of all the methods and gives some idea about how much effort might be needed to develop the class. The depth of inheritance tree of a class is defined as the maximum depth in the class hierarchy of this class, and can represent the potential of reuse that exists for a class, and the degree of coupling between the class and its parent classes. The number of children metric is the number of immediate subclasses of a class, and it can be used to capture the degree of reuse of a class. Coupling of a class is the number of classes whose methods it uses or who use its methods. It can be used to represent the lack of modularity of design. The response for a class metric is the number of methods that can be invoked by sending a message to this class. It tries to capture the strength of interconnection between classes. Finally, the lack of cohesion metric represents the number of method pairs whose set of access variables have nothing in common minus the number of method pairs that have some common instance variable.

Unlike in previous chapters, we have not discussed verification methods here. The reason is that verification methods of reviews and so on discussed in the previous chapters are general techniques that are not specific to function-oriented approaches. Hence, the same general techniques can be used for object-oriented design. Verification techniques that are specific to object-oriented systems have not evolved yet (though work has been done on verification of abstract data types).

Exercises

1. What is the relationship between abstract data types and classes?

2. Why are private parts of a superclass generally not made accessible to subclasses?

3. In C++, *friends* of a class C can access the private parts of C. For declaring a class F a friend of C, where should it be declared—in C or in F? Why?

4. What are the different ways in which an object can access another object in a language like C++? (Do not consider the access allowed by being a friend.)

5. Can we have inheritance without polymorphism? Explain.

6. What are the potential problems that can arise in software maintenance due to different types of inheritance?

7. What is the relationship between OOA, SRS, and OOD?

8. In the word-counting example, a different functional model was used from the one proposed in Chapter 5. Use the model given in Chapter 5 and modify the OO design.

9. Apply the OMT methodology to create a design for an ATM.

10. Suppose a simulator for a disk is to be written (for teaching an Operating Systems course). Use OMT to design the simulator.

11. If an association between classes has some attributes of its own, how will you implement it?

12. If we were to use the method described in Chapter 5 to identify error-prone and complex modules, which of the metrics will you use and why (you may also combine the metrics).

13. Design an experiment to validate your proposal for predicting error-prone modules. Specify data collection and analysis.

14. Compare the OO designs and the structured design of the case study to obtain some observations for comparing the two design strategies (this can be considered a research problem).

CASE STUDY

As with previous chapters, we end this chapter by performing the object-oriented design of the case study. First we discuss the application of the design process on the case study, i.e., how the design for the case study is created, and then we give the specifications of the final design that is created. While discussing the creation of design, we provide only the main steps to give an idea of the design activity.

Object-Oriented Design

We start the design activity by performing the object modeling. During object modeling, the basic focus is on identifying the object classes in the problem domain, relationships between them, hierarchies, attributes of classes, and major services that are evident from studying the problem. From the problem specification, given in Chapter 3, we can clearly identify the following objects: TimeTable, Course, Room, LectureSlot, CToBeSched (course to be scheduled), InputFile_1, and InputFile_2. From the problem, it is clear that TimeTable, an important object in the problem domain, is an aggregation of many TimeTableEntry, each of which is a collection of a Course, a Room where the course is scheduled, and a LectureSlot in which the course is scheduled.

On looking at the description of file 1, we find that it contains a list of rooms, courses, and time slots that is later used to check the validity of entries in file 2. This results in the objects RoomDB, CourseDB, and SlotDB, each of which is an aggregation of many members of Room, Course, and Slot, respectively. Similarly, on looking at the description of file 2, we find that it contains a TableOfCToBeSched, which is an aggregation of many CToBeSched.

On studying the problem further and considering the scheduling constraints imposed by the problem, it is clear that for scheduling, the courses have to be divided into four different types—depending on whether the course is a UG course or a PG course, and whether or not preferences are given. In other words, we can specialize CToBeSched to produce four different subclasses: PGwithPref, UGwithPref, PGwithoutPref, and UGwithoutPref. The classes that represent courses with preferences will contain a list of preferences, which is a list of LectureSlots. This is the only hierarchy that is evident from examining the problem.

Considering the attributes of the object classes, the problem clearly specifies that a Room has the attributes *roomNo* and *capacity*; a LectureSlot has one major attribute, the *slot* it represents; and a Course has *courseName* as an attribute. A CToBeSched contains a Course and has *enrollment* as an attribute.

Considering the services for the object classes, we can clearly identify from the problem specification some services like *scheduleAll()* on TableOfCToBeSched, which schedules all the courses, *printTable()* for the TimeTable, *setentry()* and *getentry()* for a TimeTableEntry, and *insert()* and *lookup()* operations for the various lists. The initial object diagram after object modeling is shown in Figure 6.13.

The system here is not an interactive system; hence dynamic modeling is rather straightforward. The normal scenario is that the inputs are given and the outputs are produced. There are at least two different normal scenarios possible, depending on whether there are any conflicts (requiring conflicts and their reasons to be printed) or not (in which case only the timetable is printed). The latter normal scenario does not reveal any new operations. However, a natural way to model the first scenario is to have an object ConflictTable into which different conflicts for the different time slots of different courses are stored, and from where they are later printed. Hence, we add this object and model it as an aggregation of ConflictTableEntry, with an operation *insertEntry()* to add a conflict entry in the table and an operation *printTable()* to print the conflicts. Then there are a number of exception scenarios—one for each possible error in the input. In each case, the scenario shows that a proper error message is to be output. This requires that operations needed on objects like Room, Course and Slot check their formats for correctness. Hence, validation operations are added to these objects.

The functional model for the problem was given in Chapter 5. It shows that from file 1, roomDB, courseDB, and slotDB need to be formed and the entries for each of these have to be obtained from the file and validated. As validation functions are already added, this adds the function for producing the three lists, called *build_CRS_DBs()*. Similarly, the DFD clearly shows that on InputFile_2 a function to build the table of courses to be scheduled is needed, leading to the adding of the operation *buildCtoBeSched()*. While building this table, this operation also divides them into the four groups of courses, as done in the DFD. The DFD shows that an operation to schedule the courses is needed. This operation (*scheduleAll()*) is already there. Although the high-level DFD does not show, but a further refinement of the bubble for "schedule" shows that bubbles are needed for scheduling PG courses with preferences, UG courses with preferences, PG courses without preferences, and UG courses without preferences (they are reflected in the structure chart as modules). These bubbles get reflected as *schedule()* operations on all four subclasses—PGwithPref, UGwithPref, PGwihoutPrefs, and UGwithoutPrefs. The DFD also has bubbles for printing the timetable and conflicts. These get translated into print operations on TimeTable, TimeTableEntry, ConflictTable, and ConflictTableEntry.

Now we come to the last steps of considering implementation concerns. Many new issues come up here. First, we decided to have a generic template class, which can be used to implement the various DBs, as all DBs are performing similar functions. Hence, we defined a template class List. When considering the main issue of scheduling, we notice that scheduling UG courses with preferences, as discussed in the Chapter 5, is not straightforward, as the system has to ensure that it does not

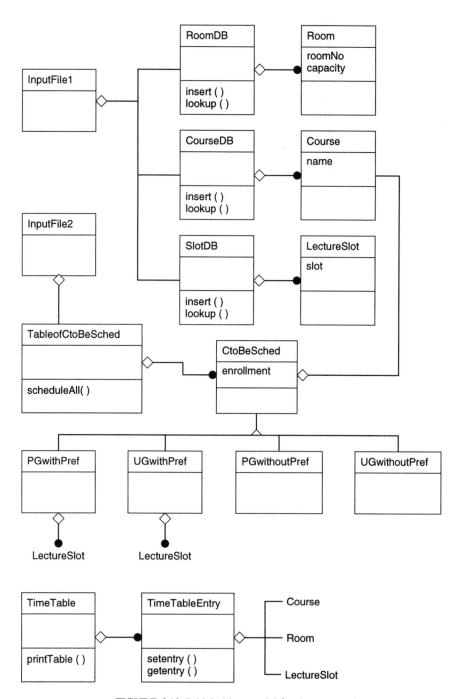

FIGURE 6.13. Initial object model for the case study.

make any PG course without preference "unschedulable." To handle this, we take a simple approach of having a data structure that will reserve slots for PG courses and will then be used to check for the safety of an assignment while scheduling PG courses with preferences. This adds an internal class PGReserve, with operations like *isAllotmentSafe()* (to check if making an allotment for UG course is "safe"), *Initialize()* (to initially "mark" all possible slots where PGwithoutPref courses can be scheduled). The structure is then used to schedule the PG courses without preferences after the UG courses with prefences are scheduled, leading to the operation *getSuitableSchedule()*.

To implement the scheduling operation, we decided to use the dynamic binding capability. For each subclass, the *schedule()* operation that has been defined is made to have the same signature, and a corresponding virtual function is added in the superclass CtoBeScheduled. With this, when the courses are to be scheduled, we can just go over all the courses that need to be scheduled and call the schedule operation. Dynamic binding will make sure that the appropriate schedule operation is called, depending on the type of course (i.e., which of the four subclasses it belongs to). All schedule operations will interact with the TimeTable for checking the conditions specified in the requirements. Various functions are added on TimeTable for this.

Having considered the scheduling operation, we considered the major operation on the files. It becomes clear that to implement these operations, various parsing functions are needed on the two files. These functions are then added. As these operations are only needed to implement the externally visible operations on the class, they are defined as private operations. Considering the public operations on these files reinforce the need for *insert()* and *lookup()* operations in the different DBs, these operations require operations to set the attributes of the independent object of which they are an aggregation. Hence, these operations are added. In a similar manner, while considering implementation issues various other operations on the different object classes were revealed. Various other operations are revealed when considering implementation of other operations. The final object diagram after the design is shown in Figure 6.14. As can be noticed, many of the relationships between the classes that were earlier aggregations have now been modeled as links rather than as contained objects, largely for efficiency reasons.

Design Specification

As we can see, the object diagram, even for this relatively small system, is quite complex and not easily manageable. Furthermore, it is not practical to properly capture the parameters of the various operations in object diagrams. The types of the various attributes is also frequently not shown to keep the diagram compact. Similarly, all associations do not get reflected. Hence, for specifying the design

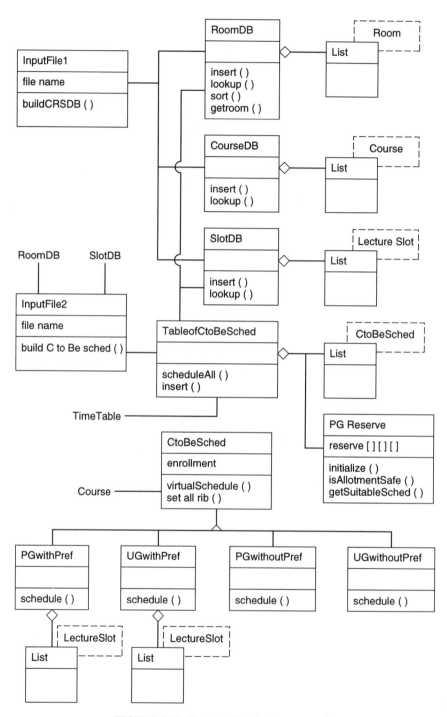

FIGURE 6.14. Object design for the case study.

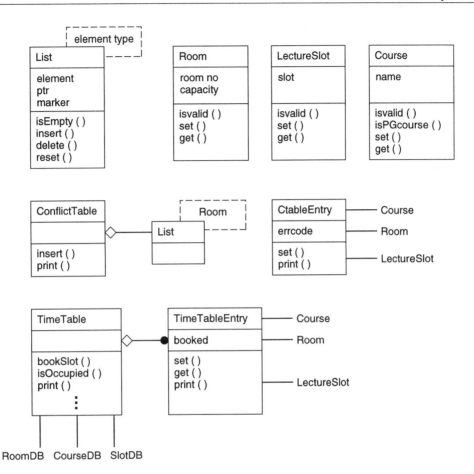

precisely, the object diagram is translated to a precise specification of the classes, and a specification of the *main()* function to show how objects are created and passed between different operations. Here we specify the design shown in Figure 6.14 precisely. As we have been doing, we use C++ structures to specify the design.

```
// This is the specification for the Object-Oriented Design for the Case Study.
// It gives all the major classes and most of the major data members and
// operations for these classes. The major parameters of the various operations
// are also given, which shows how objects are being made visible. All the
// major object declarations are also given. Comments are added only where
// they are needed over and above the discussions above.

class Course {
  private:
    char *courseID;
  public:
```

```
    *tellCourseID ();
    isAValidID ();  // To test whether courseID is invalid
    bool isAPGCourse ();
    void  setAttr (char *);
};

class Room  {
  private:
    int roomNo;
    int capacity;
  public:
    Room (int num, int cap);
    bool tellAttrib (int &num, int &cap);
    bool  areAttribValid ();  // Atrribute validation
};

class LectureSlot {
  private:
    char  *slotID;
  public:
    char  *tellSlotID ();
    bool  isAValidSlot ();
    void  setAttr (char *id);
};

//  Generic List Abstraction
template  <class Element_t>
class List {
  private:
    Element_t listElem[ MAX_ELEMENTS ];
    int currentPtr;
    int stateMarker;
  public:
    bool isListEmpty ();
    bool insertElement (Element_t  element);
    // Next two operations needed to traverse the list
    void reset (); // Reset the CurrentPtr, if you want to scan from start
    bool getNextElement (Element_t  &element);
    // In tables we will represent a room, course, etc. as an index in its DB.
    // Operations for random access in the list are therefore needed.
    bool getIthElement (int, Element_t &);
    bool setIthElement (int, Element_t);
};

// Abstraction  for  room database
class RoomDB {
  private:
    List<Room *> roomDB;
```

```
  public:
    bool insert (Room *);
    void sortRooms (); // Sort on capacity - makes looking for a room easier
    bool getSuitableRoom (enrol); // get smallest room that fits
};

// Abstraction  for  course database
class CourseDB {
  private:
    List<Course  *>  courseDB;
  public:
    bool insert (Course  *);
    bool lookUp (int &, Course &);  // Search the DB and return the index
};

// Abstraction  for  class database
class SlotDB {
  private:
    List<LectureSlot *> slotDB;
  public:
    bool insert (LectureSlot *);
    bool lookUp (int &, LectureSlot &);  // Return index of the lecture slot
};

// Object for File 1
class InputFile_1 {
  private:
    ifstream inFile;
    char *fileName;
    // Parsing functions
    bool semicolonExists (char *); // TRUE if semicolon is present in the line
    bool buildRoomDB (RoomDB  &);  // Parse file until roomDB is built
    bool build_CS_DB (CourseDB &, SlotDB &); // Build course and slot DBs
    char skipOverWhiteSpaces ();
    void getNextRoomEntry (int &, int &, int &);
    void  getNextToken (int &, char *&);
  public:
    build_CRS_DBs (char *fName,CourseDB &cDB, RoomDB &rDB, SlotDB &sDB);
};

// A course that has to be scheduled - from file 2. Forms the base class
class CtoBeSched {
  protected:
    int enrollment;
    int coursePtr;
  public:
    virtual void getScheduled (TimeTable *&, RoomDB *, SlotDB *,
    ConflictTable *&, TableOfCtoBeSched  *&, PGReserve *&);
```

```
      int setAttr (int enrollment, int course);
      bool tellAttr (int &cptr, int &enroll);
};

class PGwithPref: public CtoBeSched {
  private:
    List<int> prefList; // List of preferences
    void getScheduled (TimeTable *&, RoomDB *, SlotDB *,
    ConflictTable *&, TableOfCtoBeSched *&, PGReserve *&);
  public:
    bool insertPref (int); // into prefList
};

class UGwithPref: public CtoBeSched {
  private:
    List<int> prefList; // List of preferences
  public:
    void getScheduled (TimeTable *&, RoomDB *, SlotDB *,
    ConflictTable *&, TableOfCtoBeSched *&, PGReserve *&);
    bool insertPref (int); // into prefList
};

class PGwithoutPref: public CtoBeSched {
  public:
    void getScheduled (TimeTable *&, RoomDB *, SlotDB *,
    ConflictTable *&, TableOfCtoBeSched *&, PGReserve *&);
};

class UGwithoutPref: public CtoBeSched {
  public:
    void getScheduled (TimeTable *&, RoomDB *, SlotDB *,
    ConflictTable *&, TableOfCtoBeSched *&, PGReserve *&);
};

class PGReserve {
  private:
    int reserve[ MAX_COURSES ] [ MAX_SLOTS ] [ MAX_ROOMS ];

  public:
    void initialize (List<CtoBeSched *> *,SlotDB *,RoomDB *,TimeTable *);
    bool isAllotmentSafe (List<CtoBeSched *> *, int room, int slot);
    // given the PG courses without prefs, is this allotment safe?
    bool getSuitableSchedule (TimeTable *&,List<CtoBeSched *> *,int cPtr, int rNum,
    int &slot, int &room,bool &); // To schedule PGwithoutPref courses
};

class TableOfCtoBeSched {  // Table of courses to be scheduled
  private:
```

```
      List<CtoBeSched *> table [NUM_OF_CATEGORIES];
      PGReserve *pgReserve;  // Reservation chart for PGsansP
  public:
      bool scheduleAll (TimeTable *&, SlotDB *,RoomDB *, ConflictTable *&);
      // Sends getScheduled message to all courses
      bool insert (int, CtoBeSched *);
};


class  TimeTableEntry { // One entry in the timetable
  private:
      int coursePtr;  // Index into Course DB
      bool booked;  // Some other course booked it?
  public:
      void setAttr (int cptr, bool mark);
      bool isThisBooked ();
      int tellWho ();
      void printEntry (CourseDB *cDB);
};


class TimeTable {
  private:
      int PGOccupied[ MAX_SLOTS ];
      TimeTableEntry table[ MAX_ROOMS ][ MAX_SLOTS ];
  public:
      bool bookASlot (int, int, int); // Set table[i][j] = ptr;
      bool isColumnEmpty (int colIndex);
      bool setPGOccupied (int slotIndex,int coursePtr);
      int PGwho (int  coursePtr);
      int who (int roomPtr, int slotPtr);
      void printTimeTable (CourseDB *, RoomDB *, SlotDB *);
      bool isAlreadyOccupied (int roomPtr, int slotPtr);
      huntForSuitableRoom (int, int, RoomDB *,  int &);
};


class ConflictTable_Entry {
  private:
      int errorCode;
      int coursePtr;
      int conflictCourse;
      int preference;
      int roomPtr;
  public:
      void setAttr (int E, int c,int cc,int p,int r);
      void printAttr (CourseDB *,SlotDB *,RoomDB *);
};


class  ConflictTable {
  private:
```

```
    List< ConflictTable_Entry *>  table;
  public:
    bool insertEntry (int, int, int, int, int);
    void printTable (CourseDB *,SlotDB *,RoomDB *);
};

class InputFile_2 {
  private:
    char *fileName;
    // Parsing functions
    char skipOverWhiteSpaces ();
    char *getNextToken ();
    char *getNextPref ();
    bool prefGiven ();
  public:
    bool buildCtoBeSched (char *fName, TableOfCtoBeSched &, CourseDB *, SlotDB *);
};

main (int argc, char *argv[]) {
  InputFile_1 in1;
  InputFile_2 in2;
  TableOfCtoBeSched tbl;
  CourseDB cDB;
  RoomDB rDB;
  SlotDB sDB;
  TimeTable *timeTable;
  ConflictTable *conflictTable;

  // From main, first the databases are built by in1.build_CRS_DBs()
  // Then table from file 2 is built by in2.buildCtoBeSched()
  // Rooms are then sorted, and scheduling is done by tbl.scheduleAll()
  // Timetable and conflict table are then printed.
}
```

7

Detailed Design

In previous chapters we discussed two different approaches for system design. In system design we concentrate on the modules in a system and how they interact with each other. The specifications of a module are often communicated by its name, the English phrase with which we label the module. In previous examples we have used words like "sort" and "assign" to communicate the functionality of the modules. The specifications of a module are conveyed by our understanding of the phrases that label the modules. In a design document, a more detailed specification is given by explaining in natural language what a module is supposed to do.

These nonformal methods of specification can lead to problems during coding, particularly if the coder is a different person from the designer, which is often the case. The reason is that the correct implementation of the module depends on the coder interpreting the nonformal specifications of the modules in precisely the manner the designer intended. Even if the designer and the coder are the same person, problems can occur, as the design can take a long time, and the designer may not remember precisely what the module is supposed to do.

The first step before the detailed design or code for a module can be developed is that the specification of the module be given precisely. Once the module is precisely specified, the internal logic for the module that will implement the given specifications can be decided.

In the next section we will discuss some formal methods for specifying modules. We consider specification methods for modules supporting functional abstraction and modules supporting data abstraction. Then we discuss methods for specifying the detailed design of a module. It should, however, be emphasized that in practice, semiformal specifications of the type we have used for the case study are the ones that are most widely used.

7.1   Module Specifications

Informal means of "specifying" what a module is supposed to do are likely to lead to different interpretations of the specifications, which can lead to incorrect implementations. Formal methods of specification can ensure that the specifications are precise and not open to multiple interpretations.

As discussed in the previous chapters, two types of abstraction are commonly used: functional abstraction and data abstraction. This means that if a system design is modular and modules support a well-defined abstraction, most modules will support either functional or data abstraction. In this section we consider a formal specification method for both types of modules.

Let us first discuss the desirable properties that module specifications should have. First, the specifications should be *complete*. That is, the given specifications should specify the entire behavior of the module that only correct implementations satisfy the specifications. A related property is that the specifications should be *unambiguous*. Formal specifications usually are unambiguous while specifications written in natural languages are likely to be ambiguous. The specifications should be easily *understandable* and the specification language should be such that specifications can be easily written. This is required for practical reasons and is a very desired property if the specification method is to be used in actual software development. It is lack of this feature that makes formal specifications less widely used. Formal specifications are often hard to understand and equally hard to write.

An important property of specifications is that they should be *implementation-independent*. Specifications should be given in an abstract manner independent of the eventual implementation of the module and should not specify or suggest any particular method for implementation of the module. This property specifically rules out algorithmic methods for specification. The specification should only give the external behavior; the internal details of the module should be decided later by the programmer.

Independence of implementation is also a property on which there is no universal agreement. One line of thought is that one can never provide specifications that do not suggest anything about the internals of the module. In this case, it is argued, it is best to provide *operational specifications*, where the specifications are given in a very high-level specification language. The specifications in this case are essentially implementation of the module in this high level language. If an interpreter or compiler is available for the specification language, then the added advantage of operational specifications is that a prototype is available once the specifications are provided. This prototype can be used for either testing actual implementations or building a prototype of the entire system.

7.1.1 Specifying Functional Modules

The most abstract view of a functional module is to treat it as a black box that takes in some inputs and produces some outputs such that the outputs have a specified relationship with the inputs. Most modules are designed to operate only on inputs that satisfy some constraints. The constraints may be on the type of input and the range of the inputs. For example, a function that finds the square root of a number may be designed to operate only on the real numbers. In addition, it may require that inputs are positive real numbers.

If the inputs satisfy the desired constraints, the goal of a module is to produce outputs that satisfy some constraints that are often related to the inputs.

Hence, to specify the external behavior of a module supporting functional abstraction, one needs to specify the inputs on which the module operates, the outputs produced by the module, and the relationship of the outputs to the inputs.

One method for specifying modules was proposed by Hoare [Hoa69], based on pre- and post-conditions. The specification method was chosen more for verification of modules (i.e., verifying that a given implementation of a module satisfies its specifications) rather than specifying modules during design. In this method constraints on the input of a module were specified by a logical assertion on the input state called *pre-condition*. The output was specified as a logical assertion on the output state called *post-condition*. The post-condition is specified as an assertion on the final state of the module. No relationship is explicitly specified between the input and the output. Validity of the output is specified entirely by the post-condition assertion. We will discuss this method in more detail in a later chapter when we discuss verification of programs. As an example, consider a module `sort` to be written to sort a list L of integers in ascending order. The pre- and post-condition of this module are:

Pre-condition: non-null L
Post-condition: **forall** i, $1 \leq i < size(L), L[i] \leq L[i+1]$

The specification states that if the input state for the module `sort` is non-null L, the output state should be such that the elements of L are in increasing order.

These specifications are not complete. They only state that the final state of the list L (which is the output of the module `sort`) should be such that the elements are in ascending order. It does not state anything about the implicit requirement of the `sort` module that the final state of the list L should contain the same elements as the initial list. In fact, this specification can be satisfied by a module that takes the first element of the list L and copies it on all the other elements.

A variation of this approach is to specify assertions for the input and output states, but the assertions for the output can be stated as a relation between the final state and the initial state. In such methods, while specifying the condition on the output, the final state of an entity E is referred to as $Eprime$ (the initial state is referred by E itself). Using this notation, a possible specification of the module sort is

sort (L: list of integers)
 input: non-null L
 output: **forall** i, $1 \leq i < size(L')$
  L'[i] $\leq$ L'[i+1] **and**
  L' = permutation(L)

This specification, besides the ordering requirement, states that elements of the final list are a permutation of elements of the initial list. This specification will be complete if the module is to be designed only to operate on non-null lists. Often the modules check if the input satisfies the desired constraints. If the constraints are not satisfied, it is treated as an *exception condition*, and some special code is executed. If we want the module to handle exceptions, we need to specify the *exceptional behavior* of the modules. Some work has been done in specifying and verifying modules with exceptions, and the reader is referred to [Cri84, BJ89] for more information.

7.1.2 Specifying Classes

Data abstraction is considered one of the most important language concepts of recent times. It comprises a group of related operations that act on a particular class of objects, with the constraint that the behavior of the objects can only be observed by applying the operations. Data abstractions, when supported as types in a language, are also called abstract data types (ADTs). Data abstraction is extremely useful for hiding information and providing high-level abstraction. Many languages, including Simula, CLU, and Ada, support abstract data types. As mentioned in Chapter 6, a class without inheritance is an ADT, and an object of such a class is essentially an instance of an ADT. Here we discuss the specification of classes without inheritance, that is, abstract data types.

Various specification techniques have evolved for specifying abstract data types. Here we will describe the axiomatic specification technique [GH78]. In the axiomatic specification method the operations are not directly specified by specifying the behavior of each operation independently. Instead, axioms are used that specify the behavior of different interaction of operations. The interactions for which axioms are chosen are such that they completely describe the behavior of the operations.

Before we proceed, let us demonstrate the axiomatic method by writing specifications for a stack of integers. We define a stack that has four operations:

* Create: to create a new stack.
* Push: to push an element on a stack.

1. stack [integer]
    declare
2.   create ( ) → stack ;
3.   push (stack , integer)→ stack ;
4.   pop (stack) → stack ;
5.   top (stack) → integer U undefined ;
    var
6.   s : stack ; i : integer ;
    forall
7.   top (create ( )) = undefined ;
8.   top (push (s , i)) = i ;
9.   pop (create ( )) = create ( ) ;
10.   pop (push (s , i)) = s ;
    end

FIGURE 7.1. Axiomatic specifications of a stack.

- Pop: to pop the top element from the stack.
- Top: returns the element on top of the stack.

If we were to just specify the stack in this manner, to convey the semantics of the operations, we have to rely on the meaning of words like Stack, Push, and Pop. Based on our understanding of these words, we may derive proper semantics of operations in this simple case. However, for absolutely new data types, this assumption may not hold. Axiomatic specifications remove this reliance on the meaning of words and intuition by precisely specifying the data type. The specifications of the stack are shown in Figure 7.1.

For axiomatic specifications to be used properly, we must agree on some language to be used for specifications. Here we present the specification language that we will use in this chapter, which has two major components: syntactic specifications and semantic specifications. The syntactic specifications provide the syntactic and type checking information such as variable names, variable types, and the domain and range of operations. Semantic specifications define the meaning of the operations by stating, in the form of axioms, relationships of the operations among each other.

The syntactic part of the specifications has three components: the header, operation declarations, and variable declaration. The header specifies the name of the data type and any parameters it may have. All the operations of the ADT must have a declaration in the operation declaration part. For an operation, the declaration has to specify the type of the input parameters and the result. The type can be the ADT itself, any of the type parameters of the ADT, or a standard type like Boolean or integer. In the variable declaration part, variables can be declared only of the types that have appeared before. The variables are declared for use in semantic specifications.

The semantics of the operations in the axiomatic specification technique are specified in the semantic part by enumerating axioms for operations. Axioms attach meaning to operations by specifying the relationship between operations. The following constructs are allowed for writing the axioms:

- Free variables
- If-then-else
- Recursion
- Boolean expressions.

Once we have constructed the specifications for a data type, we have to consider if a sufficient number of consistent axioms have been provided. Consistency means that partial semantics of different operations, specified by the axioms, is not contradictory. Determining consistency is theoretically an undecidable problem, but in practice it is often relatively simple to demonstrate the consistency of a set of axioms. One method of demonstrating consistency is to implement the data type. If the type can be implemented, its consistency is established.

Determining the completeness of a given set of axioms is usually a more difficult problem than determining consistency. For completeness we use the notion of *sufficient completeness* [GH78, Gut80]. To define sufficient completeness, we divide the set of operations defined on the ADT into two sets, S and O. The set S contains the operations whose range is ADT, returning a value of the type being specified. The set O contains operations that map values of the type ADT into other types, returning values of types other than the type being specified. The operations in O are often called behavior operations, while we sometimes use the term nonbehavior operations to mean operations in the set S. In the example of the stack, the operation "top" is the only behavior operation.

Behavior operations provide a window into the state of instances of the abstract type. Behavior functions allow the actual behavior of an instance to be viewed from the outside. In principle, an abstract type can be defined without having any behavior operations, but for such types there is no way of distinguishing one instance of the abstract type from another, as there are no operations provided to observe the behavior of an instance of the abstract type from the outside. The ability to distinguish two instances depends solely on the result of behavior operations performed on the instances. Instances of the abstract type, on the other hand, are created and manipulated solely by the nonbehavior operations.

A set of axioms specifying an abstract type is considered *sufficiently complete* if and only if for every possible instance (such as an instance that can be created by some sequence of nonbehavior operations) of the abstract type, the result of all the behavior operations of the type is defined by the specifications [GH78]. This notion of sufficient completeness is from the external point of view; external behavior of the ADT should always be specified. The specifications for the type stack given earlier can be shown to be sufficiently complete. However, the general problem of determining if a set of axioms is sufficiently complete is undecidable.

The most obvious reason for incompleteness is that some axioms are not provided. Incompletion results when some of the axioms required to specify a type are omitted. Even though completeness is defined from the point of view of externally observable behavior of the type, incompleteness will result even if the missing axioms are for nonbehavior operations, because this could lead to construction of an instance on which the result of some behavior operation is not defined.

A heuristic for generating complete specifications was provided by Guttag. For this we further divide the set S into two categories—constructors and extension operators. Constructors are those operations with which we can construct any instance of the ADT. In other words, any instance of a data type, regardless of what sequence of operations created it, can be created by a sequence of operations consisting solely of constructors. Extension operators are those operations that are not constructors but that return a value of type ADT. In the case of the stack the operations "create" and "push" are constructors, while "pop" is an extension operator. Consider the following instance of the type stack:

   push(pop(push(push(create(), 1), 2)), 3)

Even though this instance is created by three different operations, the instance can be created by the following expression of constructors:

   push(push(create(), 1), 3)

Identifying constructors cannot be done mechanically. It depends on the data type, and we have to use our judgment to separate constructors from the extension operators. But, for most cases, identifying constructors is relatively easy.

With constructors, another definition can be given for sufficient completeness. When a set of axioms is complete, any expression of the abstract type is reduced to an expression consisting solely of constructors by the application of the axioms. In other words, if axioms are treated as rewrite rules, then in an expression a pattern matching the left-hand side of an axiom can be replaced by the expression on the right-hand side of the axiom. The set of axioms is complete if by rewriting the expression using the axioms, we eventually reach an irreducible expression that consists solely of constructors.

Once the constructors are identified, a sufficiently complete set of axioms can be generated. Consider an expression consisting of a nonconstructor applied to a constructor. Form all such different expressions. These expressions form the left side of the axioms. Such a set of axioms is guaranteed to be sufficiently complete. So, for a data type with n operations, if there are m constructors, the total number of axioms generated by this will be $m * (n - m)$. Thus, in the case of the stack we have $2 * 2 = 4$ axioms, and the left sides are formed by combining "top" and "pop" with the two constructors "create" and "push."

Note that this method does not specify what the right side of the axiom should be. We have to determine that ourselves. If we do not properly state the right side for each case, we may end up with a set of axioms that is inconsistent or that represents a data type different from what we wanted to specify. Clearly, no rules can be given to specify the right side, as it depends on the type being specified.

Now let us consider a queue. We define the following operations on the type queue:

- newq: creates a new queue.
- addq: adds a new element at the end of the queue.
- deleteq: deletes the element at the front of the queue.
- emptyq: tells if the queue is empty or not.
- appendq: appends another queue at the end of a queue.
- frontq: returns the item at the front of the queue.

The constructors are "newq," and "addq." Any instance, whether created by using "appendq," or "deleteq," can be created by these two operations. Using the preceding technique, we will have $4 * 2 = 8$ axioms to obtain a sufficiently complete set of axioms. For each of these eight expressions, we have to specify the right side correctly so that they represent the type queue. The axioms are shown in Figure 7.2.

Line 1 of the specification is the header of the ADT that states that this is the specification of a queue of type Items. Lines 2 through 7 specify the different operations defined on the type queue and their domain and range. It should be noted that this type is parameterized with type Item. Lines 8 and 9 declare some variables to be used in the axioms. Lines 1 through 9 form the syntactic specifications. Lines 10 and 11 specify the behavior of the function "emptyq"; if "emptyq" is performed on a "newq," it returns true, and if its performed on a queue to which an element has been added, it returns false. Lines 12 and 13 specify the behavior of the operation "frontq"; lines 14 and 15, the behavior of "deleteq"; and lines 16 and 17, the behavior of "appendq." The set of axioms given here can be shown to be complete. It might be pointed out that systems exist that can synthesize implementation from the axiomatic specifications [Jal87] or automatically test the completeness of axioms [JC88, Jal89a].

7.2 Detailed Design

We have seen some techniques for system design. Most design techniques, like structured design, identify the major modules and the major data flow among them. The methods used to specify the system design typically focus on the external interfaces of the modules and cannot be extended to specify the internals. Process design language (PDL) is one way in which the design can be communicated precisely and completely to whatever degree of detail desired by the designer. That

1. queue [Item]
    declare
2.   newq ( ) → queue ;
3.   addq (queue , Item) → queue ;
4.   deleteq (queue) → queue ;
5.   emptyq (queue) → boolean ;
6.   appendq (queue , queue) → queue ;
7.   frontq (queue) → Item U undefined ;
    var
8.   q , r : queue ;
9.   i : Item ;
    forall
10.   emptyq (newq ( )) = true ;
11.   emptyq (addq (q , i)) = false ;
12.   frontq (newq ( )) = undefined ;
13.   frontq (addq (q , i)) = if emptyq (q) then i
            else frontq (q) ;
14.   deleteq (newq ( )) = newq ( ) ;
15.   deleteq (addq (q , i)) = if emptyq (q) then newq ( )
            else addq (deleteq (q) , i) ;
16.   appendq (q , newq ( )) = q ;
17.   appendq (r , addq (q , i)) = addq (appendq (r , q) , i) ;
    end

FIGURE 7.2. Specifications of the type queue.

is, it can be used to specify the system design and to extend it to include the logic design. PDL is particularly useful when using top-down refinement techniques to design a system or module.

7.2.1 PDL

One way to communicate a design is to specify it in a natural language, like English. This approach often leads to misunderstanding, and such imprecise communication is not particularly useful when converting the design into code. The other extreme is to communicate it precisely in a formal language, like a programming language. Such representations often have great detail, which is necessary for implementation but not important for communicating the design. These details are often a hindrance to easy communication of the basic design. Ideally we would like to express the design in a language that is as precise and unambiguous as possible without having too much detail and that can be easily converted into an implementation. This is what PDL attempts to do.

minmax(infile)

ARRAY a

```
DO UNTIL end of input
    READ an item into a
ENDDO
max, min := first item of a
DO FOR each item in a
    IF max < item THEN set max to item
    IF min > item THEN set min to item
ENDDO
END
```

FIGURE 7.3. PDL description of the minmax program.

PDL has an overall outer syntax of a structured programming language and has a vocabulary of a natural language (English in our case). It can be thought of as "structured English". Because the structure of a design expressed in PDL is formal, using the formal language constructs, some amount of automated processing can be done on such designs. As an example, consider the problem of finding the minimum and maximum of a set of numbers in a file and outputting these numbers in PDL as shown in Figure 7.3.

Notice that in the PDL program we have the entire logic of the procedure, but little about the details of implementation in a particular language. To implement this in a language, each of the PDL statements will have to be converted into programming language statements. Let us consider another example. Text is given in a file with one blank between two words. It is to be formatted into lines of 80 characters, except the last line. A word is not to be divided into two lines, and the numbers of blanks needed to fill the line are added at the end, with no more than two blanks between words. The PDL program is shown in Figure 7.4. Notice the use of procedure to express the design.

With PDL, a design can be expressed in whatever level of detail that is suitable for the problem. One way to use PDL is to first generate a rough outline of the entire solution at a given level of detail. When the design is agreed on at this level, more detail can be added. This allows a successive refinement approach, and can save considerable cost by detecting the design errors early during the design phase. It also aids design verification by phases, which helps in developing error-free designs. The structured outer syntax of PDL also encourages the use of structured language constructs while implementing the design.

The basic constructs of PDL are similar to those of a structured language. The first is the IF construct. It is similar to the if-then-else construct of Pascal. However,

```
Initialize buf to empty
DO FOREVER
    DO UNTIL (#chars in buf ≥ 80 & word boundary is reached)
         OR (end-of-text reached)
       read chars in buf
    ENDDO
    IF #chars > 80 THEN
       remove last word from buf
       PRINT-WITH-FILL (buf)
       set buf to last word ELSEIF #chars = 80 THEN
       print (Buf)
       set buf to empty
    ELSE EXIT the loop
ENDDO


PROCEDURE PRINT-WITH-FILL (buf)

Determine #words and #character in buf
#of blanks needed = 80 - #character
DO FOR each word in the buf
    print (word)
    if #printed words ≥ (#word - #of blanks needed) THEN
       print (two blanks)
    ELSE print (single blank)
ENDDO
```

FIGURE 7.4. PDL description of text-formatter.

the conditions and the statements to be executed need not be stated in a formal language. For a general selection, there is a CASE statement. Some examples of CASE statements are:

    CASE OF transaction type
    CASE OF operator type

The DO construct is used to indicate repetition. The construct is indicated by:

        DO iteration criteria
           one or more statements
        ENDDO

The iteration criteria can be chosen to suit the problem, and unlike a formal programming language, they need not be formally stated. Examples of valid uses are:

        DO WHILE there are characters in input file
        DO UNTIL the end of file is reached

DO FOR each item in the list EXCEPT when item is zero

A variety of data structures can be defined and used in PDL such as lists, tables, scalar, and integers. Variations of PDL, along with some automated support, are used extensively for communicating designs.

7.2.2   Logic/Algorithm Design

The basic goal in detailed design is to specify the logic for the different modules that have been specified during system design. Specifying the logic will require developing an algorithm that will implement the given specifications. Here we consider some principles for designing algorithms or logic that will implement the given specifications.

The term *algorithm* is quite general and is applicable to a wide variety of areas. Essentially, an algorithm is a sequence of steps that need to be performed to solve a given problem. The problem need not be a programming problem. We can, for example, design algorithms for such activities as cooking dishes (the recipes are nothing but algorithms) and building a table. In the software development life cycle we are only interested in algorithms related to software. For this, we define an algorithm to be an unambiguous procedure for solving a problem [GH77]. A *procedure* is a finite sequence of well-defined steps or operations, each of which requires a finite amount of memory and time to complete. In this definition we assume that termination is an essential property of procedures. From now on we will use procedures, algorithms, and logic interchangeably.

There are a number of steps that one has to perform while developing an algorithm [GH77]. The starting step in the design of algorithms is *statement of the problem*. The problem for which an algorithm is being devised has to be precisely and clearly stated and properly understood by the person responsible for designing the algorithm. For detailed design, the problem statement comes from the system design. That is, the problem statement is already available when the detailed design of a module commences. The next step is development of a mathematical *model* for the problem. In modeling, one has to select the mathematical structures that are best suited for the problem. It can help to look at other similar problems that have been solved. In most cases, models are constructed by taking models of similar problems and modifying the model to suit the current problem. The next step is the *design of the algorithm*. During this step the data structure and program structure are decided. Once the algorithm is designed, its correctness should be verified.

No clear procedure can be given for designing algorithms. Having such a procedure amounts to automating the problem of algorithm development, which is not possible with the current methods. However, some heuristics or methods can be provided to help the designer design algorithms for modules. The most common method for designing algorithms or the logic for a module is to use the *stepwise refinement technique* [Wir71].

The stepwise refinement technique breaks the logic design problem into a series of steps, so that the development can be done gradually. The process starts by converting the specifications of the module into an abstract description of an algorithm containing a few abstract statements. In each step, one or several statements in the algorithm developed so far are decomposed into more detailed instructions. The successive refinement terminates when all instructions are sufficiently precise that they can easily be converted into programming language statements. During refinement, both data and instructions have to be refined. A guideline for refinement is that in each step the amount of decomposition should be such that it can be easily handled and that represents one or two design decisions.

The stepwise refinement technique is a top-down method for developing detailed design. We have already seen top-down methods for developing system designs. To perform stepwise refinement, a language is needed to express the logic of a module at different levels of detail, starting from the specifications of the module. We need a language that has enough flexibility to accommodate different levels of precision. Programming languages typically are not suitable as they do not have this flexibility. For this purpose, PDL is very suitable. Its formal outer syntax ensures that the design being developed is a "computer algorithm" whose statements can later be converted into statements of a programming language. Its flexible natural language–based inner syntax allows statements to be expressed with varying degrees of precision and aids the refinement process.

An Example: Let us again consider the problem of counting different words in a text file. Suppose that in the high-level structure chart of a large text processing system, a COUNT module is specified whose job is to determine the count of different words. During detailed design we have to determine the logic of this module so that the specifications are met. We will use the stepwise refinement method for this. For specification we will use PDL, adapted to C-style syntax. A simple strategy for the first step is shown in Figure 7.5.

This strategy is simple and easy to understand. This is the strategy that we proposed in the data flow graph earlier. The "primitive" operations used in this strategy

```
int count (file)
FILE file;
word_list wl;
{
  read file into wl
  sort (wl);
  count = different_words (wl);
  printf (count);
}
```

FIGURE 7.5. Strategy for the first step in stepwise refinement.

```
read_from_file (file, wl)
FILE file;
word_list wl;
{
  initialize wl to empty;
  while not end-of-file {
  get_a_word from file
  add word to wl
}
```

FIGURE 7.6. Refinement of the reading operation.

are very high-level and need to be further refined. Specifically, there are three operations that need refinement. These are (1) read file into the word list, whose purpose is to read all the words from the file and create a word list, (2) sort(wl), which sorts the word list in ascending order, and (3) count different words from a sorted word list. So far, only one data structure is defined: the word list. As refinement proceeds, more data structures might be needed.

In the next refinement step, we should select one of the three operations to be refined and further elaborate it. In this step we will refine the reading procedure. One strategy of implementing the read module is to read words and add them to the word list. This is shown in Figure 7.6.

This is a straightforward strategy, simple enough to be easily handled in one refinement step. Another strategy could be to read large amounts of data from the file in a buffer and form the word list from this buffer. This might lead to a more efficient implementation. For the next refinement step we select the counting function. A strategy for implementing this function is shown in Figure 7.7.

Similarly, we can refine the sort function. Once these refinements are done, we have a design that is sufficiently detailed and needs no further refinement. For more complex problems many successive refinements might be needed for a single operation. Design for such problems can proceed in two ways—depth first or breadth first. In the depth first approach, when an operation is being refined, its refinement is completely finished (which might require many levels of refinement) before refinement of other operations begins. In the breadth first approach, all operations needing refinement are refined once. Then all the operations specified in this refinement are refined once. This is done until no refinement is needed. A combination of the two approaches could also be followed.

It is worth comparing the structure of the PDL programs produced by this method as compared to the structure produced using the structured design methodology. The two structures are not the same. The basic difference is that in stepwise refinement, the function sort is subordinate to the main module, while in the design produced by using structured design methodology, it is a subordinate module to the input

```
int different_words (wl)
word_list wl;
{
  word last, cur;
  int cnt;

  last = first word in wl
  cnt = 1;
  while not end of list {
    cur = next word from wl
    if (cur <> last) {
      cnt = cnt + 1;
      last = cur;
    }
  }
  return (cnt)
}
```

FIGURE 7.7. Refinement of the function different_words.

module. This is not just a minor point; it points to a difference in approaches. In stepwise refinement, in each refinement step we specify the operations that are needed (as we do while drawing the data flow diagram). In structured design, the focus is on partitioning the problem into input, output, and transform modules, which usually results in a different structure.

7.2.3 State Modeling of Classes

For object-oriented design, the approach just discussed for obtaining the detailed design may not be sufficient. In the method, the focus is on specifying the logic or the algorithm for the modules identified in the (function-oriented) high-level design. But a class is not a functional abstraction and cannot be viewed as an algorithm. A method of a class can be viewed as a functional module, and the methods can be used to specify the logic for the methods.

The technique for getting a more detailed understanding of the class as a whole, without talking about the logic of different methods, has to be fundamentally different from the PDL-based approach. An object of a class has some state and many operations on it. To better understand a class, the relationship between the state and various operations and the effect of interaction of various operations have to be understood. This can be viewed as one of the objectives of the detailed design activity for object-oriented development. Once the overall class is better understood, the algorithms for its various methods can be developed. Note that the axiomatic specification approach for a class, discussed earlier in this chapter, also takes this view. Instead of specifying the functionality of each operation, it specifies, through axioms, the interaction between different operations.

A method to understand the behavior of a class is to view it as a finite state automata (FSA). An FSA consists of states and transitions between states, which take place when some events occur. When modeling an object, the state is the value of its attributes, and an event is the performing of an operation on the object. A *state diagram* relates events and states by showing how the state changes when an event is performed. A state diagram for an object will generally have an initial state, from which all states in the FSA are reachable (i.e., there is a path from the initial state to all other states).

A state diagram for an object does not represent all the actual states of the object, as there are many possible states. A state diagram attempts to represent only the logical states of the object. A *logical state* of an object is a combination of all those states from which the behavior of the object is similar for all possible events. Two logical states will have different behavior for at least one event. For example, for an object that represents a stack, all states that represent a stack of size more than 0 and less than some defined maximum are similar as the behavior of all operations defined on the stack will be similar in all such states (e.g., push will add an element, pop will remove one, etc.). However, the state representing an empty stack is different as the behavior of top and pop operations are different now (an error message may be returned). Similarly, the state representing a full stack is different. The state model for this bounded size stack is shown in Figure 7.8.

The finite state modeling of objects is an aid to understand the effect of various operations defined on the class on the state of the object. A good understanding of this can aid in developing the logic for each of the operations. To develop the logic of operations, regular approaches for algorithm development can be used. The model can also be used to validate if the logic for an operation is correct. As we have seen, for a class, typically the input-output specification of the operations

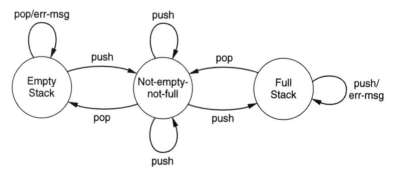

FIGURE 7.8. FSA model of a stack.

is not provided. Hence, the FSA model can be used as a reference for validating the logic of the different methods.

State modeling of classes has also been proposed as a technique for analysis [R⁺91]. However, we believe that it has limited use during analysis, and its role is more appropriate during detailed design when the detailed working of a class needs to be understood. Even here, the scope of this modeling is limited. It is likely to be more of use if the interaction between the methods through the state is heavy and there are many states in which the methods need to behave differently.

7.3 Verification

There are a few techniques available to verify that the detailed design is consistent with the system design. The focus of verification in the detailed design phase is on showing that the detailed design meets the specifications laid down in the system design. Validating that the system as designed is consistent with the requirements of the system is not stressed during detailed design. The three verification methods we consider are design walkthroughs, critical design review, and consistency checkers.

7.3.1 Design Walkthroughs

A *design walkthrough* is a manual method of verification. The definition and use of walkthroughs change from organization to organization. Here we describe one walkthrough model. A design walkthrough is done in an informal meeting called by the designer or the leader of the designer's group. The walkthrough group is usually small and contains, along with the designer, the group leader and/or another designer of the group. The designer might just get together with a colleague for the walkthrough or the group leader might require the designer to have the walkthrough with him.

In a walkthrough the designer explains the logic step by step, and the members of the group ask questions, point out possible errors or seek clarification. A beneficial side effect of walkthroughs is that in the process of articulating and explaining the design in detail, the designer himself can uncover some of the errors.

Walkthroughs are essentially a form of peer review. Due to its informal nature, they are usually not as effective as the design review.

7.3.2 Critical Design Review

The purpose of *critical design review* is to ensure that the detailed design satisfies the specifications laid down during system design. As mentioned earlier, it is very desirable to detect and remove design errors early, as the cost of removing them later can be considerably more than the cost of removing them at design time. Detecting errors in detailed design is the aim of critical design review.

The critical design review process is similar to the other reviews, in that a group of people get together to discuss the design with the aim of revealing design errors or undesirable properties. The review group includes, besides the author of the detailed design, a member of the system design team, the programmer responsible for ultimately coding the module(s) under review, and an independent software quality engineer.

The review can be held in the same manner as the requirement review or system design review. That is, each member studies the design beforehand and with the aid of a checklist marks items that the reviewer feels are incorrect or need clarification. The members ask questions and the designer tries to explain the situation. During the discussion design errors are revealed.

As with any review, it should be kept in mind that the aim of the meeting is to uncover design errors, not try to fix them. Fixing is done later. Also, the psychological frame of mind should be healthy, and the designer should not be put in a defensive position. The meeting should end with a list of action items, to be acted on later by the designer.

The use of checklists, as with other reviews, is considered important for the success of the review. The checklist is a means of focusing the discussion or the "search" of errors. Checklists can be used by each member during private study of the design and during the review meeting. For best results, the checklist should be tailored to the project at hand, to uncover project-specific errors. Here we list a few general items that can be used to construct a checklist for a design review [Dun84].

A Sample Checklist

- Does each of the modules in the system design exist in detailed design?
- Are there analyses to demonstrate that the performance requirements can be met?
- Are all the assumptions explicitly stated, and are they acceptable?
- Are all relevant aspects of system design reflected in detailed design?
- Have the exceptional conditions been handled?
- Are all the data formats consistent with the system design?
- Is the design structured, and does it conform to local standards?
- Are the sizes of data structures estimated? Are provisions made to guard against overflow?
- Is each statement specified in natural language easily codable?
- Are the loop termination conditions properly specified?

- Are the conditions in the loops OK?
- Are the conditions in the if statements correct?
- Is the nesting proper?
- Is the module logic too complex?
- Are the modules highly cohesive?

7.3.3 Consistency Checkers

Design reviews and walkthroughs are manual processes; the people involved in the review and walkthrough determine the errors in the design. If the design is specified in PDL or some other formally defined design language, it is possible to detect some design defects by using consistency checkers.

Consistency checkers are essentially compilers that take as input the design specified in a design language (PDL in our case). Clearly, they cannot produce executable code because the inner syntax of PDL allows natural language and many activities are specified in the natural language. However, the module interface specifications (which belong to outer syntax) are specified formally. A consistency checker can ensure that any modules invoked or used by a given module actually exist in the design and that the interface used by the caller is consistent with the interface definition of the called module. It can also check if the used global data items are indeed defined globally in the design.

Depending on the precision and syntax of the design language, consistency checkers can produce other information as well. In addition, these tools can be used to compute the complexity of modules and other metrics, because these metrics are based on alternate and loop constructs, which have a formal syntax in PDL. The trade-off here is that the more formal the design language, the more checking can be done during design, but the cost is that the design language becomes less flexible and tends towards a programming language.

7.4 Metrics

After the detailed design the logic of the system and the data structures are largely specified. Only the implementation-oriented details, which are often specific to the programming language used, need to be further defined. Hence, many of the metrics that are traditionally associated with code can be used effectively after detailed design. During detailed design all the metrics covered during the system design are applicable and useful. With the logic of modules available after detailed design, it is meaningful to talk about the complexity of a module. Traditionally, complexity metrics are applied to code, but they can easily be applied to detailed design as well. Here we describe some metrics applicable to detailed design.

7.4.1 Cyclomatic Complexity

Based on the capability of the human mind and the experience of people, it is generally recognized that conditions and control statements add complexity to a program. Given two programs with the same size, the program with the larger number of decision statements is likely to be more complex. The simplest measure of complexity, then, is the number of constructs that represent branches in the control flow of the program, like if then else, while do, repeat until, and goto statements.

A more refined measure is the *cyclomatic complexity measure* proposed by Mc-Cabe, which is a graph-theoretic–based concept. For a graph G with n nodes, e edges, and p connected components, the cyclomatic number V(G) is defined as

$$V(G) = e - n + p.$$

To use this to define the cyclomatic complexity of a module, the control flow graph G of the module is first drawn. To construct a control flow graph of a program module, break the module into blocks delimited by statements that affect the control flow, like if, while, repeat, and goto. These blocks form the nodes of the graph. If the control from a block i can branch to a block j, then draw an arc from node i to node j in the graph. The control flow of a program can be constructed mechanically. As an example, consider the C-like funtion for bubble sorting, given next. The control flow graph for this is given in Figure 7.9.

```
0.  {
1.      i = 1;
2.      while (i <= n) {
3.          j = i;
4.          while (j <= i) {
5.              if (A[i] < A[j])
6.                  swap(A[i], A[j]);
7.              j = j + 1; }
8.          i = i + 1; }
9.  }
```

The graph of a module has an entry node and an exit node, corresponding to the first and last blocks of statements (or we can create artificial nodes for simplicity, as in the example). In such graphs there will be a path from the entry node to any node and a path from any node to the exit node (assuming the program has no anomalies like unreachable code). For such a graph, the cyclomatic number can be 0 if the code is a linear sequence of statements without any control statement. If we draw an arc from the exit node to the entry node, the graph will be strongly connected because there is a path between any two nodes. The cyclomatic number of a graph for any program will then be nonzero, and it is desirable to have a nonzero complexity for a simple program without any conditions (after all, there is some complexity in such a program). Hence, for computing the cyclomatic complexity

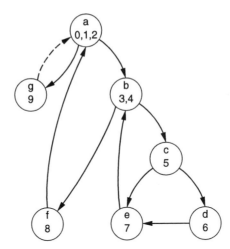

FIGURE 7.9. Flow graph of the example.

of a program, an arc is added from the exit node to the start node, which makes it a strongly connected graph. For a module, the *cyclomatic complexity* is defined to be the cyclomatic number of such a graph for the module.

As it turns out the cyclomatic complexity of a module (or cyclomatic number of its graph) is equal to the maximum number of linearly independent circuits in the graph. A set of circuits is linearly independent if no circuit is totally contained in another circuit or is a combination of other circuits. So, for calculating the cyclomatic number of a module, we can draw the graph, make it connected by drawing an arc from the exit node to the entry node, and then either count the number of circuits or compute it by counting the number of edges and nodes. In the graph shown in Figure 7.9, the cyclomatic complexity is

$$V(G) = 10 - 7 + 1 = 4.$$

The independent circuits are:

>   ckt 1: b c e b
>   ckt 2: b c d e b
>   ckt 3: a b f a
>   ckt 4: a g a

It can also be shown that the cyclomatic complexity of a module is the number of decisions in the module plus one, where a decision is effectively any conditional statement in the module [CDS86]. Hence, we can also compute the cyclomatic complexity simply by counting the number of decisions in the module. For this example, as we can see, we get the same cyclomatic complexity for the module if we add 1 to the number of decisions in the module. (The module has three decisions: two in the two while statements and one in the if statement.)

The cyclomatic number is one quantitative measure of module complexity. It can be extended to compute the complexity of the whole program, though it is more suitable at the module level. McCabe proposed that the cyclomatic complexity of modules should, in general, be kept below 10. The cyclomatic number can also be used as a number of paths that should be tested during testing. Cyclomatic complexity is one of the most widely used complexity measures. Experiments indicate that the cyclomatic complexity is highly correlated to the size of the module in LOC (after all, the more lines of code the greater the number of decisions). It has also been found to be correlated to the number of faults found in modules.

7.4.2   Data Bindings

We have seen that coupling and cohesion are important concepts for evaluating a design. However, to be truly effective, metrics are needed to "measure" the coupling between modules or the cohesion of a module. During system design, we tried to quantify coupling based on information flow between modules. Now that the logic of modules is also available, we can come up with metrics that also consider the logic. One metric that attempts to capture the module-level concept of coupling is data binding. Data bindings are measures that capture the data interaction across portions of a software system [HB85]. In other words, data bindings try to specify how strongly coupled different modules in a software system are. Different types of data bindings are possible [HB85].

A *potential data binding* is defined as a triplet (p, x, q), where p and q are modules and x is a variable within the static scope of both p and q. This reflects the possibility that the modules p and q may communicate with each other through the shared variable x. This binding does not consider the internals of p and q to determine if the variable x is actually accessed in any of the modules. This binding is based on data declaration.

A *used data binding* is a potential binding where both p and q use the variable x for reference or assignment. This is harder to compute than potential data binding and requires more information about the internal logic of a module.

An *actual data binding* is a used data binding with the additional restriction that the module p assigns a value to x and q references x. It is the hardest to compute, and it signifies the situation where information may flow from the module p to module q through the shared variable x. Computation of actual data binding requires detailed logic descriptions of modules p and q.

All of these data bindings attempt to represent the strength of interconnections among modules. The greater the number of bindings between two modules, the higher the interconnection between these modules. For a particular type of binding, a matrix can be computed that contains the number of bindings between different modules. This matrix can be used for further statistical analysis to determine the interconnection strength of the system or a subsystem.

7.4. Metrics   351

7.4.3 Cohesion Metric

Here we discuss one attempt at quantifying the cohesion of a module [Eme84]. To compute the value of the cohesion metric for a module M, a flow graph G is constructed for M. Each vertex in G is an executable statement in M. For each node, we also record the variable referenced in the statement. An arc exists from a node s_i to another node s_j if the statement s_j can immediately follow the statement s_i in some execution of the module. In addition to these, we add an initial node I from where the execution of the module starts, and a final node T, at which the execution of the module terminates. For termination statements (e.g., return, exit) we draw an arc from the statement to T.

From G a *reduced* flow graph is constructed by deleting those nodes that do not refer to any variable (such as unconstrained gotos). All the arcs coming in the deleted node are redirected to the node that is the successor of the deleted node (such nodes will have only one successor).

Assume that the variables are sequentially numbered as $1, 2, \ldots, n$. For a variable i, R_i is the reference set, which is the set of all the executable statements that refer to the variable i. The union of all the R_is is the set of all the nodes in the graph (minus the node for T, which is a nonexecuting node). Let $|G|$ refer to the (number of nodes $- 1$) for the reduced graph.

The cohesion of a set of statements S is defined as

$$C(S) = \frac{|S| \dim(S)}{|G| \dim(G)}$$

where dim() is the dimension of a set of statements, which is the maximum number of linearly independent paths from I to T that pass through any element of S. Thus, the dimension of a set of statements S is the count of all the independent paths from the start statement to the end statement of a module that includes at least one statement from the set. If S is the set of all the statements in the module (if S is the same as G), then dim S is the same as the cyclomatic complexity of the module.

The cohesion of a module is defined as the average cohesion of the reference sets of the different statements or nodes in (reduced) G. Hence the cohesion of the module $C(M)$ is

$$C(M) = \frac{\sum_{i=1}^{i=n} C(R_i)}{n}.$$

Essentially, this metric is trying to measure cohesion of a module by seeing how many independent paths of the module go through the different statements. The idea is that if a module has high cohesion, most of the variables will be used by statements in most paths. Hence for a high-cohesion module, the cohesion of the reference set of each variable will be high. The highest cohesion number achievable by this is when the dimension of all the reference sets is all the independent paths, thus the same as the cyclomatic complexity. In other words, the highest cohesion is when all the independent paths use all the variables of the module.

7.5 Summary

Detailed design starts after the system design phase is completed and the system design has been certified through a review. The goal of this phase is to develop the internal logic of each of the modules identified during system design.

Before deciding on the logic of a module, formal specifications of the module may be developed. The specifications should be such that they are complete, unambiguous, and precise, and they do not suggest any particular implementation. Two module units are frequently chosen for formal specifications: functional modules and data abstraction modules. Both of these formal methods can specify the behavior of the modules without assuming any implementation for the module. We have discussed some such methods. However, most formal methods for specifications tend to be rather cumbersome, not very expressive, and hard to understand or write. For this reason, formal specifications are not often used.

To express the internal logic of a module, we need a design language. The design language should be such that it is flexible enough to be easily usable, yet precise enough to be easily convertible into code. We have described a language, process design language (PDL), that satisfies the bill. PDL can be used to express the detailed design of systems. It has a formal outer syntax and a flexible inner syntax and vocabulary, giving it a balance between formalism and ease of expression.

Like any phase, we need some metrics to evaluate the effectiveness of the phase and to evaluate the output of that phase. We considered a metric called cyclomatic complexity for evaluating the complexity of modules from their detailed design. This metric can be also used to assess the overall complexity of the system, or it can be used to identify the most complex modules, which are more likely to be "error-prone." In a module the cyclomatic complexity equals the number of decisions in the module plus one. We also discussed the data binding metric and a cohesion metric.

A few techniques exist for verifying the detailed design. The most common are design walkthroughs and critical design review. Automated tools can be used for some consistency checking if a well-defined design language, like PDL, is used. Even with automated consistency checkers, reviews and walkthroughs remain the most important methods for verifying the detailed design. We have described the review process and given a sample checklist that can be used in the review.

A final word about the use of the detailed design phase. This is one of the phases that is frequently not performed formally and completely because it is not always the case that a detailed design description of the modules adds much value, and experienced programmers feel that they can go directly to coding. Furthermore, the detailed design document has little archival value during maintenance, unlike the requirements document or the system design document. The main reason for this is that it is not practical to keep the detailed design document consistent with the code as the code changes during the coding and testing activities. A logic description that does not describe the code accurately is of little use; hence the primary use of the detailed design phase is to design the logic and get it verified before proceeding. With this as the basic goal, it might be practical to only develop the detailed design for the more complex and important modules rather than for the entire system. Another approach that is sometimes followed is to make the detailed design phase informal, where the programmer prepares the detailed design as a step toward coding, but no formal detailed design document is produced. In other words, the detailed design is used primarily as an aid for coding. For these reasons, we will not give the detailed design of the case study. We will proceed straight from the design to coding, and detailed design will be used by the programmer as a step in coding, which is not being formalized for this project as it is not a very large and critical project.

Exercises

1. The detailed design of a system can involve many persons, each developing the detailed design of a set of modules. Draw a process diagram for this method of detailed design development.

2. Why are formal specifications of modules desirable? What are the limitations of current formal methods and why have they not come into common use?

3. Formally specify the following modules and write their detailed design:
   (a) reverse(L): reverses the input list L.
   (b) insert(S, i): inserts the element i in the set S.
   (c) strcat(s1, s2): concatenates string $s2$ at the end of $s1$.
   (d) strlen(s): determines the length of a string s.
   (e) min(S): determines the minimum of the set S.

4. Provide axioms for the data types described here. The name of each type and operations on that type are given.
   (a) type String
       null () $\rightarrow$ String
       isnull (String) $\rightarrow$ boolean
       len(String) $\rightarrow$ integer
       addchar(String, char) $\rightarrow$ String
       index(String, char) $\rightarrow$ integer
   (b) type Set
       emptyset() $\rightarrow$ Set
       isempty(Set) $\rightarrow$ boolean
       insert(Set, item) $\rightarrow$ Set

        delete(Set, item) → Set
        has(set, item) → boolean

(c) type Btree /* a simple binary tree */
        emptytree() → Btree
        make(Btree, item, Btree) → Btree
        isempty(Btree) → boolean
        left(Btree) → Btree
        right(Btree) → Btree
        isin(Btree, item) → boolean
        insert(Btree, item) → Btree

(d) type SymbolTable
        init() → SymbolTable
        enterblock(SymbolTable) → SymbolTable
        addid(SymbolTable, identifier, attributelist) → SymbolTable
        leaveblock(SymbolTable) → SymbolTable
        isinblock(SymbolTable, identifier) → boolean
        retrieve(SymbolTable, identifier) → attributelist

(e) type Library
        create() → Library
        add(Library, book) → Library
        checkout(Library, book) → Library
        return(Library, book) → Library
        isin(Library, book) → boolean
        isempty(Library) → boolean

5. Extend the PDL with constructs to support classes. Then write the detailed design for the classes just described.

6. What features would you like to add to PDL if the target source language supports data abstraction?

7. If cyclomatic complexity of a module is much higher than the suggested limit of 10, what will you do? Give reasons and guidelines for whatever you propose.

8. Consider an implementation of the type Btree as a set of procedures and functions (without data encapsulation). From the detailed design obtained earlier, determine the cohesion of different procedures/functions and coupling between them using the metrics described in this chapter.

9. Design an experiment to study the relationship between the cyclomatic complexity and size in LOC of modules. Collect a set of programs and then perform the experiment and determine the nature of the relationship between them for these programs.

10. Design an experiment to study the relation between cyclomatic complexity and "error-proneness" of modules. If you can collect error data, execute the experiment on the data you can collect.

8

Coding

The goal of the coding or programming phase is to translate the design of the system produced during the design phase into code in a given programming language, which can be executed by a computer and that performs the computation specified by the design. For a given design, the aim is to implement the design in the best possible manner.

The coding phase affects both testing and maintenance profoundly. As we saw earlier, the time spent in coding is a small percentage of the total software cost, while testing and maintenance consume the major percentage. Thus, it should be clear that the goal during coding should *not* be to reduce the implementation cost, but the goal should be to reduce the cost of later phases, even if it means that the cost of this phase has to increase. In other words, the goal during this phase is *not* to simplify the job of the programmer. Rather, the goal should be to simplify the job of the tester and the maintainer.

This distinction is important, as most programmers are individualistic, and mostly concerned about how to finish their job quickly, without keeping the later phases in mind. During implementation, it should be kept in mind that *the programs should not be constructed so that they are easy to write, but so that they are easy to read and understand*. A program is read a lot more often and by a lot more people during the later phases. Often, making a program more readable will require extra work by the programmers. For example, sometimes there are "quick fixes" to modify a given code easily, which result in a code that is more difficult to understand. In such cases, in the interest of simplifying the later phases, the easy "quick fixes" should not be adopted.

There are many different criteria for judging a program, including readability, size of the program, execution time, and required memory. Having readability

	Resulting Rank (1 = Best)				
	O1	O2	O3	O4	O5
Minimize effort to complete (O1)	1	4	4	5	3
Minimize number of statements (O2)	2–3	1	2	3	5
Minimize memory required (O3)	5	2	1	4	4
Maximize program clarity (O4)	4	3	3	2	2
Maximize output clarity (O5)	2–3	5	5	1	1

FIGURE 8.1. The Weinberg experiment.

and understandability as a clear objective of the coding activity can itself help in producing software that is more maintainable. A famous experiment by Weinberg showed that if programmers are specified a clear objective for the program, they usually satisfy it [WS74]. In the experiment, five different teams were given the same problem for which they had to develop programs. However, each of the teams was specified a different objective, which it had to satisfy. The different objectives given were: minimize the effort required to complete the program, minimize the number of statements, minimize the memory required, maximize the program clarity, and maximize the output clarity. It was found that in most cases each team did the best for the objective that was specified to it. The rank of the different teams for the different objectives is shown in Figure 8.1.

The experiment clearly shows that if objectives are clear, programmers tend to achieve that objective. Hence, if readability is an objective of the coding activity, then it is likely that programmers will develop easily understandable programs. For our purposes, ease of understanding and modification should be the basic goals of the programming activity. This means that simplicity and clarity are desirable, while cleverness and complexity are not.

8.1 Programming Practice

As we have said, the primary goal of the coding phase is to translate the given design into source code in a given programming language, so that code is simple, easy to test, and easy to understand and modify. Simplicity and clarity are the properties a programmer should strive for.

Good programming is a skill that can only be acquired by practice. However, much can be learned from the experience of others, and some general rules and guidelines can be laid for the programmer. Good programming (producing correct and simple programs) is a practice independent of the target programming language, although some well-structured languages like Pascal, ADA, and Modula make the programmer's job simpler. In this section, we will discuss some concepts related to coding in a language-independent manner.

8.1.1   Top-Down and Bottom-Up

All designs contain hierarchies, as creating a hierarchy is a natural way to manage complexity. Most design methodologies for software also produce hierarchies. The hierarchy may be of functional modules, as is the case with the structured design methodology where the hierarchy of modules is represented by the structure chart. Or the hierarchy may be an object hierarchy as is produced by object-oriented design methods and frequently represented by object diagrams. The question at coding time is: given the hierarchy of modules produced by design, in what order should the modules be built—starting from the top level or starting from the bottom level?

In a top-down implementation, the implementation starts from the top of the hierarchy and proceeds to the lower levels. First the main module is implemented, then its subordinates are implemented, and their subordinates, and so on. In a bottom-up implementation, the process is the reverse. The development starts with implementing the modules at the bottom of the hierarchy and proceeds through the higher levels until it reaches the top.

Top-down and bottom-up implementation should not be confused with top-down and bottom-up design. Here, the design is being implemented, and if the design is fairly detailed and complete, its implementation can proceed in either the top-down or the bottom-up manner, even if the design was produced in a top-down manner. Which of the two is used mostly affects testing.

If there is a complete design, why is the order in which the modules are built an issue? The main reason is that we want to *incrementally build* the system. That is, we wnat to build the system in parts, even though the design of the entire system has been done. This is necessitated by the fact that for large systems it is simply not feasible or desirable to build the whole system and then test it. All large systems must be built by assembling validated pieces together. The case with software systems is the same. Parts of the system have to first be built and tested before putting them together to form the system. Because parts have to be built and tested separately, the issue of top-down versus bottom-up arises.

The real issue in which order the modules are coded comes in testing. If all the modules are to be developed and then put together to form the system for testing purposes, as is done for small systems, it is immaterial which module is coded first. However, when modules have to be tested separately, top-down and bottom-up lead to top-down and bottom-up approaches to testing. And these two approaches have different consequences. Essentially, when we proceed top-down, for testing a set of modules at the top of the hierarchy, *stubs* will have to be written for the lower-level modules that the set of modules under testing invoke. On the other hand, when we proceed bottom-up, all modules that are lower in the hierarchy have been developed and *driver* modules are needed to invoke these modules under testing.

Top-down versus bottom-up is also a pertinent issue when the design is not detailed enough. In such cases, some of the design decisions have to be made during development. This may be true, for example, when building a prototype. In such cases, top-down development may be preferable to aid the design while the implementation is progressing. On the other hand, many complex systems, like operating systems or networking software systems, are naturally organized as layers. In a layered architecture, a layer provides some services to the layers above, which use these services to implement the services it provides. For a layered architecture, it is generally best for the implementation to proceed in a bottom-up manner.

In practice, in large systems, a combination of the two approaches is used during coding. The top modules of the system generally contain the overall view of the system and may even contain the user interfaces. Starting with these modules and testing them gives some feedback regarding the functionality of the system and whether the "look and feel" of the system is OK. For this, it is best if development proceeds top-down. On the other hand, the bottom-level modules typically form the "service routines" that provide the basic operations used by higher-level modules. It is therefore important to make sure that these service modules are working correctly before they are used by other modules. This suggests that the development should proceed in a bottom-up manner. As both issues are important in a large project, it may be best to follow a combination approach for such systems.

Finally, it should be pointed out that incremental building of code is a different issue from the one addressed in the incremental enhancement process model. In the latter, the whole software is built in increments. Hence, even the SRS and the design for an increment focus on that increment only. However, in incremental building, which we are discussing here, the design itself is complete for the system we are building. The issue is in which order the modules specified in the design should be coded.

8.1.2   Structured Programming

As stated earlier the basic objective of the coding activity is to produce programs that are easy to understand. It has been argued by many that structured programming practice helps develop programs that are easier to understand. The structured programming movement started in the 1970s, and much has been said and written about it. Now the concept pervades so much that it is generally accepted—even implied—that programming should be structured. Though a lot of emphasis has been placed on structured programming, the concept and motivation behind structured programming are often not well understood. Structured programming is often regarded as "goto-less" programming. Although extensive use of gotos is certainly not desirable, structured programs *can* be written with the use of gotos. Here we provide a brief discussion on what structured programming is.

A program has a static structure as well as a dynamic structure. The static structure is the structure of the text of the program, which is usually just a linear organization of statements of the program. The dynamic structure of the program is the sequence of statements executed during the execution of the program. In other words, both the static structure and the dynamic behavior are sequences of statements; where the sequence representing the static structure of a program is fixed, the sequence of statements it executes can change from execution to execution.

The general notion of correctness of the program means that when the program executes, it produces the desired behavior. To show that a program is correct, we need to show that when the program executes, its behavior is what is expected. Consequently, when we argue about a program, either formally to prove that it is correct or informally to debug it or convince ourselves that it works, we study the static structure of the program (i.e., its code) but try to argue about its dynamic behavior. In other words, much of the activity of program understanding is to understand the dynamic behavior of the program from the text of the program.

It will clearly be easier to understand the dynamic behavior if the structure in the dynamic behavior resembles the static structure. The closer the correspondence between execution and text structure, the easier the program is to understand, and the more different the structure during execution, the harder it will be to argue about the behavior from the program text. The goal of structured programming is to ensure that the static structure and the dynamic structures are the same. That is, the objective of structured programming is to write programs so that the sequence of statements executed during the execution of a program is the same as the sequence of statements in the text of that program. As the statements in a program text are linearly organized, the objective of structured programming becomes developing programs whose control flow during execution is linearized and follows the linear organization of the program text.

Clearly, no meaningful program can be written as a sequence of simple statements without any branching or repetition (which also involves branching). So, how is the objective of linearizing the control flow to be achieved? By making use of structured constructs. In structured programming, a statement is not a simple assignment statement, it is a structured statement. The key property of a structured statement is that it has a *single-entry and a single-exit*. That is, during execution, the execution of the (structured) statement starts from one defined point and the execution terminates at one defined point. With single-entry and single-exit statements, we can view a program as a sequence of (structured) statements. And if all statements are structured statements, then during execution, the sequence of execution of these statements will be the same as the sequence in the program text. Hence, by using single-entry and single-exit statements, the correspondence between the static and dynamic structures can be obtained. The most commonly used single-entry and single-exit statements are:

Selection:	if B then S1 else S2
	if B then S1
Iteration:	While B do S
	repeat S until B
Sequencing:	S1; S2; S3; ...

It can be shown that these three basic constructs are sufficient to program any conceivable algorithm. Modern languages have other such constructs that help linearize the control flow of a program, which, generally speaking, makes it easier to understand a program. Hence, programs should be written so that, as far as possible, single-entry, single-exit control constructs are used. The basic goal, as we have tried to emphasize, is to make the logic of the program simple to understand. No hard-and-fast rule can be formulated that will be applicable under all circumstances. Structured programming practice forms a good basis and guideline for writing programs clearly.

It should be pointed out that the main reason structured programming was promulgated is formal verification of programs. As we will see later in this chapter, during verification, a program is considered a sequence of executable statements, and verification proceeds step by step, considering one statement in the statement list (the program) at a time. Implied in these verification methods is the assumption that during execution, the statements will be executed in the sequence in which they are organized in the program text. If this assumption is satisfied, the task of verification becomes easier. Hence, even from the point of view of verification, it is important that the sequence of execution of statements is the same as the sequence of statements in the text.

A final note about the structured constructs. Any piece of code with a single-entry and single-exit cannot be considered a structured construct. If that is the case, one could always define appropriate units in any program to make it appear as a sequence of these units (in the worst case, the whole program could be defined to be a unit). The basic objective of using structured constructs is to linearize the control flow so that the execution behavior is easier to understand and argue about. In linearized control flow, if we understand the behavior of each of the basic constructs properly, the behavior of the program can be considered a composition of the behaviors of the different statements. For this basic approach to work, it is implied that we can clearly understand the behavior of each construct. This requires that we be able to succinctly capture or describe the behavior of each construct. Unless we can do this, it will not be possible to compose them. Clearly, for an arbitrary structure, we cannot do this merely because it has a single-entry and single-exit. It is from this viewpoint that the structures mentioned earlier are chosen as structured statements. There are well-defined rules that specify how these statements behave during execution, which allows us to argue about larger programs.

Overall, it can be said that structured programming, in general, leads to programs that are easier to understand than unstructured programs, and that such programs are easier (relatively speaking) to formally prove. However, it should be kept in mind that structured programming is not an end in itself. Our basic objective is that the program be easy to understand. And structured programming is a safe approach for achieving this objective. Still, there are some common programming practices that are now well understood that make use of unstructured constructs (e.g., break statement, continue statement). Although efforts should be made to avoid using statements that effectively violate the single-entry single-exit property, if the use of such statements is the simplest way to organize the program, then from the point of view of readability, the constructs should be used. The main point is that any unstructured construct should be used only if the structured alternative is harder to understand. This view can be taken only because we are focusing on readability. If the objective was formal verifiability, structured programming will probably be necessary.

8.1.3   Information Hiding

A software solution to a problem always contains data structures that are meant to represent information in the problem domain. That is, when software is developed to solve a problem, the software uses some data structures to capture the information in the problem domain. With the problem information represented internally as data structures, the required functionality of the problem domain, which is in terms of information in that domain, can be implemented as software operations on the data structures. Hence, any software solution to a problem contains data structures that represent information in the problem domain.

In the problem domain, in general, only certain operations are performed on some information. That is, a piece of information in the problem domain is used only in a limited number of ways in the problem domain. For example, a ledger in an accountant's office has some very defined uses: debit, credit, check the current balance, etc. An operation where all debits are multiplied together and then divided by the sum of all credits is typically not performed. So, any information in the problem domain typically has a small number of defined operations performed on it.

When the information is represented as data structures, the same principle should be applied, and only some defined operations should be performed on the data structures. This, essentially, is the principle of information hiding. The information captured in the data structures should be hidden from the rest of the system, and only the access functions on the data structures that represent the operations performed on the information should be visible. In other words, when the information is captured in data structures and then on the data structures that represent some information, for each operation on the information an access function should be provided. And as the rest of the system in the problem domain only performs these defined operations on the information, the rest of the modules in the software should only use these access functions to access and manipulate the data structures.

If the information hiding principle is used, the data structure need not be directly used and manipulated by other modules. All modules, other than the access functions, access the data structure through the access functions.

Information hiding can reduce the coupling between modules and make the system more maintainable. If data structures are directly used in modules, then all modules that use some data structures are coupled with each other and if change is made in one of them, the effect on all the other modules needs to be evaluated. With information hiding, the impact on the modules using the data need to be evaluated only when the data structure or its access functions are changed. Otherwise, as the other modules are not directly accessing the data, changes in these modules will have little direct effect on other modules using the data. Also, when a data structure is changed, the effect of the change is generally limited to the access functions if information hiding is used. Otherwise, all modules using the data structure may have to be changed.

Information hiding is also an effective tool for managing the complexity of developing software. As we have seen, whenever possible, problem partitioning must be used so that concerns can be separated and different parts solved separately. By using information hiding, we have separated the concern of managing the data from the concern of using the data to produce some desired results. Now, to produce the desired results, only the desired operations on the data need to be performed, thereby making the task of designing these modules easier. Without information hiding, this module will also have to deal with the problem of properly accessing and modifying the data.

Another form of information hiding is to let a module see only those data items needed by it. The other data items should be "hidden" from such modules and the modules should not be allowed to access these data items. Thus, each module is given access to data items on a "need-to-know" basis. This level of information hiding is usually not practical, and most languages do not support this level of access restriction. However, the information hiding principle discussed earlier, is supported by many modern programming languages in the form of *data abstraction*. We discussed the concept of data types and classes earlier, and we have seen that it forms the basis of the object-oriented design approach.

With support for data abstraction, a package or a module is defined that encapsulates the data. Some operations are defined by the module on the encapsulated data. Other modules that are outside this module can only invoke these predefined operations on the encapsulated data. The advantage of this form of data abstraction is that the data is entirely in the control of the module in which the data is encapsulated.

Other modules cannot access or modify the data; the operations that can access and modify are also a part of this module.

Many of the older languages, like Pascal, C, and FORTRAN, do not provide mechanisms to support data abstraction. With such languages, data abstraction can be supported only by a disciplined use of the language. That is, the access restrictions will have to be imposed by the programmers; the language does not provide them. For example, to implement a data abstraction of a stack in C, one method is to define a struct containing all the data items needed to implement the stack and then to define functions and procedures on variables of this type. A possible definition of the struct and the interface of the "push" operation is given next:

```
typedef struct {
  int elts[100];
  int top;
} stack;

void push (s, i)
stack s; int i;
{
  :
}
```

Note that in implementing information hiding in languages like C and Pascal, the language does not impose any access restrictions. In the example of the stack earlier, the structure of a variable s declared of the type stack, can be accessed from procedures other than the ones defined for stack. That is why discipline by the programmers is needed to emulate data abstraction. Regardless of whether or not the language provides constructs for data abstraction, it is desirable to support data abstraction in cases where the data and operations on the data are well defined. Data abstraction is one way to increase the clarity of the program. It helps in clean partitioning of the program into pieces that can be separately implemented and understood.

8.1.4 Programming Style

It is impossible to provide an exhaustive list of what to do and what not to do to produce simple readable code. Being able to do this will amount to providing an algorithm for writing good code. Next we will list some general rules that usually apply.

Names: Selecting module and variable names is often not considered important by novice programmers. Only when one starts reading programs written by others where the variable names are cryptic and not representative does one realize the importance of selecting proper names. Most variables in a program reflect some entity in the problem domain, and the modules reflect some process. Variable names should be closely related to the entity they represent, and module names should reflect their activity. It is bad practice to choose cryptic names (just to avoid typing) or totally unrelated names. It is also bad practice to use the same name for multiple purposes.

Control Constructs: As discussed earlier, it is desirable that as much as possible single-entry, single-exit constructs be used. It is also desirable to use a few standard control constructs rather than using a wide variety of constructs, just because they are available in the language.

Gotos: Gotos should be used sparingly and in a disciplined manner (this discussion is not applicable to gotos used to support single-entry, single-exit constructs in languages like FORTRAN). Only when the alternative to using gotos is more complex should the gotos be used. In any case, alternatives must be thought of before finally using a goto. If a goto must be used, forward transfers (or a jump to a later statement) is more acceptable than a backward jump. Use of gotos for exiting a loop or for invoking error handlers is quite acceptable (many languages provide separate constructs for these situations, in which case those constructs should be used).

Information Hiding: As discussed earlier, information hiding should be supported where possible. Only the access functions for the data structures should be made visible while hiding the data structure behind these functions.

User-Defined Types: Modern languages allow users to define types like the enumerated type. When such facilities are available, they should be exploited where applicable. For example, when working with dates, a type can be defined for the day of the week. In Pascal, this is done as follows:

type days = (Mon, Tue, Wed, Thur, Fri, Sat, Sun);

Variables can then be declared of this type. Using such types makes the program much clearer than defining codes for each day and then working with codes.

Nesting: The different control constructs, particularly the if-then-else, can be nested. If the nesting becomes too deep, the programs become harder to understand. In case of deeply nested if-then-elses, it is often difficult to determine the if statement to which a particular else clause is associated. Where possible, deep nesting should be avoided, even if it means a little inefficiency. For example, consider the following construct of nested if-then-elses:

        if C1 then S1
          else if C2 then S2
            else if C3 then S3
              else if C4 then S4;

If the different conditions are disjoint (as they often are), this structure can be converted into the following structure:

```
if C1 then S1;
if C2 then S2;
if C3 then S3;
if C4 then S4;
```

This sequence of statements will produce the same result as the earlier sequence (if the conditions are disjoint), but it is much easier to understand. The price is a little inefficiency in that the latter conditions will be evaluated even if a condition evaluates to true, while in the previous case the condition evaluation stops when one evaluates to true. Other such situations can be constructed where alternative program segments can be constructed to avoid a deep level of nesting. In general, if the price is only a little inefficiency, it is more desirable to avoid deep nesting.

Module Size: We discussed this issue during system design. A programmer should carefully examine any routine with very few statements (say fewer than 5) or with too many statements (say more than 50). Large modules often will not be functionally cohesive, and too-small modules might incur unnecessary overhead. There can be no hard-and-fast rule about module sizes the guiding principle should be cohesion and coupling.

Module Interface: A module with a complex interface should be carefully examined. Such modules might not be functionally cohesive and might be implementing multiple functions. As a rule of thumb, any module whose interface has more than five parameters should be carefully examined and broken into multiple modules with a simpler interface if possible.

Program Layout: How the program is organized and presented can have great effect on the readability of it. Proper indentation, blank spaces, and parentheses should be used to enhance the readability of programs. Automated tools are available to "pretty print" a program, but it is good practice to have a clear layout of programs.

Side Effects: When a module is invoked, it sometimes has side effects of modifying the program state beyond the modification of parameters listed in the module interface definition, for example, modifying global variables. Such side effects should be avoided where possible, and if a module has side effects, they should be properly documented.

Robustness: A program is robust if it does something planned even for exceptional conditions. A program might encounter exceptional conditions in such forms as incorrect input, the incorrect value of some variable, and overflow. A program should try to handle such situations. In general, a program should check for validity of inputs, where possible, and should check for possible overflow of the data structures. If such situations do arise, the program should not just "crash" or "core dump"; it should produce some meaningful message and exit gracefully.

8.1.5   Internal Documentation

In the coding phase, the output document is the code itself. However, some amount of internal documentation in the code can be extremely useful in enhancing the understandability of programs. Internal documentation of programs is done by the use of comments. All languages provide a means for writing comments in programs. *Comments* are textual statements that are meant for the program reader and are not executed. Comments, if properly written and kept consistent with the code, can be invaluable during maintenance.

The purpose of comments is not to explain in English the logic of the program—the program itself is the best documentation for the details of the logic. The comments should explain what the code is doing, not how it is doing it. This means that a comment is not needed for every line of the code, as is often done by novice programmers who are taught the virtues of comments. Comments should be provided for blocks of code, particularly those parts of code that are hard to follow. In most cases, only comments for the modules need to be provided.

Providing comments for modules is most useful, as modules form the unit of testing, compiling, verification and modification. Comments for a module are often called *prologue* for the module. It is best to standardize the structure of the prologue of the module. It is desirable if the prologue contains the following information:

1. Module functionality, or what the module is doing.
2. Parameters and their purpose.
3. Assumptions about the inputs, if any.
4. Global variables accessed and/or modified in the module.

An explanation of parameters (whether they are input only, output only, or both input and output; why they are needed by the module; how the parameters are modified) can be quite useful during maintenance. Stating how the global data is affected and the side effects of a module is also very useful during maintenance.

In addition other information can be included, depending on the local coding standards. Examples are the name of the author, the date of compilation, and the last date of modification.

It should be pointed out that the prologues are useful only if they are kept consistent with the logic of the module. If the module is modified, then the prologue should also be modified, if necessary. A prologue that is inconsistent with the internal logic of the module is probably worse than no prologue at all.

8.1.6   Law of Demeter for OO Programs

Much of the preceding discussion implicitly assumed that the implementation language is procedural. As most of the code in a class is in the methods of the class and methods can be treated as functions or procedures, most of the principles discussed hold for object-oriented programming (OOP) also. Guidelines for structured programming and programming style regarding nesting, user-defined types, names, and so on. should be followed while writing code for methods for developing readable object-oriented programs.

However, even though most of the code in a class resides in its methods, a class is not just its methods. And though by using good methods to develop functions and procedures we can ensure that each method is written properly, this does not ensure that the overall class, as a unit, is properly developed. In OOP, a class is the basic unit, so some additional guidelines for the class as a whole will be useful for the programmer. Here we present one such guideline called the *law of demeter* [LH89].

The primary goal of OO programming is the same as for function-oriented programming: readability. That is, readability or comprehensibility of the programs is the foremost criteria for judging the program quality. In an object-oriented program, an object may interact with other objects by sending messages (as defined in its class definition). As can be imagined, the more message passing between objects and the more indirect the message passing, the harder it will be to understand the class. Hence, the law of demeter tries to restrict the message sending structures in a class by stipulating that a method of a class send messages only to a limited set of objects. By doing this, the dependency between different classes is reduced, thereby making comprehending or modifying a class easier.

Let us give a few definitions first [LH89]. A method M is a *client* of a class C if within M a message is sent to some object of class C. The class C is then called a *supplier class*. That is, a class C is a supplier to a method M if its methods are called from M. A class C is an *acquaintance class* to a method M (of a class C') if C is a supplier to M and C is neither the class of an argument of M nor the class of an instance variable declared within C' (or its ancestors). In other words, the set of acquaintance classes of a method M is the set of those classes whose objects M sends messages to, but which are not the class of an argument of M and are not the class of an instance variable of the class to which M belongs. A *preferred-acquaintance class* of a method M is a supplier class of M that is either the class of an object created directly in M or the class of a global object used in M. As can be clearly seen, the set of preferred-acquaintance classes will be a subset of the set of acquaintance classes. A class C is *preferred-supplier class* to a method M (of class C') if C is the class of an instance variable of C' (or its ancestor) or if C is the class of an argument of M or C is a preferred acquaintance of M.

We can now state the law of demeter. The law comes in a few different forms. The minimization form of the law is [LH89]:

Minimize the number of acquaintance classes over all methods.

According to this law, it is desirable to have a method M send messages to a class that is either the class of a parameter of M or is class of an instance variable of the class to which M belongs. In other words, if the method M is invoked on an object O (of class C), it is most desirable that M sends messages to another object O' only if O' is a parameter that is passed to M or if O' is declared within C. All other forms of access, represented by acquaintance classes, should be minimized.

Let us see why access to acquaintance classes is not desirable. The most common ways by which a class C can become an acquaintance class are (1) C is a friend class, (2) C is the class of an object created within M and hence the object is accessible from M, or (3) C is the class of a global object accessible to M. In the first approach, a class that is declared as a friend can access all the internals of the declaring class, including the private features. This is clearly undesirable, as it violates the fundamental property of encapsulation that objects support and that is one of the major strengths of object-oriented approaches. In the second form, an object is created within M and is then accessed. Either this object dies when the method M terminates or it stays alive to be used later by other objects. In the latter case, we have a situation where a local variable of a method is being used by other objects—something that is clearly undesirable as it violates common scope rules, and is likely to make understanding the programs much more difficult. The third form has the same drawback as global variables: they are accessible to all and hence are potentially coupled with all. It should be clear that it is desirable to minimize these forms of interaction, as suggested by the law of demeter.

Now let us look at the two forms of interaction recommended by the law. The first form is that the object is passed as a parameter. This is consistent with the approach proposed in function-oriented approaches; all variables on which a function acts should be passed as parameters. This makes the interface of the object clear and explicit, which makes comprehension easier. The second form is where an object is declared in the class and then accessed by the methods. The instance variables in a class are declared so that they can be shared by the different operations on the object. This is just an extension of this view, saying that objects to be accessed by a method should be declared as instance variables so that they are reflected in the state of the objects.

The implementation of this law requires that we be able to count the number of acquaintance classes for each method. It is possible to do this at compile time if acquaintance classes are explicitly declared (e.g., friends in C++). The second form of this law is the *strict version*, which is:

> *All methods may have only preferred supplier classes.*

Strict form is essentially saying that all interactions must be to the preferred suppliers only. The common ways a class C can become a preferred supplier for a method M in C' are: (1) C is the class of an instance variable declared in C', (2) C is the class of a parameter passed to M, (3) C is the type of local object to M created within M, (4) C is the type of global object, and (5) C and C' are the same and M sends a message to itself. The strict form of the law says that only these five methods of interaction with a class should be used. Other forms of interaction (e.g., through *friends*) should not be used. Taken together, the two forms seem to suggest that the first two forms of interaction are the most preferred, though the latter three are also acceptable.

8.2   Verification

Verification of the output of the coding phase is primarily intended for detecting errors introduced during this phase. That is, the goal of verification of the code produced is to show that the code is consistent with the design it is supposed to implement. It should be pointed out that by verification we do not mean proving correctness of programs, which for our purposes is only *one* method for program verification.

Program verification methods fall into two categories—static and dynamic methods. In dynamic methods the program is executed on some test data and the outputs of the program are examined to determine if there are any errors present. Hence, dynamic techniques follow the traditional pattern of testing, and the common notion of testing refers to this technique.

Static techniques, on the other hand, do not involve actual program execution on actual numeric data, though it may involve some form of conceptual execution. In static techniques, the program is not compiled and then executed, as in testing. Common forms of static techniques are program verification, code reading, code reviews and walkthroughs, and symbolic execution. In static techniques often the errors are detected directly, unlike dynamic techniques where only the presence of an error is detected. This aspect of static testing makes it quite attractive and economical.

It has been found that the types of errors detected by the two categories of verification techniques are different. The type of errors detected by static techniques are often not found by testing, or it may be more cost-effective to detect these errors by static methods. Consequently, testing and static methods are complimentary in nature, and both should be used for reliable software.

8.2.1   Code Reading

Code reading involves careful reading of the code by the programmer to detect any discrepancies between the design specifications and the actual implementation. It involves determining the abstraction of a module and then comparing it with its specifications. The process is the reverse of design. In design, we start from an abstraction and move toward more details. In code reading we start from the details of a program and move toward an abstract description.

The process of code reading is best done by reading the code inside-out, starting with the innermost structure of the module. First determine its abstract behavior and specify the abstraction. Then the higher-level structure is considered, with the inner structure replaced by its abstraction. This process is continued until we reach the module or program being read. At that time the abstract behavior of the program/module will be known, which can then be compared to the specifications to determine any discrepancies.

Code reading is very useful and can detect errors often not revealed by testing. Reading in the manner of stepwise-abstraction also forces the programmer to code in a manner conducive to this process, which leads to well-structured programs. Code reading is sometimes called *desk review*.

8.2.2 Static Analysis

Analysis of programs by methodically analyzing the program text is called *static analysis*. Static analysis is usually performed mechanically by the aid of software tools. During static analysis the program itself is not executed, but the program text is the input to the tools. The aim of the static analysis tools is to detect errors or potential errors or to generate information about the structure of the program that can be useful for documentation or understanding of the program. Different kinds of static analysis tools can be designed to perform different types of analyses.

Many compilers perform some limited static analysis. More often, tools explicitly for static analysis are used. Static analysis can be very useful for exposing errors that may escape other techniques. As the analysis is performed with the help of software tools, static analysis is a very cost-effective way of discovering errors. An advantage is that static analysis sometimes detects the errors themselves, not just the presence of errors, as in testing. This saves the effort of tracing the error from the data that reveals the presence of errors. Furthermore, static analysis can provide "warnings" against potential errors and can provide insight into the structure of the program. It is also useful for determining violations of local programming standards, which the standard compilers will be unable to detect. Extensive static analysis can considerably reduce the effort later needed during testing.

Data flow analysis [FO78] is one form of static analysis that concentrates on the uses of data by programs and detects some data flow anomalies. Data flow anomalies are "suspicious" use of data in a program. In general, data flow anomalies are technically not errors, and they may go undetected by the compiler. However, they are often a symptom of an error, caused due to carelessness in typing or error in coding. At the very least, presence of data flow anomalies implies poor coding. Hence, if a program has data flow anomalies, it is a cause of concern, which should be properly addressed.

```
x = a;
    :
x does not appear in any right hand side
    :
x = b;
```

FIGURE 8.2. A code segment.

An example of the data flow anomaly is the *live variable problem*, in which a variable is assigned some value but then the variable is not used in any later computation. Such a live variable and assignment to the variable are clearly redundant. Another simple example of this is having two assignments to a variable without using the value of the variable between the two assignments. In this case the first assignment is redundant. For example, consider the simple case of the code segment shown in Figure 8.2.

Clearly, the first assignment statement is useless. The question is why is that statement in the program? Perhaps the programmer meant to say y := b in the second statement, and mistyped y as x. In that case, detecting this anomaly and directing the programmer's attention to it can save considerable effort in testing and debugging.

In addition to revealing anomalies, data flow analysis can provide valuable information for documentation of programs. For example, data flow analysis can provide information about which variables are modified on invoking a procedure in the caller program and the value of the variables used in the called procedure (this can also be used to make sure that the interface of the procedure is minimum, resulting in lower coupling). This analysis can identify aliasing, which occurs when different variables represent the same data object. This information can be useful during maintenance to ensure that there are no undesirable side effects of some modifications to a procedure.

Other examples of data flow anomalies are *unreachable code, unused variables*, and *unreferenced labels*. Unreachable code is that part of the code to which there is not a feasible path; there is no possible execution in which it can be executed. Technically this is not an error, and a compiler will at most generate a warning. The program behavior during execution may also be consistent with its specifications. However, often the presence of unreachable code is a sign of lack of proper understanding of the program by the programmer (otherwise why would a programmer leave the unreachable code), which suggests that the presence of error's is likely. Often, unreachable code comes into existence when an existing program is modified. In that situation unreachable code may signify undesired or unexpected side effects of the modifications. Unreferenced labels and unused variables are like unreachable code in that they are technically not errors, but often are symptoms of errors; thus their presence often implies the presence of errors.

Data flow analysis is usually performed by representing a program as a graph, sometimes called the flow graph. The nodes in a flow graph represent statements of a program, while the edges represent control paths from one statement to another. Correspondence between the nodes and statements is maintained, and the graph is analyzed to determine different relationships between the statements. By use of different algorithms, different kinds of anomalies can be detected. Many of the algorithms to detect anomalies can be quite complex and require a lot of processing time. For example, the execution time of algorithms to detect unreachable code increases with the square of the number of nodes in the graph. Consequently, this analysis is often limited to modules or to a collection of some modules and is rarely performed on complete systems.

To reduce processing times of algorithms, the search of a flow graph has to be carefully organized. Another way to reduce the time for executing algorithms is to reduce the size of the flow graph. Flow graphs can get extremely large for large programs, and transformations are often performed on the flow graph to reduce their size. The most common transformation is to have each node represent a sequence of contiguous statements that have no branches in them, thus representing a block of code that will be executed together. Another transformation often done is to have each node represent a procedure or function. In that case, the resulting graph is often called the *call graph*, in which an edge from one node n to another node m represents the fact that the execution of the module represented by n directly invokes the module m.

Other Uses of Static Analysis

We have seen that data flow analysis is a technique for statically analyzing a program to reveal some types of anomalies. Other forms of static analysis to detect different errors and anomalies can also be performed. Here we list some of the other common uses of static analysis tools.

An error often made, especially when different teams are developing different parts of the software, is mismatched parameter lists, where the argument list of a module invocation is different in number or type from the parameters of the invoked module. This can be detected by a compiler if no separate compilation is allowed and the entire program text is available to the compiler (as is the case with standard Pascal). However, if the programs are separately developed and compiled, which is almost always the case with large software developments, this error will not be detected. A static analyzer with access to the different parts of the program can easily detect this error. Such errors can also be detected during code review, but it is more economical to do it mechanically. An extension of this is to detect calls to nonexistent program modules. Essentially, the interfacing of different modules, developed and compiled separately, can be checked for mutual consistency easily through static analysis. In some limited cases, static analysis can also detect infinite or potentially infinite loops, and illegal recursion (e.g., no termination condition for recursion).

There are different kinds of documents that static analyzers can produce, which can be useful for maintenance or increased understanding of the program. The first is the cross-reference of where different variables and constants are used. Often, looking at the cross-reference can help one detect subtle errors, like many constants defined (with perhaps somewhat different values) to represent the same entity. For example, the value of pi could be defined as constant in different routines with slightly different values. A report with cross-references can be useful to detect such errors. To reduce the size of such reports, it may be more useful to limit it to the use of constants and global variables.

Information about the frequency of use of different constructs of the programming language can also be obtained by static analyses. Such information is useful for statistical analysis of programs, such as what types of modules are more prone to defect. Another use is to evaluate the complexity. There are some complexity measures that are a function of the frequency of occurrence of different types of statements. To determine complexity from such measures, this information can be useful.

Static analysis can also produce the structure chart of programs. The actual structure chart of a system is a useful documentation aid. It can also be used to determine the changes made in design during the coding phase by comparing it to the structure chart produced during system design. A static nesting hierarchy of procedures can also be easily produced by static analysis.

There are some coding restrictions that the programming language imposes. However, different organizations may have further restrictions on the use of different language features for reliability, portability, or efficiency reasons. Examples of these include mixed type arithmetic, type conversion, using features that are machine-dependent, and too many gotos. Such restrictions cannot be checked by the compiler, but static analysis can be used to enforce these standards. Such violations can also be checked in code review, but it is more efficient and economical to let a program do this checking.

8.2.3 Symbolic Execution

In the last section we considered techniques in which the program text is scanned to determine possible errors. In this section we will consider another approach where the program is not executed with actual data. Instead, the program is "symbolically executed" with symbolic data. Hence the inputs to the program are not numbers but symbols representing the input data, which can take different values. The execution of the program proceeds like normal execution, except that it deals with values that are not numbers but formulas consisting of the symbolic input values. The outputs are symbolic formulas of input values. These formulas can be checked to see if the program will behave as expected. This approach is called by different names like symbolic execution, symbolic evaluation, and symbolic testing [CHT79, Cla76, How77, Kin76].

Although the concept is simple and promising for verifying programs, we will see that performing symbolic-execution of even modest-size programs is very difficult. The problems basically come due to the conditional execution of statements in programs. As conditions of a symbolic expression cannot usually be evaluated to true or false without substituting actual values for the symbols, a case-by-case analysis becomes necessary, and all possible cases with a condition have to be considered. In programs with loops, this can result in an unmanageably large number of cases.

To introduce the basic concepts of symbolic execution, let us first consider a simple program without any conditional statements. A simple program to compute the product of three positive integers is shown in Figure 8.3.

Let us consider that the symbolic inputs to the function are xi, yi, and zi. We start executing this function with these inputs. The aim is to determine the symbolic values of different variables in the program after "executing" each statement, so that eventually we can determine the result of executing this function. The trace of the symbolic execution of the function is shown in Figure 8.4.

After statement 6, the value of the product is (xi*yi*)*(yi*zi)/yi. Because this is a symbolic value, we can simplify this formula. Simplification yields product = $xi * yi^2 d * zi/yi = xi * yi * zi$, the desired result. In this simple example, there is

```
1.   function product (x, y, z: integer): integer;
2.   var tmp1, tmp2: integer;
3.   begin
4.       tmp1 := x*y;
5.       tmp2 := y*z;
6.       product := tmp1*tmp2/y;
7.   end;
```

FIGURE 8.3. Function to determine product.

| After | Values of the Variables | | | | | |
Statement	x	y	z	tmp1	tmp2	Product
1	xi	yi	zi	?	?	?
4	xi	yi	zi	xi*yi	?	?
5	xi	yi	zi	xi*yi	yi*zi	?
6	xi	yi	zi	xi*yi	yi*zi	(xi*yi)*(yi*zi)/yi

FIGURE 8.4. Symbolic execution of the function product.

only one path in the function, and this symbolic execution is equivalent to checking for all possible values of x, y, and z. (Note that the implied assumption is that input values are such that the machine will be able to perform the product and no overflow will occur.) Essentially, with only one path and an acceptable symbolic result, we can claim that the program is correct.

Path Conditions

In symbolic execution, when dealing with conditional execution, it is not sufficient to look at the state of the variables of the program at different statements, as a statement will only be executed if the inputs satisfy certain conditions in which the execution of the program will follow a path that includes the statement. To capture this concept in symbolic execution, we require a notion of "path condition." Path condition at a statement gives the conditions the inputs must satisfy for an execution to follow the path so that the statement will be executed.

Path condition is a Boolean expression over the symbolic inputs that never contains any program variables. It will be represented in a symbolic execution by pc. Each symbolic execution begins with pc initialized to true. As conditions are encountered, for different cases referring to different paths in the program, the path condition will take different values. For example, symbolic execution of an `if` statement of the form

```
if C then S1 else S2
```

will require two cases to be considered, corresponding to the two possible paths; one where C evaluates to true and S1 is executed, and the other where C evaluates to false and S2 is executed. For the first case we set the path condition pc to

$$pc \leftarrow pc \wedge C$$

which is the path condition for the statements in S1. For the second case we set the path condition to

$$pc \leftarrow pc \wedge \sim C$$

which is the path condition for statements in S2.

On encountering the `if` statement, symbolic execution is said to fork into two executions: one following the `then` part, the other following the `else` part. Both these paths are independently executed, with their respective path conditions. However, if at any `if` statement we can show that *pc* implies C or ∼C, we do not need to follow both paths, and only the relevant path need be executed. Such an `if` statement is a nonforking conditional statement compared to the former case, which is a forking conditional statement.

Let us consider an example involving `if` statements. Figure 8.5 shows a program to determine the maximum of three numbers. The trace of the symbolic execution

```
1.    function max ( x, y, x: integer ): integer;
2.    begin
3.        if x ≤ y then
4.            max := y
5.        else
6.            max := x;
7.        if max < z then
8.            max := z;
9.    end;
```

FIGURE 8.5. The code for function max.

Stmt	pc	max
1.	true	?
Case (x > y)		
2.	(xi > yi)	?
3.	—	xi
	case (max < z)	
4.	(xi>yi) ∧ (xi<zi)	zi
	return this value of max	
	case (max ≥ z)	
4.	(xi>yi) ∧ (xi≤zi)	xi
	return this value of max	

Case (x ≤ y)
    Similar to the above.

FIGURE 8.6. Symbolic execution of the function max.

of this program is shown in Figure 8.6. As before, we assume that the symbolic inputs of the variables x, y, and z are xi, yi, and zi respectively.

Notice how at each `if` statement the symbolic execution forked into two cases, with each case having a different path condition. There are a total of four paths in this symbolic execution. We can see that for each path, the value returned is consistent with the specifications of the program. For example, when the inputs satisfy the condition zi>xi>yi, the value zi is the maximum, which is what is returned in symbolic execution. Similarly, we can check other paths.

Loops and Symbolic Execution Trees

The different paths followed during symbolic execution can be represented by an "execution tree." A node in this tree represents the execution of a statement, while an arc represents the transition from one statement to another. For each `if` statement where both the paths are followed, there are two arcs from the node corresponding

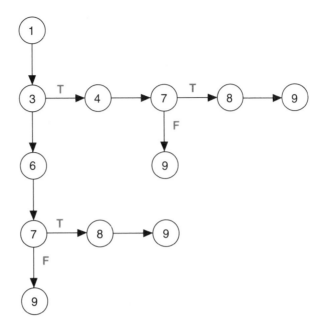

FIGURE 8.7. Execution tree for the function max

to the if statement, one labeled with T (true) and the other with F (false), for the then and else paths. At each branching, the path condition is also often shown in the tree. Note that the execution tree is different from the flow graph of a program, where nodes represent a statement, while in the execution tree nodes represent the execution of a statement. The execution tree of the program discussed earlier is shown in Figure 8.7.

The execution tree of a program has some interesting properties. Each leaf in the tree represents a path that will be followed for some input values. For each terminal leaf there exists some actual numerical inputs such that the sequence of statements executed with these inputs is the same as the sequence of statements in the path from the root of the tree to the leaf. An additional property of the symbolic execution tree is that path conditions associated with two different leaves are distinct. Thus there is no execution for which both path conditions are true. This is due to the property of sequential programming languages that in one execution we cannot follow two different paths.

If the symbolic output at each leaf in the tree is correct, it is equivalent to saying that the program is correct. Hence, if we can consider all paths, the correctness of the program can be established by symbolic execution. However, even for modest-size programs the tree can be infinite. The infinite trees result from the presence of loops in the programs.

Because of the presence of infinite execution trees, symbolic execution should not be considered a tool for proving correctness of programs. A program to perform symbolic execution may not stop. For this reason, a more practical approach is to build tools where only some of the paths are symbolically executed, and the user can select the paths to be executed. One must selectively execute some paths, as all cannot be executed.

A symbolic execution tool can also be useful in selecting test cases to obtain branch or statement coverage (discussed in the next chapter). Suppose that results of testing reveal that a certain path has not been executed, and it is desired to test that path. To execute a particular path, input test data has to be carefully selected to ensure that the given path is indeed executed. Selecting such test cases can often be quite difficult. A symbolic execution tool can be useful here. By symbolically executing that particular path, the path condition for the leaf node for that path can be determined. The input test data can then be selected using this path condition. The test case data that will execute the path are what will satisfy the path condition.

8.2.4   Proving Correctness

Many techniques for verification aim to reveal errors in the programs, because the ultimate goal is to make programs correct by removing the errors. In proof of correctness, the aim is to prove a program correct. So, correctness is directly established, unlike the other techniques in which correctness is never really established but is implied (and hoped) by the absence of detection of any errors. Proofs are perhaps more valuable during program construction, rather than after the program has been constructed. Proving while developing a program may result in more reliable programs that can be proved more easily. Proving a program not constructed with formal verification in mind can be quite difficult.

Any proof technique must begin with a formal specification of the program. No formal proof can be provided if what we have to prove is not stated or is stated informally in an imprecise manner. So, first we have to state formally what the program is supposed to do. A program will usually not operate on an arbitrary set of input data and may produce valid results only for some range of inputs. Hence, it is often not sufficient merely to state the goal of the program, but we should also state the input conditions in which the program is to be invoked and for which the program is expected to produce valid results. The assertion about the expected final state of a program is called the *post-condition* of that program, and the assertion about the input condition is called the *pre-condition* of the program. We discussed this form of specification in Chapter 7. Often, determining the pre-condition for which the post-condition will be satisfied is the goal of proof. Here we will briefly describe a technique for proving correctness called the *axiomatic method*, which was proposed by Hoare [Hoa69]. It is often also called the *Floyd-Hoare proof method*, as it is based on Floyd's inductive assertion technique.

The Axiomatic Approach

In principle, all the properties of a program can be determined statically from the text of the program, without actually executing the program. The first requirement in reasoning about programs is to state formally the properties of the elementary operations and statements that the program uses. In the axiomatic model of Hoare [Hoa69], the goal is to take the program and construct a sequence of assertions, each of which can be inferred from previously proved assertions and the rules and axioms about the statements and operations in the program. For this, we need a mathematical model of a program and all the constructs in the programming language. Using Hoare's notation, the basic assertion about a program segment is of the form:

$$P\{S\}Q.$$

The interpretation of this is that if assertion P is true before executing S, then assertion Q will be true after executing S, if the execution of S terminates. Assertion P is the pre-condition of the program and Q is the post-condition. These assertions are about the values taken by the variables in the program before and after its execution. The assertions generally do not specify a particular value for the variables, but they specify the general properties of the values and the relationships among them.

To prove a theorem of the form $P\{S\}Q$, we need some rules and axioms about the programming language in which the program segment S is written. Here we consider a simple programming language, which deals only with integers and has the following types of statements: (1) assignment, (2) conditional statement, and (3) an iterative statement. A program is considered a sequence of statements. We will now discuss the rules and axioms for these statements so that we can combine them to prove the correctness of programs.

Axiom of Assignment: Assignments are central to procedural languages. In our language no state change can be accomplished without the assignment statement. The axiom of assignment is also central to the axiomatic approach. In fact, only for the assignment statement do we have an independent axiom; for the rest of the statements we have rules. Consider the assignment statement of the form

$$x := f$$

where x is an identifier and f is an expression in the programming language without any side effects. Any assertion that is true about x after the assignment must be true of the expression f before the assignment. In other words, because after the assignment the variable x contains the value computed by the expression f, if a condition is true after the assignment is made, then the condition obtained by replacing x by f must be true before the assignment. This is the essence of the axiom of assignment. The axiom is stated next:

$$P_f^x\{x := f\}P$$

P is the post-condition of the program segment containing only the assignment statement. The pre-condition is P_f^x, which is an assertion obtained by substituting f for all occurrences of x in the assertion P. In other words, if P_f^x is true before the assignment statement, P will be true after the assignment.

This is the only axiom we have in Hoare's axiomatic model besides the standard axioms about the mathematical operators used in the language (such as commutativity and associativity of the + operator). The reason that we have only one axiom for the assignment statement is that this is the only statement in our language that has any effect on the state of the system, and we need an axiom to define what the effect of such a statement is. The other language constructs, like alternation and iteration, are for flow control, to determine which assignment statements will be executed. For such statements rules of inference are provided.

Rule of Composition: Let us first consider the rule for sequential composition, where two statements S1 and S2 are executed in sequence. This rule is called *rule of composition*, and is shown next:

$$\frac{P\{\,S1\}Q,\ Q\{S2\}R}{P\{S1;\,S2\}R}$$

The explanation of this notation is that if what is stated in the numerator can be proved, the denominator can be inferred. Using this rule, if we can prove P{S1}Q and Q{S2}R, we can claim that if before execution the pre-condition P holds, then after execution of the program segment S1;S2 the post-condition R will hold. In other words, to prove P{S1;S2}R, we have to find some Q and prove that P{S1}Q and Q{S2}R. This rule is dividing the problem of determining the semantics of a sequence of statements into determining the semantics of individual statments. In other words, from the proofs of simple statements, proofs of programs (i.e., sequence of statements) will be constructed. Note that the rule handles a strict sequence of statements only (recall the earlier discussion on structured programming.)

Rule for Alternate Statement: Let us now consider the rules for an `if` statement. For formal verification, the entire `if` statement is treated as one construct, the semantics of which have to be determined. This is the way in which other structured statements are also handled. There are two types of `if` statement, one with an `else` clause and one without. The rules for both are given next:

$$\frac{P \wedge B\{S\}Q,\ P\wedge \sim B \Rightarrow Q}{P\{\text{if B then S}\}Q}$$
$$\frac{P \wedge B\{S1\}Q,\ P \wedge B\{S2\}Q}{P\{\text{if B then S1 else S2}\}Q}$$

Let us consider the if-then-else statement. We want to prove a post-condition for this statement. However, depending on the evaluation of B, two different statements can be executed. In both cases the post-condition must be satisfied. Hence if we can show that starting in the state where $P \wedge B$ is true and executing S1 or starting in a state where $P \wedge \sim B$ is true and executing the statement S2, both lead to the post-condition Q, then the following can be inferred: if the if-then-else statement is executed with pre-condition P, the post-condition Q will hold after execution of the statement. Similarly, for the if-then statement, if B is true then S is executed; otherwise the control goes straight to the end of the statement. Hence, if we can show that starting from a state where $P \wedge B$ is true and executing S leads to a state where Q is true and before the `if` statement if $P \wedge \sim B$ implies Q, then we can say that starting from P before the `if` statement we will always reach a state in which Q is true.

Rules of Consequence: To be able to prove new theorems from the ones we have already proved using the axioms, we require some rules of inference. The simplest inference rule is that if the execution of a program ensures that an assertion Q is true after execution, then it also ensures that every assertion logically implied by Q is also true after execution. Similarly, if a pre-condition ensures that a post-condition is true after execution of a program, then every condition that logically implies the pre-condition will also ensure that the post-condition holds after execution of the program. These are called *rules of consequence*, and they are formally stated here:

$$\frac{P\{S\}R, R \Rightarrow Q}{P\{S\}Q}$$

$$\frac{P \Rightarrow R, R\{S\}Q}{P\{S\}Q}$$

Rule of Iteration:

Now let us consider iteration. Loops are the trickiest construct when dealing with program proofs. We will consider only the `while` loop of the form `while B do S`. We have to determine the semantics of the whole construct.

In executing this loop, first the condition B is checked. If B is false, S is not executed and the loop terminates. If B is true, S is executed and B is tested again. This is repeated until B evaluates to false. We would like to be able to make an assertion that will be true when the loop terminates. Let this assertion be P. As we do not know how many times the loop will be executed, it is easier to have an assertion that will hold true irrespective of how many times the loop body is executed. In that case P will hold true after every execution of statement S, and will be true before every execution of S, because the condition that holds true after an execution of S will be the condition for the next execution of S (if S is executed again). Furthermore, we know that the condition B is false when the loop terminates and is true whenever S is executed. These properties have been used in the rule for iteration:

$$\frac{P \wedge B\{S\}P}{P\{\text{while B do S}\}P \wedge \sim B}$$

As the condition P is unchanging with the execution of the statements in the loop body, it is called the *loop invariant*. Finding loop invariants is the thorniest problem in constructing proofs of correctness. One method for getting the loop invariant that often works is to extract ~B from the post-condition of the loop and try the remaining assertion as the loop invariant. Another method is to try replacing the variable that binds the loop execution with the loop counter. Thus if the loop has a counter i, which goes from 0 to n, and if the post-condition of the loop contains n, then replace n by i and try the assertion as a loop invariant.

An Example

Although in a theorem of the form $P\{S\}Q$, we say that if P is true at the start and the execution of S terminates, Q will be true after executing S, to prove a theorem of this sort we work backwards. That is, we do not start with the pre-condition; we work our way to the end of the program to determine the post-condition. Instead we start with the post-condition and work our way back to the start of the program, and determine the pre-condition. We use the axiom of assignment and other rules to determine the pre-condition of a statement for a given post-condition. If the pre-condition we obtain by doing this is implied by P, then by rules of consequence we can say that P{S}Q is a theorem. Let us consider a simple example of determining the remainder in integer division, by repeated subtraction. The program is shown in Figure 8.8.

The pre-condition and post-condition of this program are given as

$$P = \{x \geq 0 \wedge y > 0\}$$
$$Q = \{x = qy + r \wedge 0 \leq r < y\}$$

We have to prove that P {Program} Q is a theorem. We start with Q. The first statement before the end of the program is the loop. We invent the loop invariant by removing ~B from the Q, which is also the output assertion of the loop. For this we factor Q into a form like $I \wedge \sim B$, then choose I as the invariant. For this program we have $\sim B = \{r < y\}$, and $Q = \{x = qy + r \wedge 0 \leq r \wedge r < y\}$, hence our trial invariant I is $\{x = qy + r \wedge 0 \leq r\}$.

```
(* Remainder of x/y *)
1. begin
2.    q := 0;
3.    r := x;
4.    while r ≥ y do
5.    begin
6.        r := r - y ;
7.        q := q + 1 ;
8.    end;
9. end.
```

FIGURE 8.8. Program to determine the remainder.

Let us now see if this invariant is appropriate for this loop, that is, starting with this, we get a pre-condition of the form $I \wedge B$. Starting with I, we use the assignment axiom and the pre-condition for statement 7 is

$$x = (q + 1)y + r \wedge 0 \le r\{q := q + 1\}I$$

Using the assignment axiom for statement 6, we get the pre-condition for 6 as

$$x = (q + 1)y + (r - y) \wedge 0 \le (r - y),$$

which is the same as $x = qy + r \wedge y \le r$. Using the rule of composition (for statements 6 and 7), we can say

$$x = qy + r \wedge y \le r\{r := r - y; q := q + 1\}I.$$

Because $x = qy + r \wedge y \le r \Rightarrow I \wedge B$, by rule of consequence and the rule for the while loop, we have

$$I\{\text{while loop in program}\}I \wedge \sim (r \ge y)$$

where I is $x = qy + r \wedge 0 \le r$.

Now let us consider the statements before the loop (i.e., statements 2 and 3). The post-condition for these statements is I. Using the axiom of assignment, we first replace r with x, and then we replace q with 0 to get

$$(x = x \wedge 0 \le x) \Rightarrow (0 \le x).$$

By composing these statements with the while statement, we get

$$0 \le x\{\text{the entire program}\}I \wedge \sim B.$$

Because, $(I \wedge \sim B)$ is the post-condition Q of the program and $0 \le x$ is the pre-condition, we have proved the program to be correct.

Discussion

In the axiomatic method, to prove P{S}Q, we assume that S will terminate. So, by proving that the program will produce the desired post-condition using the axiomatic method, we are essentially saying that *if* the program terminates, it will provide the desired post-condition. The axiomatic proof technique cannot prove whether or not a program terminates. For this reason, the proof using the axiomatic technique is called the proof of *partial correctness*.

This is in contrast to the proof of *total correctness*, where termination of a program is also proved. Termination of programs is of considerable interest for obvious reason of avoiding infinite loops. With the axiomatic method, additional techniques have to be used to prove termination. One common method is to define a well-ordered set that has a smallest member and then add an expression to the assertions that produces a value in the set. If after an execution of the loop body, it can be shown that the value of the expression is less than it was on the entry, then the loop must terminate. There are other methods of proving correctness that aim to prove total correctness.

Proofs of correctness have obvious theoretical appeal and a considerable body of literature exists in the area. Despite this, the practical use of these formal methods of verification has been limited. In the software development industry proving correctness is not generally used as a means of verification. Their use, at best, is limited to proving correctness of some critical modules.

There are many reasons for the lack of general use of formal verification. Constructing proofs is quite hard, and even for relatively modest problems, proofs can be quite large and difficult to comprehend. As much of the work must be done manually (even if theorem provers are available), the techniques are open to clerical errors. In addition, the proof methods are usually limited to proving correctness of single modules. When procedures and functions are used, constructing proofs of correctness becomes extremely hard. In essence, the technique of proving correctness does not scale up very well to large programs. Despite these shortcomings, proof techniques offer an attractive formal means for verification and hold promise for the future.

8.2.5 Code Inspections or Reviews

The review process was started with the purpose of detecting defects in the code. Though design reviews substantially reduce defects in code, reviews are still very useful and can considerably enhance reliability and reduce effort during testing. Code reviews are designed to detect defects that originate during the coding process, although they can also detect defects in detailed design. However, it is unlikely that code reviews will reveal errors in system design or requirements.

Code inspections or reviews are usually held after code has been successfully completed and other forms of static tools have been applied but before any testing has been performed. Therefore, activities like code reading, symbolic execution, and static analysis should be performed, and defects found by these techniques corrected before code reviews are held. The main motivation for this is to save human time and effort, which would otherwise be spent detecting errors that a compiler or static analyzer can detect. In other words, the entry criteria for code review is that the code must compile successfully and has been "passed" by other static analysis tools.

The documentation to be distributed to the review team members includes the code to be reviewed and the design document. The review team for code reviews should include the programmer, the designer, and the tester. The review starts with the preparation for the review and ends with a list of action items. We discussed the general method for conducting reviews in Chapter 3.

The aim of reviews is to detect defects in code. One obvious coding defect is that the code fails to implement the design. This can occur in many ways. The function implemented by a module may be different from the function actually defined in the design or the interface of the modules may not be the same as the interface specified in the design. In addition, the input-output format assumed by a module may be inconsistent with the format specified in the design.

Other code defects can be divided into two broad categories: logic and control and data operations and computations. Some examples of logic and control defects are infinite loops, unreachable code, incorrect predicate, missing or unreferenced labels, and improper nesting of loops and branches. Examples of defects in computation and data operations are missing validity tests for external data, incorrect access of array components, improper initialization, and misuse of variables.

In addition to defects, there are quality issues, which the review also addresses. The first is efficiency. A module may be implemented in an obviously inefficient manner and could be wasteful of memory or the computer time. The code could also be violating the local coding standards. Although nonadherence to coding standards cannot be classified as a defect, it is desirable to maintain the standard. Standards can have restrictions on annotations, internal documentation, use of global variables, use of recursion, naming of variables, maximum nesting of loops, and alternative constructs.

A Sample Checklist: The following are some of the items that can be included in a checklist for code reviews [Dun84].

- Do data definitions exploit the typing capabilities of the language?
- Do all the pointers point to some object? (Are there any "dangling pointers"?)
- Are the pointers set to NULL, where needed?
- Are all the array indexes within bound?
- Are indexes properly initialized?
- Are all the branch conditions correct (not too weak, not too strong)?
- Will a loop always terminate (no infinite loops)?
- Is the loop termination condition correct?
- Is the number of loop executions "off by one"?
- Where applicable, are the divisors tested for zero?
- Are imported data tested for validity?
- Do actual and formal interface parameters match?
- Are all variables used? Are all output variables assigned?
- Can statements placed in the loop be placed outside the loop?
- Are the labels unreferenced?
- Will the requirements of execution time be met?

- Are the local coding standards met?

8.2.6   Unit Testing

All the methods discussed earlier are static methods in that the program is not compiled and executed. The program text was the input to these techniques and the text was evaluated and analyzed manually or with the aid of tools. Even symbolic execution is a static method where the program text is "executed." In fact, symbolic execution could be done manually; the use of a symbolic execution tool is essentially to eliminate the potentially cumbersome manual procedure.

In contrast to these methods, unit testing is a dynamic method for verification, where the program is actually compiled and executed. It is one of the most widely used methods, and the coding phase is sometimes called the "coding and unit testing phase." As in other forms of testing, unit testing involves executing the code with some test cases and then evaluating the results.

The goal of unit testing is to test modules or "units," not the entire software system. Other levels of testing are used to test the system. Unit testing is most often done by the programmer himself. The programmer, after finishing the coding of a module, tests it with some test data. The tested module is then delivered for system integration and further testing.

Testing of modules or software systems is a difficult and challenging task. Selection of test cases and deciding how much testing is enough are two important aspects of testing. Unit testing is dealt with in the next chapter, after the fundamentals of testing and the selection of test cases have been discussed.

8.3   Metrics

Traditionally, work on metrics has focused on the final product, namely the code. In a sense, all metrics for intermediate products of requirements and design are basically used to ensure that the final product has a high quality and the productivity of the project stays high. That is, the basic goal of metrics for intermediate products is to predict or get some idea about the metrics of the final product. For the code, the most commonly used metrics are size, complexity, and reliability. We will discuss reliability, in the next chapter as most reliability models use test data to assess reliability. Here we discuss a few size and complexity measures.

8.3.1   Size Measures

Size of a product is a simple measure, which can be easy to calculate. The main reason for interest in size measures is that size is the major factor that affects the cost of a project. Size in itself is of little use; it is the relation of size with the cost and quality that makes size an important metric. At the end of the project, size is measured primarily to record it, along with total cost, for future use. As we saw earlier, this type of data is used to determine the cost estimation models for a process. It is also used to measure productivity during the project. As mentioned earlier, a common measure of productivity is DLOC per person-month. When the coding is finished, size can also be to plan the testing activity for the project, as testing effort is also governed by the size of the project. Final quality delivered by a process is also frequently normalized with respect to size. A commonly used approach to specify the quality being delivered by a process is to characterize the process by the number of defects per KLOC. For these reasons, size is one of the most important and frequently used metrics. At the end of the coding phase, the size of the project is likely to be very close to the final delivered size. Hence, here the size is measured (as opposed to estimated).

The most common measure of size is delivered lines of source code, or the number of lines of code (LOC) finally delivered. The trouble with LOC is that the number of lines of code for a project depends heavily on the language used. For example, a program written in assembly language will be large compared to the same program written in a higher-level language, if LOC is used as a size measure. Even for the same language, the size can vary considerably depending on the programmer and other factors. What forms a line in determining the size is also not universally accepted and depends on the use of the size measure. For example, if we are interested in size to determine the total effort, then it might be reasonable to include comment and data lines. On the other hand, if we are interested in function size, it is better to include only the executable statements. Despite these deficiencies, LOC remains a handy and reasonable size measure that is used extensively. Currently, perhaps the most widely used counting method for determining the size is to count noncomment, nonblank lines only.

Halstead [Hal77] has proposed metrics for length and volume of a program based on the number of operators and operands. In a program we define the following measurable quantities:

- n_1 is the number of distinct operators.
- n_2 is the number of distinct operands.
- $f_{1,j}$ is the number of occurrences of the jth most frequent operator.
- $f_{2,j}$ is the number of occurrences of the jth most frequent operand.

Then the vocabulary n of a program is defined as

$n = n_1 + n_2.$

With the measurable parameters listed earlier, two new parameters are defined:

$$N_1 = \sum f_{1,j}, \, N_2 = \sum f_{2,j}.$$

N_1 is the total occurrences of different operators in the program and N_2 is the total occurrences of different operands. The length of the program is defined as

$N = N_1 + N_2$.

From the length and the vocabulary, the volume V of the program is defined as

$V = N \log_2(n)$.

This definition of the volume of a program represents the minimum number of bits necessary to represent the program. $\text{Log}_2(n)$ is the number of bits needed to represent every element in the program uniquely, and N is the total occurrences of the different elements. Volume is used as a size metric for a program.

Experiments have shown that the volume of a program is highly correlated with the size in LOC. Some experiments have also shown that the volume metric has a very high correlation with the error-proneness of modules [MJ95], i.e., in the experiments it was found that the modules in which the programmer had made more errors generally had a high volume. The same is true for the LOC measure. Overall, due to the high correlation, we can say that despite the theoretical appeal of volume as a size measure, for statistical studies it does not offer any strong advantages over the LOC measure.

8.3.2   Complexity Metrics

The productivity, if measured only in terms of lines of code per unit time, can vary a lot depending on the complexity of the system to be developed. Clearly, a programmer will produce a lesser amount of code for highly complex system programs, as compared to a simple application program. Similarly, complexity has great impact on the cost of maintaining a program. To quantify complexity beyond the fuzzy notion of the ease with which a program can be constructed or comprehended, some metrics to measure the complexity of a program are needed.

Some metrics for complexity were discussed in Chapter 7. The same metrics that are applicable to detailed design can be applied to code. One such complexity measure discussed in the previous chapter is *cyclomatic complexity*, in which the complexity of a module is the number of independent cycles in the flow graph of the module. A number of metrics have been proposed for quantifying the complexity of a program [HMKD82], and studies have been done to correlate the complexity with maintenance effort. Here we discuss a few more complexity measures. Most of these have been proposed in the context of programs, but they can be applied or adapted for detailed design as well.

Size Measures

A complexity measure tries to capture the level of difficulty in understanding a module. In other words, it tries to quantify a cognitive aspect of a program. It is well known that, in general, the larger a module, the more difficult it is to comprehend. Hence, the size of a module can be taken as a simple measure of the complexity of the module. It can be seen that, on an average, as the size of the module increases, the number of decisions in it are likely to increase. This means that, on an average, as the size increases the cyclomatic complexity also increases. Though it is clearly possible that two programs of the same size have substantially different complexities, in general, size is quite strongly related to some of the complexity measures.

Extension to Cyclomatic Complexity

The cyclomatic complexity measure proposed by McCabe considers each decision in the program as a single unit (in the flow graph, one node is created for each condition). With this, the cyclomatic complexity is the same as (under some conditions) the number of decisions plus one. Myers [Mye77] has extended the notion of cyclomatic complexity noting that decisions with multiple conditions (combined into a predicate by Boolean operators) are typically more complex than decisions with one condition. In this extension, complexity is measured as an interval rather than a single value. The lower bound of the interval is the number of decisions plus one or the cyclomatic complexity of the program. The upper bound of the interval is the number of individual conditions plus one. Specifying the complexity as an interval accounts for both the decisions and the conditions in a program.

Halstead's Measure

Halstead also proposed a number of other measures based on his software science [Hal77]. Some of these can be considered complexity measures. As given earlier, a number of variables are defined in software science. These are n_1 (number of unique operators), n_2 (number of unique operands), N_1 (total frequency of operators), and N_2 (total frequency of operands). As any program must have at least two operators—one for function call and one for end of statement—the ratio $n_1/2$ can be considered the relative level of difficulty due to the larger number of operators in the program. The ratio N_2/n_2 represents the average number of times an operand is used. In a program in which variables are changed more frequently, this ratio will be larger. As such programs are harder to understand, *ease of reading or writing* is defined as

$$D = \frac{n_1 * N_2}{2 * n_2}.$$

Halstead's complexity measure focused on the internal complexity of a module, as does McCabe's complexity measure. Thus the complexity of the module's connection with its environment is not given much importance. In Halstead's measure, a module's connection with its environment is reflected in terms of operands and operators. A call to another module is considered an operator, and all the parameters are considered operands of this operator.

Live Variables

In a computer program, a typical assignment statement uses and modifies only a few variables. However, in general the statements have a much larger context. That is, to construct or understand a statement, a programmer must keep track of a number of variables, other than those directly used in the statement. For a statement, such data items are called *live variables*. Intuitively, the more live variables for statements, the harder it will be to understand a program. Hence, the concept of live variables can be used as a metric for program complexity.

First let us define *live variables* more precisely. A variable is considered live from its first to its last reference within a module, including all statements between the first and last statement where the variable is referenced. Using this definition, the set of live variables for each statement can be computed easily by analysis of the module's code. The procedure of determining the live variables can easily be automated.

For a statement, the number of live variables represents the degree of difficulty of the statement. This notion can be extended to the entire module by defining the average number of live variables. The average number of live variables is the sum of the count of live variables (for all executable statements) divided by the number of executable statements. This is a complexity measure for the module.

Live variables are defined from the point of view of data usage. The logic of a module is not explicitly included. The logic is used only to determine the first and last statement of reference for a variable. Hence, this concept of complexity is quite different from cyclomatic complexity, which is based entirely on the logic and considers data as secondary.

Another data usage–oriented concept is *span*, the number of statements between two successive uses of a variable. If a variable is referenced at n different places in a module, then for that variable there are $(n - 1)$ spans. The average span size is the average number of executable statements between two successive references of a variable. A large span implies that the reader of the program has to remember a definition of a variable for a larger period of time (or for more statements). In other words, span can be considered a complexity measure; the larger the span, the more complex the module.

Knot Count

A method for quantifying complexity based on the locations of the control transfers of the program has been proposed in [WHH79]. It was designed largely for FORTRAN programs, where explicit transfer of control is shown by the use of goto statements. A programmer, to understand a given program, typically draws arrows from the point of control transfer to its destination, helping to create a mental picture of the program and the control transfers in it. According to this metric, the more intertwined these arrows become, the more complex the program. This notion is captured in the concept of a "knot."

A *knot* is essentially the intersection of two such control transfer arrows. If each statement in the program is written on a separate line, this notion can be formalized as follows. A jump from line a to line b is represented by the pair (a, b). Two jumps (a, b) and (p, q) give rise to a knot if either min (a, b) < min (p, q) < max (a, b) and max (p, q) > max (a, b); or min (a, b) < max (p, qa) < max (a, b) and min (p, q) < min (a, b).

Problems can arise while determining the knot count of programs using structured constructs. One method is to convert such a program into one that explicitly shows control transfers and then compute the knot count. The basic scheme can be generalized to flow graphs, though with flow graphs only bounds can be obtained.

Topological Complexity

A complexity measure that is sensitive to the nesting of structures has been proposed in [Che78]. Like cyclomatic complexity, it is based on the flow graph of a module or program. The complexity of a program is considered its maximal intersect number *min*.

To compute the maximal intersect, a flow graph is converted into a strongly connected graph (by drawing an arrow from the terminal node to the initial node). A strongly connected graph divides the graph into a finite number of regions. The number of regions is (edges − nodes + 2). If we draw a line that enters each region exactly once, then the number of times this line intersects the arcs in the graph is the maximal intersect *min*, which is taken to be the complexity of the program.

8.3.3 Style Metrics

Earlier in this chapter, we discussed many issues relating to programming style. The programming style affects the readability of a program. Hence, it will be very useful if we can quantify the programming style. In general, what is considered a "good" style will also depend on the local coding conventions and the coding standards of the organization. However, some general guidelines for style can be formulated. Here we discuss an approach to quantify the programming style of a program [BM85]. In this approach, the following factors are considered to affect the programming style:

1. **Module length:** the average length of modules in the program (measured in noncommented, nonblank lines).

2. **Identifier length:** the average length, in characters, of the user-defined identifiers.

3. **Comments:** the percentage of total lines that are comment lines.

4. **Indentation:** the ratio of initial spaces to total number of characters.

5. **Blank lines:** the percentage of lines that are blank. As blank lines are used by programmers to highlight the structure of the program, their usage affects readability.

6. **Line length:** the average number of nonblank characters in a line.

7. **Embedded spaces:** the average number of embedded spaces in a line. These are significant for the readability of arithmetic and logical expressions and declarations.

8. **Constants definitions:** the percentage of all user identifiers that are defined as constants.

9. **Reserved words:** the number of reserved words (and standard library functions) used. A high value shows a better use of facilities available to the programmer.

10. **Include files:** the number of files included in a program. This represents how a program has been divided into files.

11. **Gotos:** the number of occurrences of the goto statement. It is assumed that a figure of 0 is best.

Each of these features is considered as affecting the readability or style of the program. A very high or very low value is considered undesirable. For example, understandability increases as the number of comments increases. However, after a certain point, the understandability decreases, as excessive comments can obscure the semantics of the program. The same is the situation with other factors. Hence, for each factor, a low and a high value is attached. If the value of the feature is less than low or higher than high its contribution to the style "score" of the program is considered 0. Between low and high, two other threshold values are defined: lot and hit. If the value of the feature is between these, the score contribution of this feature is the specified max value. If it is between low and lot or between hit and high, a proportional score between 0 and max is given. The general curve for the score contribution of a feature is shown in Figure 8.9.

For each feature, the values for low, high, lot, hit, and max are specified. For C programs, the specific values are shown in Table 8.1 [BM85]. The style score of the program is the sum of all the score contributions of all the features. A score higher than 60 is considered good, while a score less than 20 is considered poor. A program to evaluate the style score of C programs has been developed and used for the case study. It is available from the home page of the book, as described in the preface.

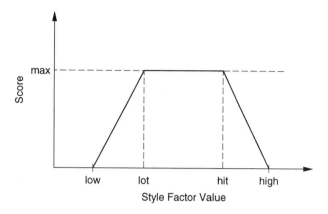

FIGURE 8.9. Programming style scoring

	max	low	lot	hit	high
Module length	15	4	10	25	35
Identifier length	14	4	5	10	14
Comment lines (%)	12	8	15	25	35
Indentation (%)	12	8	24	48	60
Blank lines (%)	11	8	15	30	35
Characters per line	9	8	12	25	30
Spaces per line	8	1	4	10	12
Defines (%)	8	10	15	25	30
Reserved words	6	4	16	30	36
Include files	5	0	3	3	4
Gotos	-20	1	3	99	99

TABLE 8.1. Style metric values.

8.4 Summary

In the coding phase, the design of a system is translated into code that can be compiled and executed. Although the coding phase does not affect the structure of the system, it has great impact on the internal structure of modules, which affects the testability and understandability of the system.

The goal of the coding phase is to produce clear and simple programs. The aim is not to reduce the coding effort, but to program in a manner so that testing and maintenance costs are reduced. Programs should not be constructed so that they are easy to write; they should be easy to read and understand. Reading programs (mostly by people other than the programmer) is a much more common activity than writing programs. Hence, the goal of the coding phase is to produce simple programs that are clear to understand and modify.

To enhance the readability of programs, structured programming should be used. In structured programs, the program is a sequence of single-entry, single-exit statements, and the control flow during execution is linearized. This makes the dynamic structure of a program similar to the static structure. Such programs are easy to understand and verify.

Information hiding is another principle that can be used to enhance program clarity. In information hiding, the data structures are hidden behind access functions. Different modules are given access to data on a "need to know" basis. When supported by language mechanisms, information hiding is a very useful construct that limits coupling between modules by ensuring that the data encapsulated in a module is accessible only to operations defined on that module. From the outside, the data cannot be directly accessed, and only operations on the data can be performed.

Internal documentation is also essential for readable programs. Comments in programs should be written to aid understanding and should provide supplementary information. Usually, comments should be written for blocks of code such as procedures and functions. A prologue for a module should define what the module is doing and the logic of the module. It should also describe the side effects and other information about the module.

Verification of code can be done in a number of ways, including code reading or desk reviews, data flow analysis, symbolic execution, proving correctness, code reviews and walkthroughs, and unit testing. Of all these, code reviews and unit testing are the most common. In code reviews, a team of persons reviews the code as in a requirement or design review. During testing the program is executed with test cases to determine the presence of errors. Except for testing, all other methods discussed in the chapter are static methods where the program is not executed. Static methods often directly find the error in the program, while testing detects only the presence of errors.

A number of metrics exist for quantifying different qualities of the code. The most commonly used are size metrics, because they are used to assess the productivity of people and are often used in cost estimation. The most common size measure is lines of code (LOC), which is also used in most cost models. There are also other measures for size.

The goal of complexity metrics is to quantify the complexity of software. Complexity is an important factor affecting the productivity of projects and is a factor in cost estimation. A number of different metrics exist. Perhaps the most common is the cyclomatic complexity, which is based on the internal logic of the program and defines complexity as the number of independent cycles in the flow graph of the program.

Exercises

1. What is structured programming and why is it important?

2. What are the major concepts that help make a program more readable?

3. Consider the following program, which takes in the values A, B, and C in sorted order and determines the type of triangle represented by A, B, and C:

```
read(a, b, c);
if (a < b) or (b < c) then
    print("Illegal inputs");
    return;
if (a=b) or (b=c) then
    if (a=b) and (b=c) then print("equilateral triangle")
    else print("isoscles triangle")
else begin
    a := a*a; b := b*b; c := c*c;
    d := b+c;
    if (a = d) then print("right triangle")
    else if (a<d) then print("acute triangle")
    else print("obtuse triangle");
end;
```

Symbolically execute this program and show that it is correct (or incorrect). Draw the execution tree.

4. Consider the following program to determine the product of two integers *x* and *y*:

```
if (x = 0) or (y = 0) then
    p := 0
else begin
    p := x;
    i := 1;
    while (i != y) do begin
        p := p * x;
        i := i + 1;
    end;
end;
```

Write formal specifications for a program to compute the product of two numbers. Then, using the axiomatic method, prove that this program is correct.

5. Consider the following two algorithms for searching an element *E* in a sorted array *A*, which contains *n* integers. The first procedure implements a simple linear search algorithm. The second performs a binary search. Binary search is generally much more efficient in terms of execution time compared to the linear search.

```
        function lin_search (A, E): boolean
        var
            i : integer;
            found: boolean;
        begin
            found := false;
            i := 1;
            while (not found) and (i ≤ n) do begin
            if (A[i] = E) then found := true;
            i := i + 1;
            end;
            lin_search := found;
        end;
        function bin_search (A, E): boolean
        var
            low, high, mid, i, j : integer;
            found : boolean;
        begin
            low := 1;
            high := n;
            found := false;
            while (low ≤ high) and (not found) do begin
                mid := (low + high)/2;
                if E < A[mid] then high := mid − 1
                    else if E > A[mid] then low := mid + 1
                    else found := true;
            end;
            bin_search := found;
        end;
```

Determine the cyclomatic complexity and live variable complexity for these two functions. Is the ratio of the two complexity measures similar for the two functions?

6. What is Halstead's size measure for these two modules? Compare this size with the size measured in LOC.

7. Consider the size measure as the number of bytes needed to store the object code of a program. How useful is this size measure? Is it closer to LOC or Halstead's metric? Explain.

8. Not all control statements are equally complex. Assign complexity weights (0–10) to different control statements in Pascal, and then determine a formula to calculate the complexity of a program. How will you determine if this measure is better or worse than other complexity measures?

9. A combination of conditions in a decision makes a decision more complex. Such decisions should be treated as a combination of different decisions.

Compared to the simple measure where each decision is treated as one, how much will the difference in the cyclomatic complexity of a program with 20% of its conditional statements having two conditions and 20% having three conditions be, when evaluated by this new approach?

10. Suppose multiple methods must be used for verification, as is usually done. Select at least three methods you want to apply. In what order will you apply these?

11. Design an experiment to study the correlation between some of the complexity measures and between some of the size measures.

12. Design an experiment to study if the "error-proneness" of a module is related to a complexity measure for the module.

CASE STUDY

Implementation of Structured Design

The programs were written in C on a Sun workstation, as required. The first version almost directly implemented the modules specified in the function-oriented design (given earlier and available from the home page). The first thing that came up during coding was that our view of the data expanded. To write the code of the modules, data like total number of courses, starting index for the different type of courses, etc. were needed.

The total size of the program was about 1320 lines. We determined various code based complexity and size metrics for this code using the tool complexity that we developed (and which is available from the home page, as described in the preface). The metrics that were collected were cyclomatic complexity, Halstead metrics, and live variables and span of variables. The tools output these in descending order. Part of the output from these tools is given here:

MODULE	SIZE	CYCLOMATIC COMPLEXITY
validate_file2	111	18
validate_dept_courses	88	17
sched_ug_pref	104	16
validate_class_rooms	92	15
validate_lec_times	84	15
print_conflicts	50	11
print_TimeTable	42	10
chk_fmt_time_slot	36	10
sched_pg_pref	82	9
separate_courses	46	9

Total Size: 1322   Total Cyclomatic Complexity: 243
Avg. size: 33   Avg. Cyclomatic Complexity: 6

Module	size	Volume	Ease of reading	Prog. effort
sched_ug_pref	104	1764	76	134
validate_file2	111	1725	131	225
sched_pg_pref	82	1352	55	74
validate_class_rooms	92	1329	111	147
validate_dept_courses	88	1271	103	130

```
main                        30    1180     36      42
validate_lec_times          84    1147     95     108
separate_courses            46     923     36      33
print_TimeTable             42     891     38      33
print_explanation           49     864     30      25
------------------------------------------------------------
Total Size:   1322    Total Volume:   21115
Avg.  size:     33    Avg.  Volume:     527
------------------------------------------------------------
```

From these metrics, it was clear that some of the modules were too large and had a high complexity value. Based on this information, we carefully reviewed some of these modules to see if their size or complexity could be reduced. During the reviews we found that in these modules some parts of the code were actually implementing some support functions that can be separated by forming clean, functionally cohesive modules. The basic guiding rule while trying to "break" the modules was to partition a module only if the new modules were all functionally cohesive modules. That is, parts of the code were taken to form new modules if the new modules were functionally cohesive and if the complexity of the parent module was reduced.

As a result of this, a few new modules were formed. The complexity of many of the modules was reduced, and there was a general decline in the average complexity. Parts of the cyclomatic complexity analysis of the modules in the new code is given soon. After reviewing the code again, we felt that further reducing the size and complexity of modules would result in a structure that is not modular. Note that the total size and complexity reduced by this exercise, besides the reduction in the complexity and size of the individual modules. That is, by this exercise we did not just redistribute the complexity, we actually reduced the overall complexity.

```
------------------------------------------------------------
MODULE                      SIZE    CYCLOMATIC COMPLEXITY
------------------------------------------------------------
sched_ug_pref               85          14
validate_class_rooms        89          14
validate_dept_courses       80          13
validate_lec_times          83          13
print_conflicts             50          11
print_TimeTable             42          10
chk_fmt_time_slot           33          10
print_explanation           49           9
separate_courses            47           9
sched_pg_no_pref            53           9
sched_ug_no_pref            46           8
sched_pg_pref               67           8
chk_file2_header            27           8
chk_fmt_course_no           17           7
```

```
        form_pref_list              46              7
        validate_file2              44              7
        -----------------------------------------------------------
        Total Size:   1264    Total Cyclomatic Complexity:   235
        Avg.  Size:     30    Avg.  Cyclomatic Complexity:     5
        -----------------------------------------------------------
```

The style of the final program was also analyzed by the `style` tool (which is also available from the home page). The tool gives the style metrics for the whole program, and for each module. The metrics for the entire program are shown soon. As we can see, the overall score is quite good. However, it does say that the amount of blank lines and spaces per line are fewer. As there are not too many arithmetic expressions, we do not consider lack of blank spaces important. Similarly, for structuring and organization, we have used some non-blank pattern lines. Hence we do not consider highlighting of lack of blank lines important.

```
    SCORE FOR THE PROGRAMMING STYLE : 70/100    ****    GOOD

    STYLE METRICS FOR THE WHOLE PROGRAM
    -----------------------------------------------------------
        Average size of the module            30  ACCEPTABLE
        Average identifier length              8  ACCEPTABLE
        Percentage of comment lines           20  ACCEPTABLE
        Percentage of blank lines             14  LESS
        Average number of chars per line      12  ACCEPTABLE
        Average number of embedded
        spaces per line                        0  VERY LESS
        Total no. of reserved words used      29  ACCEPTABLE
        Number of files included               4  ACCEPTABLE
        Number of goto's used                  0
    -----------------------------------------------------------
```

Both versions of the code for the case study (i.e., the initial implementation and the implementation after complexity reduction) are available from the home page, whose address is given in the preface.

Implementation of the OO Design

The object-oriented design of the case study, given earlier in Chapter 6, was implemented in C++. The implementation did extend the design a little, as is to be expected, but the extension was mostly in addition of data members and some methods. No major design changes were required due to implementation issues. The code could have been analyzed by using some of the metrics and then modified, as was done in the code implementing the structured design. However, this was not done for this implementation for three reasons. First, we did not have tools to analyze the C++ programs. Secondly, some of the tools that were available for use through other sources worked on a different version of C++ (our implementation is in GNU C++). And finally, the OO metrics are still relatively new, and not much data about their use is available.

The C++ code for the case study is also available from the home page of the book.

9

Testing

In a software development project, errors can be injected at any stage during development. For each phase, we have discussed different techniques for detecting and eliminating errors that originate in that phase. However, no technique is perfect, and it is expected that some of the errors of the earlier phases will finally manifest themselves in the code. This is particularly true because in the earlier phases most of the verification techniques are manual because no executable code exists. Ultimately, these remaining errors will be reflected in the code. Hence, the code developed during the coding activity is likely to have some requirements errors and design errors, in addition to errors introduced during the coding activity. Because code is frequently the only product that can be executed and whose actual behavior can be observed, testing is the phase where the errors remaining from all the previous phases must be detected. Hence, testing performs a very critical role for quality assurance and for ensuring the reliability of software.

During testing, the program to be tested is executed with a set of test cases, and the output of the program for the test cases is evaluated to determine if the program is performing as expected. Due to its approach, dynamic testing can only ascertain the presence of errors in the program; the exact nature of the errors is not usually decided by testing. Testing forms the first step in determining the errors in a program. Clearly, the success of testing in revealing errors in programs depends critically on the test cases. Much of this chapter is devoted to test case selection, criteria for selecting test cases, and their effect on testing.

Testing a large system is a complex activity, and like any complex activity it has to be broken into smaller activities. Due to this, for a project, *incremental testing* is generally performed, in which components and subsystems of the system are tested separately before integrating them to form the system for system testing. This form of testing, though necessary to ensure quality for a large system, introduces new issues of how to select components for testing and how to combine them to form subsystems and systems. In other words, integration of the various components of the system is an important issue that the testing phase has to deal with. For this reason, this phase is sometimes called "integration and testing."

We begin this chapter by discussing some definitions and concepts pertinent to testing. Then we discuss the two basic approaches to testing—black box or functional testing and white box or structural testing. Following this we discuss some of the special issues involved in testing object-oriented programs. The overall testing process is discussed next, followed by reliability estimation, as reliability estimation is the main metric of interest during testing. This chapter ends with the test plan and test case specification for the case study.

9.1   Testing Fundamentals

In this section we will first define some of the terms that are commonly used when discussing testing. Then we will discuss some basic issues relating to how testing can proceed, the need for oracles for testing, the importance of psychology of the tester, and some desirable properties for the criteria used for testing. Once these are discussed, we will proceed with the issue of selection of test cases.

9.1.1   Error, Fault, and Failure

So far, we have used the intuitive meaning of the term *error* to refer to problems in requirements, design, or code. Sometimes error, fault, and failure are used interchangeably, and sometimes they refer to different concepts. Let us start by defining these concepts clearly. We follow the IEEE definitions [IEE87] for these terms.

The term *error* is used in two different ways. It refers to the discrepancy between a computed, observed, or measured value and the true, specified, or theoretically correct value. That is, error refers to the difference between the actual output of a software and the correct output. In this interpretation, error is essentially a measure of the difference between the actual and the ideal. Error is also used to refer to human action that results in software containing a defect or fault. This definition is quite general and encompasses all the phases.

Fault is a condition that causes a system to fail in performing its required function. A fault is the basic reason for software malfunction and is synonymous with the commonly used term *bug*. The term error is also often used to refer to defects (taking a variation of the second definition of error). In this book we will continue to use the terms in the manner commonly used, and no explicit distinction will be made between errors and faults, unless necessary. It should be noted that the only faults that a software has are "design faults"; there is no wear and tear in software.

Failure is the inability of a system or component to perform a required function according to its specifications. A software failure occurs if the behavior of the software is different from the specified behavior. Failures may be caused due to functional or performance reasons. A failure is produced only when there is a fault in the system. However, presence of a fault does not guarantee a failure. In other words, faults have the potential to cause failures and their presence is a necessary but not a sufficient condition for failure to occur. Note that the definition does not imply that a failure must be *observed*. It is possible that a failure may occur but not be detected.

There are some implications of these definitions. Presence of an error (in the state) implies that a failure must have occurred, and the observance of a failure implies that a fault must be present in the system. However, the presence of a fault does not imply that a failure must occur. The presence of a fault in a system only implies that the fault has a *potential* to cause a failure to occur. Whether a fault actually manifests itself in a certain time duration depends on many factors. This means that if we observe the behavior of a system for some time duration and we do not observe any errors, we cannot say anything about the presence or absence of faults in the system. If, on the other hand, we observe some failure in this duration, we can say that there are some faults in the system.

There are direct consequences of this on testing. In testing, system behavior is observed, and by observing the behavior of a system or a component during testing, we determine whether or not there is a failure. Because of this fundamental reliance on external behavior observation, testing can only reveal the presence of faults, not their absence. By observing failures of the system we can deduce the presence of faults; but by not observing a failure during our observation (or testing) interval we cannot claim that there are no faults in the system. An immediate consequence of this is that it becomes hard to decide for how long we should test a system without observing any failures before deciding to stop testing. This makes "when to stop testing" one of the hard issues in testing.

During the testing process, only failures are observed, by which the presence of faults is deduced. The actual faults are identified by separate activities, commonly referred to as "debugging." In other words, for identifying faults, after testing has revealed the presence of faults, the expensive task of debugging has to be performed. This is one of the reasons why testing is an expensive method for identification of faults, compared to methods that directly observe faults.

9.1.2 Test Oracles

To test any program, we need to have a description of its expected behavior and a method of determining whether the observed behavior conforms to the expected behavior. For this we need a *test oracle*.

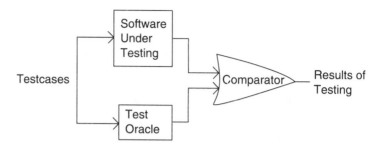

FIGURE 9.1. Testing and test oracles.

A test oracle is a mechanism, different from the program itself, that can be used to check the correctness of the output of the program for the test cases. Conceptually, we can consider testing a process in which the test cases are given to the test oracle and the program under testing. The output of the two is then compared to determine if the program behaved correctly for the test cases. This is shown in Figure 9.1.

Test oracles are necessary for testing. Ideally, we would like an automated oracle, which always gives a correct answer. However, often the oracles are human beings, who mostly compute by hand what the output of the program should be. As it is often extremely difficult to determine whether the behavior conforms to the expected behavior, our "human oracle" may make mistakes. As a result, when there is a discrepancy between the results of the program and the oracle, we have to verify the result produced by the oracle, before declaring that there is a fault in the program. This is one of the reasons testing is so cumbersome and expensive.

The human oracles generally use the specifications of the program to decide what the "correct" behavior of the program should be. To help the oracle determine the correct behavior, it is important that the behavior of the system or component be unambiguously specified and that the specification itself is error-free. In other words, the specifications should actually specify the true and correct system behavior. These conditions are hard to satisfy. After all, it is the activity of some earlier phase that determines these specifications, and these activities might be error-prone. Hence, the specifications themselves may contain errors, be imprecise, or contain ambiguities. Such shortcomings in the specifications are the major cause of situations where one party claims that a particular condition is not a failure while the other claims it is. However, there is no easy solution to this problem. Testing does require some specifications against which the given system is tested.

There are some systems where oracles are automatically generated from specifications of programs or modules [Jal87]. With such oracles, we are assured that the output of the oracle is consistent with the specifications. However, even this approach does not solve all our problems, because of the possibility of errors in the specifications. Consequently, an oracle generated from the specifications will only produce correct results if the specifications are correct, and it will not be dependable in the case of specification errors. Furthermore, such systems that generate oracles from specifications are likely to require formal specifications, which are frequently not generated during design.

9.1.3   Top-Down and Bottom-Up Approaches

Generally, parts of the program are tested before testing the entire program. Besides partitioning the problem of testing, another reason for testing parts separately is that if a test case detects an error in a large program, it will be extremely difficult to pinpoint the source of the error. That is, if a huge program does not work, determining which module has errors can be a formidable task. Furthermore, it will be extremely difficult to construct test cases so that different modules are executed in a sufficient number of different conditions so that we can feel fairly confident about them. In many cases, it is even difficult to construct test cases so that all the modules will be executed. This increases the chances of a module's errors going undetected. Hence it is clear that for a large system, we should first test different parts of the system independently, before testing the entire system.

In incremental testing, some parts of the system are first tested independently. Then these parts are combined to form a (sub) system, which is then tested independently. This combination can be done in two ways: either only the modules that have been tested independently are combined or some new untested modules are combined with tested modules. Both of these approaches require that the order in which modules are to be tested and integrated be planned before commencing testing.

We assume that a system is a hierarchy of modules. For such systems, there are two common ways modules can be combined, as they are tested, to form a working program: top-down and bottom-up. In top-down strategy, we start by testing the top of the hierarchy, and we incrementally add modules that it calls and then test the new combined system. This approach of testing requires *stubs* to be written. A stub is a dummy routine that simulates a module. In the top-down approach, a module (or a collection) cannot be tested in isolation because they invoke some other modules. To allow the modules to be tested before their subordinates have been coded, stubs simulate the behavior of the subordinates.

The bottom-up approach starts from the bottom of the hierarchy. First the modules at the very bottom, which have no subordinates, are tested. Then these modules are combined with higher-level modules for testing. At any stage of testing all the subordinate modules exist and have been tested earlier. To perform bottom-up testing, *drivers* are needed to set up the appropriate environment and invoke the module. It is the job of the driver to invoke the module under testing with the different set of test cases.

Notice that both top-down and bottom-up approaches are incremental, starting with testing single modules and then adding untested modules to those that have been tested, until the entire system is tested. In the first case, stubs must be written to perform testing, and in the other, drivers need to be written. Top-down testing is advantageous if major flaws occur toward the top of the hierarchy, while bottom-up is advantageous if the major flaws occur toward the bottom. Often, writing stubs can be more difficult than writing drivers, because one may need to know beforehand the set of inputs for the module being simulated by the stub and to determine proper responses for these inputs. In addition, as the stubs often simulate the behavior of a module over a limited domain, the choice of test cases for the superiordinate module is limited, and deciding test cases is often very difficult.

It is often best to select the testing method to conform with the development method. Thus, if the system is developed in a top-down manner, top-down testing should be used, and if the system is developed in a bottom-up manner, a bottom-up testing strategy should be used. By doing this, as parts of the system are developed, they are tested, and errors are detected as development proceeds. It should be pointed out that we are concerned with actual program development here, not the design method. The development can be bottom-up even if the design was done in a top-down manner.

9.1.4   Test Cases and Test Criteria

Having test cases that are good at revealing the presence of faults is central to successful testing. The reason for this is that if there is a fault in a program, the program can still provide the expected behavior for many inputs. Only for the set of inputs that exercise the fault in the program will the output of the program deviate from the expected behavior. Hence, it is fair to say that testing is as good as its test cases.

Ideally, we would like to determine a set of test cases such that successful execution of all of them implies that there are no errors in the program. This ideal goal cannot usually be achieved due to practical and theoretical constraints. Each test case costs money, as effort is needed to generate the test case, machine time is needed to execute the program for that test case, and more effort is needed to evaluate the results. Therefore, we would also like to minimize the number of test cases needed to detect errors. These are the two fundamental goals of a practical testing activity—maximize the number of errors detected and minimize the number of test cases (i.e., minimize the cost). As these two are frequently contradictory, the problem of selecting the set of test cases with which a program should be tested becomes more complex.

While selecting test cases the primary objective is to ensure that if there is an error or fault in the program, it is exercised by one of the test cases. An ideal test case set is one that succeeds (meaning that its execution reveals no errors) only if there are no errors in the program. One possible ideal set of test cases is one that includes all the possible inputs to the program. This is often called *exhaustive* testing. However, exhaustive testing is impractical and infeasible, as even for small programs the number of elements in the input domain can be extremely large (i.e., it is not practical due to cost constraints).

Hence, a realistic goal for testing is to select a set of test cases that is close to ideal. How should we select our test cases? On what basis should we include some element of the program domain in the set of test cases and not include others? For this *test selection criterion* (or simply *test criterion*) can be used. For a given program P and its specifications S, a test selection criterion specifies the conditions that must be satisfied by a set of test cases T. The criterion becomes a basis for test case selection. For example, if the criterion is that all statements in the program be executed at least once during testing, then a set of test cases T satisfies this criterion for a program P if the execution of P with T ensures that each statement in P is executed at least once.

There are two aspects of test case selection—specifying a criterion for evaluating a set of test cases, and generating a set of test cases that satisfy a given criterion. As we will see, many test case criteria have been proposed. However, generating test cases for most of these is not easy and cannot, in general, be automated fully. Often, a criterion is specified and the tester has to generate test cases that satisfy the criterion. In some cases, guidelines are available for deciding test cases. Overall, the problem of test case selection is very challenging, and current solutions are limited in scope.

There are two fundamental properties for a testing criterion: reliability and validity [GG75]. A criterion is reliable if all the sets (of test cases) that satisfy the criterion detect the same errors. That is, it is insignificant which of the sets satisfying the criterion is chosen; every set will detect exactly the same errors. A criterion is valid if for any error in the program there is some set satisfying the criterion that will reveal the error. A fundamental theorem of testing is that if a testing criterion is valid and reliable, if a set satisfying the criterion succeeds (revealing no faults) then the program contains no errors [GG75]. However, it has been shown that no algorithm exists that will determine a valid criterion for an arbitrary program.

As getting an ideal test criterion (that is both valid and reliable) is not generally possible, other more practical properties of test criteria have been proposed. Some axioms capturing some of the desirable properties of test criteria have been proposed in [Wey86]. We discuss some of the axioms proposed in [Wey86] here.

The first axiom is the *applicability axiom*, which states that for every program (and its specification) there exists a test set T that satisfies the criterion. This is clearly desirable for a general-purpose criterion; a criterion that can be satisfied only for some types of programs is of limited use in testing. The axiom is not saying anything about whether it is feasible to actually generate the test cases to satisfy the criterion. All it is saying is that it should be possible for all programs to have a set of test cases that will satisfy the criterion.

The *antiextensionality* axiom states that there are programs P and Q, both of which implement the same specifications, such that a test set T satisfies the criterion for P but does not satisfy the criterion for Q. This axiom ensures that the program structure has an important role to play in deciding the test cases. This axiom should hold for those criteria based on the program structure but not necessarily for those criteria based on specifications only. For program structure–based criteria, this axiom says that if there are multiple ways to implement a specification, the same set of test cases should not necessarily satisfy the criterion for both implementations.

The *antidecomposition* axiom states that there exists a program P and its component Q such that a test case set T satisfies the criterion for P and T' is the set of values that variables can assume on entering Q for some test case in T and T' does not satisfy the criterion for Q. Essentially, the axiom says that just because the criterion is satisfied for the entire program, it does not mean that the criterion has been satisfied for its components. For example, T might be such that the variables assume only a very limited set of values when entering Q. In this case, the criterion may not be satisfied for Q even when T satisfies the criterion for P.

The *anticomposition* axiom states that there exist programs P and Q such that T satisfies the criterion for P and the outputs of P for T (represented by P(T)) satisfy the criterion for Q, but T does not satisfy the criterion for P;Q. In other words, separately satisfying the criterion for the parts P and Q does not imply that the criterion has been satisfied by the program comprising P;Q. This is the dual of the antidecomposition axiom and should hold as the complexity of P;Q is more than the sum of complexities P and Q due to the interactions between P and Q. For example, the number of paths in a program comprising of P and Q is frequently far more than the sum of the number of paths in the two programs.

A total of eight axioms were proposed in [Wey86] (more were added in [Wey88]). We have discussed only a few key ones here. These axioms, which are for criteria based on the structure of the program, only provide some desirable properties that the test criteria should have. If all the axioms are satisfied by a test criterion, it does not imply that a set of test cases that satisfies the criterion will guarantee correctness. These are only some theoretically desired properties that a test criterion should have. If a test criterion does not even satisfy these axioms, then its applicability is even more limited, and the confidence one can have in testing based on that test criterion is presumably lower.

As it turns out, it is very difficult to get a criterion that satisfies even these axioms. This is largely due to the fact that a program may have paths that are infeasible, and one cannot determine these infeasible paths algorithmically as the problem is undecidable. Hence, one cannot have any criterion that tries to ensure some "coverage" of program structures, which will satisfy even the most fundamental applicability axiom. For example, the criterion of executing all statements does not satisfy the applicability axiom for this reason.

Hence, getting a criterion that is reliable and valid and that can be satisfied by a manageable number of test cases is usually not possible, and it is not easy to have a criterion that will satisfy the axioms in [Wey86]. Even devising a precise criterion is a very difficult task. So, often criteria are chosen that are not valid or reliable and that do not satisfy the axioms, like "90% of the statements should be executed at least once." Often a criterion is not even clearly specified, as in "all special values in the domain must be included" (what is a "special value"?).

Even when the criterion is specified, generating test cases to satisfy a criterion is not simple. In general, generating test cases for most of the criteria cannot be automated. For example, even for a simple criterion like "each statement of the program should be executed," it is extremely hard to construct a set of test cases that will satisfy this criterion for a large program, even if we assume that all the statements can be executed (i.e., there is no part that is not reachable).

Let us now consider the issue of comparison of criteria, that is, is a criterion "better" or "more powerful" than another. One relationship between criteria is that of *inclusion* (or *subsumption*). A criterion C_1 includes (or subsumes) the criterion C_2 if for every program P and its specification S, any set of test cases that satisfy C_1 also satisfy C_2 [FW93b]. This relation is represented as $C_1 \Rightarrow C_2$, and is a transitive relation. One may think that if $C_1 \Rightarrow C_2$, testing based on C_1 will always be better than testing based on C_2. Unfortunately, this is not the case. The reason is that the fault-detection capability of a set of test cases T that satisfy a criterion C depends on the actual test cases in T and not just C (i.e., the criterion is not valid). In other words, if T_1 and T_2 both satisfy C for a program P, it does not mean that T_1 and T_2 will execute the same paths of P and detect the same faults in P. Because the actual test cases also play a role in whether or not an error in a program is detected, in general, it is possible to have a situation where $C_1 \Rightarrow C_2$, T_1 satisfies C_1, T_2 satisfies C_2, but T_2 detects an error that T_1 does not. However, if similar methods are used for test case generation then, generally speaking, C_1 will be better for testing than C_2 if $C_1 \Rightarrow C_2$.

The intent of the preceding discussion is to illustrate that no single criterion will serve the purpose of detecting a reasonable number of errors in a program. And though frequently the focus is on the criterion, to use a criterion for testing, the strategy for generating test cases to satisfy a criterion is also important. As it is generally known that all the faults in a program cannot be practically revealed by testing, and due to the limitations of the test criterion, it is best that during testing more than one criterion be used. One can also say that precise criterion-based testing that will provide a determinable level of confidence in testing is generally not possible.

9.1.5   Psychology of Testing

As we have seen, devising a set of test cases that will guarantee that all errors will be detected is not feasible. Moreover, there are no formal or precise methods for selecting test cases. Even though there are a number of heuristics and rules of thumb for deciding the test cases, selecting test cases is still a creative activity, that relies on the ingenuity of the tester. Due to this reason, the psychology of the person performing the testing becomes important.

The aim of testing is often to demonstrate that a program works by showing that it has no errors. This is the *opposite* of what testing should be viewed as. The basic purpose of the testing phase is to detect the errors that may be present in the program. Hence, one should not start testing with the intent of showing that a program works; but the intent should be to show that a program does not work. With this in mind we define testing as follows: *testing is the process of executing a program with the intent of finding errors* [Mye79].

This emphasis on proper intent of testing is not a trivial matter because test cases are designed by human beings, and human beings have a tendency to perform actions to achieve the goal they have in mind. So, if the goal is to demonstrate that a program works, we may consciously or subconsciously select test cases that will try to demonstrate that goal and that will beat the basic purpose of testing. On the other hand, if the intent is to show that the program does not work, we will challenge our intellect to find test cases toward that end, and we are likely to detect more errors. Testing is essentially a destructive process, where the tester has to treat the program as an adversary that must be beaten by the tester by showing the presence of errors. With this in mind, a test case is "good" if it detects an as-yet-undetected error in the program, and our goal during designing test cases should be to design such "good" test cases.

One of the reasons many organizations require a product to be tested by people not involved with developing the program before finally delivering it to the customer is this psychological factor. It is hard to be destructive to something we have created ourselves, and we all like to believe that the program we have written "works." So, it is not easy for someone to test his own program with the proper frame of mind for testing. Another reason for independent testing is that sometimes errors occur because the programmer did not understand the specifications clearly. Testing of a program by its programmer will not detect such errors, whereas independent testing may succeed in finding them.

9.2   Functional Testing

There are two basic approaches to testing: functional and structural. In functional testing the structure of the program is not considered. Test cases are decided solely on the basis of the requirements or specifications of the program or module, and the internals of the module or the program are not considered for selection of test cases. Due to its nature, functional testing is often called "black box testing." In the structural approach, test cases are generated based on the actual code of the program or module to be tested. This structural approach is sometimes called "glass box testing." In this section, we will present some techniques for generating test cases for functional testing. Structural testing is discussed in the next section.

The basis for deciding test cases in functional testing is the requirements or specifications of the system or module. For the entire system, the test cases are designed from the requirements specification document for the system. For modules created during design, test cases for functional testing are decided from the module specifications produced during the design.

The most obvious functional testing procedure is exhaustive testing, which as we have stated, is impractical. One criterion for generating test cases is to generate them randomly. This strategy has little chance of resulting in a set of test cases that is close to optimal (i.e., that detects the maximum errors with minimum test cases). Hence, we need some other criterion or rule for selecting test cases. There are no formal rules for designing test cases for functional testing. In fact, there are no precise criteria for selecting test cases. However, there are a number of techniques or heuristics that can be used to select test cases that have been found to be very successful in detecting errors. Here we mention some of these techniques.

9.2.1 Equivalence Class Partitioning

Because we cannot do exhaustive testing, the next natural approach is to divide the domain of all the inputs into a set of equivalence classes, so that if any test in an equivalence class succeeds, then every test in that class will succeed. That is, we want to identify classes of test cases such that the success of one test case in a class implies the success of others. If we can indeed identify such classes and guarantee that each class forms such an equivalence class, the success of one test case from each equivalence class is equivalent to successfully completing an exhaustive test of the program.

However, without looking at the internal structure of the program, it is impossible to determine such ideal equivalence classes (even with the internal structure, it usually cannot be done). The equivalence class partitioning method [Mye79] tries to approximate this ideal. Different equivalence classes are formed by putting inputs for which the behavior pattern of the module is specified to be different into similar groups and then regarding these new classes as forming equivalence classes. The rationale of forming equivalence classes like this is the assumption that if the specifications require exactly the same behavior for each element in a class of values, then the program is likely to be constructed so that it either succeeds or fails for each of the values in that class. For example, the specifications of a module that determines the absolute value for integers specify one behavior for positive integers and another for negative integers. In this case, we will form two equivalence classes—one consisting of positive integers and the other consisting of negative integers.

For robust software, we must also test for incorrect inputs by generating test cases for inputs that do not satisfy the input conditions. With this in mind, for each equivalence class of valid inputs we define equivalence classes for invalid inputs.

Equivalence classes are usually formed by considering each condition specified on an input as specifying a valid equivalence class and one or more invalid equivalence classes. For example, if an input condition specifies a range of values (say, 0 < count < Max), then form a valid equivalence class with that range and two invalid equivalence classes, one with values less than the lower bound of the range (i.e., count < 0) and the other with values higher than the higher bound (count > Max). If the input specifies a set of values and the requirements specify different behavior for different elements in the set, then a valid equivalence class is formed for each of the elements in the set and an invalid class for an entity not belonging to the set.

Essentially, if there is reason to believe that the entire range of an input will not be treated in the same manner, then the range should be split into two or more equivalence classes. Also, for each valid equivalence class, one or more invalid equivalence classes should be identified. For example, an input may be specified as a character. However, we may have reason to believe that the program will perform different actions if a character is an alphabet, a number, or a special character. In that case, we will split the input into three valid equivalence classes.

It is often useful to consider equivalence classes in the output. For an output equivalence class, the goal is to generate test cases such that the output for that test case lies in the output equivalence class. Determining test cases for output classes may be more difficult, but output classes have been found to reveal errors that are not revealed by just considering the input classes.

9.2.2   Boundary Value Analysis

It has been observed that programs that work correctly for a set of values in an equivalence class fail on some special values. These values often lie on the boundary of the equivalence class. Test cases that have values on the boundaries of equivalence classes are therefore likely to be "high-yield" test cases, and selecting such test cases is the aim of the boundary value analysis. In boundary value analysis [Mye79], we choose an input for a test case from an equivalence class, such that the input lies at the edge of the equivalence classes. Boundary values for each equivalence class, including the equivalence classes of the output, should be covered. Boundary value test cases are also called "extreme cases." Hence, we can say that a boundary value test case is a set of input data that lies on the edge or boundary of a class of input data or that generates output that lies at the boundary of a class of output data.

In case of ranges, for boundary value analysis it is useful to select the boundary elements of the range and an invalid value just beyond the two ends (for the two invalid equivalence classes). So, if the range is $0.0 \leq x \leq 1.0$, then the test cases are 0.0, 1.0 (valid inputs), and −0.1, and 1.1 (for invalid inputs). Similarly, if the input is a list, attention should be focused on the first and last elements of the list. We should also consider the outputs for boundary value analysis. If an equivalence class can be identified in the output, we should try to generate test cases that will produce the output that lies at the boundaries of the equivalence classes. Furthermore, we should try to form test cases that will produce an output that does not lie in the equivalence class. (If we can produce an input case that produces the output outside the equivalence class, we have detected an error.)

9.2.3 Cause-Effect Graphing

One weakness with the equivalence class partitioning and boundary value methods is that they consider each input separately. That is, both concentrate on the conditions and classes of one input. They do not consider combinations of input circumstances that may form interesting situations that should be tested. One way to exercise combinations of different input conditions is to consider all valid combinations of the equivalence classes of input conditions. This simple approach will result in an unusually large number of test cases, many of which will not be useful for revealing any new errors. For example, if there are n different input conditions, such that any combination of the input conditions is valid, we will have 2^n test cases.

Cause-effect graphing [Mye79] is a technique that aids in selecting combinations of input conditions in a systematic way, such that the number of test cases does not become unmanageably large. The technique starts with identifying causes and effects of the system under testing. A *cause* is a distinct input condition, and an *effect* is a distinct output condition. Each condition forms a node in the cause-effect graph. The conditions should be stated such that they can be set to either true or false. For example, an input condition can be "file is empty," which can be set to true by having an empty input file, and false by a nonempty file. After identifying the causes and effects, for each effect we identify the causes that can produce that effect and how the conditions have to be combined to make the effect true. Conditions are combined using the Boolean operators "and," "or," and "not," which are represented in the graph by &, |, and ∼. Then for each effect, all combinations of the causes that the effect depends on which will make the effect true, are generated (the causes that the effect does not depend on are essentially "don't care"). By doing this, we identify the combinations of conditions that make different effects

Causes:
   c1. Command is credit
   c2. Command is debit
   c3. Account number is valid
   c4. Transaction_amt is valid

Effects:
   e1. Print "invalid command"
   e2. Print "invalid account_number"
   e3. Print "Debit amount not valid"
   e4. Debit account
   e5. Credit account

FIGURE 9.2. List of causes and effects.

true. A test case is then generated for each combination of conditions, which make some effect true.

Let us illustrate this technique with a small example. Suppose that for a bank database there are two commands allowed:

credit   acct_number   transaction_amount
debit   acct_number   transaction_amount

The requirements are that if the command is credit and the acct_number is valid, then the account is credited. If the command is debit, the acct_number is valid, and the transaction_amount is valid (less than the balance), then the account is debited. If the command is not valid, the account number is not valid, or the debit amount is not valid, a suitable message is generated. We can identify the following causes and effects from these requirements, shown in Figure 9.2.

The cause-effect of this is shown in Figure 9.3. In the graph, the cause-effect relationship of this example is captured. For all effects, one can easily determine the causes each effect depends on and the exact nature of the dependency. For example, according to this graph the effect e5 depends on the causes c2, c3, and c4 in a manner such that the effect e5 is enabled when all c2, c3, and c4 are true. Similarly, the effect e2 is enabled if c3 is false.

From this graph, a list of test cases can be generated. The basic strategy is to set an effect to 1 and then set the causes that enable this condition. The condition of causes forms the test case. A cause may be set to false, true, or don't care (in the case when the effect does not depend at all on the cause). To do this for all the effects, it is convenient to use a decision table. The decision table for this example is shown in Figure 9.4.

This table lists the combinations of conditions to set different effects. Each combination of conditions in the table for an effect is a test case. Together, these condition

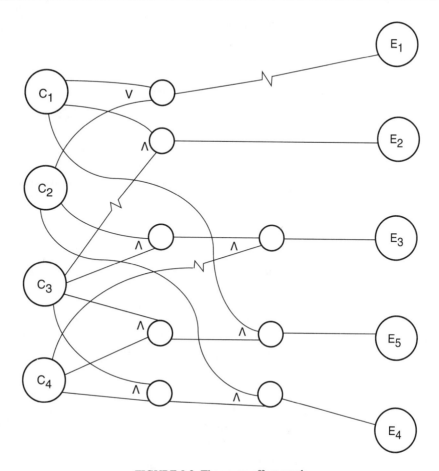

FIGURE 9.3. The cause-effect graph.

SNo.	1	2	3	4	5
c1	0	1	x	x	1
C2	0	x	1	1	x
c3	x	0	1	1	1
c4	x	x	0	1	1
e1	1				
e2		1			
e3			1		
e4				1	
e5					1

FIGURE 9.4. Decision table for the cause-effect graph.

combinations check for various effects the software should display. For example, to test for the effect e3, both c2 and c4 have to be set. That is, to test the effect "Print debit amount not valid," the test case should be: Command is debit (setting c2 to True), the account number is valid (setting c3 to False), and the transaction money is not proper (setting c4 to False).

Cause-effect graphing, beyond generating high-yield test cases, also aids the understanding of the functionality of the system, because the tester must identify the distinct causes and effects. There are methods of reducing the number of test cases generated by proper traversing of the graph. Once the causes and effects are listed and their dependencies specified, much of the remaining work can also be automated.

9.2.4   Special Cases

It has been seen that programs often produce incorrect behavior when inputs form some special cases. The reason is that in programs, some combinations of inputs need special treatment, and providing proper handling for these special cases is easily overlooked. For example, in an arithmetic routine, if there is a division and the divisor is zero, some special action has to be taken, which could easily be forgotten by the programmer. These special cases form particularly good test cases, which can reveal errors that will usually not be detected by other test cases.

Special cases will often depend on the data structures and the function of the module. There are no rules to determine special cases, and the tester has to use his intuition and experience to identify such test cases. Consequently, determining special cases is also called *error guessing*.

The psychology is particularly important for error guessing. The tester should play the "devil's advocate" and try to guess the incorrect assumptions the programmer could have made and the situations the programmer could have overlooked or handled incorrectly. Essentially, the tester is trying to identify error prone situations. Then test cases are written for these situations. For example, in the problem of finding the number of different words in a file (discussed in earlier chapters) some of the special cases can be: file is empty, only one word in the file, only one word in a line, some empty lines in the input file, presence of more than one blank between words, all words are the same, the words are already sorted, and blanks at the start and end of the file.

Incorrect assumptions are usually made because the specifications are not complete or the writer of specifications may not have stated some properties, assuming them to be obvious. Whenever there is reliance on tacit understanding rather than explicit statement of specifications, there is scope for making wrong assumptions. Frequently, wrong assumptions are made about the environments. However, it should be pointed out that special cases depend heavily on the problem, and the tester should really try to "get into the shoes" of the designer and coder to determine these cases.

9.3   Structural Testing

In the previous section we discussed functional testing, which is concerned with the function that the tested program is supposed to perform and does not deal with the internal structure of the program responsible for actually implementing that function. Thus functional testing is concerned with functionality rather than implementation of the program. Various criteria for functional testing were discussed. Structural testing, on the other hand is concerned with testing the implementation of the program. The intent of structural testing is not to exercise all the different input or output conditions (although that may be a by-product) but to exercise the different programming structures and data structures used in the program.

To test the structure of a program, structural testing aims to achieve test cases that will force the desired coverage of different structures. Various criteria have been proposed for this. Unlike the criteria for functional testing, which are frequently imprecise, the criteria for structural testing are generally quite precise as they are based on program structures, which are formal and precise. Here we will discuss three different approaches to structural testing: control flow–based testing, data flow–based testing, and mutation testing.

9.3.1   Control Flow–Based Criteria

Most common structure-based criteria are based on the control flow of the program. In these criteria, the control flow graph of a program is considered and coverage of various aspects of the graph are specified as criteria. Hence, before we consider the criteria, let us precisely define a control flow graph for a program.

Let the *control flow graph* (or simply *flow graph*) of a program P be G. A node in this graph represents a block of statements that is always executed together, i.e., whenever the first statement is executed, all other statements are also executed. An edge (i, j) (from node i to node j) represents a possible transfer of control after executing the last statement of the block represented by node i to the first statement of the block represented by node j. A node corresponding to a block whose first statement is the start statement of P is called the *start* node of G, and a node corresponding to a block whose last statement is an exit statement is called an *exit* node [RW85]. A *path* is a finite sequence of nodes $(n_1, n_2, \ldots, n_k)$, $k > 1$, such that there is an edge (n_i, n_{i+1}) for all nodes n_i in the sequence (except the last node n_k). A *complete path* is a path whose first node is the start node and the last node is an exit node.

Now let us consider control flow–based criteria. Perhaps the simplest coverage criteria is *statement coverage*, which requires that each statement of the program be executed at least once during testing. In other words, it requires that the paths executed during testing include all the nodes in the graph. This is also called the *all-nodes* criterion [RW85]. This coverage criterion is not very strong, and can leave errors undetected. For example, if there is an `if` statement in the program without having an `else` clause, the statement coverage criterion for this statement will be satisfied by a test case that evaluates the condition to true. No test case is needed that ensures that the condition in the `if` statement evaluates to false. This is a serious shortcoming because decisions in programs are potential sources of errors. As an example, consider the following function to compute the absolute value of a number:

```
int abs (x)
int x;
{
    if (x >= 0) x = 0 - x;
    return (x)
}
```

This program is clearly wrong. Suppose we execute the function with the set of test cases { x=0 } (i.e., the set has only one test case). The statement coverage criterion will be satisfied by testing with this set, but the error will not be revealed.

A little more general coverage criterion is *branch coverage*, which requires that each edge in the control flow graph be traversed at least once during testing. In other words, branch coverage requires that each decision in the program be evaluated to true and false values at least once during testing. Testing based on branch coverage is often called *branch testing*. The 100% branch coverage criterion is also called the *all-edges* criterion [RW85]. Branch coverage implies statement coverage, as each statement is a part of some branch. In other words, $C_{branch} \Rightarrow C_{stmt}$. In the preceding example, a set of test cases satisfying this criterion will detect the error.

The trouble with branch coverage comes if a decision has many conditions in it (consisting of a Boolean expression with Boolean operators *and* and *or*). In such situations, a decision can evaluate to true and false without actually exercising all the conditions. For example, consider the following function that checks the validity of a data item. The data item is valid if it lies between 0 and 100.

```
int check(x)
int x;
{
    if ((x >= ) && (x <= 200))
        check = True;
    else check = False;
}
```

The module is incorrect, as it is checking for x $\leq$ 200 instead of 100 (perhaps a typing error made by the programmer). Suppose the module is tested with the following set of test cases: { x = 5, x = -5 }. The branch coverage criterion will be satisfied for this module by this set. However, the error will not be revealed, and the behavior of the module is consistent with its specifications for all test cases in this set. Thus, the coverage criterion is satisfied, but the error is not detected. This occurs because the decision is evaluating to true and false because of the condition (x $\geq$ 0). The condition (x $\leq$ 200) never evaluates to false during this test, hence the error in this condition is not revealed.

This problem can be resolved by requiring that all conditions evaluate to true and false. However, situations can occur where a decision may not get both true and false values even if each individual condition evaluates to true and false. An obvious solution to this problem is to require decision/condition coverage, where all the decisions and all the conditions in the decisions take both true and false values during the course of testing.

Studies have indicated that there are many errors whose presence is not detected by branch testing because some errors are related to some combinations of branches and their presence is revealed by an execution that follows the path that includes those branches. Hence a more general coverage criterion is one that requires all possible paths in the control flow graph be executed during testing. This is called the *path coverage* criterion or the *all-paths* criterion, and the testing based on this criterion is often called *path testing*. The difficulty with this criterion is that programs that contain loops can have an infinite number of possible paths. Furthermore, not all paths in a graph may be "feasible" in the sense that there may not be any inputs for which the path can be executed. It should be clear that $C_{path} \Rightarrow C_{branch}$.

As the path coverage criterion leads to a potentially infinite number of paths, some efforts have been made to suggest criteria between the branch coverage and path coverage. The basic aim of these approaches is to select a set of paths that ensure branch coverage criterion and try some other paths that may help reveal errors. One method to limit the number of paths is to consider two paths the same if they differ only in their subpaths that are caused due to the loops. Even with this restriction, the number of paths can be extremely large.

Another such approach based on the cyclomatic complexity has been proposed in [McC76]. The test criterion is that if the cyclomatic complexity of a module is V, then at least V distinct paths must be executed during testing. We have seen that cyclomatic complexity V of a module is the number of independent paths in the flow graph of a module. As these are independent paths, all other paths can be represented as a combination of these basic paths. These basic paths are finite, whereas the total number of paths in a module having loops may be infinite.

It should be pointed out that none of these criteria is sufficient to detect all kind of errors in programs. For example, if a program is missing some control flow paths that are needed to check for a special value (like pointer equals nil and divisor equals zero), then even executing all the paths will not necessarily detect the error. Similarly, if the set of paths is such that they satisfy the all-path criterion but exercise only one part of a compound condition, then the set will not reveal any error in the part of the condition that is not exercised. Hence, even the path coverage criterion, which is the strongest of the criteria we have discussed, is not strong enough to guarantee detection of all the errors. None of the three major criteria discussed earlier satisfy the applicability axiom or the antidecomposition axiom. All of them satisfy the antiextensionality axiom, and the anticomposition axiom is satisfied only by the path coverage criterion. It is left as an exercise to the reader to determine which axioms are met and which are not.

9.3.2   Data Flow–Based Testing

Now we discuss some criteria that select the paths to be executed during testing based on data flow analysis, rather than control flow analysis. In the previous chapter, we discussed use of data flow analysis for static testing of programs. In the data flow–based testing approaches, besides the control flow, information about where the variables are defined and where the definitions are used is also used to specify the test cases. The basic idea behind data flow–based testing is to make sure that during testing, the definitions of variables and their subsequent use is tested. Just like the all-nodes and all-edges criteria try to generate confidence in testing by making sure that at least all statements and all branches have been tested, the data flow testing tries to ensure some coverage of the definitions and uses of variables. Approaches for use of data flow information have been proposed in [LK83, RW85]. Our discussion here is based on the family of data flow–based testing criteria that were proposed in [RW85]. We discuss some of these criteria here.

For data flow–based criteria, a *definition-use graph* (*def/use* graph, for short) for the program is first constructed from the control flow graph of the program. A statement in a node in the flow graph representing a block of code has variable occurrences in it. A variable occurrence can be one of the following three types [RW85]:

- *def* represents the definition of a variable. The variable on the left-hand side of an assignment statement is the one getting defined.

- *c-use* represents computational use of a variable. Any statement (e.g., read, write, an assignment) that uses the value of variables for computational purposes is said to be making c-use of the variables. In an assignment statement, all variables on the right-hand side have a c-use occurrence. In a read and a write statement, all variable occurrences are of this type.

- *p-use* represents predicate use. These are all the occurrences of the variables in a predicate (i.e., variables whose values are used for computing the value of the predicate), which is used for transfer of control.

Based on this classification, the following can be defined [RW85]. Note that c-use variables may also affect the flow of control, though they do it indirectly by affecting the value of the p-use variables. Because we are interested in the flow of data between nodes, a c-use of a variable x is considered *global c-use* if there is no def of x within the block preceding the c-use. With each node i, we associate all the global c-use variables in that node. The p-use is associated with edges. If $x_1, x_2, \ldots, x_n$ had p-use occurrences in the statement of a block from where two edges go to two different blocks j and k (e.g., with an if then else), then $x_1, \ldots, x_n$ are associated with the two edges (i, j) and (i, k).

A path from node i to node j is called a *def-clear* path with respect to (w.r.t.) a variable x if there is no def of x in the nodes in the path from i to j (nodes i and j may have a def). Similarly, a def-clear path w.r.t. x from a node i to an edge (j, k) is one in which no node on the path contains a definition of x. A def of a variable x in a node i is a *global def*, if it is the last def of x in the block being represented by i, and there is a def-clear path from i to some node with a global c-use of x. Essentially, a def is a global def if it can be used outside the block in which it is defined.

The def/use graph for a program P is constructed by associating sets of variables with edges and nodes in the flow graph. For a node i, the set *def(i)* is the set of variables for which there is a global def in the node i, and the set *c-use(i)* is the set of variables for which there is a global c-use in the node i. For an edge (i, j), the set *p-use(i, j)* is the set of variables for which there is a p-use for the edge (i, j).

Suppose a variable x is in $def(i)$ of a node i. Then, $dcu(x, i)$ is the set of nodes, such that each node has x in its c-use, $x \in def(i)$, and there is a def-clear path from i to j. That is, dcu(x, i) represents all those nodes in which the (global) c-use of x uses the value assigned by the def of x in i. Similarly, $dpu(x, i)$ is the set of edges, such that each edge has x in its p-use, $x \in def(i)$, and there is a def-clear path from i to (j, k). That is, dpu(x, i) represents all those edges in which the p-use of x uses the value assigned by the def of x in i.

Based on these definitions proposed in [RW85], a family of test case selection criteria were proposed in [RW85], a few of which we discuss here. Let G be the def/use graph for a program, and let P be a set of complete paths of G (i.e., path representing a complete execution of the program). A test case selection criterion defines the contents of P.

P satisfies the *all-defs* criterion if for every node i in G and every x in $def(i)$, P includes a def-clear path w.r.t. x to some member of $dcu(x, i)$ or some member of $dpu(x, i)$. This criterion says that for the def of every variable, one of its uses (either p-use or c-use) must be included in a path. That is, we want to make sure that during testing the use of the definitions of all variables is tested.

The *all-p-uses* criterion requires that for every $x \in def(i)$, P include a def-clear path w.r.t. x from i to some member of $dpu(x, i)$. That is, according to this criterion all the p-uses of all the definitions should be tested. However, by this criterion a c-use of a variable may not be tested. The *all-p-uses, some-c-uses* criterion requires that all p-uses of a variable definition must be exercised, and some c-uses must also be exercised. Similarly, the *all-c-uses, some-p-uses* criterion requires that all c-uses of a variable definition be exercised, and some p-uses must also be exercised.

The *all-uses* criterion requires that all p-uses and all c-uses of a definition must be exercised. That is, the set P must include, for every node i and every $x \in def(i)$, a def-clear path w.r.t. x from i to all elements of $dcu(x, i)$ and to all elements of $dpu(x, i)$. A few other criteria have been proposed in [RW85].

In terms of the number of test cases that might be needed to satisfy the data flow–based criteria, it has been shown that though the theoretical limit on the size of the test case set is up to quadratic in the number of two-way decision statements in the program, the actual number of test cases that satisfy a criterion is quite small in practice [Wey90]. Empirical observation in [Wey90] seems to suggest that in most cases the number of test cases grows linearly with the number of two-way decisions in the program.

As mentioned earlier, a criterion C_1 includes another criterion C_2 (represented by $C_1 \Rightarrow C_2$) if any set of test cases that satisfy criterion C_1 also satisfy the criterion C_2. The inclusion relationship between the various data flow criteria and the control flow criteria is given in Figure 9.5 [RW85].

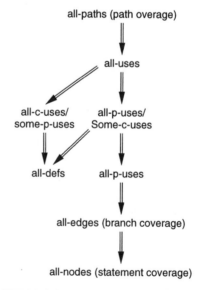

FIGURE 9.5. Relationship between different criteria.

It should be quite clear that all-paths will include all-uses and all other structure–based criteria. All-uses, in turn, includes all-p-uses, all-defs, and all-edges. However, all-defs does not include all-edges (and the reverse is not true). The reason is that all-defs is focusing on all definitions getting used, while all-edges is focusing on all decisions evaluating to both true and false. For example, a decision may evaluate to true and false in two different test cases, but the use of a definition of a variable x may not have been exercised. Hence, the all-defs and all-edges criteria are, in some sense, incomparable.

As mentioned earlier, inclusion does not imply that one criterion is always better than another. At best, it means that if the test case generation strategy for two criteria C_1 and C_2 is similar, and if $C_1 \Rightarrow C_2$, then statistically speaking, the set of test cases satisfying C_1 will be better than a set of test cases satisfying C_2. The experiments reported in [FW93b] show that no one criterion (out of a set of control flow–based and data flow–based criteria) does significantly better than another consistently. However, it does show that testing done by using all-branch or all-uses criterion generally does perform better than randomly selected test cases.

9.3.3 An Example

Let us illustrate the use of some of the control flow–based and data flow–based criteria through the use of an example. Consider the following example of a simple program for computing x^y for any integer x and y [RW85]:

```
1. scanf(x, y); if (y $<$ 0)
2.    pow = 0 - y;
3. else pow = y;
4. z = 1.0;
5. while (pow != 0)
6.    { z = z * x; pow = pow - 1; }
7. if (y $<$ 0)
8.    z = 1.0/z;
9. printf(z);
```

The def/use graph for this program is given in the Figure 9.6 [RW85]. In the graph, the line numbers given in the code segment are used to number the nodes (each line contains all the statements of that block). For each node, the def set (i.e., the set of variables defined in the block) and the c-use set (i.e., the set of variables that have a c-use in the block) are given along with the node. For each edge, if the p-use set is not empty, it is given in the graph.

The various sets are easily determined from the block of code representing a node. To determine the dcu and dpu the graph has to be traversed. The dcu for various

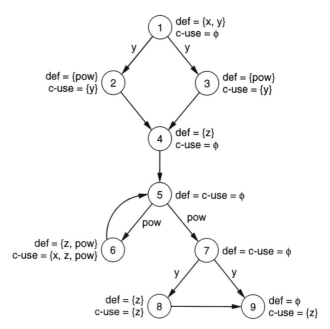

FIGURE 9.6. def/use graph for the example [RW85].

node and variable combination is given next:

(node, var)	dcu	dpu
(1, x)	{6}	ϕ
(1, y)	{2, 3}	{(1,2), (1,3), (7, 8), (7, 9)}
(2, pow)	{6}	{(5, 6), (5, 7)}
(3, pow)	{6}	{(5, 6), (5, 7)}
(4, z)	{6, 8, 9}	ϕ
(6, z)	{6, 8, 9}	ϕ
(6, pow)	{6}	{(5, 6), (5, 7)}
(8, z)	{9}	ϕ

Now let us discuss the issue of generating test cases for this program using various criteria. We can divide the problem of test case selection into two parts. First we identify some paths that together satisfy the chosen criterion. Then we identify the test cases that will execute those paths. As the first issue is more relevant when discussing coverage criteria, frequently in testing literature only the paths that satisfy the criterion are discussed. While selecting paths that satisfy a given coverage brings us to the question of whether the path is *feasible*, that is, if it is possible to have some test data that will execute that path. It is known that a program may contain paths that are not feasible. A simple example is in a program with a for loop. In such a program, no path that executes the loop fewer than the number of times specified by the for loop is feasible. In general, the issue of feasibility of paths cannot be solved algorithmically, as the problem is undecidable. However, the programmer can use his judgment and knowledge about the program to decide whether or not a particular path is infeasible. With the presence of infeasible paths, it is not possible to fully satisfy the criterion like all-uses, and the programmer will have to use his judgment to avoid considering the infeasible paths.

Let us first consider the all-edges criterion, which is the same as 100% branch coverage. In this we want to make sure that each edge in the graph is traversed during testing. For this, if the paths executed by the test cases include the following paths, we can see that all edges are indeed covered:

$$(1; 2; 4; 5; 6; 7; 8; 9), (1; 3; 4; 5; 7; 9)$$

Here we could have chosen a set of paths with $(1; 2; 4; 5; 6; 7; 9)$ as one of them. But a closer examination of the program will tell us that this path is not feasible, as going from 1 to 2 implies that y is negative, which in turn implies that from 7 we must go to 8 and cannot go directly to 9. As can be seen even from this simple example, it is very easy to have paths that are infeasible. To execute the selected paths (or paths that include these paths), the following two test cases will suffice: $(x = 3, y = 1)$ and $(x = 3, y = -1)$. That is, a set consisting of these two test cases will satisfy the all-edges criterion.

Now let us consider the all-defs criterion, which requires that for all definitions of all variables, at least one use (c-use or p-use) must be exercised during testing. First let us observe that the set of paths given earlier for the all-edges criterion does not satisfy the all-uses criterion. The reason is that to satisfy all-uses, we must have some path in which the defs in node 6 (i.e., for z and pow) also get used. As the only way to get the def of pow in node 6 to be used is to visit 6 again, these paths fail to satisfy the criterion. The following set of paths will satisfy the all-defs criterion:

$$(1; 2; 4; 5; 6; 5; 6; 7; 8; 9), (1; 3; 4; 5; 6; 7; 9)$$

Let's consider the first path in this. The prefix 1; 2; 4; 5; 6; ensures that all the defs of nodes 1, 2, and 4 have been used. Having another 5; 6 after this ensures that the defs in node 6 are used. This is not needed by the branch coverage, but it comes because of the def-use constraints. It can also be easily seen that the set of test cases selected for the branch coverage will not suffice here. The following two test cases will satisfy the criteria: $(x = 3, y = 4)$ and $(x = 3, y = -2)$.

Let us finally consider the all-uses criterion, which requires that all p-uses and all c-uses of all variable definitions be tried during testing. In other words, we have to construct a set of paths that include a path from any node having a def to all nodes in its dcu and its dpu. The dcu and dpu sets for all nodes were given earlier. In this example, as it turns out, the paths given earlier for all-defs also satisfy the all-uses criterion. Hence, the corresponding test cases will also suffice. We leave the details of this as an exercise for the reader.

9.3.4 Mutation Testing

Mutation testing is another structural testing technique that differs fundamentally from the approaches discussed earlier. In control flow–based and data flow–based testing, the focus was on which paths to execute during testing. Mutation testing does not take a path-based approach. Instead, it takes the program and creates many mutants of it by making simple changes to the program. The goal of testing is to make sure that during the course of testing, each mutant produces an output different from the output of the original program. In other words, the mutation testing criterion does not say that the set of test cases must be such that certain paths are executed; instead it requires the set of test cases to be such that they can distinguish between the original program and its mutants. The description of mutation testing given here is based on [DLS78, Mat94].

In hardware, testing is based on some fault models that have been developed and that model the actual faults closely. The fault models provide a set of simple faults, combination of which can model any fault in the hardware. In software, however, no usch fault model exists. That is why most of the testing techniques try to guess where the faults might lie and then select the test cases that will reveal those faults. In mutation testing, faults of some predecided types are introduced in the program being tested. Testing then tries to identify those faults in the mutants. The idea is that if all these "faults" can be identified, then the original program should not have these faults; otherwise they would have been identified in that program by the set of test cases.

Clearly this technique will be successful only if the changes introduced in the main program capture the most likely faults in some form. This is assumed to hold due to the *competent programmer hypothesis* and the *coupling effect*. The competent programmer hypothesis says that programmers are generally very competent and do not create programs at random, and for a given problem, a programmer will produce a program that is very "close" to a correct program. In other words, a correct program can be constructed from an incorrect program with some minor changes in the program. The coupling effect says that the test cases that distinguish programs with minor differences with each other are so sensitive that they will also distinguish programs with more complex differences. In [Mat94], some experiments are cited in which it has been shown that the testdata that can distinguish mutants created by simple changes can also distinguish up to 99% of the mutants that have been created by applying a series of simple changes.

Now let us discuss the mutation testing approach in a bit more detail. For a program under test P, mutation testing prepares a set of *mutants* by applying *mutation operators* on the text of P. The set of mutation operators depends on the language in which P is written. In general, a mutation operator makes a small unit change in the program to produce a mutant. Examples of mutation operators are: replace an arithmetic operator with some other arithmetic operator, change an array reference (say, from A to B), replace a constant with another constant of the same type (e.g., change a constant to 1), change the label for a goto statement, and replace a variable by some special value (e.g., an integer or a real variable with 0). Each application of a mutation operator results in one mutant. As an example, consider a mutation operator that replaces an arithmetic operator with another one from the set { +,-,*,**, / }. If a program P contains an expression

$$a = b * (c - d),$$

then this particular mutation operator will produce a total of eight mutants (four by replacing '*' and four by replacing '-'). The mutation operators that make exactly one syntactic change in the program to produce a mutant are said to be of *first order*. If the coupling effect holds, then the first-order mutation operators should be sufficient, and there is no need for higher-order mutation operators.

Mutation testing of a program P proceeds as follows. First a set of test cases T is prepared by the tester, and P is tested by the set of test cases in T. If P fails, then T reveals some errors, and they are corrected. If P does not fail during testing by T, then it could mean that either the program P is correct or that P is not correct but T is not sensitive enough to detect the faults in P. To rule out the latter possibility (and therefore to claim that the confidence in P is high), the sensitivity of T is evaluated through mutation testing and more test cases are added to T until the set is considered sensitive enough for "most" faults. So, if P does not fail on T, the following steps are performed [Mat94]:

1. Generate mutants for P. Suppose there are N mutants.

2. By executing each mutant and P on each test case in T, find how many mutants can be distinguished by T. Let D be the number of mutants that are distinguished; such mutants are called *dead*.

3. For each mutant that cannot be distinguished by T (called a *live* mutant), find out which of them are equivalent to P. That is, determine the mutants that will always produce the same output as P. Let E be the number of equivalent mutants.

4. The *mutation score* is computed as $D/(N - E)$.

5. Add more test cases to T and continue testing until the mutation score is 1.

In this approach, for the mutants that have not been distinguished by T, their equivalence with P has to be determined. As determining the equivalence of two programs is undecidable, this cannot be done algorithmically and will have to be done manually (tools can be used to aid the process). There are many situations where this can be determined easily. For example, if a condition $x \ <= 0$ (in a program to compute the absolute value, say) is changed to $x \ < \ 0$, we can see immediately that the mutant produced through this change will be equivalent to the original program P, as it does not matter which path the program takes when the value of x is 0. In other situations, it may be very hard to determine equivalence. One thing is clear: the tester will have to compare P with all the live mutants to determine which are equivalent to P. This analysis can then be used to add further test cases to T in an attempt to kill those live mutants that are not equivalent.

Determining test cases to distinguish mutants from the original program is also not easy. In an attempt to form a test case to kill a mutant, a tester will have to examine the mutant (and the original program) and then reason which test case is likely to distinguish the mutant. This can be a complex exercise, depending on the complexity of the program being tested and the exact nature of the difference between the mutant and the original program. Suppose that a statement at line l of the program P has been mutated to produce the mutant M. The first property that a test case t needs to have to distinguish M and P is that the test case should force the execution to reach the statement at l. Clearly, without this, M and P will not behave differently. The test case t should also be such that after execution of the statement at l, different states are reached by P and M. Before reaching l, the state while executing the programs P and M will be the same as the programs are same until l. If the test case is such that after executing the statement at l, the execution of the programs P and M either takes a different path or the values in the state are different, then there is a possibility that this difference will be manifested in output being different. If the state after executing the statement at l continues to be the same in P and M, we will not be able to distinguish P and M. Finally, t should be such that when P and M terminate, their states are different (assuming that P and M output their complete state at the end only). As one can imagine, constructing a test case that will satisfy these three properties is not going to be, in general, an easy task.

Finally, let us discuss the issue of detecting errors in the original program P, which is one of the basic goals of testing. In mutation testing, errors in the original program are frequently revealed when test cases are being designed to distinguish mutants from the original program. If no errors are detected and the mutation score reaches 1, then the testing is considered *adequate* by the mutation testing criterion. It should be noted that even if no errors have been found in the program under test during mutation testing, the confidence in the testing increases considerably if the mutation score of 1 is achieved, as we know that the set of test case with which P has been tested has been able to kill all (nonequivalent) mutants of P. This suggests that if P had an error, one of its mutants would have been closer to the correct program, and then the test case that distinguished the mutant from P would have also revealed that P is incorrect (it is assumed that the output of all test cases are evaluated to see if P is behaving correctly).

Some studies have been done to show that mutation testing does increase the confidence in testing and that it performs quite well compared to other methods of testing. Like other structural testing methods, it does not satisfy the applicability axiom because of the undecidability of determining equivalence. However, as determining equivalence is made a part of the testing activity, it can also be viewed as satisfying the applicability axiom. It also satisfies the antiextensionality, antidecomposition, and anticomposition axioms, as well as other axioms [Wey86]. It has also been used to compare the test cases generated by different test case generation schemes—the mutation score is used as the metric for comparison; the higher the mutation score, the better the test case set or the test case generation strategy.

One of the main problems of mutation testing relates to its performance. The number of mutants that can be generated by applying first-order mutation operators is quite large and depends on the language and the size of the mutation operator set. For a FORTRAN program containing L lines of code to which the mutation operator can be applied, the total number of mutants is of the order of L^2 [Mat94]. These many programs have to be compiled and executed on the selected test case set. This requires an enormous amount of computer time. For example, for a 950-line program, it was estimated that a total of about 900,000 mutants will be produced, the testing of which would take more than 70,000 hours of time on a Sun SPARC station [Mat94]. Further, the tester might have to spend considerable time doing testing, as he will have to examine many mutants, besides the original program, to determine whether or not they are equivalent. These performance issues make mutation testing impractical for large programs.

9.3.5 Test Case Generation and Tool Support

Once a coverage criterion is decided on, two problems have to be solved to use the chosen criterion for testing. The first is to decide if a set of test cases satisfy the criterion, and the second is to generate a set of test cases for a given criterion. Deciding whether a set of test cases satisfy a criterion without the aid of any tools is a cumbersome task, though it is theoretically possible to do manually. For almost all the structural testing techniques, tools are used to determine whether the criterion has been satisfied. Generally, these tools will provide feedback regarding what needs to be tested to fully satisfy the criterion.

To generate the test cases, tools are not that easily available, and due to the nature of the problem (i.e., undecidability of "feasibility" of a path), a fully automated tool for selecting test cases to satisfy a criterion is generally not possible. Hence, tools can, at best, aid the tester. One method for generating test cases is to randomly select test data until the desired criterion is satisfied (which is determined by a tool). This can result in a lot of redundant test cases, as many test cases will exercise the same paths.

As test case generation cannot be fully automated, frequently the test case selection is done manually by the tester by performing structural testing in an iterative manner, starting with an initial test case set and selecting more test cases based on the feedback provided by the tool for test case evaluation. The test case evaluation tool can tell which paths need to be executed or which mutants need to be killed. This information can be used to select further test cases. For example, to select a test case to execute some path, static data flow analysis tools can be used to decide what input values should be chosen so that when the program is executed this particular path is executed. Symbolic evaluation (discussed in Chapter 8) tools can also be quite useful here. The paths that need to be executed during testing can be treated as programs in their own right and symbolically executed. With symbolic execution, the conditions on input variables that will enable this path to be executed can be determined.

However, even with the aid of tools, selecting test cases is not a simple mechanical process. Ingenuity and creativity of the tester are still important, even with the availability of the tools to determine the coverage. Because of this, and for other reasons, the criteria are often weakened. For example, instead of requiring 100% coverage of statements and branches, the goal might be to achieve some acceptably high percentage (but less than 100%).

Consider a tool for statement or branch coverage, which collects information about which statements or branches have been executed during testing. To achieve this, the execution of the program during testing has be closely monitored. This requires that the program be instrumented so that required data can be collected. Perhaps the most common method of instrumenting is to insert some statements called *probes* in the program. The sole purpose of the probes is to generate data about program execution during testing that can be used to compute the coverage. With this, we can identify three phases in generating coverage data:

1. Instrument the program with probes.
2. Execute the program with test cases.
3. Analyze the results of the probe data.

Probe insertion can be done automatically by a *preprocessor*. The analysis of the probe data can be done automatically by a *postprocessor*. The first question is where the probes should be inserted. Probes can be inserted after each line of code, but that would be wasteful and inefficient. We want to identify segments of statements that must be executed together and insert one probe for the segment. A common technique is to insert probes where a path splits into multiple paths and where multiple paths merge. A different probe is inserted for each path. Different kinds of probes can be constructed, and one simple method is to insert probes that keep track of the number of times a segment is executed. For example, at some place in the program, the preprocessor can insert a probe of the nature count[10] = count[10] + 1, which will tell us how many times the particular segment (which was numbered 10 by the preprocessor) was executed.

Note that such a preprocessor also inserts proper declarations for the data used by the probes and has to insert a routine in the end to print the data or invoke the postprocessor. The postprocessor, to determine the statement or branch coverage, will need to know where the probes were introduced. Based on the knowledge of counts and the placement of the probes, statistics about the coverage is produced. In addition, tools point out the statements or branches that have not yet been executed during testing. These can then be used to determine the paths that still need to be executed. One such coverage tool for C programs is available for the readers from the home page of the book.

Tools for data flow–based testing and mutation testing are even more complex. Some tools have been built for aiding data flow–based testing [FWW85, HK92]. A data flow testing tool has to keep track of definitions of variables and their uses, besides keeping track of the control flow graph. For example, the ASSET tool for data flow testing [FWW85] first analyzes a Pascal program unit to determine all the definition-use associations. It then instruments the program so that the paths executed during testing are recorded. After the program has been executed with the test cases, the recorded paths are evaluated for satisfaction of the chosen criterion using the definition-use associations generated earlier. The list of definition-use associations that have not yet been executed is also output, which can then be used by the tester to select further test cases.

It should be pointed out that when testing a complete program that consists of many modules invoked by each other, the presence of procedures considerably complicates data flow testing. The main reason is that the presence of global variable creates def-use pairs in which the statements may exist in different procedures, e.g., a (global) variable may be defined in one procedure and then used in another. To use data flow–based testing on complete programs (rather than just modules), inter-procedural data flow analysis will be needed. Though some methods have been developed for performing data flow–based testing on programs with procedures [HS89], the presence of multiple procedures complicates data flow–based testing. It should be noted that this problem does not arise with statement coverage and branch coverage, where there are no special linkages between modules. The statement or branch coverage of a program can be computed simply from the statement or branch coverage of its modules. This is one of the reasons for the popularity of these coverage measures and tools.

In mutation testing, the tool is generally given a program P and a set of test cases T. The tool has to first use the mutation operations for the language in which P is written to produce the mutants. Then P and all the mutants and P are executed with T. Based on the output of different programs, the mutation score, and the number and identity of dead and live mutants are determined and reported to the tester. The score tells the tester the quality of T according to the mutation criterion, and the set of live mutants give the feedback to the tester for selecting further test cases to increase the mutation score. Some mutation testing tools have also been built [B⁺78, D⁺88].

9.4   Testing Object-Oriented Programs

A software typically undergoes many levels of testing, from unit testing to system or acceptance testing. Typically, in unit testing small "units," or modules, of the software are tested separately with focus on testing the code of that module. In higher-order testing (e.g., acceptance testing), the entire system (or a subsystem) is tested with the focus on testing the functionality or external behavior of system. Generally, only black box testing is performed at higher levels, while at lower levels white box testing is also done.

If black box testing is to be done, by definition, the test cases are selected independently of the internal structure of the code. In this case, it clearly does not matter whether the software is object-oriented or function-oriented. All the techniques mentioned earlier for black box testing can be applied to object-oriented systems. However, if the testing is white box, then the test cases are determined based on the structure of the code. Consequently, for such testing, the object-oriented structure can impact the testing activity. As unit testing is the place where white box testing is most likely to be used, it is at the unit testing level where different approaches may be required for object-oriented software. As the basic unit in object-oriented software is typically a class, here we focus on the testing of classes.

Testing classes is a fundamentally different problem than testing functions, as a function (or a procedure) has a clearly defined input-output behavior, while a class does not have an input-output behavior specification. We can test a method of a class using approaches for testing functions, but we cannot test the class using these approaches. So, for testing methods individually, the control flow–based and data flow–based structural testing techniques can easily be applied. New problems do crop up while doing data flow–based testing, but some solutions for these have been proposed [HR94, PBC93]. However, as one can imagine, and as has been formally argued in [PK90], testing of all the methods separately is not equivalent to testing the class. Hence, appropriate techniques are needed for testing classes.

Efforts were made earlier for testing abstract data types (ADTs) [GMH81, JC88, Jal89b, Jal92]. As we mentioned earlier, an abstract data type is equivalent to classes without inheritance. Hence, these approaches are somewhat limited in scope. More recent work has focused on testing of classes, with and without inheritance. In this section, we will look at some of these recent approaches. But before we do that, let us clearly understand the problems that come in testing classes.

9.4.1 Issues in Testing Classes

Testing classes brings in some new issues that are not present in testing functions. First, a class cannot be tested directly; only an instance of a class can be tested. This means that we test a class indirectly by testing its instances, and a tester must create different instances of the class and test them to test the class. An immediate problem due to this is how to test an abstract class, which cannot be instantiated (e.g., a class in C++ that has pure virtual operations).

In object-oriented programs, control flow is characterized by message passing among objects, and the control flow switches from one object to another by inter-object communication. Consequently, there is no sequential control flow within a class like in functions. This lack of sequential control flow within a class requires different approaches for testing. Furthermore, in a function, arguments passed to the function with global data determine the path of execution within the procedure. But, in an object, the state associated with object also influences the path of execution, and methods of a class can communicate among themselves through this state, because this state is persistent across invocations of methods. Hence, for testing objects, the state of an object has to play an important role.

Thirdly, new issues are introduced due to inheritance. There are basically two reasons for problems that arise from inheritance: the structure of inheritance hierarchy and the kind of inheritance [SR90]. Let us first consider the structure of the inheritance hierarchy. Problems start if the hierarchy is a lattice instead of a tree or a forest of trees. In such a case, a class at the bottom may inherit some of the features more than once (repeated inheritance), or it may inherit a feature that appears with the same name in two different ancestors (multiple inheritance). These make the classes more complex and error-prone. And the second kind of problem is owing to the type of inheritance. Suppose the derived class is redefining some of the inherited features and there are other inherited features that make use of those redefined features, then invocation of such features may give run-time errors. The reason is, as we discussed earlier in Chapter 6, due to dynamic binding of operations it may not be known until run time whether or not the operation is defined (on the object to which a variable is bound). This type of problem does not arise if there is only strict inheritance. A detailed discussion on the problems in the validation of object-oriented programs can be found in [SR90].

Overall, testing of objects can be defined as the process of exercising the routines provided by an object with the goal of uncovering errors in the implementation of the routines or state of the object or both [SR92]. To test an object, we have to test the interaction between the methods provided on the object. For this, the problem of object testing can be viewed as a search problem for finding the patterns of method invocation of the object under test with different arguments, which will yield errors [SR92]. This is particularly important, as there is no order imposed on the invocation of the methods of the objects and they can be invoked in any random order leading to a large number of patterns. In some sense, by executing various patterns, we are testing the communication between the different methods of the object. Directly testing various patterns of method invocation was the approach used in [Jal89b, Jal92] for testing abstract data types. The state-based testing approach that we discuss here tests for interaction by changing the state of the object under which the methods are tested. An overview of the state based testing method is given in [KJ96]. Some of the following discussion is based on this report.

9.4.2   State-Based Testing

State-based testing is a technique to test whether or not the methods of a class interact correctly among themselves by monitoring the data members of the class [TR92]. By checking whether or not the state of an object is changed in the expected way by any particular method of the object, we can exercise the path between the definition and use all instance variables of the object. The testing technique is to test all the methods of a class, one by one, against the set of states that the object can take. If any of the features does not change the state of the object in the expected way, then that method is declared as containing errors.

In the state-based testing technique suggested in [TR92], all methods of an object are tested one at a time. A method is invoked in all possible states that the object can assume, and after each invocation the resulting state is checked to see whether or not the method takes the object under test to the expected state. In this form of testing, emphasis is on the interaction between methods, that is, whether the method is communicating properly with other methods of the object through the state of the object.

Reducing the State Space

The state space of an object is the Cartesian product of domains of all the data members of the object. Clearly, performing state-based testing in all possible states of the object is impractical. For state-based testing to be practical, we have to reduce the state space without affecting the "coverage" too much. For this, it is proposed that for a data member, instead of considering all possible values, consider the domain as consisting of some specific values and some general value groups [TR92].

The *specific values* are the special values for the data member that are treated differently in the code or are described as being of special significance by the specification or design. These values can be easily identified by looking at the code and the specifications for classes produced in design. A *general value group* is the group of values of a data member that are all considered in the same manner in the code and the design specification. Due to this, there is no need to distinguish the different values of this group.

By using these two approaches, the domain of each data member that needs to be considered can be reduced, thereby reducing the overall state space of the object. The basic idea behind these approaches is similar to that of equivalence class partitioning. We are trying to identify those groups of values so that if we test with one member of the group, we can be fairly sure that the outcome will be the same if we test with other data members of the group. The group formation is done by looking at the code or design specifications, and the basic idea is to reduce the number of test cases. As an example, consider the following:

```
class Account {
  char *name ;
  int accNum ;
  int balance ;
}
```

The specific values of interest for this class are:

```
name = NULL,
accNum = 0,
balance = 0
```

And the general value groups are:

```
name != NULL
accNum < 0, accNum > 0
balance < 0, balance > 0
```

If we use these specific values and general group values, the state space of account object will become:

```
{NULL, non-NULL} X
{ SomeValue < 0, SomeValue > 0 } X
{ SomeValue < 0, SomeValue > 0 }
```

which is considerably smaller than the original state space, which was

```
DOMAIN{string} X DOMAIN{accNum} X DOMAIN{balance}
```

State-based testing, as discussed so far, focuses on the changes in state and hence may not be suitable for checking changes in the structure of data, which happens with objects that have dynamic data structures. In such cases, not only the contents, but the structure of the data also changes. For this, the tester needs to analyze the data structure to find when and how it is changing and derive some scenarios from the analysis that are significant for the structure. These *data scenarios* are then used to test an object [TR92]. These scenarios basically provide more specific values of interest for some data member. They then increase the number of values to be considered in the domain of the data member when specifying the states for the object. The construction of data scenarios is similar to the technique of special cases we discussed earlier, except that the special cases are being identified from the point of view of the structure of the data. Consider the example of the class List, given next [TR92].

```
template <EltType>
class List {
  private :
    EltType listElem[ MAX_ELEMENTS ] ;
      // Repository to store elements
    int currentPtr ;
      // Points to the top element in the list

  public :
    bool insertElement ( EltType element ) ;
    EltType getElement( EltType element ) ;
    bool isListEmpty() ;
}
```

This is a generic class, that models a list of objects. We analyze the data structures to get some data scenarios that will help in the correct construction of the data structures. For this class, we can say that the following scenarios are important for the correct construction of the list data structure:

```
List is empty, Only one element in the list
List is full, Partially filled list,
curPtr=-1, curPtr=0, curPtr=MAX_ELEMENTS,
curPtr between 0 and MAX_ELEMENTS
```

These can be used to form the extra entities in the domain of the particular data elements (curPtr and listElement). The domains are then used to define the state space in which the object will be tested.

Performing State Based Testing

To perform state-based testing on a class, we first need to derive a class under test from the class. This new class will be the class with some additional features to examine the state of the object and to set the state of the object. Sometimes it is better to have a separate method for setting the state of each instance variable, especially when the number of instance variables is higher, because most of the time testers will be testing varying values of one instance variable hence setting other variables each time will be redundant. The next step is to write a test driver, which will constitute a main program to create the object, send messages to set the states as dictated by the test cases, send messages to invoke methods of the class under test, and then send messages to check the final state. While testing a method that sends messages to some untested objects, the tester needs to write stubs to focus on testing the method. Testing such a method involves more work, because they tend to increase the test state space. The overall process of generating the test cases using this approach is [TR92]:

1. For each data member of the class under test, decide on the special values and general value groups to specify the domain values to be used for testing.
2. Determine the data scenarios for the class.
3. Augment the domain using data scenarios.
4. Add operations to set and test state values.
5. For each operation, determine which of the states form valid inputs. These states are to be used for testing the operation.
6. Start by testing operations at the bottom of the call graph. Each operation is tested.
7. For each state in which an operation is to be tested, determine all significant values that can be passed as parameters. The operation is tested with each of these parameters.

Remarks

State-based testing takes a different approach from black box testing or coverage-based testing. It does not replace these, but should be considered complimentary [TR92]. This testing approach seems to do well when the operations interact heavily through the state of the object. If an object is a mere repository of information, it is not very effective, as the number of states under which testing done will be small.

As a tester cannot set the state of the object before the constructor is invoked, this approach cannot be used to test a constructor. Similar is the case for destructors. A tester can set the state of the object before the destructor is invoked, but there is no way to test whether the destructor is working properly.

State-based testing is greatly influenced by the number of data members the object has, because the cardinality of the state space of the object is directly dependent on that. As the number of data members increases, more effort might be needed in performing state-based testing on that object. Hence, the number of data members of a class can be treated as a metric to measure the state-based testing effort that needs be put in [KJ96].

State-based testing has the tendency to detect only those errors associated with the instance variables of the object and those associated with the signature variables (arguments to the methods plus return value) and ignore other errors. So, if the object has no instance variables or has methods with zero signature variables or there are no errors in the methods of the object that influence instance variables or signature variables, then this method will be of little use. Some recent experiments indicate that state-based testing is effective in detecting errors that affect the state of the object or faults that lead to run-time errors, but is not very effective in detecting errors involving local variables of methods and errors in the logical conditions of the code [KJ96].

To decide which method to test first, an approach could be to build a call graph of methods, where each node represents a method, and an arc from node A to node B represents the fact that method B is called from method A. Once the graph is built, testing can commence from those features that fall at the bottom of graph.

9.4.3   Incremental Testing for Subclasses

Testing each class individually when the class is part of a class hierarchy can be wasteful as there might be an operation in a subclass that is the same as the base class and hence might not require any testing if the base class has been tested. In other words, when testing class hierarchies, it can be wasteful to test each class individually and separately. When a class inherits from a base class that has been tested, testing of this subclass requires testing only some features; for some features no testing might be needed. It will clearly reduce the testing effort if what features need to be tested can be clearly identified and for what features previous testing is sufficient. That is, just like a subclass inherits features from the base class, it should also inherit some test history of the base class, leading to reuse of testing effort. This form of testing can be viewed as *incremental testing*, where the testing of a class is done incrementally, depending on the testing history of the base class.

Here we discuss one approach for incremental testing of subclasses proposed in [HMF92]. There are two aspects to incremental testing. First is which features of a subclass need to be tested and which don't need to be tested. The second issue deals with reuse of test cases. That is, can the test case designed for a base class be reused to test some feature in the derived class. The aim of the second aspect is to reduce the effort required in selecting test cases; it does not reduce the other activities of testing (i.e., executing test cases or checking for presence of errors). Reuse of test cases also requires documenting whether the test case was selected based on the specifications or on the code. Then, in some cases where the specifications stay the same and the implementation changes, the test cases based on specifications can be reused. Both of the issues have been discussed in [HMF92]. In our discussion here, we will focus mostly on the first part, that is, deciding which features need to be tested and for which feature testing can be avoided.

For incremental testing, we consider a subclass R to be defined as the base class P plus the modifier M. That is, the class under test, R, is formed by applying the modifier M to the base class P. We limit our attention to single inheritance. The features or attributes of a (sub)class under test are classified into following categories [HMF92]:

- *New.* These features are specific only to the class under test and do not exist in the base class. Note that a feature is different if either its name is different or its parameters are different (i.e., a feature is different from another if its signature is different).

- *Virtual-new.* These are the features specific to the class under test that have their implementation dynamically bound, that is, the feature is defined but its implementation is not completely defined to allow for redefinition by the subclasses of this class.

- *Redefined.* These are the features inherited from the base class whose definitions are modified in the class under test. That is, the signature is the same, but the implementation is different.

- *Virtual-redefined.* These are the features inherited from the base class whose implementation is dynamically bound.

- *Recursive.* These are the features inherited from the base class of the class under test. That is, the definition and implementation of these are defined in the base class.

- *Virtual-recursive.* These are the features inherited from the base class of the class under test whose implementations are dynamically bound.

This classification of features will be used to determine which features need to be tested. For example, if the feature to be tested is *new* or *virtual-new*, we know that it is specific to the class under test and there is no information regarding this recorded in the testing history of the base class. Hence, we have to test these features thoroughly. On the other hand, if a feature is of the type *recursive*, we know its definition and implementation is defined in the base class, hence we can reuse the testing history of this feature. However, if this feature interacts with new features of the class under test, then this interaction has clearly not been tested in the base class and needs to be tested while testing this class.

This clearly shows that we have to separate individual testing of features and interaction of features. As mentioned earlier, testing of features independently is not sufficient to claim that the class has been tested properly [PK90]. To test a class, besides testing the features independently, their interaction needs to be tested. For a feature A of the class under test, we group the test cases with which the feature is tested into feature-test-set (FTS(A)) and integration-test-set (ITS(A)). FTS(A) is the set of test cases that test A independently, while ITS(A) is the set of test cases that test the interaction of A with other features. Note that some features, which do not directly interact with other features, may have ITS as a null set.

One way to identify what other features the feature under test is interacting with is to build a graph, whose nodes represent features of the class and an arc from node A to node B indicates the usage of B in A's implementation. This graph will show interactions between the features. Features that have arcs going to other nodes are candidates for integration testing.

Now let us consider the testing of the class R that was formed from the base class P and the modifier M. We assume that the base class P has been tested, and for each

> **foreach** feature A ∈ M **do**
>> **case** A is *New* or *Virtual-new*
>>> Generate FTS(A)
>>> Generate ITS(A)
>>> FTS(A) ∪ ITS(A) is the set of test cases for testing A
>>
>> **case** A is *Recursive* or *Virtual-recursive*
>>> Generate ITS(A), if needed, for new interactions
>>> ITS(A) is the set of test cases for testing A
>>
>> **case** A is *Redefined* or *Virtual-redefined*
>>> Generate FTS(A) – the specifcation based test cases of
>>>> FTS(A) in the test history of *P* can be reused
>>> Generate ITS(A) – again specification based test cases of
>>>> ITS(A) in the test history of *P* can be reused
>>> FTS(A) ∪ ITS(A) is the set of test cases for testing A

FIGURE 9.7. Algorithm for incremental testing.

feature of P, the test history gives the FTS and ITS. The algorithm in Figure 9.7 describes the incremental testing for subclass R [HMF92].

As stated in the algorithm, if a feature is *New* (or *Virtual-new*), it has to be fully tested by selecting proper test cases for feature testing as well as integration testing. Here its integration with all other features need to be tested. If the feature is *Recursive*, it was defined, and therefore tested, in the base class. Hence, no feature testing needs to be done for this. However, if the feature is interacting with some new features, then test cases for testing these interactions need to be generated. Finally, if the feature is *Redefined*, both the feature and its interactions need to be tested. However, for both sets of test cases, from the testing history of the base class, the test cases of this feature that were derived from the specifications can be reused, because the specifications have not changed.

This approach to testing reduces the testing effort by reducing what needs to be tested when testing a subclass and by reusing some of the test cases that were designed for testing the base class. The incremental approach clearly suggests that the testing should proceed in a top-down manner starting from the base classes in the inheritance hierarchy, so that the test history of these classes can be reused while testing derived classes.

9.5   Testing Process

The basic goal of the software development process is to produce software that has no errors or very few errors. In an effort to detect errors soon after they are introduced, each phase ends with a verification activity such as a review. However, most of these verification activities in the early phases of software development are based on human evaluation and cannot detect all the errors. This unreliability of the quality assurance activities in the early part of the development cycle places a very high responsibility on testing. In other words, as testing is the last phase before the final software is delivered, it has the enormous responsibility of detecting any type of error that may be in the software.

Furthermore, we know that software typically undergoes changes even after it has been delivered. And to validate that a change has not affected some old functionality of the system, regression testing is done. In regression testing, old test cases are executed with the expectation that the same old results will be produced. Need for regression testing places additional requirements on the testing phase; it must provide the "old" test cases and their outputs.

In addition, as we have seen in the discussions in this chapter, testing has its own limitations. These limitations require that additional care be taken while performing testing. As testing is the costliest activity in software development, it is important that it be done efficiently.

All these factors mean that testing cannot be done on-the-fly, as is often done by programmers. It has to be carefully planned and the plan has to be properly executed. The testing process focuses on how testing should proceed for a particular project. Having discussed various methods of selecting test cases, we turn our attention to the testing process. But before we discuss the various aspects of the process, let us compare the different techniques for verification and validation.

9.5.1 Comparison of Different Techniques

After discussing various techniques for verification and validation in Chapters 7 and 8, it is natural to ask how these techniques compare with each other. The major techniques we have covered in this chapter and Chapter 8 are: code reviews, static analysis, proof of correctness, structural testing, and functional testing.

It is not easy to compare the effectiveness of the different techniques. By effectiveness, we mean the fault detecting capability. The effectiveness of a technique for testing a particular software will, in general, depend on the type of errors that exist in the software. Various studies have been done to evaluate or compare some techniques. Techniques to partition the input domain for testing purposes, as is generally done by any testing criterion, were evaluated against random testing, in which test cases are selected randomly, through simulation in [DN84]. The simulation results seem to indicate that random testing may be quite cost effective. The work in [HT90] suggests that partition testing performs well only if the subdomains with a high failure probability can be identified. This implies that faults are localized and the inputs that cause the faults to manifest themselves can be guessed. Similar results were found in [WJ91], which also concluded that the effectiveness of partition testing depends on how the inputs that cause failures to occur are distributed in the subdomains defined by the strategy for partitioning. Some studies reported in [Mat94] show that mutation testing can be quite effective in revealing errors. An experimental comparison of control flow–based testing and data flow–based testing reported in [FW93a] found that the all-uses criterion was more effective in some cases and branch-coverage was more effective in some others.

Overall, it is safe to say that no one strategy does better than another strategy in all situations. And the exact situations in which one strategy performs better is also not well understood yet; at least not to the level that it can be generalized for practitioners. However, based on the nature of the techniques, one can make some general observations about the effectiveness for different types of errors. For comparison, it is best to first classify the errors into different categories and then compare the effectiveness of these techniques for the different categories. One such comparison is given in Figure 9.8 [Dun84].

As we can see, according to this comparison, different techniques have different strengths and weaknesses. For example, structural testing, as one would expect, is good for detecting logic errors, but not very good for detecting data handling errors. For data handling type errors, static analysis is quite good. Similarly, functional testing is good for input/output errors as it focuses on the external behavior, but it is not as good for detecting logic errors. As the figure shows, no one technique is good at detecting all types of errors, and hence no one technique can suffice for proper verification and validation. If high reliability is desired for the software, a combination of these techniques will have to be used. From the table, one can see that if code reviews, structural testing, and functional testing are all used, then together they have a high capability of detecting errors in all the categories described earlier.

Defect	Technique				
	Code Review	Static Analysis	Proof	Structural Test	Functional Test
Computational	Med	Med	High	High	Med
Logic	Med	Med	High	High	Med
I/O	High	Med	Low	Med	High
Data handling	High	High	Med	Low	High
Interface	High	High	low	High	Med
Data Definition	Med	Med	Med	Low	Med
Database	High	Low	Low	Med	Med

FIGURE 9.8. Comparison of the different techniques.

It is clear from the comparison in Figure 9.8 and from the nature of functional and structural testing approaches, that the two basic approaches to testing are actually complimentary. One looks at one program from the outside, the other from the inside. Hence, for effective testing of programs, both techniques should be applied. It should also be noted that the two approaches are often suited for different kinds of testing. Structural testing is not suitable for testing entire programs, because it is extremely difficult to generate test cases to get the desired coverage. It is well suited for module testing. So, structural testing is often done only for modules, and only functional testing is done for systems.

If both structural and functional testing are to be used for testing some program, an approach to combine them could be to to start with selecting a set of test cases using the functional criteria. In general, these test cases will provide some coverage but will not completely satisfy the chosen coverage criterion. This set of test cases is then augmented with additional test cases so that the coverage criterion is satisfied. This final set of test cases can then be used for testing.

Another way of measuring effectiveness is to consider the "cost effectiveness" of different strategies, that is, the cost of detecting an error by using a particular strategy. And the cost includes all the effort required to plan, test, and evaluate. In cost effectiveness, static analysis fares the best, as without any human effort it can detect anomalies that have a high probability of containing errors. Hence, if static analysis tools are available, they should be used first for detecting errors. However, static analysis can detect only a very few types of errors.

Next in cost effectiveness is code reviews. As we know, in code reviews, the code is reviewed by a team of people in a formal manner. The group synergy is used to find faults in the code. In code reviews the faults are found directly, unlike in testing where only the failure is detected and the fault has to be found through debugging. Furthermore, no test case planning, test case generation, or test case execution is needed. In place of these, reviews require effort by a group of reviewers reviewing the code. Much of the experience now indicates that code reviews are an extremely cost-effective means of detecting errors. That is, cost in terms of human time per defect detected is quite low in code reviews. Testing may be the least cost-effective method of detecting errors.

9.5.2 Levels of Testing

Now let us turn our attention to the testing process. We have seen that faults can occur during any phase in the software development cycle. Verification is performed on the output of each phase, but some faults are likely to remain undetected by these methods. These faults will be eventually reflected in the code. Testing is usually relied on to detect these faults, in addition to the faults introduced during the coding phase itself. Due to this, different levels of testing are used in the testing process; each level of testing aims to test different aspects of the system.

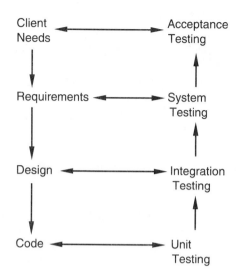

FIGURE 9.9. Levels of testing.

The basic levels are unit testing, integration testing, and system and acceptance testing. These different levels of testing attempt to detect different types of faults. The relation of the faults introduced in different phases, and the different levels of testing are shown in Figure 9.9.

The first level of testing is called *unit testing*. In this, different modules are tested against the specifications produced during design for the modules. Unit testing is essentially for verification of the code produced during the coding phase, and hence the goal is to test the internal logic of the modules. It is typically done by the programmer of the module. A module is considered for integration and use by others only after it has been unit tested satisfactorily. Due to its close association with coding, the coding phase is frequently called "coding and unit testing." As the focus of this testing level is on testing the code, structural testing is best suited for this level. In fact, as structural testing is not very suitable for large programs, it is used mostly at the unit testing level.

The next level of testing is often called *integration testing*. In this, many unit tested modules are combined into subsystems, which are then tested. The goal here is to see if the modules can be integrated properly. Hence, the emphasis is on testing interfaces between modules. This testing activity can be considered testing the design.

The next levels are *system testing* and *acceptance testing*. Here the entire software system is tested. The reference document for this process is the requirements document, and the goal is to see if the software meets its requirements. This is essentially a validation exercise, and in many situations it is the only validation activity. Acceptance testing is sometimes performed with realistic data of the client to demonstrate that the software is working satisfactorily. Testing here focuses on the external behavior of the system; the internal logic of the program is not emphasized. Consequently, mostly functional testing is performed at these levels.

These levels of testing are performed when a system is being built from the components that have been coded. There is another level of testing, called *regression testing*, that is performed when some changes are made to an existing system. We know that changes are fundamental to software; any software must undergo changes. Frequently, a change is made to "upgrade" the software by adding new features and functionality. Clearly, the modified software needs to be tested to make sure that the new features to be added do indeed work. However, as modifications have been made to an existing system, testing also has to done to make sure that the modification has not had any undesired side effect of making some of the earlier services faulty. That is, besides ensuring the desired behavior of the new services, testing has to ensure that the desired behavior of the old services is maintained. This is the task of regression testing.

For regression testing, some test cases that have been executed on the old system are maintained, along with the output produced by the old system. These test cases are executed again on the modified system and its output compared with the earlier output to make sure that the system is working as before on these test cases. This frequently is a major task when modifications are to be made to existing systems.

A consequence of this is that the test cases for systems should be properly documented for future use. Often, when we test our programs, the test cases are treated as "throw away" cases; after testing is complete, test cases and their outcomes are thrown away. With this practice, every time regression testing has to be done, the set of test cases will have to be re-created, resulting in increased cost. In fact, for many systems that are frequently changed, regression testing "scripts" are used to automatically perform the regression testing after some changes. A regression testing script contains all the inputs given by the test cases and the outputs produced by the system for these test cases. These scripts are typically produced during system testing, as regression testing is generally done only for complete systems or subsystems. When the system is modified, the scripts are executed again, giving the inputs specified in the scripts and comparing the outputs with the outputs given in the scripts. Given the scripts, through the use of tools, regression testing can be largely automated.

9.5.3 Test Plan

In general, testing commences with a *test plan* and terminates with acceptance testing. A test plan is a general document for the entire project that defines the scope, approach to be taken, and the schedule of testing as well as identifies the test items for the entire testing process and the personnel responsible for the different activities of testing. The test planning can be done well before the actual testing commences and can be done in parallel with the coding and design phases. The inputs for forming the test plan are: (1) project plan, (2) requirements document, and (3) system design document. The project plan is needed to make sure that the test plan is consistent with the overall plan for the project and the testing schedule matches that of the project plan. The requirements document and the design document are the basic documents used for selecting the test units and deciding the approaches to be used during testing. A test plan should contain the following:

- Test unit specification.
- Features to be tested.
- Approach for testing.
- Test deliverables.
- Schedule.
- Personnel allocation.

One of the most important activities of the test plan is to identify the test units. A *test unit* is a set of one or more modules, together with associated data, that are from a single computer program and that are the object of testing [IEE87]. A test unit can occur at any level and can contain from a single module to the entire system. Thus, a test unit may be a module, a few modules, or a complete system.

As seen earlier, different levels of testing have to be used during the testing activity. The levels are specified in the test plan by identifying the test units for the project. Different units are usually specified for unit, integration, and system testing. The identification of test units establishes the different levels of testing that will be performed in the project. Generally, a number of test units are formed during the testing, starting from the lower-level modules, which have to be unit tested. That is, first the modules that have to be tested individually are specified as test units. Then the higher-level units are specified, which may be a combination of already tested units or may combine some already tested units with some untested modules. The basic idea behind forming test units is to make sure that testing is being performed *incrementally*, with each increment including only a few aspects that need to be tested.

An important factor while forming a unit is the "testability" of a unit. A unit should be such that it can be easily tested. In other words, it should be possible to form meaningful test cases and execute the unit without much effort with these test cases. For example, a module that manipulates the complex data structure formed from a file input by an input module might not be a suitable unit from the point of view of testability, as forming meaningful test cases for the unit will be hard, and driver routines will have to be written to convert inputs from files or terminals that are given by the tester into data structures suitable for the module. In this case, it might be better to form the unit by including the input module as well. Then the file input expected by the input module can contain the test cases.

Features to be tested include all software features and combinations of features that should be tested. A software feature is a software characteristic specified or implied by the requirements or design documents. These may include functionality, performance, design constraints, and attributes.

The *approach* for testing specifies the overall approach to be followed in the current project. The techniques that will be used to judge the testing effort should also be specified. This is sometimes called the *testing criterion* or the criterion for evaluating the set of test cases used in testing. In the previous sections we discussed many criteria for evaluating and selecting test cases.

Testing deliverables should be specified in the test plan before the actual testing begins. Deliverables could be a list of test cases that were used, detailed results of testing, test summary report, test log, and data about the code coverage. In general, a *test case specification* report, *test summary report*, and a *test log* should always be specified as deliverables. Test case specification is discussed later. The test summary report summarizes the results of the testing activities and evaluates the results. It defines the items tested, the environment in which testing was done, and any variations from the specifications observed during testing. The test log provides a chronological record of relevant details about the execution of the test cases.

The *schedule* specifies the amount of time and effort to be spent on different activities of testing, and testing of different units that have been identified. *Personnel allocation* identifies the persons responsible for performing the different activities.

9.5.4 Test Case Specifications

The test plan focuses on how the testing for the project will proceed, which units will be tested, and what approaches (and tools) are to be used during the various stages of testing. However, it does not deal with the details of testing a unit, nor does it specify which test cases are to be used.

Test case specification has to be done separately for *each unit*. Based on the approach specified in the test plan, first the features to be tested for this unit must be determined. The overall approach stated in the plan is refined into specific test techniques that should be followed and into the criteria to be used for evaluation. Based on these, the test cases are specified for testing the unit. Test case specification gives, for each unit to be tested, all test cases, inputs to be used in the test cases, conditions being tested by the test case, and outputs expected for those test cases.

Test case specification is a major activity in the testing process. Careful selection of test cases that satisfy the criterion and approach specified is essential for proper testing. We have considered many methods of generating test cases and criteria for evaluating test cases. A combination of these can be used to select the test cases. It should be pointed out that test case specifications contain not only the test cases, but also the rationale of selecting each test case (such as what condition it is testing) and the expected output for the test case.

There are two basic reasons test cases are specified before they are used for testing. It is known that testing has severe limitations and the effectiveness of testing depends very heavily on the exact nature of the test cases. Even for a given criterion, the exact nature of the test cases affects the effectiveness of testing. Constructing "good" test cases that will reveal errors in programs is still a very creative activity that depends a great deal on the ingenuity of the tester. Clearly, it is important to ensure that the set of test cases used is of "high quality."

As with many other verification methods, evaluation of quality of test cases is done through "test case review." And for any review, a formal document or work product is needed. This is the primary reason for having the test case specification in the form of a document. The test case specification document is reviewed, using a formal review process, to make sure that the test cases are consistent with the policy specified in the plan, satisfy the chosen criterion, and in general cover the various aspects of the unit to be tested. For this purpose, the reason for selecting the test case and the expected output are also given in the test case specification document. By looking at the conditions being tested by the test cases, the reviewers can check if all the important conditions are being tested. As conditions can also be based on the output, by considering the expected outputs of the test cases, it can also be determined if the production of all the different types of outputs the unit is supposed to produce are being tested. Another reason for specifying the expected outputs is to use it as the "oracle" when the test case is executed.

Besides reviewing, another reason for formally specifying the test cases in a document is that the process of sitting down and specifying all the test cases that will be used for testing helps the tester in selecting a good set of test cases. By doing this, the tester can see the testing of the unit in totality and the effect of the total set of test cases. This type of evaluation is hard to do in on-the-fly testing where test cases are determined as testing proceeds.

Another reason for formal test case specifications is that the specifications can be used as "scripts" during regression testing, particularly if regression testing is to be performed manually. Generally, the test case specification document itself is used to record the results of testing. That is, a column is created when test cases are specified that is left blank. When the test cases are executed, the results of the test cases are recorded in this column. Hence, the specification document eventually also becomes a record of the testing results.

9.5.5 Test Case Execution and Analysis

With the specification of test cases, the next step in the testing process is to execute them. This step is also not straightforward. The test case specifications only specify the set of test cases for the unit to be tested. However, executing the test cases may require construction of driver modules or stubs. It may also require modules to set up the environment as stated in the test plan and test case specifications. If data is to be collected, then data collection forms need to be set up or data collection software developed. Only after all these are ready can the test cases be executed. Sometimes, the steps to be performed to execute the test cases are specified in a separate document called the *test procedure specification*. This document specifies any special requirements that exist for setting the test environment and describes the methods and formats for reporting the results of testing. Measurements, if needed, are also specified, along with how to obtain them.

Various outputs are produced as a result of test case execution for the unit under test. These outputs are needed to evaluate if the testing has been satisfactory. The most common outputs are the *test log*, the *test summary report*, and the *error report*. The test log describes the details of the testing. As mentioned earlier, the test case specification document itself can act as the document for logging the details of testing. The test summary report is meant for project management, where the summary of the entire test case execution is provided. The summary gives the total number of test cases executed, the number and nature of errors found, and a summary of any metrics data (e.g., effort) collected. The error report gives the summary of all the errors found. The errors might also be categorized into different levels, if such a categorization is available and its use has been planned in the test plan. This information can also be obtained from the test log, but it is usually given as a separate document. This report is frequently used to track the status of defects found during testing.

After testing is complete, the efficiency of the various defect removal techniques can be studied. The efficiency of a defect removal process can be defined if the total number of errors in the software is known. This data is not known but can be approximated more accurately after all the defects found in testing are known. The *defect removal efficiency* of a defect removing process is defined as the percentage reduction of the defects that are present before the initiation of the process [Jon78]. The *cumulative defect removal efficiency* of a series of defect removal processes is the percentage of defects that have been removed by this series, based on the number of defects present at the beginning of the series.

For example, suppose a total of 10 defects are detected during development and field operation. We can estimate the total number of errors in the software before the defect removal operations began as 10. Suppose that during reviews four defects were removed. The defect removal efficiency of reviews in this example is 40%. Suppose that during testing another four defects are removed. The defect removal efficiency of testing then is 66% (as it removed four out of the six remaining defects). The cumulative defect removal efficiency of reviews followed by testing is 80%. Defect removal efficiencies of the different methods is useful for evaluating the quality assurance process being used. It can also be used to evaluate how well the activities are performed in a given project, if process data from previous projects is available.

Testing and coding are the two phases that require careful monitoring, as these phases involve the maximum number of people. A few parameters can be observed for monitoring the testing process. *Testing effort* is the total effort spent by the project team in testing activities; and is an excellent indicator of whether or not testing is sufficient. In particular, if inadequate testing is done, it will be reflected in a reduced testing effort. From past experience we know that the total testing effort should be about 40% of the total effort for developing the software (the exact percentage will depend on the process and will have to be determined for the process). From this, the estimate of the effort required for testing, compared to coding or design, can be computed and used for monitoring. Such monitoring can catch the "miracle finish" cases, where the project "finishes" suddenly, soon after the coding is done. Such "finishes" occur for reasons such as unreasonable schedules, personnel shortages, and slippage of schedule. Such a finish usually implies that to finish the project the testing phase has been compressed too much, which is likely to mean that the software has not been evaluated properly.

Computer time consumed during testing is another measure that can give valuable information to project management. In general, in a software development project, the computer time consumption is low at the start, increases as time progresses, and reaches a peak. Thereafter it is reduced, as the project reaches its completion. Maximum computer time is consumed during the latter part of coding and testing. By monitoring the computer time consumed, one can get an idea about how thorough the testing has been. Again, by comparing the previous buildups in computer time consumption, computer time consumption of the current project can provide valuable information about whether or not the testing is adequate.

Error tracing is an activity that does not directly affect the testing of the current project, but it has many long-term quality control benefits. By error tracing we mean that when a fault is detected after testing, it should be studied and traced back in the development cycle to determine where it was introduced. This exercise has many benefits. First, it gives quantitative data about how many errors slip by the earlier quality control measures and which phases are more error-prone. If some particular phase is found to be more error prone, the verification activity of that phase should be strengthened in the future and proper standards and procedures need to be developed to reduce the occurrence of errors in the future. The volume and nature of faults slipping by the earlier quality assurance measures provide valuable input for evaluation of the quality control strategies. This evaluation can be used to determine which quality control measures should be strengthened and what sort of techniques should be added. Another benefit of error tracing is productivity improvement in the future. Error tracing is a feedback mechanism that is invaluable for learning. A designer or programmer, by seeing the mistakes that occurred during his activities, will learn from the information and is less likely to make similar mistakes in the future, thereby increasing his productivity. If this feedback is not provided, such learning will not take place.

9.6 Metrics—Reliability Estimation

After the testing is done and the software is delivered, the development is considered over. It will clearly be very desirable to know, in quantifiable terms, the reliability of the software being delivered. As testing directly impacts the reliability and most reliability models use data obtained during testing to predict reliability, reliability estimation is the main product metrics of interest at the end of the testing phase. We will focus our attention on this metric in this section.

Though reliability is the main product metric for the testing activity, there are other metrics of interest that can be evaluated after testing. Most of these are process metrics that do not directly relate to testing and are evaluated at the end of testing only because the end of testing signifies the end of the project. In other words, the *termination analysis* of the project management phase (refer to Chapter 2) is done typically at the end of testing, and some process metrics are used for this. Before we discuss the reliability modeling and estimation, let us briefly discuss a few main metrics that can be used for process evaluation at the end of the project.

Once the project is finished, one can look at the overall productivity achieved by the programmers during the project. Productivity data can be used to manage the resources and reduce cost by increasing productivity in the future. One common method for measuring productivity is *lines of code* or *function points per programmer-month*. This measure can be obtained easily from the data about the total programmer-months spent on the project and the size of the project (in LOC or function points). The use of this metric requires a precise definition of size. It should be kept in mind that productivity by this measure depends considerably on the source language (when LOC is used as size), and so data across languages may not be comparable. This productivity measure cannot handle reuse of code properly. Some other problems that must be handled properly while using this metric are discussed in [Jon78].

Another process metric of interest is *defect removal efficiency*, which was discussed earlier in the chapter. Another metric that is frequently used is *defects per thousand lines of code* or *defects per function point*. This is, in a sense, a rough measure of the "reliability" of the software as the defect density directly impacts the reliability of the software. It is also related to some of the software reliability models. We will discuss this metric more after we have discussed reliability modeling.

Let us now return to our main topic—software reliability modeling and assessment. Reliability of software often depends considerably on the quality of testing. Hence, by assessing reliability we can also judge the quality of testing. Alternatively, reliability estimation can be used to decide whether enough testing has been done. Hence, besides characterizing an important quality property of the product being delivered, reliability estimation has a direct role in project management—the reliability models being used by the project manager to decide when to stop testing.

Many models have been proposed for software reliability assessment. Some of the commonly referred models are the Jelinski and Moranda model [JM72], the Goel and Okomuto model [GO79], Musa's models [Mus75, MO84, MIO87], and the Littelwood and Verall model [LV74]. Most of these models differ in what they take as the random variable for modeling and the distributions they consider for the random variable. They also make different assumptions about the software and the underlying testing process. A discussion of the assumptions and consequent limitations on the models is given in [Goe85]. A survey of many of the different models is given in [Goe85, MIO87]. Here we will primarily discuss Musa's basic model, as it is one of the simplest models and one of the ones that has been most widely used. The discussion of the model is based largely on the book [MIO87].

9.6.1 Basic Concepts and Definitions

Reliability of a product specifies the probability of failure-free operation of that product for a given time duration. As we discussed earlier in this chapter, unreliability of any product comes due to failures or presence of faults in the system. As software does not "wear out" or "age" as a mechanical or an electronic system does, the unreliability of software is primarily due to bugs or design faults in the software. It is widely believed that with the current level of technology it is impossible to detect and remove all the faults in a large software system (particularly before delivery). Consequently, a software system is expected to have some faults in it.

Reliability is a probabilistic measure that assumes that the occurrence of failure of software is a random phenomenon. That is, if we define the life of a software system as a variable, this is a random variable that may assume different values in different invocations of the software. This randomness of the failure occurrences is necessary for reliability modeling. Here, by *randomness* all that is meant is that the failure cannot be predicted accurately. This assumption will generally hold for larger systems, but may not hold for small programs that have bugs (in which case one might be able to predict the failures). Hence, reliability modeling is more meaningful for larger systems (In [MIO87] it is suggested that it should be applied to systems larger than 5000 LOC, as such systems will provide enough data points to do statistical analysis.)

Let X be the random variable that represents the life of a system. The *failure probability*, $F(t)$, of a system is defined as the probability that the system will fail by time t, that is, the life of the system, X, is less than t:

$$F(t) = P(X \leq t).$$

As $F(t)$ specifies the failure probability up to a given time t, which changes with time, one can specify functions for $F(t)$. Such a function is called the *failure distribution function*. Each of these functions must have a value of 0 at time $t = 0$ (a system cannot fail before time 0) and a value 1 at time $t = \infty$ (all systems must fail before infinity). Reliability of a system is the probability that the system has not failed by time t. In other words,

$$R(t) = 1 - F(t).$$

If $F(t)$ is differentiable, its first derivative $f(t)$ is called the *failure density function*. The failure density function represents the instantaneous failure probability at time t. Or, the probability that a failure will occur between times t and $(t + \Delta t)$ is given by $f(t)\Delta t$.

These definitions give the failure probability, and reliability, failure density as a function of time at the initial time. That is, at time $t = 0$ we are predicting that the probability that the system will fail by some time t is $F(t)$. What if we find that by time t the system has not failed (after all $F(t)$ is only a probability)? That is, as time passes, we may find that a system has not failed by some time t. In that case, at time t, we would like to know the future failure probabilities from that time onward. In other words, we would like to know the failure probability for a system, given that the system has not failed by time t. This is generally specified for a system by its *hazard rate, z(t)*, which is the conditional failure density at time t, given that no failure has occurred between 0 and t. By this definition, the hazard rate is

$$z(t) = \frac{f(t)}{R(t)}.$$

The relationship between the hazard rate and reliability is [Tri82, MIO87] ($exp[x]$ represents e^x):

$$R(t) = \exp\left[\int_0^t z(x)dx\right].$$

The reliability of a system can also be specified as the *mean time to failure (MTTF)*. MTTF represents the expected lifetime of the system. From the reliability function, it can be obtained as [Tri82, MIO87]:

$$MTTF = \int_0^\infty R(x)dx.$$

Note that one can obtain the MTTF from the reliability function but the reverse is not always true. The reliability function can, however, be obtained from the MTTF if the failure process is assumed to be *Poisson*, that is, $F(t)$ has an *exponential distribution*. Exponential distribution is given by $F(t) = 1 - e^{-\lambda t}$, where λ is the failure rate and is equal to inverse of MTTF.

The classical definition of reliability was given earlier. However, there are other ways reliability can be specified. In the preceding definitions, the random variable was the time to next failure or the life of the system. We can define a different random variable, which represents the number of failures experienced by the system by time t. Clearly, this number will also be random as failures are random. If we use the random variable representing the number of failures by time t, we can specify reliability in a different form. If $M(t)$ represents the distribution of the number of failures experienced by time t, then the *mean value function* $\mu(t)$ for this is [MIO87]:

$$\mu(t) = E[M(t)],$$

where E is the expectation function and $\mu(t)$ represents the expected number of failures that will be experienced by time t. The function $\mu(t)$ will have a value of 0 at time $t = 0$ and will be a non-decreasing function. The *failure intensity* $\lambda(t)$ of the system is defined as [MIO87]

$$\lambda(t) = \frac{d\mu(t)}{dt}.$$

The failure intensity specifies the instantaneous change in the expected number of failures, or the expected number of failures per unit time. The number of failures that will occur between t and $t + \Delta t$ can be approximated as $\lambda(t)\Delta t$. For Poisson-type models (in which the failure probability has an exponential distribution), the probability of more than one event occurring in a small interval Δt is considered 0. Hence, $\lambda \Delta t$ represents the probability that a failure will occur between t and $(t + \Delta t)$, which is the same as the probability that the system does not fail until time t and there is a failure within Δt after that. In other words, for these types of models, the hazard rate is the same as the failure intensity function.

Having given the definitions, let us come back to some terms that are used in these definitions. In particular, it is very important to understand the notion of time and what is meant by failure and fault in the context of reliability models.

First let us clearly define what is meant by time in these reliability models. There are three common definitions of time for software reliability models [MIO87]: execution time, calendar time, and clock time. *Execution time* is the actual CPU time the software takes during its execution. *Calendar time* is the regular time we use, and *clock time* is the actual clock time that elapses while the software is executing (i.e., it includes the time the software waits in the system). Different models have used different time definitions, though the most commonly used are execution time and calendar time. It is now believed that execution time models are better and more accurate than calendar time models, as they more accurately capture the "stress" on the software due to execution.

Now let us revisit "failure" of software. In software, what is called a "failure" is dependent on the project, and its exact definition is left to the tester or project manager. For example, is a misplaced line in the output a failure or not? Clearly, it depends on the project; some will consider it a failure and others will not. Take another example. If the output is not produced within a given time period, is it a failure or not? For a real-time system this may be viewed as a failure, but for an operating system it may not be viewed as a failure. This means that there can be no general definition of failure, and it is up to the project manager or end user to decide what will be considered a failure for reliability purposes. Note that in the example of a misplaced line, a defect might be recorded, and even corrected later, but its occurrence might not be considered a failure. The failure behavior of software is primarily controlled by two factors [MIO87]:

1. The number of faults in the software being evaluated.
2. The operational profile of the execution.

Clearly, with a higher number of faults in software, one will expect the software to have a lower reliability. That is, the higher the number of faults, the higher the probability that the system will fail within time t. Due to this, the total number of defects in the software can be considered a rough guide of its reliability. This is why *defects* or *faults per KLOC* is a very commonly used metric for quantifying quality. Such a metric may be used to compare processes or products but cannot be effectively used to quantify reliability. As such a metric does not require reliability modeling, which requires a fair amount of data collection and sophistication, this metric is widely used in practice, despite its limitations. As we will see soon, the reliability models can be used to estimate the faults per KLOC metric more accurately.

The failure of software also depends critically on the environment in which it is executing. It is well known that software frequently fails only if some types of inputs are given. In other words, if software has faults, only some types of input will exercise that fault to affect failures. Hence, how often these inputs cause failures during execution will decide how often the software fails. The operational profile of software captures the relative probability of different types of inputs being given to the software during its execution. As the definition of reliability is based on failures, which in turn depends on the nature of inputs, reliability is clearly dependent on the operational profile of the software. Hence, when we say that the reliability of software is $R(t)$, it assumes that this is for some operational profile. If the operational profile changes dramatically, then we will need to either recompute $R(t)$ or recalibrate it. In other words, if we want to measure the reliability of a software system, we must observe the failures of the software in the operational profile in which it is eventually going to execute. Generally it is assumed that the profile of inputs given during system testing is similar to the inputs the software will experience during operation (i.e., the test cases during system testing are consistent with the operational profile of the software). Hence, the data of system testing is used to model the reliability of the software.

9.6.2   Musa's Basic Model

Let us now discuss one particular model—Musa's basic execution time model. The description given here of the model is based on [MIO87]. This is an execution time model, that is, the time taken during modeling is the actual CPU execution time of the software being modeled. The model is simple to understand and apply, and its predictive value has been generally found to be good.

The model focuses on failure intensity while modeling reliability. It assumes that the failure intensity decreases with time, that is, as (execution) time increases, the failure intensity decreases. This assumption is generally true as the following is assumed about the software testing activity, during which data is being collected: during testing, if a failure is observed, the fault that caused that failure is detected and the fault is removed. Even if a specific fault removal action might be unsuccessful, overall, failures lead to a reduction of faults in the software. Consequently, the failure intensity decreases. Most other models make similar assumption, which is consistent with actual observations.

In the basic model, it is assumed that each failure causes the same amount of decrement in the failure intensity. That is, the failure intensity decreases with a constant rate with the number of failures. In the more sophisticated Musa's logarithmic model [MO84, MIO87], the reduction is not assumed to be linear but logarithmic (this is the basic difference between the basic and logarithmic model). For the basic model, the failure intensity (number of failures per unit time) as a function of the number of failures is given as

$$\lambda(\mu) = \lambda_0 \left(1 - \frac{\mu}{\nu_0} \right),$$

where λ_0 is the initial failure intensity at the start of execution (i.e., at time $t = 0$), μ is the expected number of failures by the given time t, and ν_0 is the total number of failures that would occur in infinite time. The total number of failures in infinite time is finite as it is assumed that on each failure, the fault in the software is removed. As the total number of faults in a given software whose reliability is being modeled is finite, this implies that the number of failures is finite. The failure intensity, as a function of the total number of failures experienced, is shown in Figure 9.10 [MIO87].

The linear decrease in failure intensity as the number of failures observed increases is an assumption that is likely to hold for software for which the operational profile is uniform. That is, for software where the operational profile is such that any valid input is more or less equally likely, the assumption that the failure intensity decreases linearly generally holds. The intuitive rationale is that if the operational profile is uniform, any failure can occur at any time and all failures will have the same impact in failure intensity reduction. If the operational profile is not uniform, the failure intensity curves are ones whose slope decreases with the number of failures (i.e., each additional failure contributes less to the reduction in failure intensity). In such a situation the logarithmic model is better suited.

Note that the failure intensity decreases due to the nature of the software development process, in particular system testing, the activity in which reliability

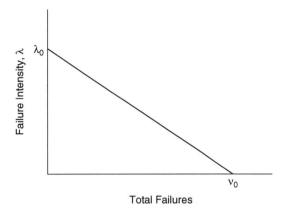

FIGURE 9.10. Failure intensity function.

modeling is applied. Specifically, during testing when a failure is detected, the fault that caused the failure is identified and removed. It is removal of the fault that reduces the failure intensity. However, if the faults are not removed, as would be the situation if the software was already deployed in the field (when the failures are logged or reported but the faults are not removed), then the failure intensity would stay constant. In this situation, the value of λ would stay the same as at the last failure that resulted in fault removal, and the reliability will be given by $R(t) = e^{-\lambda \tau}$, where τ is the execution time.

Earlier, the failure intensity was given as a function of mean number of failures experienced by the software. The expected number of failures as a function of execution time τ (i.e expected number of failures by time τ), $\mu(\tau)$, in the basic model is assumed to have an exponential distribution. That is,

$$\mu(\tau) = v_0(1 - e^{-\lambda_0/v_0 * \tau}).$$

By substituting this value in the equation for λ given earlier, we get the failure intensity as a function of time:

$$\lambda(\tau) = \lambda_0 * e^{-\lambda_0/v_0 * \tau}.$$

A typical shape of the failure intensity as it varies with time is shown in Figure 9.11 [MIO87].

This reliability model has two parameters whose values are needed to predict the reliability of given software. These are the initial failure intensity λ_0 and the total number of failures v_0. Unless the value of these are known, the model cannot be applied to predict the reliability of software. Most software reliability models are like this; they frequently will have a few parameters whose values are needed to apply the model.

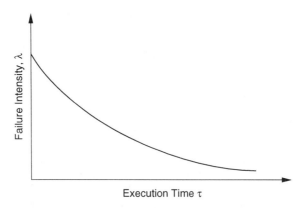

FIGURE 9.11. Failure intensity with time.

It would be very convenient if these parameters had constant values for all software systems or if they varied in a manner that their values for a particular software can be determined easily based on some clearly identified and easily obtained characteristic of the software (e.g., size or complexity). Some speculations have been made regarding how these parameters may depend on software characteristics. However, no such simple method is currently available that is dependable. The method that is currently used for all software reliability models is to *estimate* the value of these parameters for the particular software being modeled through the failure data for that software itself. In other words, the failure data of the software being modeled is used to obtain the value of these parameters. Some statistical methods are used for this, which we will discuss shortly.

The consequence of this fact is that, in general, for reliability modeling, the behavior of the software system is carefully observed during system testing and data of failures observed during testing is collected up to some time τ. Then statistical methods are applied to this collected data to obtain the value of these parameters. Once the values of the parameters are known, the reliability (in terms of failure intensity) of the software can be predicted. As statistical methods require that "enough" data points be available before accurate estimation of the parameters can be done, this implies that reliability can be estimated only after sufficient data has been collected. The requirement that there be a reasonably large failure data set before the parameters can be estimated is another reason reliability models cannot effectively be applied to software that is small in size (as it will not provide enough failure data points). Another consequence of this approach is that we can never determine the values of the parameters precisely. They will only be estimates, and there will always be some uncertainty with the values we compute. This uncertainty results in corresponding uncertainty in the reliability estimates computed using the models.

Let us assume that the failure data collection begins with system testing (as is usually the case). That is, time $\tau = 0$ is taken to be the commencement of system testing. The selection of the start of time is somewhat arbitrary. However, selecting the start of time where the assumptions about randomness and operational profile may not hold will cause the model to give incorrect estimates. This is why data of unit testing or integration testing, where the whole system is not being tested, is not considered. System testing, in which the entire system is being tested, is really the earliest point from where the data can be collected.

This reliability model can be applied to compute some other values of interest that can help decide if enough testing has been done or how much more testing needs to be done to achieve a target reliability. Suppose the target reliability is specified in terms of desired failure intensity, λ_F. If we have computed the two parameters, then at a given time, by the time a given number of failures have been experienced, the failure intensity is known. Let the present failure intensity be λ_P. Then the number of failures that we can expect to observe before the software achieves the desired reliability can be computed by computing $\lambda_F - \lambda_P$, which gives,

$$\Delta\mu = \frac{v_0}{\lambda_0}(\lambda_P - \lambda_F).$$

In other words, we can now clearly say that at any given time, we need to know how many more failures we need to observe (and correct) before the software will achieve the target reliability. Similarly, we can compute the additional time that needs to be spent before the target reliability is achieved. This is given by

$$\Delta t = \frac{v_0}{\lambda_0} \ln \frac{\lambda_P}{\lambda_F}.$$

That is, we can expect that the software needs to be executed for Δt more time before we will observe enough failures (and remove the faults corresponding to them) to reach the target reliability. This time can be converted to calendar time, which is what is used in projects, by incorporating some parameters about the software development environment. This issue will be discussed later.

9.6.3   Failure Data and Parameter Estimation

To apply the reliability model for a particular software, we need to obtain the value of the two parameters: λ_0 and v_0. These parameters are not the same for all software and have to be estimated for the software being modeled. Some efforts have been made to get an initial prediction of these values, which can later be replaced by more accurate estimated values, based on values for similar projects and process characteristics [MIO87]. Here we will discuss only the statistical estimation methods, which give more accurate values for these parameters.

For statistical approaches to parameter estimation, data has to be collected about the failures of the software being modeled. Generally, as mentioned earlier, the earliest point to start collecting data for reliability estimation is the start of system testing (a later point can also be taken, though it will reduce the number of failures that can be observed). The data can be collected in two different forms. The first form is to record the failure times (in execution time) of the failures observed during execution. This data will essentially be a sequence of (execution) times representing the first, second, and so on failures that are observed. The second form of data is to record the number of failures observed during execution in different time intervals (called *grouped failure data*). This form might sometimes be easier to collect if the unit is a clearly identified unit, like a day. In this form, the data will be in the form of a table, where the duration of the interval (in execution time) and the number of failures observed during that interval are given. We will only discuss the parameter estimation with the first form. For further details on parameter estimation, the reader is referred to [MIO87].

There are many ways in which the model can be "fitted" to the data points to obtain the parameters or coefficients. The two most common methods are the *maximum likelihood* estimation and the *least squares* approach. In the maximum likelihood approach, a likelihood function is defined, and the objective is to select the value of the parameters of the model so that the actual observed data are more probable than any other choice. For large data sets this approach frequently gives good results. We will not discuss this approach and the reader is referred to [MIO87] or any statistics text.

In the least squares approach, the goal is to select the parameters for the model so that the square of the difference between the observed value and the one predicted by the model is minimized. We saw the use of this approach for linear regression analysis in Chapter 2. This approach works well when the size of the data set is not very large.

For applying the least squares approach, we will consider the equation for the failure intensity as a function of the mean number of failures (i.e., $\lambda(\mu) = \lambda_0(1 - \mu/\nu_0)$). To determine parameters for this equation, we need a set of observed data points, each containing the value of the dependent variable and the value of the independent variable. In this case, this means that we need data points, each of which gives the failure intensity and the number of failures.

The data collected, as specified earlier, may be in the form of failure times or grouped failure data. The first thing that needs to be done is to convert the data to the desired form by determining the failure intensity for each failure. If the data about failure times is available, this conversion is done as follows [MIO87]. Let the observation interval be $(0, t_e]$ (t_e is the time when the observations are stopped; it will generally be greater than the time of the last failure). We partition this observation interval at every kth failure occurrence. That is, this time interval is partitioned into sub-intervals, each (except the last one) containing k distinct failures. If the total number of failures observed until t_e is m_e, then the number of subintervals is p, where $p = \lceil m_e/k \rceil$. The observed failure intensity for an interval can now be computed by dividing the number of failures in that interval by the duration of the interval. That is, for an interval l, the observed failure intensity r_l is given by

$$r_l = \frac{k}{t_{kl} - t_{k(l-1)}}, l = 1, \ldots, p - 1.$$

For the last interval, the failure intensity is

$$r_p = \frac{m_e - k(p - 1)}{t_e - t_{k(l-1)}}.$$

These failure intensities are *independent* of each other as the different time intervals are disjoint. The estimate for the mean value for the lth interval, m_l, can be obtained by

$$m_l = k(l - 1).$$

(This takes the start value for the interval but has been found to be better than taking the average or midpoint value [MIO87].) In this method, if k is chosen to be too small, large variations will occur in failure intensity. If the value of k is very large, too much smoothing may occur. A value of about five (i.e., $k = 5$) gives reasonable results [MIO87].

Obtaining data in this form from grouped data is even easier. For each time interval for which failures were counted, dividing the number of failures by the duration of the interval will give the failure intensity of that interval. The total number of failures for an interval is the sum of all the failures of all the intervals before this interval.

In this manner, we can get from the collected data a set of p data points, each giving a failure intensity and the total number of failures observed. As the relationship between them is linear, a regression line can be fit in these data points. The determination of the coefficients for the regression line was discussed in Chapter 2. We leave the details as an exercise.

However, the approach of simple linear regression minimizes the sum of absolute errors (between the predicted value by the model and the actual value observed). This approach gives a higher weight to the data points with larger failure intensity. In other words, the coefficients will be influenced more by data points with larger failure intensity. A better approach is to consider *relative error*, which is absolute error divided by the value given by the model. The least square approach here will be to minimize the sum of all the relative errors. With relative errors, each data point is given the same weight. However, with this, linear regression cannot be used, and closed-form equations for determining the coefficients are not available. For this approach, numerical methods must be used to determine the coefficients. The approach will be to obtain the derivatives of the equation for least squares (with relative error) with the two coefficients to be determined, set these to 0, and then solve these two simultaneous equations through some standard numerical technique like the Newton-Raphson method. For further discussion on this, the reader is referred to [MIO87] or any numerical analysis text.

Once the parameters are known, we can also predict the number of faults in the delivered software using the reliability model (which can be used to accurately predict faults per KLOC). As we don't otherwise know how many faults remain in software, generally, this data is available for a project only after the software has been in operation for a few years and most of its faults have been identified. By using the reliability model, we can predict this with some confidence.

The total failures experienced in infinity time by a software is related to the total faults in the system, as we are assuming that faults are generally removed after a failure is detected. However, the fault removal process may not be perfect and may introduce errors. In addition, each failure may not actually result in removing of a fault, as the information obtained on failure may not be sufficient for fault detection. If the total number of faults in the software is ω_0, we can get ν_0 from this by using the *fault reduction factor, B*:

$$\nu_0 = \frac{\omega_0}{B}$$

The fault reduction factor, B, is the ratio of the *net* fault reduction to the total number of failures experienced. If each failure resulted in exactly one fault being removed, then B would be 1. However, sometimes a failure is not sufficient to locate a fault or a fault removal adds some faults. Due to these, the fault reduction factor is not always 1. Currently available data suggests that B is close to 1, with an average value of about 0.95 [MIO87]. This value can be used to predict the number of faults that remain in the software. Alternatively, the value of B can be computed from the data collected (additional data about fault correction will have to be compiled).

9.6.4   Translating to Calendar Time

The model discussed here is an execution-time model: all the times are the CPU execution time of the software. However, software development and project planning works in calendar time—hours, days, months, etc. Hence, we would like to convert the estimates to calendar time, particularly when we are trying to predict the amount of time still needed to achieve the desired reliability. In this case, it is clearly desirable to specify the time in calendar time, so that the project plan can be modified appropriately, if needed.

As reliability modeling is performed from system testing onward, the execution time can be related to the effort for testing, debugging, etc. The simplest way to do this is to determine an average ratio of the amount of effort to execution time and then to use this effort to estimate the calendar time. Alternatively, instead of giving one ratio, two ratios can be specified—one for the CPU time expended and one for the failures detected. These ratios can then be used to determine the total amount of effort.

Let us explain this approach with a simple example. Generally, the main resource during testing is the test team effort. For now, we consider this as the only resource of interest for modeling calendar time. Suppose the test team runs the software for 10 CPU hours, during which it detects 25 failures. Suppose that for each hour of CPU execution time, an average of 8 person-hours of the test team are consumed (ratio of effort to CPU time), and that on an average 4 person-hours is needed on each failure to analyze it (ratio of effort to failures). Hence, the total effort required for this is

$$10 * 8 + 25 * 4 = 180 \text{ person-hours.}$$

If the quantity of test team resources (i.e., the number of members in the test team) is three persons, this means that the calendar time for this is 60 hours. As the number of failures experienced is a function of time according to the Basic model, one overall ratio could also have been given with CPU time (or with number of failures). In this example, the overall ratio will be 18 person-hours per CPU hour.

This simple approach considers only the test team resource when converting execution time to calendar time. A more elaborate method was proposed in [Mus75, MIO87], which partitions the overall testing process (during which data is being collected) into different phases and then uses different ratios for the different phases. According to this approach, at any given time there is some resource that is the "limiting resource," and this resource determines the rate at which the execution time is expended. Typically, in the beginning, when the failures are most frequent, the limiting resource is the fault-fixing personnel. Testing has to be stopped after every failure to allow the fault-fixing team to fix the fault. Later as the failure frequency decreases, the testing personnel becomes the limiting resource and the fault-fixing personnel are not fully occupied. Still later, when failures are very rare, it is the computer resources that become the limiting resources that govern how fast the execution time is expended.

With this model, we can obtain the ratios (either two ratios—one for the execution time and one for the number of failures—or just one ratio) of these resources to the execution time. These ratios will be obtained from past experience with the software development and testing process. By extracting the execution time in these phases from the collected data, these ratios can be used to determine the amount of resources needed for each of these phases. From the resource usage and the quantity of resources used in the phase (number of test personnel, number of fault-fixing personnel, number of computers available for testing), the calendar time for each phase can be determined. The calendar times for the different phases can then be added up to get the overall calendar time.

Time of Failure (in CPU sec)				
311	3089	5922	10,559	14,358
366	3565	6738	10,559	15,168
608	3623	8089	10,791	
676	4080	8237	11,121	
1098	4380	8258	11,486	
1278	4477	8491	12,708	
1288	4740	8625	13,251	
2434	5192	8982	13,261	
3034	5447	9175	13,277	
3049	5644	9411	13,806	
3085	5837	9442	14,185	
3089	5843	9811	14,229	

TABLE 9.1. Failure data for a real system [MIO87].

9.6.5   An Example

Let us illustrate the use of the reliability model discussed earlier through the use of an example. In [MIO87], times for more than 130 failures for a real system called T1 are given. For illustration purposes, we select about 50 data points from it, starting from after about 2000 CPU sec have elapsed (from the 21st failure). We define $\tau = 0$ after the first 2000 sec of [MIO87] to illustrate that the choice of $\tau = 0$ is up to the reliability estimator and to eliminate the first few data points, which are likely to show a wider variation, as they probably represent the start of testing. The times of failures with this $\tau = 0$ are given in Table 9.1.

As we can see, this is the failure times data. From this, using $k = 5$, we obtain the failure intensities and the cumulative failures as discussed earlier. The data points we get are:

(0.0045, 0), (0.0026, 5), (0.0182, 10), (0.0047, 15), (0.0040, 20),
(0.0020, 25), (0.0056, 30), (0.0032, 35), (0.0023, 40), (0.0035, 45)

For the purposes of this example, we will try to fit a regression line to this data using the regular least squares approach discussed in Chapter 2. We are doing this largely because this form of minimization and parameter determination can be done without a computer program. However, as discussed earlier, this method is likely to give poorer results compared to minimizing the square of relative errors (for which equation solving programs will be required). Using the regular regression line fitting approach, we get $\lambda_0 = 0.0074$ failure/CPU sec and $\nu_0 \approx 70$ failures. (If the complete data from [MIO87] is used, then ν_0 comes out to about 136 failures. Because we are not counting the first 20, this means that by fitting a line on the complete data using the relative error approach, ν_0 would come out to be around

110. This error in our estimate is coming due to the smaller sample and the use of absolute error for determining the coefficients.) By the reliability model, the current reliability of the software (after 50 failures have been observed) is about 0.002 failure per CPU second.

Assuming that the fault reduction factor is 1, we can see that the total number of estimated faults in the system at the start of the time is 70. Out of this, 50 faults have been removed (after observing the 50 failures). Hence, there are still 20 faults left in the software. Suppose the size of the final software was 20,000 LOC. If the failure data given earlier is until the end of system testing (i.e., the software is to be delivered after this) and this software development project is a typical project for the process that was followed, we can say that the capability of this process is to deliver software with a fault density of 1.0 per KLOC.

Now let's suppose the current failure intensity after 50 failures is not acceptable to the client. The desired failure intensity is 0.001 failure per CPU second. Using the model, we can say that to achieve this reliability, further testing needs to be done and the amount of CPU time that will be consumed in this extra testing can be estimated to be

$$70/0.0074 * \ln(0.002/0.001) = 6,527 \text{ CPU-sec.}$$

That is, approximately 1.81 CPU hours of testing needs to be performed to achieve the target reliability. Suppose the limiting resource is only the testing personnel, there is one person assigned to test this software, and on an average 20 person-hours of testing personnel effort is spent for each hour of CPU time. In this case, we can say that more than 36 person-hours of testing need to be done. In other words, the calendar time needed to achieve the target reliability is about a week.

9.7 Summary

Testing plays a critical role in quality assurance for software. Due to the limitations of the verification methods for the previous phases, design and requirement faults also appear in the code. Testing is used to detect these errors, in addition to the errors introduced during the coding phase.

Testing is a dynamic method for verification and validation, where the system to be tested is executed and the behavior of the system is observed. Due to this, testing observes the failures of the system, from which the presence of faults can be deduced. However, separate activities have to be performed to identify the faults (and then remove them).

There are two approaches to testing: functional and structural. In functional testing, the internal logic of the system under testing is not considered and the test cases are decided from the specifications or the requirements. It is often called "black box testing." Equivalence class partitioning, boundary value analysis, and cause-effect graphing are examples of methods for selecting test cases for functional testing. In structural testing, the test cases are decided entirely on the internal logic of the program or module being tested. The external specifications are not considered. Often a structural criterion is specified, but the procedure for selecting test cases is left to the tester. The most common control flow–based criteria are statement coverage and branch coverage, and the common data flow–based criteria are all-defs and all-uses. Mutation testing is another approach for structural testing that creates mutants of the original program by changing the original program. The testing criterion is to kill all the mutants by having the mutant generate a different output from the original program.

As the goal of testing is to detect any errors in the programs, different levels of testing are often used. Unit testing is used to test a module or a small collection of modules and the focus is on detecting coding errors in modules. During integration testing, modules are combined into subsystems, which are then tested. The goal here is to test the system design. In system testing and acceptance testing, the entire system is tested. The goal here is to test the system against the requirements, and to test the requirements themselves. Structural testing can be used for unit testing, while at higher levels mostly functional testing is used.

The testing process usually commences with a test plan, which is the basic document guiding the entire testing of the software. It specifies the levels of testing and the units that need to be tested. For each of the different units, first the test cases are specified and then they are reviewed. During the test case execution phase, the test cases are executed, and various reports are produced for evaluating testing. The main outputs of the execution phase are the test log, the test summary report, and the error report.

The main metric of interest during testing is the reliability of the software under testing. Reliability of software depends on the faults in the software. To assess the reliability of software, reliability models are needed. To use a model for a given software system, data is needed about the software that can be used in the model to estimate the reliability of the software. Most reliability models are based on the data obtained during the system and acceptance testing. Data about time between failures observed during testing are used by these models to estimate the reliability of the software. We discussed one such reliability model in the chapter in some detail and have discussed how the reliability model can be used in a project and what the limitations of reliability models are.

Exercises

1. Define error, fault, and failure. What is the difference between a fault and a failure? Does testing observe faults or failures?

2. What are the different levels of testing and the goals of the different levels? For each level, specify which of the testing approaches (functional, structural, or some other) is most suitable.

3. What is the goal of testing? Why is the psychology of the tester important?

4. Testing often consumes more resources than any other phase in software development. List the major factors that make testing so expensive.

5. Convince yourself that the branch coverage criterion does not satisfy the applicability, antidecomposition, and anticomposition axioms, but does satisfy the antiextensionality axiom.

6. Determine which of the axioms are satisfied by the all-defs and all-uses criteria.

7. Consider a simple text formatter problem. Given a text consisting of words separated by blanks (BL) or newline (NL) characters, the text formatter has to covert it into lines, so that no line has more than MAXPOS characters, breaks between lines occurs at BL or NL, and the maximum possible number of words are in each line. The following program has been written for this text formatter [GG75]:

```
alarm := false;
bufpos := 0;
fill := 0;
repeat
    inchar(c);
    if (c = BL) or (c = NL) or (c = EOF)
    then
        if bufpos != 0
        then begin
            if (fill + bufpos < MAXPOS) and (fill != 0)
            then begin
                outchar(BL);
                fill := fill + 1; end
            else begin
                outchar(NL);
                fill := 0; end;
            for k:=1 to bufpos do
                outchar(buffer[k]);
            fill := fill + bufpos;
            bufpos := 0; end
    else
        if bufpos = MAXPOS
        then alarm := true
        else begin
            bufpos := bufpos + 1;
```

buffer[bufpos] := c; **end**
until alarm or (c = EOF);

For this program, do the following:

(a) Select a set of test cases using the functional testing approach. Use as many techniques as possible and select test cases for special cases using the "error guessing" method.

(b) Select a set of test cases that will provide 100% branch coverage.

(c) Select a set of test cases that will satisfy the all-defs and the all-uses criteria (except the ones that are not feasible).

(d) Create a few mutants by simple transformations. Then select a set of test cases that will kill these mutants.

(e) Suppose that this program is written as a procedure. Write a driver for testing this procedure with the test cases selected in (a) and (b). Clearly specify the format of the test cases and how they are used by the driver.

8. Suppose three numbers A, B, and C are given in ascending order representing the lengths of the sides of a triangle. The problem is to determine the type of the triangle (whether it is isosceles, equilateral, right, obtuse, or acute). Consider the following program written for this problem:

```
read(a, b, c);
if (a < b) or (b < c) then
    print("Illegal inputs");
    return;
if (a=b) or (b=c) then
    if (a=b) and (b=c) then print("equilateral triangle")
    else print("isosceles triangle")
else begin
    a := a*a; b := b*b; c := c*c;
    d := b+c;
    if (a = d) then print("right triangle")
    else if (a<d) then print("acute triangle")
    else print("obtuse triangle");
end;
```

For this program, perform the same exercises as in the previous problem.

9. Do the reliability models actually measure reliability or estimate it from some other measurements?

10. Define some data flow criteria for testing an entire class (i.e., not just for testing the methods independently) (refer to [HR94]).

11. Convert Musa's reliability model for calendar time. Assume that the testing personnel resource is the only limiting factor, and that N persons are assigned for testing.

12. Another method for evaluating software reliability is to use the Mill's seeding approach. In this method some faults are seeded in the program, and reliability is assessed based on how many of these seeded faults are detected during testing. Develop a simple reliability model based on this approach. Define your parameters, and give a formula for estimating the reliability and the number of faults remaining in the system.

    What are the drawbacks and limitations of this seeding model? What are the assumptions about the seeded faults?

13. You want to find whether there is a correlation between complexity and reliability and between size and reliability. What data will you collect during and after termination of a project? Design an experiment to perform this study.

CASE STUDY

As was discussed in the chapter, testing is a fairly involved activity that is quite expensive. A number of documents are produced as a result of testing. Here we give the test plan and the test case specifications for system testing. The outcome of the testing and various reports is not included.

Test Plan

This document describes the plan for testing the course scheduling software. All major testing activities are specified here; additional testing may be scheduled later, if necessary.

1. Test Units

In this project we will perform two levels of testing: unit testing and system testing. Because the system is small, it is felt that there is no need for elaborate integration testing. The basic units to be tested are:

> Modules to input file-1
> Modules to input file-2
> Modules for scheduling

In addition, some other units may be chosen for testing. The testing for these different units will be done independently.

2. Features to Be Tested

All the functional features specified in the requirements document will be tested. No testing will be done for the performance, as the response time requirement is quite weak.

3. Approach for Testing

For unit testing, structural testing based on the branch coverage criterion will be used. The goal is to achieve branch coverage of more than 95%. The CCOV coverage analyzer tool will be used to determine the coverage. System testing will be largely functional in nature. The focus is on invalid and valid cases, boundary values, and special cases.

4. Test Deliverables

The following documents are required (besides this test plan):

- Unit test report for each unit.
- Test case specification for system testing.
- Test report for system testing.
- Error report.

The test case specification for system testing has to be submitted for review before system testing commences.

5. Schedule and Personnel Allocation

The entire testing—unit and system—will be finished within the month of April. Much of the unit testing will be done in the first two weeks of April. Test case specifications for the system testing will be produced while unit testing is going on. This schedule is consistent with the overall schedule of the project. The schedule for testing is shown here:

```
Unit testing      |******        Person-1
Unit testing      |******        Person-2
Test case specs   |   *****       Person-3
System testing    |      ********** 2 Persons
                  |—————————————————|
                          April
```

Test Case Specifications for System Testing

Here we specify all test cases that are used for system testing. First, the different conditions that need to be tested, along with the test cases used for testing those conditions and the expected outputs are given. Then the data files used for testing are given. The test cases are specified with respect to these data files. The test cases have been selected using the functional approach. The goal is to test the different functional requirements, as specified in the requirements document. Test cases have been selected for both valid and invalid inputs.

SEQ NO.	TEST_CASE [File]	CONDITION BEING CHECKED	EXPECTED OUTPUT
1	Empty_file	Empty F1	Print message and stop
2	Empty_file	Empty F2	Print message and stop
3	No file F1	Does not exist	Print message and stop

SEQ NO.	TEST_CASE [File]	CONDITION BEING CHECKED	EXPECTED OUTPUT
4	No file F2	Does not exist	Print message and stop

For checking FILE1 format error

SEQ NO.	TEST_CASE [File]	CONDITION BEING CHECKED	EXPECTED OUTPUT
5	[F1.1]	Incorrect course no. format	Print course no. and error message
6	[F1.7]	More than allowed (30) courses	Error message and skip to lecture times
7	[F1.4]	Course list empty	Error message and skip to lecture times
8	[F1.5]	Spelling of header	Error message and stop
9	[F1.1]	Lecture time format	Print time, error message, and continue
10	[F1.2]	More than allowed no. of lecture times (15)	Error message, discard extra and skip to room no.s
11	[F1.4]	Lecture times list empty	Print "No lecture times" and parse rooms
12	[F1.1]	Incorrect room no format	Print room no. and message
13	[F1.1]	No colon (:) between room# and capacity	Continue
14	[F1.1]	Capacity format	Print message with room no. and capacity and continue
15	[F1.1]	Capacity more than limit (300)	Error message, continue
16	[F1.1]	Capacity less than 10	Error message, continue
17	[F1.7]	More than 20 room#, cap entries	Error message, stop
18	[F1.4]	Room list empty	Error message, stop
19	[F1.1]	No correct room entries	Error message, no scheduling, continue parsing
20	[F1.3]	Same course_no entered more than once	Print message and discard the entry
21	[F1.3]	Duplicate lecture time	Print message, discard it, and continue
22	[F1.3]	Duplicate room entry	Print message, ignore it, and continue

FILE2 format (for FILE1, F1.8 is used)

SEQ NO.	TEST_CASE [File]	CONDITION BEING CHECKED	EXPECTED OUTPUT
23	[F2.1]	Enrollment ≤ 2	Print message, ignore it, and continue
24	[F2.1]	Enrollment in range [3–250]	Executes normally
25	[F2.1]	Enrollment exceeds 250	Print message, continue
26	[F2.2]	No preference specified	Scheduled

SEQ NO.	TEST_CASE [File]	CONDITION BEING CHECKED	EXPECTED OUTPUT
27	[F2.1]	More than allowed number of preferences (5).	Print message and discard the rest
28	[F2.1]	Duplicate course entry	Print message and ignore duplicate

Consistency of FILE2 with FILE1. File F1.8 used for file 1.

SEQ NO.	TEST_CASE [File]	CONDITION BEING CHECKED	EXPECTED OUTPUT
29	[F2.1]	Course not present in the list of offered courses	Print message, ignore it, and continue
30	[F2.1]	Preference not found in lecture time list	Print message and ignore the preference
31	[F2.1]	Enrollment > max. room capacity available	Error message
32	[F2.4]	Missing enrollment field	Ignore the course

SCHEDULING cases. File F1.8 used for file 1.

SEQ NO.	TEST_CASE [File]	CONDITION BEING CHECKED	EXPECTED OUTPUT
33	[F2.4]	No valid courses in F2	Print message and stop
34	[F2.2]	No PG course with prefs	Schedule
35	[F2.4]	No UG course with prefs	Schedule
36	[F2.4]	No PG courses with no pref	Schedule
37	[F2.2]	No two courses allotted at the same time and in the same room	The first course is given the first preference
38	[F2.2]	Room capacity is more than the classroom	Course scheduled in a room with capacity more than enrollment
39	[F2.2]	PG courses given priority over UG courses even if UG course appears before the PG course in input	PG course is scheduled; UG course faces conflict
40	[F2.2]	Courses scheduled in the order they appear in the input file	The first course is given the best pref., second the next pref., and so on
41	[F2.2]	Highest possible preference of a course is honored	The nth pref. honored with explanation for all the earlier n-1 preferences
42	[F2.3]	No two PG courses scheduled in the same slot even if same pref. given	The first one scheduled and conflict shown for the second course
43	[F2.3]	PG course with pref. given priority over PG courses with no preference	Courses with pref.s are scheduled before

| 44 | [F2.2] | PG courses with no pref.s are guaranteed a room even if some UG course has to be "unscheduled" | PG course scheduled and conflict generated for the UG course |
| 45 | [F2.2] | No room with required capacity available for UG course with no preference | Error message |

Data Files for Test Cases

Note: To present these files compactly, all the new line characters are not included. Some formatting has been done to enhance readability.

File F1.1

rooms
    F-101 30 105 : 40 1052 : 25 F30:50 301 :9 311: 325 320 200
    310 : 211 312 2a 313 : 34 201 :00 678 ;
courses
    XC539 x29 53ABc cs5394 csa59 cs250 CS 245 CS665 ;
times
    TT TW10 TT10:30 MWF10:30 MWF9 MWF09 MWF789 10253 TTL2
       TT11 TT10-30 ;

File F1.2

rooms
    100 20 200 39 201 45 202 50 203 50 204 60 205 200 206 299
    207 10 208 300 209 100 301 11 302 25 303 15 304 56 305 77
    306 30 307 40 308 60 309 90 400 95 404 44 405 67 ;
courses
    cs444 cs_233 CS555,cs3423 cs665 ;
times
    TT8 TT9 MWF8 MWF9 MWF10 MWF11 MWF12 MWF2 MWF3 MWF4
       TT1:30
    TT11:30 TT1 TT3 TT5 TT12:30 TT3:30 ;

File F1.3

rooms
    101 :250 303 49 401 40 101 30 303 45 202 50 ;
courses
    cs320 cs741 cs201 cs320 cs622 ;
times
    TT9 MWF12 TT10:30 MWF12 TT10:30 ;

File F1.4

rooms
    ;
courses

```
    ;
times
    ;
```

File F1.5

```
rooms
    202 34 100 10 ;
course
    cs330 ;
timeslot
    TT1 MWF12 ;
```

File F1.6

```
rooms
    202:39 300 56 ;
courses
    ;
times
    TT3 ;
```

File F1.7

```
rooms
    101:25 456:78 345 90 346 90 347 90 348 90 349 90
    355 90 365 90 375 90 385 90 395 90 305 90 335 90
    495 90 545 90 645 90 745 90 945 90 946 90 155 90 ;
courses
    cs301, cs302, cs303, cs304, cs305, cs306 cs307 cs308
    cs309 cs201 cs601 cs602 cs603 cs604 cs605 cs606 cs607
    cs608 cs609 cs611 cs641 cs751 cs752 cs753 cs754 cs755
    cs756 cs757 cs758 cs759 cs123 ;
times
    MWF1, MWF2, MWF3, MWF4 MWF5 MWF6 MWF7 MWF8 MWF9
        MWF91
    MWF92 MWF93 MWF94 MWF98 MWF99 MWF56
```

File F1.8

```
rooms
    201:50 202 75 203 30 204 150 ;
courses
    cs310, cs320, cs330, cs340 cs350 cs315 cs335 cs365 cs325 cs345,
    cs355 cs305 cs360 cs370 cs380 cs375, cs610 cs620 cs605 cs615,
    cs630, cs625, cs635 cs640 cs650 cs645 cs660, cs655 cs665 cs670 ;
times
    MWF9, MWF11, MWF2 TT8:30 TT1 TT11:30 ;
```

File F2.1

```
course
    cs305 25 TT8 TT6 TT9 MWF8
```

```
cs344 45 TT1
cd456 56 Tw56
cs365 200 TT1 MWF9
cs3a0 301 TT1
cs345 0 TT11:30
cs601 267 TT4
cs665 140 TT1
cs305 45 TT1
cs335 df TT1
cs645 45 TT1 TT11:30 TT8:30 MWF2 MWF11 MWF9
cs330 100 TT1 MWF9,
MWF2 MWF11
```

File F2.2

course	enrollment	preferences
cs355	35	TT1
cs660	70	
cs310	79	MWF11
cs640	100	
cs315	50	TT11:30
cs320	100	MWF9
cs305	50	TT1
cs325	70	TT1
cs345	35	
cs365	70	

File F2.3

course	enrollment	preferences
cs605	70	TT1
cs310	50	TT11:30, TT1
cs625	35	TT11:30
cs615	70	
cs325	35	MWF9
cs330	55	MWF9
cs610	100	TT1, TT11:30, MWF9
cs335	50	MWF9, TT11:30, TT1
cs650	150	MWF2 MWF9
cs635	50	
cs660	150	
cs655	30	TT1, MWF2 MWF9
cs315	52	
cs320	75	
cs305	70	MWF11
cs340	150	TT8:30
cs345	70	TT8:30 MWF11
cs350	50	TT8:30 MWF11
cs355	50	TT8:30 MWF11, MWF2
cs360	50	MWF9 MWF11

cs365	30
cs370	50
cs375	50
cs620	155

File F2.4

course	enrollment	preferences
cs635	45	MWF11,TT11:30
cs620	36	TT1
cs330		
cs320	26	

References

[AC94]   F. B. Abreu and R. Carapuca. Candidate metrics for object-oriented software within a taxonomy framework. *Journal of Systems and Software*, 26(1):87–96, Jan. 1994.

[AG83]   A. J. Albrecht and J. E. Gaffney. Software function, source lines of code, and development effort prediction: A software science validation. *IEEE Transactions on Software Engineering*, 9(6):639–648, Nov. 1983.

[Alf77]   M. Alford. A requirement engineering methodology for real-time processing requirements. *IEEE Transactions on Software Engineering*, 3(1):60–69, Jan. 1977.

[B⁺78]   T. A. Budd et al. The design of a prototype mutation system for program testing. In *National Computer Conference*, 1978.

[Bas80]   V. R. Basili. *Tutorial on models and metrics for software management and engineering*. IEEE Press, 1980.

[BBM95]   Victor R. Basili, Lionel Briand, and Walcelio L. Melo. A validation of object-oriented design metrics. Technical Report CS-TR-3443, University of Maryland, Dept. of Computer Science, College Park, MD, April 1995.

[BCR94]   V. R. Basili, G. Caldiera, and H. D. Rombach. Goal question metric paradigm. In *Encyclopedia of Software Engineering*. John Wiley and Sons, 1994.

[Ber84]   E. H. Bersoff. Elements of software configuration management. *IEEE Transactions of Software Engineering*, pages 79–87, Jan. 1984.

[BHS79]   E. H. Bersoff, V. D. Henderson, and S. G. Siegel. Software configuration management: A tutorial. *IEEE Computer*, pages 6–14, Jan. 1979.

[BHS80]   E. H. Bersoff, V. D. Henderson, and S. G. Siegel. *Software configuration management—an investment in product integrity*. Prentice-Hall, Inc., Englewood Cliffs, NJ, 1980.

[BJ89]   J. C. Bolot and P. Jalote. Formal verification of programs with exceptions. In *Proc.19th Fault Tolerant Computing Symposium*, pages 283–290, Chicago, 1989.

[BM85]   R. E. Berry and B. A. E. Meeking. A style analysis of C programs. *Communications of the ACM*, Jan. 1985.

[Boe76]   B. Boehm. Software engineering. *IEEE Transactions on Computers*, 25(12), Dec. 1976.

[Boe81]   B. W. Boehm. *Software engineering economics*. Prentice Hall, Englewood Cliffs, NJ, 1981.

[Boe84a] B. Boehm. Verifying and validating software requirements and design specifications. *IEEE Software*, pages 75–88, Jan. 1984.

[Boe84b] B. W. Boehm. Software engineering economics. *IEEE Transactions on Software Engineering*, 10(1):135–152, Jan. 1984.

[Boe87]   B. W. Boehm. Improving software productivity. *IEEE Computer*, pages 43–57, Sept. 1987.

[Boe88]   B. Boehm. A spiral model of software development and enhancement. *IEEE Computer*, pages 61–72, May 1988.

[Boe89]   B. Boehm. *Tutorial: software risk management*. IEEE Computer Socity, Washington D.C., 1989.

[Boo94]   G. Booch. *Object-oriented analysis and design*. The Benjamin/Cummings Publishing Company, Santa Clara, CA, 1994.

[BR88]   V. R. Basili and H. D. Rombach. The TAME project: Towards improvement-oriented software environments. *IEEE Transactions on Software Engineering*, 14(6):758–773, June 1988.

[BR94]   V. R. Basili and H. D. Rombach. The experience factory. In *Encyclopedia of Software Engineering*. John Wiley and Sons, 1994.

[Bro75]   F. Brooks. *The mytical man month*. Addison-Wesley, Reading, MA, 1975.

[BT75]   V. R. Basili and A. Turner. Iterative enhancement, a practical technique for software development. *IEEE Transactions on Software Engineering*, SE-1(4), Dec. 1975.

[BW81]   V. R. Basili and D. M. Weiss. Evaluation of a software requirements document by analysis of change data. In *5th Int. Conf. on Software Engineering*, pages 314–323. IEEE, 1981.

[BW84]   V. R. Basili and D. M. Weiss. A methodology for collecting valid software engineering data. *IEEE Transactions on Software Engineering*, 10(6):728–738, Nov. 1984.

[C$^+$83]   J. Celko et al. A demonstration of three requirement language systems. *ACM SIGPLAN Notices*, 18(1):9–14, Jan. 1983.

[CDS86]   S. D. Conte, H. E. Dunsmore, and V. Y. Shen. *Software engineering metrics and models*. The Benjamin/Cummings Publishing Company, 1986.

[Che76]   P. Chen. The entity relationship model: Towards a unifying view of data. *ACM Transactions on Database Systems*, 1(1):9–36, March 1976.

[Che78]   E. Chen. Program complexity and programmer productivity. *IEEE Transactions on Software Engineering*, SE-4:187–194, May 1978.

[CHT79]   T. E. Cheatham, G. H. Holloway, and J. A. Townley. Symbolic evaluation and the analysis of programs. *IEEE Transactions on Software Engineering*, SE-5(4), July 1979.

[CK94]   S. R. Chidamber and C. F. Kemerer. A metrics suite for object-oriented design. *IEEE Transactions on Software Engineering*, 20(6):476–493, June 1994.

[Cla76]   L . A. Clarke. A system to generate test data and symbolic execute programs. *IEEE Transactions on Software Engineering*, SE-2(3), July 1976.

[CM78]   J. P. Cavano and J. A. McCall. A framework for the measurement of software quality. In *Proc. ACM Software Quality Assurance Workshop*, pages 133–139. ACM, Nov. 1978.

[Cri84]   F . Cristian. Correct and robust programs. *IEEE Transactions on Software Engineering*, SE-10(2), March 1984.

[CY90]   P. Coad and E. Yourdon. *Object-oriented analysis*. Prentice Hall, 1990.

[CY91]   P. Coad and E. Yourdon. *Object-oriented design*. Prentice Hall, 1991.

[D⁺88]   R. A. DeMillo et al. An extended overview of the MOTHRA testing environment. In *Workshop on Software Testing, Verification, and Analysis*, July 1988.

[D⁺93]   A. Davis et al. Identifying and measuring quality in a software requirements specification. In *First Int. Software Metrics Symposium*, pages 141–152. IEEE, 1993.

[Dav89]   J. S. Davis. Identification of errors in software requirements through use of automated requirements tools. *Information and Software Technology*, 31(9):472–476, Nov. 1989.

[Dav92]   A. M. Davis. Operational prototyping: A new development approach. *IEEE Software*, pages 70–78, Sept. 1992.

[Dav93]   A. M. Davis. *Software Requirements: Objects, Functions, and States*. Prentice Hall, Englewood Cliffs, NJ, 1993.

[Dav95]   A. M. Davis. Software prototyping. In *Advances in Computers, Vol. 40*, pages 39–63. Academic Press, 1995.

[DeM79]   T. DeMarco. *Structured analysis and system specification*. Yourdon Press, 1979.

[DeM82]   T. DeMarco. *Controlling software projects*. Yourdon Press, 1982.

[DLS78]   R. A. DeMillo, R. A. Lipton, and F. G. Sayward. Hints on test data selection: Help for the practicing programmer. *IEEE Computer*, pages 34–41, Apr. 1978.

[DN84]   J. W. Duran and S. C. Ntafos. An evaluation of random testing. *IEEE Transactions on Software Engineering*, 10(4):438–444, July 1984.

[Dun84]   R. H. Dunn. *Software defect removal*. McGraw-Hill Inc., 1984.

[EJW95]   D. W. Embley, R. B. Jackson, and S. N. Woodfield. OO systems analysis: Is it or isn't it. *IEEE Software*, 12(4):19–33, July 1995.

[EKW92]   D. W. Embley, B. D. Kurtz, and S. N. Woodfield. *Object-oriented systems analysis: A model-driven approach*. Prentice Hall, 1992.

[Eme84]   T. J. Emerson. A discriminating metric for module cohesion. In *Proc. of the 7th Int. Conf. on Software Engineering*, pages 294–303, 1984.

[EN89]   R. Elmasri and S. B. Navathe. *Fundamentals of Database Systems*. The Benjamin/Cummings Publishing Company, 1989.

[Fag76]   M. E. Fagan. Design and code inspections to reduce errors in program development. *IBM System Journal*, (3):182–211, 1976.

[Fai85]   R. E. Fairly. *Software engineering concepts*. McGraw-Hill Inc., 1985.

[Fel79]   S. I. Feldman. Make—a program for maintaining computer programs. *Software Practice and Experience*, 9(3):255–265, March 1979.

[Fir93]   D. G. Firesmith. *Object-oriented requirements analysis and logical design*. John Wiley and Sons, 1993.

[FO78]   L. D. Fosdick and L. J. Osterweil. Dataflow analysis in software reliability. *ACM Computing Surveys*, 8(3), Sept. 1978.

[FW93a]   P. G. Frankl and S. N. Weiss. An experimental comparison of the effectiveness of branch testing and data flow testing. *IEEE Transactions on Software Engineering*, 19(8):774–787, Aug. 1993.

[FW93b]   P. G. Frankl and E. J. Weyuker. Provable improvements on branch testing. *IEEE Transactions on Software Engineering*, 19(10):962–975, Oct. 1993.

[FWW85]   P. G. Frankl, S. Weiss, and E. J. Weyuker. ASSET: A system to select and evaluate tests. In *Proc. IEEE Conference on Software Tools*, pages 72–79, Apr. 1985.

[G⁺94]   E. Gamma et al. *Design Patterns—Elements of Reusable Object-Oriented Software*. Addison-Wesley, 1994.

[GG75]   J. Goodenough and S. L. Gerhart. Towards a theory of test data selection. *IEEE Transactions on Software Engineering*, SE-1:156–173, 1975.

[GG94]   T. Gilb and D. Graham. *Software Inspection*. Addison-Wesley, 1994.

[GH77]   S. E. Goodman and S. T. Hedetniemi. *Introduction to the design and analysis of algorithms*. McGraw-Hill Inc., 1977.

[GH78]   J. V. Guttag and J. J. Horning. The algebraic specifications for abstract data types. *Acta Informatica*, 10:27–62, 1978.

[GMH81]   J. D. Gannon, P. McMullin, and R. Hamlet. Data abstraction implementation specification and testing. *ACM Transactions Prog. Lang. Sys.*, 3(3):211–223, July 1981.

[GO79]   A. L. Goel and K. Okumoto. A time dependent error detection rate model for software reliability and other performance measures. *IEEE Transactions on Reliability*, R-28:769–774, 1979.

[Goe85]   A. L. Goel. Software reliability models: Assumptions, limitations and applicability. *IEEE Transactions on Software Engineering*, SE-11:1411–1423, Dec. 1985.

[GS81]   H. Gomma and D. B. H. Scott. Prototyping as a tool in the specification of user requirements. In *Fifth Int. Conf. on Software Engineering*, pages 333–341, 1981.

[Gut80]   J. V. Guttag. Notes on type abstraction (version 2). *IEEE Transactions on Software Engineering*, SE-6(1):13–23, Jan. 1980.

[Hal77]   M. Halstead. *Elements of software science*. Eslevier North-Holland, New York, 1977.

[HB85]   D. H. Hutchens and V. R. Basili. System structure analysis: clustering with data bindings. *IEEE Transactions on Software Engineering*, SE-11(8):749–757, Aug. 1985.

[HK81]   S. Henry and D. Kafura. Software structure metrics based on information flow. *IEEE Transactions on Software Engineering*, 7(5):510–518, 1981.

[HK84]   S. Henry and D. Kafura. The evaluation of software systems' structures using quantitative software metrics. *Software Practice and Experience*, 14(6):561–573, June 1984.

[HK92]   M. J. Harrold and P. Kolte. Combat: A compiler based data flow testing system. In *Proc. of the Pacific Northwest Quality Conference*, pages 311–323, 1992.

[HMF92]   M. J. Harrold, John D. McGregor, and Kevin J. Fitzpatrick. Incremental testing of object-oriented class structures. *Proc. of 14th International Conference on Software Engineering*, pages 68–79, 1992.

[HMKD82] W. Harrison, K. Magel, R. Kluczny, and A. DeKock. Applying software complexity metrics to program maintenance. *IEEE Computer*, pages 65–79, Sept. 1982.

[Hoa69]   C. A. R. Hoare. An axiomatic basis for computer programming. *Communications of the ACM*, 12(3):335–355, 1969.

[How77]   W. E. Howden. Symbolic testing and the DISSECT symbolic evaluation system. *IEEE Transactions on Software Engineering*, SE-3(4):13–23, July 1977.

[HR94]   M. J. Harrold and G. Rothermel. Performing data flow testing on classes. In *ACM Foundations on Software Engineering*, pages 154–163, 1994.

[HS89]   M. J. Harrold and M. L. Soffa. Interprocedural data flow testing. In *Proc. of the 3rd Testing, Analysis, and Verification Symposium*, pages 158–167, 1989.

[HT90]   D. Hamlet and R. Taylor. Partition testing does not inspire confidence. *IEEE Transactions on Software Engineering*, 16(12):1402–1411, Dec. 1990.

[Hum89]   W. E. Humphrey. *Managing the software process*. Addison Wesley, 1989.

[IEE87]   IEEE. *Software Engineeing Standards*. IEEE Press, 1987.

[IEE94]   IEEE. *IEEE Software Engineeing Standards Collection, 1994 Edition*. IEEE Press, 1994.

[Ing86]   F. S. Ingrass. *Tutorial: Software Management*, chapter The unit development folder (UDF): An effective management tool for software development. IEEE Computer Society, 3 edition, 1986.

[Jac92]   I. Jacobson. *Object-oriented software engineering—A use case driven approach*. Addison Wesley Publishing Co., 1992.

[Jal87]   P. Jalote. Synthesizing implementations of abstract data types from axiomatic specifications. *Software Practice and Experience*, 17(11):847–858, Nov. 1987.

[Jal89a] P. Jalote. Functional refinement and nested objects for object-oriented design. *IEEE Transactions on Software Engineering*, 15(3):264–270, March 1989.

[Jal89b] P. Jalote. Testing the completeness of specifications. *IEEE Transactions on Software Engineering*, 15(5):526–531, May 1989.

[Jal92]   P. Jalote. Specification and testing of abstract data types. *Computer Languages*, 17(1):75–82, 1992.

[JC88]   P. Jalote and M. Caballero. Automated testcase generation of abstract data types from axiomatic specifications. In *Proc. COMPSAC 88, Chicago*, pages 205–210, Chicago, Oct. 1988. COMPSAC.

[JF88]   R. E. Johnson and B. Foote. Designing reusable classes. *Journal of Object Oriented Programming*, 1(2):22–25, 1988.

[JM72]   Z. Jelinski and P. Moranda. Software reliability research. In W. Freiberger, editor, *Statistical Computer Performance Evaluation*, pages 465–484. New York: Academic, New York, 1972.

[Jon78]   T. C. Jones. Measuring program quality and productivity. *IEEE Systems Journal*, 17(1), 1978.

[Kem87]   C. F. Kemerer. An empirical validation of software cost estimation models. *CACM*, 30(5):416–429, May 1987.

[KG90]   T. Korson and J. D. Gregor. Understanding object-oriented: A unifying paradigm. *Commn. of the ACM*, 33(9):40–60, Sept. 1990.

[Kin76]   J. C. King. Symbolic execution and program testing. *Communications of the ACM*, 19(7), July 1976.

[KJ96]   G. A. Kiran and P. Jalote. State based testing of object-oriented programs. Technical Report TRCS-96-237, Dept. of Computer Sc. and Engineering I. I. T., Kanpur, India, 1996.

[Kon94]   J. Kontio. Software engineering risk management: A technology review report. Technical Report PI 4.1, NOKIA Research Center, 1994.

[LH89]   Karl J. Lieberherr and Ian M. Holland. Assuring good style for object-oriented programs. *IEEE Software*, pages 38–48, Sept. 1989.

[LH93]   W. Lie and S. Henry. Object-oriented metrics that predict maintainability. *Journal of Systems and Software*, 23(2):111–122, 1993.

[LJ90]   G. C. Low and D. R. Jeffery. Function points in the estimation and evaluation of the software process. *IEEE Transactions on Software Engineering*, 16(1):64–71, Jan. 1990.

[LJZ94]   H. Lichter, M. S. Jufschmidt, and H. Zullighoven. Prototyping in industrial software projects—bridging the gap between theory and practice. *IEEE Transactions on Software Engineering*, 20(11):825–832, Nov. 1994.

[LK83]   J. W. Laski and B. Korel. A data flow oriented program testing strategy. *IEEE Transactions on Software Engineering*, 9(3):347–354, May 1983.

[LV74]   B. Littlewood and J. L. Verall. A bayesian reliability model with a stochastically monotone failure rate. *IEEE Transactions on Reliability*, 23(2):108–114, 1974.

[Man81]   M. Mantei. The effect of programming team structure on programming tasks. *Communications of the ACM*, 24(3), March 1981.

[Mat94]   A. P. Mathur. Mutation testing. In *Encyclopedia of Software Engineering*, pages 707–713. John Wiley, 1994.

[MBM94]   J. E. Matson, B. E. Barrett, and J. Me. Mellichamp. Software development cost estimation using function points. *IEEE Transactions on Software Engineering*, 20(4):275–287, April 1994.

[McC76]   T. J. McCabe. A complexity measure. *IEEE Transactions on Software*, SE-2(4):308–320, Dec. 1976.

[Mcf89]   F. W. Mcfarlan. Portfolio approach to information systems. In B. W. Boehm, editor, *Tutorial: Software Risk Management*, pages 17–25. IEEE Computer Society, 1989.

[MIO87]   J. D. Musa, A. Iannino, and K. Okumoto. *Software reliability—measurement, prediction, application*. McGraw Hill Book Company, 1987.

[MJ95]   K. K. Mantri and P. Jalote. Identifying error prone modules during software development. Technical report, Indian Institute of Technology Kanpur, Dept. of Computer Science and Engineering, 1995.

[MO84]   J. D. Musa and K. Okumoto. A logarithmic poisson execution time model for software reliability measurement. In *Proc. 7th Int. Conf. on Software Engineering*, pages 230–238, 1984.

[MP92]   D. E. Monarchi and G. I. Puhr. A research topology for object-oriented analysis and design. *Communications of the ACM*, 35(9):35–47, Sept. 1992.

[Mus75]   J. D. Musa. A theory of software reliability and its applications. *IEEE Transactions on Software Engineering*, 1(3):312–327, Sept. 1975.

[Mye77]   G. Myers. An extension to the cyclomatic measure of program complexity. *ACM SIGPLAN Notices*, pages 61–64, Oct. 1977.

[Mye79]   G. Myers. *The art of software testing*. Wiley-Interscience, New York, 1979.

[Neu88]   P. G. Neumann. Risks to the public in computers and related systems. *Software engineering notes*, 13(2):5–18, April 1988.

[P+93]   M. C. Paulk et al. Capability maturity model for software, version 1.1. Technical Report ESC-TR-93-177, Software Engineering Institute, Carnegie Mellon University, Pittsburgh, PA, Feb 1993.

[PBC93]   A. S. Parrish, R. B. Borie, and D. W. Cordes. Automated flow graph based testing of object-oriented software modules. *Journal of Systems and Software*, 23:95–109, 1993.

[PK90]   D. E. Perry and G. E. Kaiser. Adequate testing and object-oriented programming. *Journal of Object Oriented Programming*, pages 13–19, Jan./Feb. 1990.

[Put78]   L. H. Putnam. A general empirical solution to the macro software sizing and estimation problem. *IEEE Transactions on Software Engineering*, pages 345–361, July 1978.

[R+91]   J. Rumbaugh et al. *Object-Oriented Modeling and Design*. Prentice Hall, Englewood Cliffs, NJ, 1991.

[Ros77]   D. T. Ross. Structured analysis: A language for communicating ideas. *IEEE Transactions on Software Engineering*, 3(1):16–34, Jan. 1977.

[Rot89]   J. Rothfeder. Its late, costly, incompetent—but try firing a computer system. In B. W. Boehm, editor, *Tutorial: Software Risk Management*, pages 63–64. IEEE Computer Society, 1989.

[RS77]   D. T. Ross and K. E. Schoman. Structured analysis for requirements definition. *IEEE Transactions on Software Engineering*, 3(1):6–15, Jan. 1977.

[RV95]   H. D. Rombach and M. Verlage. Directions in software process research. In M. V. Zelkowitz, editor, *Advances in Computers, Vol. 41*, pages 1–63. Academic Press, 1995.

[RW85]   S. Rapps and E. J. Weyuker. Selecting software test data using data flow information. *IEEE Transactions on Software Engineering*, 11(4):367–375, Apr. 1985.

[SMC74]   W. P. Stevens, G. J. Myers, and L. Constantine. Structured design. *IBM Systems Journal*, 13(2), 1974.

[SR90]   M. D. Smith and D. J. Robson. Object oriented programming: The problems of validation. *Proc. of 6th International IEEE Conference on Software Maintenance*, pages 272–282, Nov. 1990.

[SR92]   M. D. Smith and D. J. Robson. A framework for testing object-oriented programs. *Jounal of Object-Oriented Programming (JOOP)*, pages 45–53, June 1992.

[TH77]   D. Teichroew and E. A. Hershey. PSL/PSA: A computer aided technique for structured documentation and analysis of information processing systems. *IEEE Transactions on Software Engineering*, 3(1):41–48, Jan. 1977.

[TR92]   C. D. Turner and D. J. Robson. The testing of object-oriented programs. Technical Report TR-13/92, University of Durham, Durham, England, Feb. 1992.

[Tri82]   K. S. Trivedi. *Probability and statistics with reliability, queuing, and computer science applications*. Prentice-Hall, Inc., Englewood Cliffs, NJ, 1982.

[Wey86]   E. J. Weyuker. Axiomatizing software test data adequacy. *IEEE Transactions on Software Engineering*, 12(12):1128–1138, Dec. 1986.

[Wey88]   E. J. Weyuker. The evaluation of program based software test data adequacy criteria. *Communications of the ACM*, 31(6):668–675, June 1988.

[Wey90]   FE. J. Weyuker. The cost of data flow testing: An empirical study. *IEEE Transactions on Software Engineering*, 16(2):121–128, Feb 1990.

[WF77]   C. Watson and C. Felix. A method of programming measurement and estimation. *IBM Systems Journal*, 16(1), Jan. 1977.

[WHH79]   M. Woodward, M. Hennell, and D. Hedley. A measure of control flow complexity in program text. *IEEE Transactions on Software Engineering*, SE-5:45–50, Jan. 1979.

[Whi91]   D. Whitgift. *Methods and tools for software configuration management*. John Wiley and Sons, 1991.

[Wir71]   N. Wirth. Program development by stepwise refinement. *Communications of the ACM*, 14(4):221–227, April 1971.

[WJ91]   E. J. Weyuker and B. Jeng. Analyzing partition testing strategies. *IEEE Transactions on Software Engineering*, 17(7):703–711, July 1991.

[WS74]   G. M. Weinberg and E. L. Schulman. Goals and performance in computer programming. *Human Factors*, 16(1):70–77, 1974.

[YC79]   E. Yourdon and L. Constantine. *Structured design*. Prentice Hall, 1979.

[YC85]   S. S. Yau and J. S. Collofello. Design stability measures for software maintenance. *IEEE Transactions on Software Engineering*, 11(9):849–856, Sept. 1985.

[YW78]   B. H. Yin and J. W. Winchester. The establishment and use of measures to evaluate the quality of designs. *Software Engineering Notes*, 3:45–52, 1978.

[YZ80]   R. T. Yeh and P. Zave. Specifying software requirements. *Proceedings of the IEEE*, 68(9):1077–1088, Sept. 1980.

[ZZ93]   W. M. Zage and D. M. Zage. Evaluating design metrics on large-scale software. *IEEE Software*, pages 75–81, July 1993.

Index